Learning to Teach
in post-apartheid South Africa

Student Teachers' Encounters with Initial Teacher Education

EDITORS
Yusuf Sayed | Nazir Carrim | Azeem Badroodien | Zahraa McDonald | Marcina Singh

Learning to Teach in post-apartheid South Africa - Student Teacher' Encounters with Initial Teacher Encounters

Published by AFRICAN SUN MeDIA under the SUN PReSS imprint

All rights reserved

Copyright © 2018 AFRICAN SUN MeDIA and the editors

This publication was subjected to an independent double-blind peer evaluation by the publisher.

The editors and the publisher have made every effort to obtain permission for and acknowledge the use of copyrighted material. Refer all enquiries to the publisher.

No part of this book may be reproduced or transmitted in any form or by any electronic, photographic or mechanical means, including photocopying and recording on record, tape or laser disk, on microfilm, via the Internet, by e-mail, or by any other information storage and retrieval system, without prior written permission by the publisher.

Views reflected in this publication are not necessarily those of the publisher.

First edition 2018

ISBN 978-1-928357-96-4
ISBN 978-1-928357-97-1 (e-book)
https://doi.org/10.18820/9781928357971

Set in Californian FB 9.5/12.5
Cover design, typesetting and production by AFRICAN SUN MeDIA

SUN PReSS is a licensed imprint of AFRICAN SUN MeDIA. Scholarly, professional and reference works are published under this imprint in print and electronic format.

This publication can be ordered directly from:
www.sun-e-shop.co.za
africansunmedia.snapplify.com (e-books)
www.store.it.si (e-books)
www.africansunmedia.co.za

Table of Contents

List of Figures ix
List of Tables ix
List of Abbreviations xv
List of Authors xix
Acknowledgments xxi
Foreword xxiii

Chapter 1: Initial Teacher Education in & for the 21st Century

Yusuf Sayed, Nazir Carrim, Azeem Badroodien & Marcina Singh

1.1 Introduction 1
1.2 The Importance of Initial Teacher Education (ITE) Preparation 1
1.3 Developing the Conceptual Framework: ITE Programmes as Knowledge Sets 5
1.4 Developing the Conceptual Framework: Translating ITE as Knowledge Sets into Programmes 9
1.5 ITE and the Phases of Learning and Teacher Preparation in the Context of South Africa 11
1.6 The Genesis of the Book: Building Partnerships and Networks of Collaboration ... 15
1.7 Research Context and Approach of the Broader Study 16
1.8 Overview of the Book 18
    1.8.1 Section 1: Setting the Context 18
    1.8.2 Section 2: Teachers' Professional Knowledge 19
    1.8.3 Section 3: Learning to Teach 20
    1.8.4 Section 4: ITE in the 21st Century 21
1.9 Conclusion 21
References 23

Chapter 2
Policy & Legislative Context of Initial Teacher Education in South Africa

Yusuf Sayed, Nazir Carrim, Azeem Badroodien, Zahraa McDonald & Marcina Singh

2.1	Introduction	27
2.2	ITE under Apartheid	28
2.3	(Re)Spatialisation of ITE in Post-Apartheid South Africa: Changing the ITE Landscape	29
2.4	(Re)Curriculation of ITE in Post-Apartheid South Africa: Changing Roles and Specifications	31
2.5	Global Context of Teachers and Teacher Education	34
2.6	Conclusion	36
References		38

Chapter 3
Who Becomes a Teacher & Why

Yusuf Sayed, Chiwimbiso Kwenda, Harry Rampa & Thelma Mort

3.1	Introduction		41
3.2	Situating the Debate		42
3.3	Extrinsic Motivation to Become a Teacher		43
3.4	Intrinsic Motivation to Become a Teacher		44
3.5	Research Design		44
3.6	Findings and Discussion		46
	3.6.1	Who Becomes a Teacher in Post-apartheid South Africa?	46
	3.6.2	Motivation for Becoming a Teacher	48
		3.6.2.1 Extrinsic Motivation	48
		3.6.2.2 Financial Incentives: Bursaries	50
		3.6.2.3 Conditions of Work: Work, Security and Salaries	52
		3.6.2.4 Inspiration and Modelling: From Teachers to Family	53
		3.6.2.5 Teaching as a Gateway Career Choice	56
		3.6.2.6 Teaching as Work-Life Balance	58
		3.6.2.7 Intrinsic Reasons	59
		3.6.2.8 Teaching as a Civic Duty/Commitment to Society	60

		3.6.2.9	Working with Children	61
		3.6.2.10	Developing Learners' Cognitive Skills	62
		3.6.2.11	Developing Learners' Cognitive Skills by Mathematics and Languages	63
3.7	Conclusion			65
References				67

Chapter 4: Beliefs about Professional Knowledge

Marcina Singh, Helena Wessels & Anil Kanjee

4.1	Introduction		73
4.2	Methodology		79
4.3	Themes Related to Beliefs about Knowledge: General Beliefs about Teaching		81
	4.3.1	Bachelor of Education (BEd)	81
	4.3.2	Postgraduate Certificate in Education (PGCE)	83
	4.3.3	BEd And PGCE	84
	4.3.4	Qualitative Data	85
		4.3.4.1 BEd	85
4.4	Beliefs about Domain-Specific Subject Knowledge (Language and Mathematics)		86
	4.4.1	BEd: Language	86
	4.4.2	PGCE: Language	89
	4.4.3	BEd: Mathematics	91
	4.4.4	PGCE: Mathematics	94
	4.4.5	Analysis	97
4.5	Competence to Teach (Language and Mathematics)		98
	4.5.1	BEd: Language	98
	4.5.2	BEd: Mathematics	99
4.6	Confidence to Teach (Language and Mathematics)		100
	4.6.1	BEd: Language	100
	4.6.2	PGCE: Language	101
4.7	Discussion		102
4.8	Limitations		104
4.9	Conclusion		105
References			105

Chapter 5: Ways of Knowing: Developing Professional Knowledge of Foundation Phase Student Teachers

Rada Jancic Mogliacci, Maureen Robinson & Nicoline Rousseau

5.1	Introduction	113
5.2	Debates in the Literature	114
5.3	Methodology	117
5.4	Analysis of Findings	118
5.5	Conclusion	126
References		128

Chapter 6: Developing Student Teachers' Professional Knowledge (Including Teaching Practice) in the Further Education & Training Phase

Trevor Moodley, Melanie Sadeck & Melanie Luckay

6.1	Introduction		131
6.2	The PGCE Programme		132
6.3	Theoretical Framework		134
6.4	Methodology		134
6.5	Findings and Discussion		135
	6.5.1	The Role of a Teacher	136
	6.5.2	Perceptions of the PGCE Programme in Preparing Students for the Teaching Profession (Theory/Practice Praxis)	137
	6.5.3	Teaching Practice Experiences	139
		6.5.3.1 Experiences of Teacher Mentors	140
		6.5.3.2 Demonstrating Agency during Teaching Practice	141
		6.5.3.3 Reflections of Lesson Planning and Delivery during Teaching Practice	142
		6.5.3.4 Experiences of Classroom Management	145
6.6	Conclusion		146
References			147

Teaching & Learning Foundation Phase Mathematics — Chapter 7

Sharon McAuliffe, Hamsa Venkatakrishnan & Jeanette Ramollo

7.1	Introduction	149
7.2	Literature Review: Student Teacher Knowledge Perspectives in Mathematics Education	151
7.3	Methodology	153
7.4	Data Analysis	154
7.5	Results	155
	7.5.1 Case Study 1	155
	Common Content Knowledge (CCK)	155
	Specialised Content Knowledge (CCK)	155
	7.5.2 Case Study 2	156
	CCK	156
	SCK	157
	7.5.3 Case Study 3	157
	CCK	157
	SCK	158
	7.5.4 Case Study 4	159
	CCK	159
	SCK	159
7.6	Discussion	160
	7.6.1 Supporting the Orchestration of Tasks, Resources, Talk and Children's Offers	160
	7.6.2 Understanding of Progression	161
7.7	Conclusion	161
	References	162

Chapter 8
Learning to Teach Language in the Foundation Phase

Zelda Barends & Shelley Aronstam

8.1	Introduction	165
8.2	Language and Literacy in the Foundation Phase	166
8.3	Literacy in the Foundation Phase	168
8.4	Content or Subject Matter Knowledge for Literacy	169
	8.4.1 Pedagogical Content Knowledge (PCK)	171
8.5	Methodology	172
8.6	Student Teachers' Experiences in Learning to Teach Languages in the Foundation Phase	172
	8.6.1 Student Teachers' Language Demographics	172
	8.6.2 Student Teachers' Exposure to Language in the BEd Programmes	174
8.7	Conclusion	184
References		185

Chapter 9
Engaging Further Education & Training Mathematics Student Teachers' Knowledge

Rajendran Govender, Conrad Potberg & Jacques Verster

9.1	Introduction	189
9.2	Mathematical Learning in Policy Context	189
	9.2.1 Research Question	192
	9.2.2 Conceptual Framework for the Study with FET MPTs: Generalisation	192
	9.2.3 Inductive Generalisations	193
	9.2.4 Counter-Examples	194
	9.2.5 Conjecturing, Generalising, and Justifying within a Dynamic Geometry Context	196
	9.2.5.1 The Geometer's Sketchpad (GSP): What it is and What Can You Do With it	196
	9.2.5.2 Research Related to Conjecturing, Generalising, and Justifying in a GSP Context	198
9.3	Methodology	200

9.4 Results and Discussion ... 201
    9.4.1 Making an Initial Conjecture in a Non-Geometer Sketchpad (GSP) Context ... 201
        9.4.1.1 Findings Based on Making an Initial Conjecture ... 204
    9.4.2 Making a Conjecture by Empirical Induction from Dynamic Cases in a GSP Context ... 205
        9.4.2.1 Validating the Conjecture for New Particular Cases ... 206
        9.4.2.2 Mathematics Pre-Service Teachers' (MPTs) Formulations of their Conjecture Generalisations ... 207
        9.4.2.3 Findings Based on GSP Context ... 208
    9.4.3 Certainty ... 208
        9.4.3.1 Findings Based on Certainty ... 211
    9.4.4 Heuristic Counter-Examples ... 211
    9.4.5 Refinement/Modification of an MPT's Initial Non-GSP Conjecture ... 211
9.5 Discussion of Findings ... 211
9.6 Conclusion ... 214
References ... 214

Chapter 10
Learning to Teach Language in the Further Education & Training Phase

Hanlie Dippenaar, Azeem Badroodien & Nomakhaya Mashiyi

10.1 Introduction ... 223
10.2 Teaching Languages Post-Apartheid ... 224
    10.2.1 Challenges for Teaching ... 224
    10.2.2 Dilemmas Tied to Language Policy ... 225
    10.2.3 Approaches and Concerns Tied to the Teaching of Language ... 226
    10.2.4 Teacher Education Policy for the FET Phase ... 227
10.3 Methodology ... 228
10.4 Student Teacher Reflections on Language Teaching Preparation ... 229
    10.4.1 Student Teacher Beliefs ... 229
        10.4.1.1 Beliefs about the Role of Language in Teaching and Learning ... 229
        10.4.1.2 Beliefs about the Teaching of Language and its Role in Developing the Skills of Reading, Writing, Speaking and Listening ... 230

10.4.2	Student Teacher Confidence in Developing the Four Skills of Language and in Teaching these Skills	232
	10.4.2.1 Teaching Strategies and Resources for Teaching English	232
10.4.3	Student Teacher Experiences of ITE Programmes and Views about their Development of Key Pedagogical Skills	233
	10.4.3.1 Student Teachers Indicate what They were Taught, and its Value to them	233
	10.4.3.2 Student Teachers' Responses Regarding Their Confidence to Implement and Teach Different Strategies	235
	10.4.3.3 Assessment Preparation as Indicative of Confidence, Ability and Intent	237
10.5 Student Teacher Preparedness to Teach Language in the FET Phase		240
10.5.1 Curriculum and Subject Content Matter		242
10.5.2 Pedagogy and PCK		242
10.6 Conclusion		243
References		245

Chapter 11: A Prospective 21st-Century Post-Apartheid Teacher Education Agenda

Yusuf Sayed, Nazir Carrim & Azeem Badroodien

11.1 Introduction		249
11.2 Emerging Themes		249
11.3 Teacher Education Models and Approaches in the Post-Apartheid 21st Century		257
11.4 Moving Forward with Policy, Practice and Research		261
11.4.1 A Democratic Public-Good Approach		261
11.4.2 A Joined up and Comprehensive Teacher Education Policy Approach		262
11.4.3 High-Quality ITE Programmes		262
11.4.4 Strong and Capable ITE Providers		262
11.4.5 Credible Prospective Teacher Evaluation Systems in ITE		263
11.4.6 Developing the Knowledge Base		264
References		265

Appendices

Appendix 1	Session one Task-Based Activity – Equilateral Triangle Problems	221
Appendix 2	Mapping Education Policies Relating to Teachers and Teacher Education in South Africa	269
Appendix 3	Overview of Research Questionnaires	273

List of Figures

Figure 1.1	Knowledge in ITE	5
Figure 1.2	A Composite Model of Teacher Quality	8
Figure 1.3	A Programmatic Approach to ITE	10
Figure 1.4	Teacher Career Phases	12
Figure 4.1	Mathematical Knowledge for Teaching (MKT)	74
Figure 4.2	Model of Teacher Knowledge	75
Figure 9.1	Dynamic Sketch	196
Figure 9.2	An Illustration of a Successful Conjecture	199
Figure 9.3	Equilateral Triangle	202
Figure 9.4	Victor's Initial Response to the Shipwreck Problem	202
Figure 9.5	A Trajectory of the MPTs' Inductive Generalisation	212

List of Tables

Table 1.1	Higher Education Institutions (HEIs) Offering ITE Programmes in South Africa	12
Table 1.2	Phase-specific Specialisation Fields	14
Table 1.3	Overview of the Data for this Book	18
Table 3.1	Combined Institutional Demographic Profiles of Participants	47
Table 3.2	Extrinsic Motivation for Choosing Teaching as a Career	49
Table 3.3	Perceptions of the Significance of Bursaries by Racial Group	51
Table 3.4	Perceptions of the Importance of Teacher Salaries as an Extrinsic Motivator (by Race)	52

Table 3.5	Inspiration to Become Teachers (by race): A Teacher Inspired Me	54
Table 3.6	Inspiration to Become Teachers (by race): A Family Member Inspired Me	54
Table 3.7	Inspiration to Become Teachers (by race): Someone Else Inspired Me	56
Table 3.8	Teaching will Open up Opportunities in Other Careers (by race)	57
Table 3.9	Balance Between Personal and Professional Life (by race)	58
Table 3.10	Intrinsic Reasons for Choosing Teaching as a Career	59
Table 3.11	I Can Help Society (by race)	60
Table 3.12	Enjoy working with children (by race)	61
Table 3.13	Developing Children's Cognitive Skills (by race)	63
Table 3.14	Developing Children's Mathematical Knowledge Skills (by race)	64
Table 3.15	Developing Children's Language Knowledge Skills (by race)	64
Table 4.1	Beliefs about Teaching – Q1 Teacher Motivation and Beliefs (BEd)	81
Table 4.2	Beliefs about Teaching – Q1 Teacher Motivation and Beliefs (PGCE)	83
Table 4.3	Most Powerful Determinant of a Learner's Success – Q1 Teacher Motivation and Beliefs (BEd)	84
Table 4.4	Beliefs about Language as a Subject – Q1 Teacher Motivation and Beliefs (BEd)	86
Table 4.5	Views about Teaching Language – Q1 Teacher Motivation and Beliefs (BEd)	87
Table 4.6	Importance of Developing Language Skills - Q1 Teacher Motivation and Beliefs(BEd)	88
Table 4.7	Beliefs about Language as a Subject – Q1 Teacher Motivation and Beliefs (PGCE)	89
Table 4.8	Views about Teaching Language – Q1 Teacher Motivation and Beliefs (PGCE)	89
Table 4.9	Importance of Developing Language Skills – Q1 Teacher Motivation and Beliefs (PGCE)	90
Table 4.10	Beliefs about Mathematics as a Subject – Q1 Teacher Motivation and Beliefs (BEd)	91
Table 4.11	Beliefs about the Goals of Mathematics – Q1 Teacher Motivation and Beliefs (BEd)	92
Table 4.12	Views about Mathematics Teaching – Q1 Teacher Motivation and Beliefs (BEd)	92
Table 4.13	Importance of Developing Mathematical Knowledge – Q1 Teacher Motivation and Beliefs (BEd)	93
Table 4.14	Beliefs about Mathematics as a Subject – Q1 Teacher Motivation and Beliefs (PGCE)	94

Table 4.15	Beliefs about Goals for Mathematics Teaching – Q1 Teacher Motivation and Beliefs (PGCE)	95
Table 4.16	Views about Teaching Mathematics – Q1 Teacher Motivation and Beliefs (PGCE)	95
Table 4.17	Importance of Developing Mathematical Knowledge – Q1 Teacher Motivation and Beliefs (PGCE)	97
Table 4.18	Competence to Teach Language Skills – Q1 Teacher Motivation and Beliefs (BEd)	98
Table 4.19	Competence to Teach Mathematical skills – Q1 Teacher Motivation and Beliefs (BEd)	99
Table 4.20	Confidence to Teach Language Skills – Q1 Teacher Motivation and Beliefs (BEd)	100
Table 4.21	Confidence to Teach Mathematics – Q1 Teacher Motivation and Beliefs (BEd)	101
Table 4.22	Confidence to Teach Language – Q1 Teacher Motivation and Beliefs (PGCE)	101
Table 4.23	Confidence to Teach Mathematics – Q1 Teacher Motivation and Beliefs (PGCE)	102
Table 5.1	Do You Develop the Following Mathematical Knowledge and Skill in Learners?: The Correct use of Basic Terminology	119
Table 5.2	Do You Require Additional Development to Teach the Following Mathematical Knowledge Skills to Learners: The Correct use of Basic Terminology	119
Table 5.3	Learners' Assessment	120
Table 5.4	To what Extent Have You Learned about the Following during Teaching Practice?: Learned to Train Learners to Conduct Self-assessment	120
Table 5.5	Knowledge and Skills in Assessing Language: Learned to Develop Assessments	121
Table 5.6	Knowledge and Skills Gained in Assessing Mathematics: Learned to Develop Assessments	121
Table 5.7	Activities Able to Participate in during Teaching Practice: General Administrative work	122
Table 5.8	Activities Able to Participate in during Teaching Practice: Substituting for a Teacher other than my Mentor Teacher	123
Table 5.9	To what Extent Have You Learned about the Following during Teaching Practice?: Learned to Teach in Multilingual Classrooms	124
Table 5.10	Teachers are Accountable for what Learners Learn	125
Table 5.11	Determinants of Learner Success	125

Table 6.1	Professional Knowledge Components Covered in the Course (N=45)	135
Table 6.2	Perceptions of Experiences of Learning in the PGCE Programme (N=45)	137
Table 6.3	Teaching Practice Experiences (N=45)	139
Table 7.1	Comparison of the Shulman and Ball Models	152
Table 8.1	The Four Language Systems which Learners must Acquire	168
Table 8.2	The Disciplinary Knowledge Base Required to Teach the Reading Literacy Components	170
Table 8.3	Primary Home Language of Student Teachers	173
Table 8.4	Home Language in Grade 12	173
Table 8.5	First Additional Language (FAL) in Grade 12	174
Table 8.6	Beliefs about Language	175
Table 8.7	How Important is Developing these Skills during Language Teaching?	176
Table 8.8	How useful was the coverage of knowledge of the CAPS curriculum in the programme?	176
Table 8.9	Competence in Developing Reading Skills in Learners during Language Teaching	177
Table 8.10	Confidence in Developing Reading Skills in Learners during Language Teaching	177
Table 8.11	Confidence in Developing Reading Skills in Learners during Language Teaching (Q3)	178
Table 8.12	Extent that have You been Prepared to use the 'Start from Learners' Prior Knowledge' Teaching Strategy	178
Table 8.13	Medium of Instruction Year 1	180
Table 8.14	Medium of Instruction Year 2	181
Table 8.15	Medium of Instruction Year 3	181
Table 8.16	Medium of Instruction Year 4	182
Table 8.17	To what Extent have You Learned to Teach Languages in Teaching Practice?	183
Table 8.18	Learning Experiences Facilitated by Mentor	183
Table 9.1	Five Kinds of Mathematical Competencies or 'Strands'	191
Table 10.1	Student Teacher Beliefs about Language as a Subject	230
Table 10.2	Student Teacher Beliefs about Teaching Language	230
Table 10.3	Beliefs about the Importance of Developing Language Teaching Skills	231
Table 10.4	Student Teacher Confidence in Developing Language Teaching Skills	232
Table 10.5	Student Teacher Views of Teaching Strategies	234
Table 10.6	Student Teacher Confidence to Teach Specific Teaching Strategies	236

Table 10.7	Student Teachers' Views on whether they will Implement Teaching Strategies	237
Table 10.8	Student Teachers' Views on whether they were Taught the Necessary Skills during Language Teaching	238
Table 10.9	Student Teacher Preparedness to Perform certain Tasks	238
Table 10.10	Confidence to Assess the Skills during Language Teaching	239
Table 10.11	Knowledge and Skills Gained to Assess Language	239
Table 10.12	Envisaged CPD as a Language Teacher	240

List of Abbreviations

ANA	Annual National Assessment
BA	Bachelor of Arts
BCom	Bachelor of Commerce
BEd	Bachelor of Education
BSc	Bachelor of Science
BSocSc	Bachelor of Social Science
C2005	Curriculum 2005
CAPS	Curriculum and Assessment Policy Statement
CCK	Common content knowledge
CHE	Council on Higher Education
CHED	Centre for Higher Education Development
CITE	Centre for International Teacher Education
CK	Content knowledge
CPD	Continuing professional development
CPUT	Cape Peninsula University of Technology
CUT	Central University of Technology
DBE	Department of Basic Education
DGS	Dynamic geometry software
DHET	Department of Higher Education and Training
DoE	Department of Education
DST	Department of Science and Technology
DUT	Durban University of Technology
FET	Further Education and Training
FLBP	Funza Lushaka Bursary Programme
FP	Foundation Phase
GPK	General pedagogical knowledge
GSP	Geometer Sketchpad
HEI	Higher education institution
HEQF	High Education Qualifications Framework
HK	Horizon knowledge
ICT	Information and communications technology
ILO	International Labor Organization

ITE	Initial teacher education
KCC	Knowledge of content and curriculum
KCS	Knowledge of content and students
KCT	Knowledge of content and teaching
LiEP	Language-in-Education Policy
LoLT	Language of learning and teaching
MDG	Millennium Development Goal
MKT	Mathematical knowledge for teaching
MPT	Mathematics pre-service teacher
MRTEQ	Minimum Requirements for Teacher Education Qualifications
NAEYC	National Association for the Education of Young Children
NCATE	National Council for the Accreditation of Teacher Education
NCS	National Curriculum Statement
NCTAF	National Commission on Teaching & America's Future
NDP	National Development Plan
NEEDU	National Education Evaluation and Development Unit
NES	National Evaluation Series
NMU	Nelson Mandela University
NPFTED	National Policy Framework for Teacher Education and Development
NQF	National Qualifications Framework
NQT	Newly qualified teacher
NRF	National Research Foundation
NRP	National Reading Panel
NSE	Norms and Standards of Educators
NSFAS	National Student Financial Aid Scheme
NWU	North-West University
OBE	Outcomes-based education
OECD	Organization for Economic Co-operation and Development
PCK	Pedagogical content knowledge
PGCE	Postgraduate Certificate in Education
PIRLS	Progress in International Reading Literacy Study
PUFM	Profound understanding of fundamental mathematics

RNCS	Revised National Curriculum Statement
RU	Rhodes University
SACE	South African Council for Educators
SACMEQ	Southern and Eastern Africa Consortium for Monitoring Educational Quality
SAQA	South African Qualifications Authority
SARChI	South African Research Chair
SCK	Subject content knowledge
SCS	Senior Civil Servant
SDG	Sustainable Development Goal
SES	Socio-economic status
SETA	Sector Education and Training Authority
SMK	Subject matter knowledge
SPSS	Statistical Package for the Social Sciences
SPU	Sol Plaatjie University
Stats SA	Statistics South Africa
SU	Stellenbosch University
TFA	Teach for All
TIMSS	Trends in International Mathematics and Science Study
TPACK	Technological pedagogical content knowledge
TRIS	Teacher Rural Incentive Scheme
TUT	Tshwane University of Technology
UCT	University of Cape Town
UFH	University of Fort Hare
UFS	University of the Free State
UJ	University of Johannesburg
UK	United Kingdom
UKZN	University of KwaZulu-Natal
UL	University of Limpopo
UN	United Nations
UNA-GP	United Nations Association of Greater Philadelphia
UNESCO	United Nations Educational, Scientific and Cultural Organization
UNISA	University of South Africa
Univen	University of Venda

Unizulu	University of Zululand
UP	University of Pretoria
USA	United States of America
UWC	University of the Western Cape
WCED	Western Cape Education Department
Wits	University of the Witwatersrand
WSU	Walter Sisulu University

List of Authors

	Name and Surname	Designation	Institution
1	Prof Yusuf Sayed	Professor of International Education and Development Policy, University of Sussex, UK & South African Research Chair in Teacher Education, Centre for International Teacher Education (CITE), CPUT	University of Sussex, UK & Centre for International Teacher Education (CITE), CPUT
2	Prof Nazir Carrim	HOD	University of Witwatersrand
3	Prof Azeem Badroodien	Deputy Director: CITE Currently Professor of Education, University of Cape Town	Cape Peninsula University of Technology
4	Ms Marcina Singh	Doctoral Candidate & Research Officer, CITE	Cape Peninsula University of Technology
5	Dr Zahraa McDonald	Postdoctoral Fellow: CITE	Cape Peninsula University of Technology
6	Dr Chiwimbiso Kwenda	Lecturer	Cape Peninsula University of Technology
7	Prof Harry Rampa	Professor of Education	Tshwane University of Technology
8	Ms Thelma Mort	Doctoral Candidate: CITE	Cape Peninsula University of Technology
9	Dr Helena Wessels	Lecturer	Stellenbosch University
10	Prof Anil Kanjee	Research Professor	Tshwane University of Technology
11	Dr Rada Jancic Mogliacci	Postdoctoral Fellow: UCT	Cape Peninsula University of Technology
12	Prof Maureen Robinson	Professor of Education	Stellenbosch University
13	Dr Nicoline Rousseau	Lecturer	Cape Peninsula University of Technology
14	Dr Trevor Moodley	Lecturer	University of the Western Cape
15	Ms Melanie Sadeck	HOD & Doctoral Candidate	Cape Peninsula University of Technology
16	Dr Melanie Luckay	Lecturer	University of the Western Cape
17	Dr Sharon McAuliffe	Senior Lecturer	Cape Peninsula University of Technology
18	Prof Hamsa Venkatakrishnan	SA Numeracy Chair	University of Witwatersrand

	Name and Surname	Designation	Institution
19	Ms Jeanette Ramollo	Lecturer	Tshwane University of Technology
20	Dr Zelda Barends	Lecturer	Stellenbosch University
21	Ms Shelley Aronstam	Lecturer	Cape Peninsula University of Technology
22	Prof Rajendran Govender	Deputy-Dean	University of the Western Cape
23	Dr Conrad Potberg	Lecturer	University of the Western Cape
24	Mr Jacques Verster	Doctoral Candidate: CITE	Cape Peninsula University of Technology
25	Dr Hanlie Dippenaar	Lecturer	Cape Peninsula University of Technology
26	Ms Nomakhaya Mashiyi	Lecturer	Cape Peninsula University of Technology

Acknowledgments

We would like to express our gratitude and thanks to:

- Colleagues at the Cape Peninsula University of Technology (CPUT) and the Centre for International Teacher Education (CITE) for their support, advice and encouragement in making this book possible. In particular, we would like to thank Dr Nhlapo, Deputy Vice-Chancellor: Research, Partnerships and Innovation, for his unfailing support to advancing the research project at CPUT.
- The Department of Science and Technology (DST) and the National Research Foundation (NRF) for their generous financial support to the South African Research Chair (SARChI) in Teacher Education hosted by the Faculty of Education: CPUT. Opinions expressed in this book and the conclusions arrived at are those of the authors and are not necessarily to be attributed to the NRF and CPUT and its partners.
- The CITE Advisory Board and in particular the chairperson, Prof Robert van Niekerk and Mathew Goniwe, Chair of Social Policy and Director: Institute of Social Economic Research, Rhodes University, for his sage advice and wisdom.
- The University of Sussex for supporting Prof Sayed in making his stay in South Africa possible.
- The postgraduate research students at CITE for their ongoing commitment to the academic project at CITE.
- The many contributors without whom this book would not have been possible.
- We note with deep regret that one of our contributors Dr Helena Wessels tragically passed away during the production of this book. Her article is published posthumously in this book. We wish to acknowledge her contribution to the book and to teacher education in South Africa. She was a great mentor and a pleasure to work with.
- Mrs Basheerah Simon, who, as the administrator of CITE, works tirelessly and with great patience and commitment on our many research projects at CITE.
- Last, but not least, the student teachers who participated in this project and who are the future generations of teachers upon which our education system rests.

Note

In this book, we use the racial categories of white, black, coloured and Indian for discussion relating to South Africa, as these are the dominant racial categories that marked apartheid and the inequities that the system engendered. The usage of these terms does not in any way imply that we endorse racial categorisation and we argue that race is socially constructed and embedded in systems of privilege and inequity.

Foreword

Pam Christie

Emeritus Professor of Education and Senior Scholar,
Centre for Higher Education Development (CHED),
University of Cape Town (UCT)

How might the intellectual and professional preparation of prospective teachers best be approached in South Africa? How might initial teacher education (ITE) programmes best be structured to prepare aspirant teachers for the complexities they will certainly confront in classrooms? Is there a set of core knowledge and practices that all aspirant teachers should engage with, regardless of context? Experience shows that questions such as these are easier to ask than to answer. There exists wide-ranging literature covering research, policy and programme design in teacher education, much of it very helpful. Yet there often is a lingering sense of inadequacy on the part of those who design and conduct these programmes.

One reason for this sense of inadequacy stems from the nature of education itself, where aims are contested and often conflicting, where many different understandings of the task compete and where 'completion' is by definition always out of reach. Freud (1937) famously observed that education is one of three "impossible professions" (the other two being healing/psychoanalysis and governing) and where one could be sure of achieving unsatisfying results. There is an inherent uncertainty to the nature of education that cannot be 'fixed' or tidied away. Gert Biesta (2013) captures this well in the title of his book, *The Beautiful Risk of Education*. Education, he argues, is not something that can, or ought to be, completely controlled. Quoting Yeats, he reminds us that education is not about filling a bucket, but rather lighting a fire.

The core of education practice – pedagogical interactions of teachers and students in classrooms, mediated by context – is complex to disentangle, control and it is also very difficult to shift. The multiple and often tacit components of a successful pedagogical encounter mean that these encounters are all but impossible to script for the initial education of teachers. Instead of searching for certainty and 'completion' in teacher education programmes, it might be more appropriate to build student teachers' capacities to work creatively with risk and change, while at the same time addressing the more standard mix of content knowledge and pedagogical skills that are necessary for classroom practice.

A challenge that teacher education always confronts is that everyone who has been to school can rightly claim some knowledge of schooling. This makes it particularly difficult for teacher educators to stake out what the specialist field of education entails as against 'common-sense' conceptions of it. Students who enter teacher education programmes bring with them their own experiences and expectations of classrooms, of schools and of teaching. However, 'experience' is not sufficient for understanding. It is always partial and often incoherent and it requires critical reflection to sift and refine. In South Africa, 'learning from experience' may be particularly problematic where students' experience is of poor-quality schooling. Conversely, it is also problematic where students have experienced only the privileged and protected schools in the system. It is often extremely difficult to shift what has been learned by experience and practising teachers often 'default' to their own past experience in times of uncertainty.

Deborah Britzman's (1991) work, *Practice Makes Practice*, offers useful insights here. Teacher education programmes face the challenge of working with and against preformed notions that aspirant teachers have, with the aim of developing a critical understanding of education and the schooling system and building a different image of what 'good education' is.

The practice of teaching and its co-constitutive activity of learning are interpersonal engagements of self-and-other that go well beyond the cognitive domain to include embodied and emotion-laden encounters. It is not surprising that stepping into the classroom with a precarious sense of authority strikes terror into the hearts of many beginner teachers. Expertise in teaching depends in part on developing a deep knowledge of classrooms over time (see Berliner 1986) and it is ironic that in many countries, including South Africa, this expertise is not accorded sufficient social value. Building expertise in teaching is a long-term project that extends beyond what ITE programmes are able to provide. If ITE programmes are understood as preparation for 'classroom readiness', they may then be designed as the first part of a system of continuing professional development (CPD). The responsibility for career-long teacher professional development extends beyond the individual teacher to include professional bodies, providers and employers – particularly the state. In short, ITE should enable student teachers to enter the profession with the understanding that the task is not complete and that further professional learning will always be important.

There are a number of valuable schemata or frameworks for designing teacher education, developed from research and practitioner experience and reflected in the opening chapters of this book. However, frameworks such as these have their limits as strategies for influencing practice. As stylised ideals, they are capable of generating multiple variations in practice and many variables intervene between programme design and the contexts of classrooms in which teachers work – as is evident from later chapters in this book. The expertise of teachers is a crucial factor in classroom learning and one which teacher education rightly addresses. Equally crucial are the socio-economic contexts of schools where teachers work and the resources and support provided to them.

Decades of research in sociology of education confirm that the individual teacher makes the single largest in-school difference to pupil learning outcomes, but learners' home background has the overriding effect on their life chances (see Christie 2008). This is an unresolvable tension that teachers need to negotiate and work with. Essentially, it means that teachers bear responsibility for learner outcomes that are not within their control. It is essential that teachers take responsibility for the task that is theirs and they should not be blamed, as they sometimes are, for systemic limitations in schooling that are beyond their control. Ideally, teachers' responsibility extends beyond improvements in their own classrooms to improvements and renewal in the system as a whole. However, the responsibility of engagement falls upon them – regardless of how they find the system in which they work.

In understanding what this might entail, Iris Marion Young's (2011) distinction between different kinds of responsibility is helpful. While the liability model of responsibility emphasises blame and fault, the social connection model consists of "a shared responsibility that all members of a society have to redress structural injustice by dint of the fact that they contribute by their actions to its production and reproduction" (Young 2011:172). One way of approaching this is to recognise that teaching is a collective activity although it is all too often portrayed in individualised ways. In most schools, students are taught by a number of different teachers over the years, all of whom bear some responsibility for the overall task. The 'egg crate' design of classrooms, where teachers work behind closed doors, tends to privatise teachers' work and isolate their classroom practice from scrutiny. It also reduces teachers' opportunities to work collaboratively and to learn from one another. Young's (2011) social connectedness model of responsibility is more likely to be realised in a collectivist rather than an individualist approach to the work of teaching.

In South Africa, systemic challenges in education are particularly stark given that the apartheid legacies of segregation and inequality have not been adequately remedied. Schools in suburbs, townships and rural areas do not provide the same conditions for teachers' work and give rise to different possibilities and challenges for teacher education to engage with. The lingering and profound inequalities of coloniality are deeply embedded in South African schooling. These were made highly visible in the black student protests of 2016 in former white Model C and private schools, with black students speaking out against discrimination on matters such as hairstyles, name calling and speaking African languages in school. The protests revealed the widely held assumptions that former white schools exemplify 'excellence' and that their traditions and cultural ethos should be maintained when they admit students with different languages and cultures. These assumptions exemplify what Walter Mignolo (2011) and others call "the colonial matrix of power" – entangled intersectional inequalities of class, race, gender, sexuality, culture, language and religion that linger on after the formal administrative arrangements of colonialism are dismantled.

Alongside privileged schools, the majority of the country's schools are under-resourced and poorly served by a curriculum that does not support instruction in students' home languages beyond the fourth year, as is well illustrated by McKinney's (2017) work on "anglonormativity". The obvious structural inequalities in the state's education system – in learners' experiences, opportunities and outcomes – have become normalised or regarded as simply too difficult to tackle. Clearly, teacher education in South Africa needs to prepare student teachers to understand these structural inequalities and the complex dynamics impacting schooling so that they are able to engage ethically to work with and against them. While knowledge of context may be straightforwardly designed and scripted into teacher education programmes, alongside content knowledge and repertoires of pedagogy and assessment, new teachers also need to have a disposition of ethical engagement to grapple with these complex inequalities – this is not simple to design into teacher education programmes.

So far, in outlining challenges faced in designing and delivering ITE programmes, I have suggested a number of ethical dispositions that teacher education needs to build, alongside the knowledge and competencies of its curriculum. These include the capacity to work creatively with the risk and uncertainty that education necessarily entails the habit of critical reflection on experience and a willingness to work towards a new image of 'good education' and an expectation of their need for continuing to learn as teachers. Also important is a willingness to grapple with the complex inequalities of the education system, to hold a sense of responsibility for their individual and collective activities as teachers, as well as a sense of responsibility for improving the education system as a whole. This requires teachers to be open to challenge, to continually question and to adjust their thoughts and actions in relation to matters of good and harm for their learners and the system they share.

These often unspoken challenges facing ITE programmes may be framed in Freirean terms as follows: Teacher education programmes need to deepen student teachers' consciousness of their situation, so as to understand it as a historical reality that requires transformation (see Freire 1973 [2007]). Teacher education programmes need to provide student teachers with the knowledge and expertise to begin to work in the system and also to change it.

Viewed in this way, we as teacher educators cannot give up in the face of the 'impossibility' of our profession. ITE for this 'impossible profession' means building an ethics of engagement within a curriculum of knowledge and pedagogical skills. Lest this seems like an impossible task, it is appropriate to remember Raymond Williams' (1989) advice for a journey of hope: that if there are no easy answers, hard answers are still available and we need to make and share these.

This book provides an account of making and sharing these answers drawing from the ITE research project in post-apartheid South Africa.

References

Berliner, D.C. 1986. In pursuit of the expert pedagogue. *Educational Researcher*, 15(7): 5-13. https://doi.org/10.3102/0013189X015007007

Biesta, G. 2013. *The beautiful risk of education*. Boulder: Paradigm Press.

Britzman, D. 1991. *Practice makes practice: A critical study of learning to teach*. Albany, NY: SUNY Press.

Christie, P. 2008. *Opening the doors of learning: Changing schools in South Africa*. Johannesburg: Heinemann.

Freire, P. 1973 [2007]. *Education for critical consciousness*. London: Continuum.

Freud, S. 1937. Analysis terminable and interminable. *International Journal of Psycho-Analysis*, 18: 373-405.

McKinney, C. 2017. *Language and power in post-colonial schooling: Ideologies in practice*. New York and London: Routledge.

Mignolo, W. 2011. *The darker side of Western modernity: Global futures, decolonial options*. Durham Duke University Press. https://doi.org/10.1215/9780822394501

Williams, R. 1989. *Resources of hope: Culture, democracy, socialism*. London and New York: Verso.

Young, I.M. 2011. *Responsibility for justice*. Oxford: Oxford University Press. https://doi.org/10.1093/acprof:oso/9780195392388.001.0001

Chapter 01

Initial Teacher Education in & for the 21st Century

Yusuf Sayed, Nazir Carrim, Azeem Badroodien & Marcina Singh

1.1 Introduction

Initial teacher education (ITE) is both a knowledge system and a programme design. It is about producing quality education and quality teachers and about ensuring effective teaching. In this first chapter, we begin by considering the importance of ITE preparation by sketching the broad global and national context which informs and drives this book. It then expands on the main concepts that the book uses to engage with different ITE issues, from which we developed a conceptual framework that guided this study. This is based on a review of key debates and literature related to teacher education and what is understood to be effective teaching. This is followed by an outline of the background to the book and its genesis, after which we discuss the overall research approach based on the conceptual framework outlined in this chapter. The chapter concludes with an overview of the book.

1.2 The Importance of Initial Teacher Education (ITE) Preparation

This section considers the importance of good ITE in enhancing education quality. It highlights how, in policy and research pronouncements about equitable and quality education, much rests on teachers and teaching.

The preparation of teachers in ITE programmes has become a particular priority within the increased global and local emphasis on quality teaching and learning in the 21st century, especially with regard to specialised areas of knowledge and how to organise relations to professional knowledge and practices.

At the global level, the Sustainable Development Goals (SDGs) highlight equitable and quality education as a fundamental driver that can realise change, especially in low economic states. One of the SDG targets is to "substantially increase the supply of qualified teachers by 2030, to address the qualified teacher shortage, and to ensure that learners have access to quality primary and secondary education" (United Nations Association of Greater Philadelphia [UNA-GP] 2015).

The emphasis on ITE globally is mainly due to the importance given to quality teaching and learning in the United Nations (UN) SDGs. The concern about the contribution of schooling to quality learning for all (particularly for the marginalised) and the promotion of social cohesion and social justice in societies emerging from the long shadows of violence, conflict and fragmentation, is also emphasised. Against this background, governments across the world have re-examined ITE programmes in terms of the types and extent of investment that they believe are necessary to improve education quality. As teacher salaries are on average the single largest expenditure item (between 70% and 90%) in national budgets across diverse contexts, a preoccupation with teachers is perhaps predictable.

It is often asserted that equitable and quality education is only possible if there are "sufficient numbers of adequately and highly qualified teachers" to provide it (Bourgonje & Tromp 2011). This is particularly evident when viewed through the lens of learner performance and how different learners perform at different levels across international contexts. What international comparative tests highlight is the importance of quality teaching and learning and thus the importance of the training that teachers need to receive to provide quality teaching and learning.

In that regard, the Africa Learning Barometer (Van Fleet 2012) notes that while 97 million of Africa's 128 million school-aged children will enter school on time, in the current situation, 37 million of these children will not learn basic skills through their education. Moreover, of the 14 million that will enter school late, 3,9 million will not learn, meaning that they will "not be able to read or write with fluency or successfully complete basic numeracy tasks" (United Nations Educational, Scientific and Cultural Organization – International Labor Organization [ILO-UNESCO] 2003). This raises complex challenges for a continent like Africa, especially for sub-Saharan Africa, given the urgent demand for further and rapid development.

Equally disconcerting is the poor quality of the teachers who teach in schools in such contexts with many teachers entering the profession with inadequate core subject knowledge, because their own initial education had been so poor. ILO-UNESCO (2003) points out that this is especially the case in countries where primary education provision has expanded rapidly (in pursuit of expanding access to education) and where "many teachers have been recruited without the necessary training".

In both national and international cases, the policy imperative in focusing on teachers and encouraging more effective teaching is to achieve greater equity and quality. This, however, requires greater investment in stronger and high-quality ITE and continuing professional development (CPD). As Darling-Hammond (2000:1) notes:

> The findings of both qualitative and quantitative analyses suggest that policy investments in the quality of teachers may be related to improvements in student performance. Quantitative analyses indicate that measures of teacher preparation and certification are by far the strongest correlates of student achievement in reading and mathematics, both before and after controlling for student poverty and language status. This analysis suggests that policies adopted by states [in the United States of America (USA)] regarding teacher education, licensing, hiring, and professional development may make an important difference in the qualifications and capacities that teachers bring to their work.

It also requires teachers being granted the space to exercise their various agencies. In developing this space, teachers need to be supported in their initial teacher preparation to do the right thing and to make teaching and teachers effective. As Naylor and Sayed (2014:9-10) assert:

> The quality of the new teachers graduating from initial teacher training will depend on the selection of candidates into the program, the modality of the training, the quality of the teacher educators, the teacher education curriculum and the assessment process.

This view is reinforced by the National Commission on Teaching & America's Future (NCTAF) (2016:28-29), which argues in a review of teacher education and teachers that:

> [s]uccessful teacher preparation programs are grounded in an understanding of the skills required for K-12 students to succeed in the 21st century and the teaching practices that foster those skills; these programs integrate an extended period of robust clinical experience and help beginning teachers learn how to evaluate and improve their own practice. Successful candidates experience subject matter content and pedagogy in the authentic settings of K-12 classrooms, and reflect on what they are learning through aligned coursework that involves intensive study of child development, the science of learning, cultural contexts, culturally responsive teaching, curriculum, assessment, and subject-specific instructional strategies. Effective programs prepare candidates to address complex standards and assessments by teaching content in a way that focuses on depth over breadth, builds higher order critical thinking and problem-solving skills, and that makes connections across disciplines.

At the national level in South Africa, for example, the National Policy Framework for Teacher Education and Development (DoE 2007) acknowledges that "teachers are the largest single occupational group and profession in the country and they have serious strategic importance for the intellectual, moral, and cultural preparation of young people". In noting this, the framework observes that teachers invariably work under extremely complex conditions in South Africa, largely due to the pervasive legacies of apartheid.

In South Africa, many international comparative tests such as the Southern and Eastern Africa Consortium for Monitoring Educational Quality (SACMEQ), Trends in International Mathematics and Science Study (TIMSS), Progress in International Reading Literacy Study (PIRLS), and national assessments such as the Annual National Assessment (ANA) have been done. They reveal that learners, particularly the marginalised, perform rather poorly comparatively and that their poor attainment is closely tied to the vast majority of South African learners being schooled in dysfunctional institutions (Badat & Sayed 2014).

In that respect, as evident in TIMSS 1995, 1999 and 2003, learner performance in South Africa in literacy and numeracy is particularly shocking, with very little change in performance over an eight-year period (Martin & Kelly 1997; Mullis et al. 2000; Martin, Mullis & Chrostowski 2004). This low level of performance is best illustrated by a comparison of South Africa's average score for mathematics, 275, to the international average of 487 in 1999 and 467 in 2003. In science, the score was 243, compared to the international average of 488 in 1999 and 244 compared to the international average score of 474 in 2003 (Organization for Economic Co-operation and Development [OECD] 2005:53-54).

Data from TIMSS 2015 showed an improvement in mathematics and science in South Africa between 2003 and 2015. The average score in mathematics was 372, compared to the international average of 500. In science, the average attainment score was 358, compared to the international average of 500 (Reddy et al. 2016:3). Notwithstanding the improvement, the results of South African learners still signify extremely poor levels of understanding for both mathematics and science and South Africa remains at the bottom of the attainment list when compared to other participating countries (Reddy et al. 2016:3). Reddy et al. (2016:7) state that "[p]erformance in mathematics and science appears to have shifted from a very low level to a low level". The unequal nature of schools in South Africa is reflected in the TIMSS 2015 data – proportionally more former Model C Quintile 5 schools achieved better in mathematics than poorer, no-fee schools. This aggregation increases in learning, albeit low, masks inequities in attainment across school types (Reddy et al. 2016:7).

These low performance levels can perhaps be inferentially linked to the ways in which South African teachers perform in tests like SACMEQ and the knowledge bases that they reveal in them. In SACMEQ III (2010), for example, the results showed that while South African teachers performed relatively well on questions requiring the simple retrieval of information explicitly stated in the text (scoring an average of 75,1%), scores dropped dramatically when higher cognitive functions of inference (55,2%), interpretation (36,6%) and evaluation (39,7%) were invoked (Hungi et al. 2010). Therefore, while teachers performed at relatively acceptable levels in basic arithmetic and language, their abilities declined dramatically when more complex topics were explored or addressed (a drop from 67,2% for basic arithmetic to 49,7% for key mathematical areas such as fractions, ratios, and proportions). This issue was quite evident in a 2008 study that examined teachers using the same test items as those taken by Grade 6 learners. The study revealed very low levels of performance among teachers and that their performance levels also dropped according to the grade they taught. For mathematics, for example, Foundation Phase teachers (up to Grade 3) obtained an average score of 53%, while colleagues in the Intermediate Phase (Grades 4 to 6) obtained an average of 36%. Notably, the study also showed that when teaching arithmetic, teachers with postgraduate degrees tended to score the highest (Taylor 2013).

As such, at both national and international levels, policies fortify the view that it is high-quality teacher preparation that makes a difference in teacher quality. This makes a difference especially in getting student teachers to become teachers in ways that make them grapple with contextual problems arising from within the schooling sector. This ultimately relies on what is constituted in various ITE programmes.

This poses a serious challenge for ITE programme provisioning at the tertiary level in South Africa. Even though the term 'teachers matter' holds enormous currency in current policy, little is really known about how teachers are trained, how they experience such training and where and how investment for improving teacher quality for quality education should be done. As such, what is taught in ITE programmes remains a black box – a gap which this book seeks to address. The government and education policymakers have an immediate interest in understanding how education and teacher quality can be improved.

1.3 Developing the Conceptual Framework: ITE Programmes as Knowledge Sets

For this book, what comprises a teacher education programme is considered through the prism of the different kinds of knowledge that prospective teachers need to be equipped with prior to becoming teachers in different schooling contexts. This book takes its lead from the Department of Higher Education and Training (DHET) in South Africa, which observes that:

> [t]eaching is a complex activity that is premised upon the acquisition, integration, and application of different types of knowledge practices or learning. A purely skills-based approach, which relies almost exclusively on evidence of demonstrable outcomes as measures of success, without paying attention to how knowledge should underpin these skills for them to impact effectively on learning, will produce technicians who may be able to replicate performance in similar contexts, but who are severely challenged when the context changes. In contrast, the approach adopted in the Minimum Requirements for Teacher Education Qualifications pays close attention to the various types of knowledge that underpin teachers' practice, while encapsulating all of these in the notion of integrated and applied knowledge (DHET 2015:9).

The DHET lists five types of knowledge that should underpin all ITE programmes in South Africa, namely (i) disciplinary, (ii) pedagogical, (iii) practical, (iv) fundamental and (v) situational knowledge (DHET 2015:10). These are further discussed in Chapter 2.

Darling-Hammond and Bransford (in Darling-Hammond 2006:304) similarly approach ITE from the vantage point of 'knowledges' and identify three knowledge areas, as captured in Figure 1.1. These areas (easily) resonate with the five knowledge areas identified by the DHET.

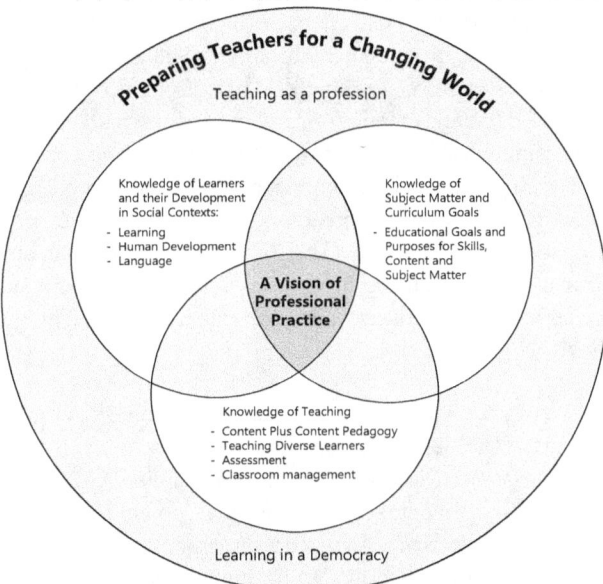

Figure 1.1   Knowledge in ITE. *Source:* Darling-Hammond and Bransford (Darling-Hammond 2006:304)

Notably, however, the idea of ITE as knowledge sets is a contested one. Fenstermacher (1994) and Cochran-Smith and Lytle (1999) ask, for example, what constitutes a knowledge set and what interrelationships exist between knowledge sets. Others also question what is understood to constitute knowledge in ITE and how this informs the design of ITE programmes. As such, there are two further frames (in addition to those noted above) by which ITE programmes are often conceptualised. These include Shulman's (1987) framework, which talks about content knowledge (CK), pedagogical content knowledge (PCK) and general pedagogical knowledge (GPK), as well as the TPACK framework, which refers to technological pedagogical content knowledge that integrates technology into thinking about what knowledge prospective teachers should possess. There are also instances where frameworks such as Shulman's has been expanded and further categorised into the teaching of particular subjects and disciplines, for example that of Ball, Bass and Hill (2004; 2005) on a subject like mathematics (see Chapter 7).

For this book, the above frameworks are analytically and heuristically framed as three interrelated knowledge sets. In the first knowledge set, specialist, specific and general knowledge are tied to teaching and learning in a particular subject, learning domain, or discipline. This is conceived as knowledge that is internal to a particular domain of learning/subject/discipline, where the knowledge set encompasses specialist and more GPK that cuts across learning domains (including classroom management). It is a knowledge set characterised by Shulman (1995; 1997), who argues that all prospective teachers need mastery of three elements tied to what they teach, namely subject content knowledge (SCK), CK, PCK, and GPK.

CK refers to the material taught to learners and that which teachers should be competent in. It is about the actual content as well as the logic of the discipline/subject and that of the particular domain of learning. PCK refers to the organisation of effective teaching for the content of a particular learning domain/discipline (Shulman 1987). This requires deep learning about the logic systems of learning domains/disciplines that then assist teachers to select, organise and present content to learners in ways that facilitate their learning. PCK involves recognising what learners know, as well as their misconceptions, in order to facilitate effective learning. This includes knowing how to use technologies in the teaching and learning process. GPK provides the broad principles and practices required to facilitate learning in classrooms. As such, GPK is not specific to a learning domain but instead refers to how learning is managed – for example through classroom management and organisation, or behaviour management. Inclusive education is often embedded in ITE programmes as part of GPK (Shulman 1986).

In the second knowledge set, the focus is on that which frames and makes it possible to effectively teach a particular subject, learning domain or discipline. It is knowledge that is external to a particular subject, learning domain or discipline and encompasses curricula knowledge, knowledge about context and knowledge about the aims and purposes of education. This includes (i) curricula frameworks, textbooks and other learning resources that become the tools that teachers utilise to be able to communicate with their learners, (ii) the particular contexts that impact what and how teachers teach and (iii) that which is intimately seen to connect what is desirable in society in general and education in particular (Shulman 1987).

With regard to context, Darling-Hammond (1994) speaks about "knowledge about learners" and "knowledge about place and space". With "knowledge about learners", Darling-Hammond observes that teachers need contextually specific knowledge about who their learners are, where they come from and what they bring to the teaching and learning process. They also need to know how learners learn and what they know about learning. With "knowledge about place and space", Darling-Hammond (1994) refers to the connection between the type of pedagogy enacted and the place and space in which it is enacted. This includes understanding the immediate school and surrounding communities and extending this to include national and global social, political, economic and culturally contextual factors. It is thus knowledge that positions the teacher as someone who knows what is happening at the micro, meso and macro level, and who understands the dialectic interplay between teaching as a pedagogic activity in the classroom and factors outside of this private world.

With regard to knowledge that connects what is desirable in society, this includes knowledge about the purposes, values and goals of education, and presupposes that teachers are both active agents in schools and are able to engage critically with the moral and ethical purposes of education. This ties knowledge to teaching as a profession and teachers as professionals (Conway et al. 2009).

In the third knowledge set, the idea of effective teaching as a purposive moral and ethical activity is given prominence, with emphasis on the affective dimensions of teaching. As a moral exercise, this knowledge set encompasses the skills and competences of teachers to model, teach, and demonstrate the values and behaviours of social cohesion and social justice in education (Sayed et al. 2015). This knowledge set thus refers to both the technical skills that prospective teachers should possess and the value dispositions they need to have to forge a social justice agenda within education. The (third) knowledge set is furthermore transversal in relation to the other two knowledge sets, given that it cuts across not just what and how teachers teach, but also how they understand the context within which they work. It positions teachers as knowing, purposive and active agents working towards the broad goals of transforming society and forging a more inclusive and equitable future for learners. It also shows teachers as acting both within their classrooms and schools, as well as outside of their education spaces (Boostrom 1998).

Notably, these three knowledge sets are analytically and heuristically held together by the following ideas:

- ✓ Knowledge in ITE is integrated and indivisible and pedagogic enactments in classrooms require an integration of knowledge sets that maximise learning and enact effective teaching (Guerriero 2014). Conceptually, this suggests that it is through professional practice enacted in diverse classroom settings that benchmarks how prospective teachers graduating from ITE programmes integrate different sets of knowledge.
- ✓ Context may encapsulate the backgrounds of learners, but it further refers to national contexts and the community contexts from which learners are drawn. Context is thus a determinant of how practice is enacted, as well as how it impacts acts of enactment (Fenwick & Cooper 2013).

✓ ITE programmes shape, and are invariably shaped by, individual visions of what is desirable in and for society (Labaree, 2000). As such, ITE programmes offer more than technical skills, but are informed by the values of prospective teachers. This encompasses how ITE programmes conceptualise their commitments to equity and redress in a democratic society, and how they position social justice as a desirable value within the programmes.

Also, within the three knowledge sets, the combination of the context of practice integrated with the context of environment in shaping practice is usefully captured in Figure 1.2. The figure shows how teacher quality is tied to professional development and the contexts of practice and environment, and how these different and interconnecting contexts shape teacher practice. Crucial to the figure is who the teachers are (their attributes, backgrounds and biographies of teaching/learning experiences), as well as who teaches them (the teacher educators and their backgrounds and biographies).

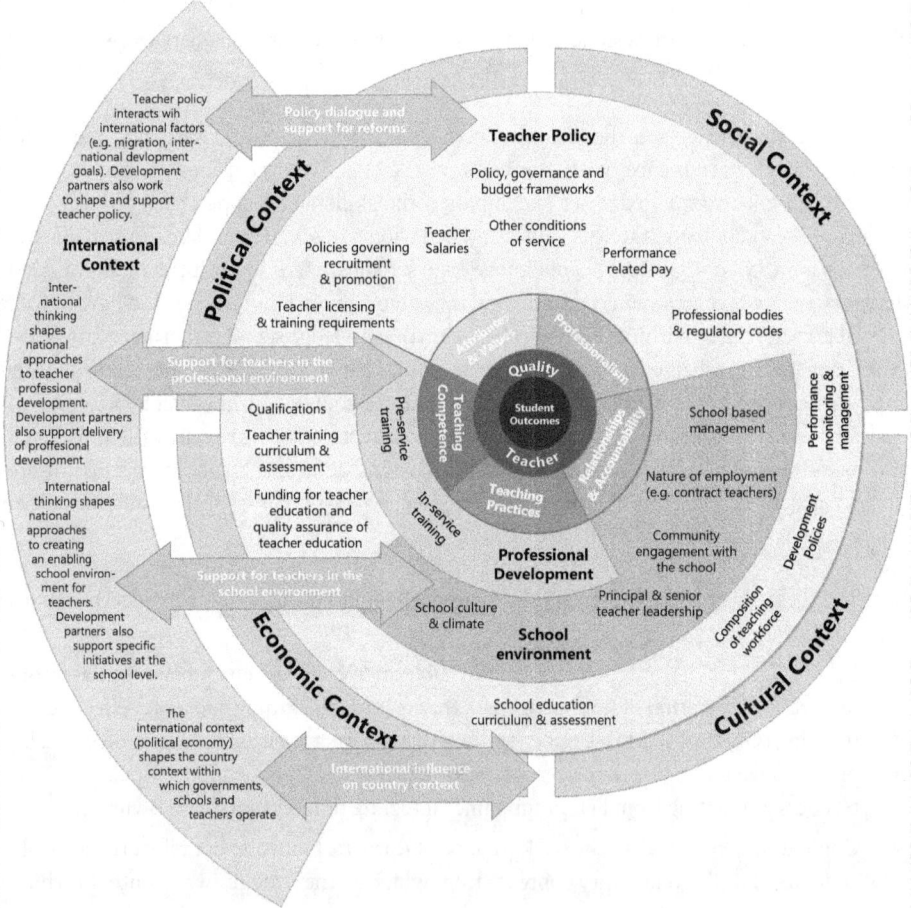

Figure 1.2   A Composite Model of Teacher Quality. *Source:* Naylor and Sayed (2014:22)

Indeed, the idea of three interrelated knowledge sets within ITE programmes is an important conceptual and heuristic tool for thinking about what ITE programmes can do. It emphasises the various issues and concerns that must be addressed if quality teaching and quality teachers are to be at the heart of the quality education goal. As Darling-Hammond (2014:7) notes:

> If one wants to ensure high-quality instruction, it is important to attend to both teacher quality and teaching quality. Teacher quality might be thought of as the bundle of personal traits, skills, and understanding an individual brings to teaching, including dispositions to behave in certain ways, such as collaborating with colleagues and adapting instruction to help students succeed. Teaching quality, as distinct from teacher quality, refers to strong instruction that enables a wide range of students to learn. Such instruction meets the demands of the discipline, the goals of instruction, and the needs of students in a particular context. Teaching quality is in part a function of teacher quality – teachers' knowledge, skills, and dispositions – but it is also strongly influenced by the context of instruction, including factors aside from what the teacher knows and can do.

For this book, the above framework identifies not just who the teachers are but also what they do, as shaped by the national, regional and international contexts within which teachers teach. Specifically, this book examines two very specific dimensions of what makes a quality teacher and what quality teaching is. First, the book focuses solely on (and is specific to) teacher preparation in mathematics and languages. Second, the book engages with ITE preparation in relation to two phases of the schooling system, namely the Foundation Phase and the Further Education and Training (FET) Phase. These phases represent the start and end of the schooling experiences of all learners – thus what knowledge ITE programmes equip teachers entering these phases with, is crucial.

1.4 Developing the Conceptual Framework: Translating ITE as Knowledge Sets into Programmes

While the idea of knowledge sets helps to understand the conceptual framing of ITE programmes, in the end it is how this translates into programme designs that determine their usefulness. Figure 1.3 links what knowledge ITE programmes offer with the design of programmes. As such, Figure 1.3 translates the knowledge that students teachers is expected to acquire into the course/modules that typically characterise ITE programmes. In Figure 1.3, the issue of practice is central to ITE provision and consequentially programme design. It reveals that while knowledge is crucial to professional practice, it is the teaching component of ITE programmes that lies at the heart of teacher preparation. This ironically stands in stark contrast to many current approaches to the design of ITE programmes, where teaching practice is often treated as marginal and disconnected from other ITE courses. In the above regard, it is notable that courses are offerings within programmes (also referred to as modules or subjects) and are delivered by teacher educators who ultimately determine what lies within them.[1] It is also important to recognise the interrelationship between the different knowledge components and with teaching practice, which is at the core of ITE programmes. Thus, ITE programme design must take a holistic and integrated approach to curriculum delivery. For

---

1   While the framework recognises the importance of teacher educators as key to the experiences of student teachers, they are not the focus of this book.

the purpose of this book, the dimensions identified are analysed in relation to the experiences of student teachers. Thus, the main focus of this book is those who are becoming teachers, as the title of this book indicates and, as such, this book focuses on the beliefs and attitudes of student teachers. In this respect, Pajares (1992) notes that the beliefs of teachers crucially impact their view of how students learn, their role and what counts as valid knowledge, which is why this is also a focus of this book.

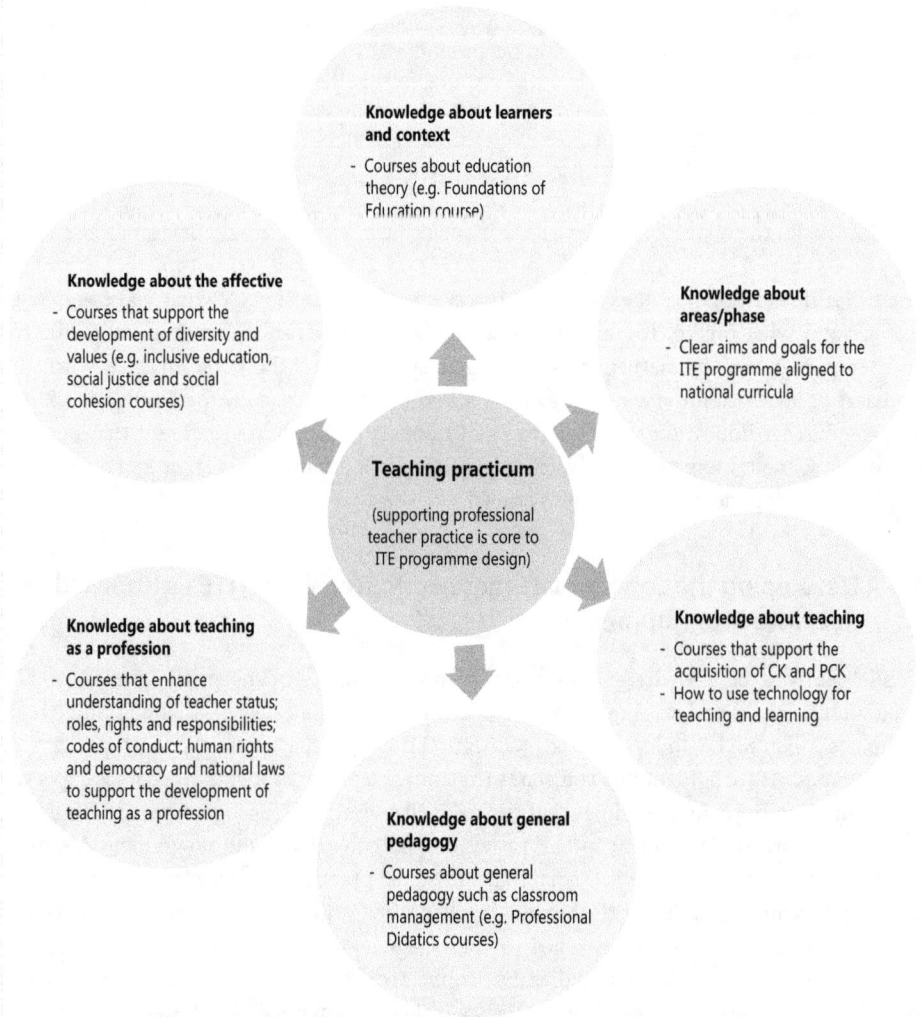

Figure 1.3   A Programmatic Approach to ITE. *Source*: Sayed (co-editor)

As such, ITE programmes are as much about representing knowledge sets as about reflecting visions of professional practice. In that regard, it is important to recognise, as Darling-Hammond (2006) notes, that:

> a good teacher education program is first of all coherent and further has a good idea about what good teaching is, and is also able to organise all of its course work and all of the clinical experiences around that coherent vision.

Indeed, ITE programmes need to be more than arbitrary collections of modules and should instead prioritise enabling student teachers to benefit from working with more experienced teachers in the classrooms. ITE programmes need to focus on teaching students effective teaching strategies, how learners learn and how to assess learning.

This (above) kind of programme design is generally lacking in South Africa. In that respect, an approach that grounds ITE within robust conceptual frameworks that also pay close attention to its form and substance within different programme designs is urgently required. It would usefully serve as a key vehicle by which professional practice, that promotes equitable and quality learning for all in diverse classroom contexts, could be advanced.

1.5 Phases of Learning and Teacher Preparation in the Context of South Africa

It is noteworthy that ITE programmes are but the first stage of ongoing journeys of professional development for teachers in South Africa. They provide prospective teachers with the knowledge, skills and dispositions to embark on their journeys as classroom teachers and are preparatory and initial, requiring a basic minimum to practise in schools. As such, ITE needs to be conceptualised as fundamental to teacher professional development – a process that is ongoing and will continue throughout the different stages of a teacher's working life, as illustrated in Figure 1.4. This figure captures the idea of teacher professional development as a continuous process but not one that is linear.[2]

---

[2] This is akin to Huberman's idea of the lifecycle of teachers.

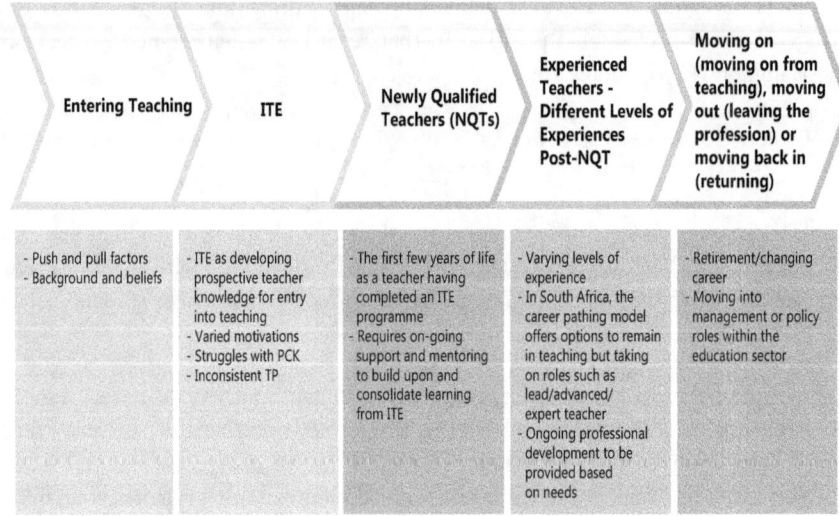

Figure 1.4 Teacher Career Phases. *Source:* Sayed (co-editor)

In South Africa, the majority of ITE programmes are offered at public higher education institutions (HEIs), as listed in Table 1.1 and are accredited by the DHET. Should students choose to attain their teaching qualifications from private colleges, it is their responsibility to check the accreditation status of that institution. This is important to consider as the quality of ITE experiences for prospective teachers in South Africa is contingent on which institutions they study at. For this book, the focus is on ITE programmes offered at universities in the Western Cape and Gauteng provinces, comprising of different provider types.[3]

Table 1.1 Higher Education Institutions (Heis) Offering ITE Programmes in South Africa

Province	HEI
Eastern Cape	Nelson Mandela University (NMU)
	Rhodes University (RU)
	University of Fort Hare (UFH)
	Walter Sisulu University (WSU)
Free State	Central University of Technology (CUT)
	University of the Free State (UFS)

---

3   It is important to note that this book focuses on public teacher educator providers and not private HEIs such as the Embury Institute of Higher Education, which offers teacher training. It should also be noted that this book does not engage with the reopening of Colleges of Education, which are argued to produce technically more competent teachers. It is argued that what is important is not which institutional type trains teachers but instead what student teachers acquire during their training.

Province	HEI
Gauteng	Tshwane University of Technology (TUT) University of Johannesburg (UJ) University of Pretoria (UP) University of the Witwatersrand (Wits)
KwaZulu-Natal	Durban University of Technology (DUT) University of KwaZulu-Natal (UKZN) University of Zululand (Unizulu)
Limpopo	University of Limpopo (UL) University of Venda (Univen)
Northern Cape	Sol Plaatjie University (SPU)
North West	North-West University (NWU)
Western Cape	Cape Peninsula University of Technology (CPUT) University of Cape Town (UCT) Stellenbosch University (SU) University of the Western Cape (UWC)
National	University of South Africa (UNISA)

Source: Department of Basic Education (DBE 2012)

In the above institutions, students can approach becoming a teacher in two ways. They can either opt to complete a Bachelor of Education (BEd) degree, which will allow them to specialise in the Foundation Phase (Grades R to 3), Intermediate Phase (Grades 4 to 6), Senior Phase (Grades 7 to 9), or FET (Grades 10 to 12); or prospective teachers can complete an initial Bachelor of Arts (BA), Bachelor of Science (BSc) or Bachelor of Social Science (BSocSc) degree and then follow this up with a one-year Postgraduate Certificate in Education (PGCE), which allows them to specialise in the same learning phases as with the BEd noted above. Table 1.2 lists the different learning areas offered within each of the four phases.

Table 1.2 Phase-specific Specialisation Fields[4]

Foundation Phase (Grades R-3)	Intermediate Phase (Grades 4-6)	Senior Phase (Grades 7-9)	FET Phase (Grades 10-12)
✓ Literacy & Numeracy ✓ Life Skills	✓ Languages ✓ Mathematics ✓ Arts & Culture ✓ Life Orientation ✓ Natural Sciences & Technology ✓ Social Sciences	✓ Arts & Culture ✓ Economic & Management Sciences ✓ Languages ✓ Life Orientation ✓ Mathematics ✓ Natural Sciences ✓ Social Sciences ✓ Technology	✓ Accounting ✓ Agricultural Management Practices ✓ Agricultural Sciences ✓ Agricultural Technology ✓ Business Studies ✓ Civil Technology ✓ Computer Applications Technology ✓ Consumer Studies ✓ Dance Studies ✓ Design Studies ✓ Dramatic Arts ✓ Economics ✓ Electrical Technology ✓ Engineering Graphics & Design ✓ Geography ✓ History ✓ Hospitality Studies ✓ Information Technology ✓ Languages ✓ Life Orientation ✓ Life Sciences ✓ Mathematics ✓ Mathematical Literacy ✓ Mechanical Technology ✓ Music ✓ Physical Sciences ✓ Religion Studies ✓ Tourism ✓ Visual Arts

Source: DBE (2012)

4 This information is likely to change as there is a review of MRTEQ and the possible introduction of the three stream curriuclum.

For this book, two types of student cohorts were followed, with data from the questionnaires analysed by the different chapter authors. The first student cohort comprised Foundation Phase BEd students in their final year of a four-year Foundation Phase programme. This included students from three universities: SU, CPUT, and TUT. The second cohort consisted of PGCE FET students who completed a one-year teacher preparation programme, following their first degree, at the UWC.

For this book, the specific focus was on languages and mathematics across the two phases. This was decided based on government prioritisation of these as core areas for improving quality education in South Africa and areas that national and international large-scale assessment studies reveal as problem subject areas.

1.6 The Genesis of the Book: Building Partnerships and Networks of Collaboration

Having outlined the framework of the study, this section provides the background and genesis of the study. This book forms part of research initiatives undertaken by the Centre for International Teacher Education (CITE) at the CPUT, which houses the South African Research Chair (SARChI) in Teacher Education. Within these initiatives, teacher education development is prioritised due to the dearth of systematically collected material about ITE preparation and CPD in South Africa. The focus is also informed by ITE being recognised internationally as an important focus within the field of teacher education research and scholarship. Still, there are very limited contributions from developing contexts in this body of international literature, especially scholarly inputs from African contexts. In South Africa, for example, there has been very limited large-scale and longitudinal research at the various HEIs in the country regarding how students develop skills, knowledge, and dispositions to become teachers.

To the latter end, CITE initiated an ITE research programme in 2015 in collaboration with various HEIs in both the Western Cape and Gauteng provinces (see Sayed et al. 2015). The partnership was aimed at strengthening and enhancing dialogue and networking between the institutions to develop a collaborative research agenda. As such, cross-institutional teams were established to work on the various dimensions of the project at the different institutions, which was then used to inform the development of each chapter of this book. While the teams collectively analysed the data and as teams produced the various draft chapters, members of CITE assisted in key ways in finalising the production of the draft book. They did this through a number of workshops that developed a common understanding for the authors of the book and that provided feedback on the writing as it evolved. This book is thus a completely collaborative effort and represents a commitment to networking and scientific exchange across various institutions in South Africa.

It is part of CITE's mission to share relevant experiences, lessons and good practices emerging from this writing partnership in ways that:
- ✓ provide a scholarly platform for discussion and dialogue about ITE in South Africa and globally; and
- ✓ contribute to the discourse on education change and school reform as it relates to ITE.

In that respect, this book represents the overall aim of CITE to systematically collect data on student teacher experiences of ITE that speak directly to issues of quality and understanding this across multiple and diverse institutional settings.

1.7   Research Context and Approach of the Broader Study

Drawing on multi-site case studies of ITE programmes at four HEIs in South Africa, this book systematically examines student teachers' experiences of their learning across their respective programmes. Specifically, it focuses on data from exit-level student teachers completing either a four-year BEd degree in Foundation Phase or a one-year PGCE, concentrating on languages and mathematics in the Foundation and FET phases. The case studies were conducted at three universities (four campuses) in the Western Cape province and one university in the Gauteng province.

Given that ITE as a form of provision greatly varies across the university landscape, the aim of this book is to show new institutional forms that have emerged in the post-apartheid period that influence student teacher experiences.

As such, the chapters of this book were informed by the following:
- ✓ The inclusion of both traditional universities and universities of technology, as well as the inclusion of one university from another province (one with high student numbers in its ITE programme).
- ✓ A focus on two different phases of the schooling system, concentrating on their 'becoming as teachers' in the two phases.
- ✓ The data used came from one component of a larger ITE project that sought to track student teachers across the four (or one) years of their ITE programme to their first year of teaching. The second volume of this book will examine the latter, namely the experiences of qualified teachers as NQTs in post-apartheid South Africa.

The specific aims of this book, across the different chapters, are to address the following questions:
- ✓ What motivates individuals to enrol in teacher education and what are their beliefs about teaching and learners?
- ✓ What are student teachers' experiences of their specific programmes in relation to the skills and knowledge they develop?
- ✓ How do student teachers experience the teaching practicum component of their ITE programmes – a component that is meant to model their practice as NQTs?

Based on the overarching research question of the larger study, namely "What are the learning experiences of student teachers enrolled in teaching education programmes in general, and how do these programmes support student teachers to teach literacy/language and numeracy/mathematics effectively in the classroom?". The larger study employs a mixed-methods approach that draws on data collected from several questionnaires and focus group interviews with student teachers in their programmes.

The questionnaires encompassed three different dimensions for the two cohorts of BEd Foundation Phase and PGCE FET students. These included the following:

- ✓ The dimension of teacher motivation (reasons to become a teacher) and beliefs about teaching. This dimension specifically considers what extrinsic and intrinsic factors drive students leaving school to enrol for a teaching qualification and what their beliefs about teaching and learners are, in general and specifically, in relation to languages and mathematics.
- ✓ Student teachers' experiences about their development of knowledge and skills in ITE programmes. This dimension specifically explored their overall perceptions of the programme and specifically the extent to which they feel competent and skilled to teach languages and mathematics.
- ✓ The dimension of teacher practicum. This dimension specifically explored student teachers' experiences of teaching practice, the support they received from the school in which they practised as teachers, as well as the support from the university and the extent to which they found this to be a valuable component of their learning.

The questionnaires included questions that captured biographic and contextual background data for each student teacher.[5] These were complemented by focus group interviews and discussions with selected student teachers at all the participating institutions and documentary data on each of the programmes at the participating institutions. Details about specific research techniques tied to individual chapters are outlined in those chapters. In some chapters authors include additional data, as appropriate, from their ongoing research.

Notably, for this book, the identity of each of the participating institutions is anonymised. This is both to protect the integrities of the different institutions and to ensure that their privacy and practices are respected. Ethical permission for the ITE project was obtained from each of the institutions with ethical clearance secured for the research project from CPUT, the institution where CITE is based. All elements of the ethics requirements were fully adhered to.

Table 1.3 provides an overview of the data that underpinned the particular component of the project covered in this book, as well as the number of participants in each.

---

5   One of the biographic questions asked student teachers to self-identify with one of the population groups legislated in the Population Registration Act of 1950 (black African, Indian, coloured, or white). In this book this is regarded as a marker of respondents' self-identification, which may be consequential given the legacy of apartheid.

Table 1.3   Overview of the Data for this Book

Institution	Questionnaire (teacher motivation and beliefs)	Questionnaire (students' experiences of development of their knowledge, skills and disposition)	Questionnaire (students' experiences of the teaching practicum)	Focus group
	(for PGCE, these two questionnaires were combined)			
Institution A	147	117	152	5
Institution B	64	58	57	3
Institution C	48	48	34	4
Institution D	66		45	4

1.8   Overview of the Book

This book, as noted above, draws on empirical research conducted at four HEIs in South Africa within the ITE programmes they have in place. This encompasses the experiences of student teachers in particular ITE programmes, including their motivation for wanting to become a teacher, what their hopes and aspirations were, how they related to professional knowledge (particularly in relation to the teaching and learning of languages and mathematics in schools) and the challenges they thought they would encounter in their teaching practices. In that regard, this book is divided into four sections, each covering an identified niche or specialist area within ITE provisioning.

1.8.1   Section 1: Setting the Context

Section 1 consists of four chapters that provide an overview of the context of ITE provision in South Africa and an insight into the profiles of students of the different institutions, as well as their professed motivation and beliefs for entering the teaching profession and wanting to teach.

Chapter 1, by Sayed, Carrim, Badroodien and Singh, provides an outline of the research that was conducted and its contribution to the genesis of this book. The chapter provides the main conceptual framework that underpins the various authors' thinking about ITE, using the notion of different knowledge sets to synthesise the literature about quality teachers and quality teaching. Consequentially it highlights what ITE programmes are expected to provide. This is explored in a later subsection of this chapter, where ITE as different knowledge forms is discussed.

Chapter 2, by Sayed, Carrim, Badroodien, McDonald and Singh, outlines the policy and legislative context of ITE in South Africa. It traces the development of ITE in post-apartheid South Africa against the background of the inheritance and legacies of the apartheid system of teacher education. The chapter positions this in relation to post-apartheid teacher education policies that have attempted to reshape the content and specification of what ITE programmes should cover, such as the Norms and Standards of Educators (NSE) and the Minimum Requirements for Teacher Education Qualifications (MRTEQ) policy. It is also positioned in relation to wider international policies and development debates that emerge from the UN's SDGs 2030, as agreed to in September 2015. This chapter pays particular attention to how ITE as a field of provision is shaped by national and global policies, by the reorganisation of teacher education within the higher education national landscape, as well as by different institutional contexts.

Chapter 3, by Sayed, Kwenda, Rampa and Mort, provides insights into the backgrounds and profiles of the different students that enter teaching in the BEd Foundation Phase and the PGCE FET Phase in languages and mathematics and explores their reasoning for doing so. It considers 'who becomes a teacher' in order to better understand the motivation of student teachers and as a way of informing how teachers could be recruited for areas and subjects with the most need in the South African context.

Chapter 4, by Singh, Wessels and Kanjee, addresses the beliefs that student teachers bring with them as prospective teachers, as well as their expectations of training in teacher education programmes. It asks to what extent such aspirations are met in relation to the beliefs they had when they entered their programmes. As such, the chapter pays particular attention to their beliefs about learners, the teaching of languages and mathematics and about teaching in transitional contexts.

1.8.2 Section 2: Teachers' Professional Knowledge

Section 2 consists of two chapters that examine the notion of professional knowledge, how this is understood in the literature and what it may mean in relation to student teachers in the context of the two ITE programmes being investigated. The chapters distinguish between general knowledge and knowledge relating to professional practice.

Chapter 5, by Mogliacci, Robinson and Rousseau, considers the development of professional knowledge among student teachers in the Foundation Phase of ITE programmes and during teaching practice. The chapter more specifically explores the perceptions of student teachers in the BEd Foundation Phase of the efficacy of the content of their programmes in enhancing their teaching experiences. As such, the chapter focuses on epistemological issues related to what constitutes professional knowledge and the kinds of knowledge deemed to be needed for professional teaching practice. It explores why student teachers express quite different views about teacher professional knowledge and suggests some implications of this for teacher education programmes.

Chapter 6, by Moodley, Sadeck and Luckay, considers the development of professional knowledge among student teachers in the FET Phase of ITE programmes and during teaching practice. Specifically, it reports on empirical research conducted with PGCE students enrolled at one HEI in the Western Cape. The chapter focuses on the value of the PGCE programme as a vehicle to develop the professional knowledge of student teachers at the institution. This is done by making them aware of their prospective roles as teachers and the kinds of professional preparation they require both in the PGCE programme and during their teaching practice experiences.

1.8.3   Section 3: Learning to Teach

Section 3 consists of four chapters that critically examine the challenges that prospective teachers encounter in learning to teach mathematics (or numeracy) and language (or literacy) within ITE programmes.

Chapter 7, by McAuliffe, Venkatakrishnan and Ramollo, focuses on teaching and learning in Foundation Phase mathematics. They argue that limited attention is paid to the learning experiences of Foundation Phase student teachers when being prepared to teach mathematics. As such, the chapter examines the mathematical knowledge of Foundation Phase ITE student teachers – both in terms of their own problem-solving skills and in terms of the choices they make while teaching to represent and explain problems, and to support and advance learning. The chapter suggests that with more relative fluency in their own mathematical problem solving and with good support, student teachers can develop the kind of confidence and fluency required to make important pedagogic choices regarding the selection and sequencing of examples, the selection and use of resources and inscriptions, as well as the accompanying explanatory talk. While the pedagogic transformations of the student teachers were regarded as tentative and fragile during task-based interviews, these seemed to improve with appropriate support and guidance. This suggests, the chapter argues, a real potential for further growth in teachers' mathematical knowledge for teaching (MKT). I also underlines the need for ITE programmes to focus more directly on developing student teachers' discursive practices, and building better connections and coherence within their selection and use of examples and resources.

Chapter 8, by Barends and Aronstam, asks what the experiences of Foundation Phase student teachers are regarding learning to teach language. They claim that teaching and learning language in the Foundation Phase in South Africa is complex. The chapter provides a description of how prospective teachers' experiences of learning to teach languages are circumscribed by education language policy on the one hand and the diverse language situations in classrooms on the other. The chapter also explains how the Foundation Phase curriculum makes provision for language to be taught via literacy (DoE 2002:15). In keeping with the theoretical framework provided in Chapter 1, knowledge sets relevant to teaching and developing language among Foundation Phase learners are discussed in this chapter. The chapter then presents data from BEd Foundation Phase student teachers relating to their perceived experiences of learning to teach language with respect to the knowledge sets. The authors argue that the relationship between the knowledges of language and literacy can thus be understood as a complex symbiosism further complicated by the requirements of the Foundation Phase Curriculum and Assessment Policy Statement (CAPS) requirements. The qualitative data presented in the chapter show that the student teachers' experience of Foundation Phase ITE programmes includes CK or subject matter knowledge (SMK), PCK, and curricula knowledge related to literacy skills. However, the qualitative data suggest that the knowledge or SMK and PCK were not adequate or sufficient given the complex symbiosis of language, literacy and the Foundation Phase curriculum in South Africa.

Chapter 9, by Govender, Potberg and Verster, focuses on teaching and learning FET mathematics. For this chapter, further complementary data were used from another study on an educational technology intervention with eight pre-service PGCE students. The chapter points to the importance of actively working with mathematical objects and to enhance advanced mathematical thinking.

This is a firm part of MRTEQ policy. It also emphasises the value of using technology, in this case Geometer's Sketchpad, to enable advanced mathematical learning in classrooms to demonstrate the complex nature of mathematical teaching and learning.

Chapter 10, by Dippenaar, Badroodien and Mashiyi, explores teaching and learning FET languages. The chapter focuses on experiences and challenges in developing the required competencies for language teaching in the FET Phase (Grades 10 to 12). It critically examines the extent to which ITE prepares student teachers to develop the linguistic and multiple literacies necessary for effective teaching.

1.8.4 Section 4: ITE in the 21st Century

Chapter 11, by Sayed, Carrim and Badroodien, offers some concluding views about current debates in ITE in South Africa and globally. It discusses the kinds of training that are required to develop context-relevant teachers for the 21st century, drawing on international comparisons of UN and World Bank indicators. It concludes that it is always necessary when assessing the efficacy of ITE programmes to understand the influence of school context on how ITE programmes are realised.

1.9 Concluding Comments: The Need for Systematic Initial Teacher Education Research

This chapter has located the research project on which this book is based in context, discussing how the data was collected and analysed, and provided a conceptual framework by which to engage with ITE provision. In closing it is important to note the importance and further need of large-scale longitudinal research about initial teacher education as a corrective to public and policy discourses which pronounce on the failures of teachers and the crisis of public education without systematically interrogating the experiences of those who are to become the future teachers.

Whilst there has been much debate about the quality of education in South Africa and concerns about the learning crisis, there has been limited systematic empirical research about teachers and teacher education as key to improving education quality. This is all the more surprising as teachers and teacher education providers are often blamed in the popular media and in policy discourses for the crisis of education quality in South Africa. Furthermore, there is a serious dearth in systematic, large-scale, and longitudinal studies within education research about how teachers are prepared to enter the profession. This means that there is very little that is systematically known about initial teacher education in the South African and regional context. In 2007 the Honourable Dr Naledi Pandor, the previous Minister of Education and currently Minister of Higher Education in South Africa, invited more studies that make available knowledge about novice and qualified teachers. In particular, more needs to be known about how those being prepared to become teachers experience their training. Indeed, whilst much is made about what teachers cannot do, there is little attention to giving voice to those who are becoming teachers specifically. These are some of the research gaps that this book addresses.

The book contributes to a growing body of knowledge in the global context about what constitutes good quality initial teacher education, especially as seen through the eyes of those who undergo such training. This particular focus on the understandings and perceptions of student teachers adds to a knowledge base that is keen to provide voice and give agency to prospective teachers. This focus on the agency of teachers is especially important given the current context of strong managerial and regulatory governmental frameworks. Increasingly, in the name of 'declining quality' and for some a need to focus on transformation, governments have sought to circumscribe and delimit teacher agency. They do so in ways that seek to secure compliance with globally determined standards of quality, outcomes, and efficiency (Tatto 2007; Anderson & Herr 2015), but in so doing offer a particularly limited conceptualisation of what constitutes education quality.

The research reported in this book further adds considerably to understanding the experiences of student teachers across diverse institutional types, especially where they reflect particular historical and structural contexts that frame not only who enters teaching but what their experiences thereof is. This book demonstrates that empirically investigating initial teacher education can significantly develop the knowledge base in a deeply neglected area of research, particularly with regard to thinking about education quality. It is after all teachers who after home background most impact learning. Who become teachers and what they experience as prospective teachers is of crucial research and policy importance.

References

Anderson, G. & Cohen, M. I. 2015. Redesigning the identities of teachers and leaders: A framework for studying new professionalism and educator resistance. *Education Policy Analysis Archives*, 23 (85). https://doi.org/10.14507/epaa.v23.2086

Badat, S. & Sayed, Y. 2014. Post-1994 South African education: The challenge of social justice. *The Annals of the American Academy of Political and Social Science*, 652(1): 127-148. https://doi.org/10.1177/0002716213511188

Ball, D.L.; Bass, H. & Hill, H.C. 2004. Knowing and using mathematical knowledge in teaching: Learning what matters. In: A. Buffler & R.C. Laugksch (eds). *Proceedings of the 12th Annual Conference of the Southern African Association for Research in Mathematics, Science and Technology Education (SAARMSTE)*. Durban: SAARMSTE, 51-65.

Ball, D.L.; Hill, H.C. & Bass, H. 2005. Knowing mathematics for teaching: Who knows mathematics well enough to teach third grade, and how can we decide? *American Educator*, 29(3): 14-46.

Boostrom, R. 1998. What makes teaching a moral activity? *The Educational Forum*, 63(1): 58-64.

Bourgonje, P. & Tromp, R. 2011. *Quality educators: An international study of teacher competencies and standards*. Brussels: Education International & Oxfam Novib.

Burnett, B. & Lampert, J. 2011. Teacher education and the targeting of disadvantage. *Creative Education*, Vol.2, No.5, 446-451. https://doi.org/10.4236/ce.2011.25064

Cochran-Smith, M. & Lytle, S.L. 1999. The teacher research movement: A decade later. *Educational Researcher*, 28(7): 15-25.

Conway, P.; Morphy, R.; Rath, A. & Hall, K. 2009. *Learning to teach and its implication for the continuum and teacher education: A nine-country cross national study*. Report commissioned by the Teaching Council. Ireland: Teaching Council. Available at: https://www.teachingcouncil.ie/en/Publications/Research/Documents/Learning-to-Teach-and-its-Implications-for-the-Continuum-of-Teacher-Education.pdf

Darling-Hammond, L (ed.). 1994. *Professional development schools: Schools for developing a profession*. New York: Teachers College Press.

Darling-Hammond, L. 1997a. *The right to learn: A blueprint for creating schools that work*. San Francisco: Jossey-Bass.

Darling-Hammond, L. 1997b. *Doing what matters most: Investing in quality teaching*. New York: The National Commission on Teaching & America's Future (NCTAF).

Darling-Hammond, L. 1999. *Reshaping teaching policy, preparation, and practice: Influences of the National Board for Professional Teaching Standards*. New York: American Association of Colleges for Teacher Education (AACTE) Publications.

Darling-Hammond, L. 2000. Teacher quality and student achievement: A review of state policy evidence. *Education Policy Analysis Archives*, 8(1): 1-44. https://doi.org/10.14507/epaa.v8n1.2000

Darling-Hammond, L. 2006. Securing the right to learn: Policy and practice for powerful teaching and learning. *Educational Researcher*, 35(7): 13-24. https://doi.org/10.3102/0013189X035007013

Darling-Hammond, L. 2014. One piece of the whole: Teacher evaluation as part of a comprehensive system for teaching and learning. *American Educator*, 38(1): 4-13.

Darling-Hammond, L. & McLaughlin, M.W. 1995. Policies that support professional development in an era of reform. *Phi Delta Kappan*, 76(8): 597-604.

Department of Basic Education (DBE). 2012. *Information guide on Initial Teacher Education*. Available at: https://www.dhet.gov.za/Funza%20Lushaka%20Bursary%20Scheme/Brochure%20 Information%20about%20Initial%20Teacher%20Education.pdf

Department of Education (DoE). 2002. *Revised National Curriculum Statement for Schools: Grades R-9*. Pretoria: DoE.

Department of Education (DoE). 2007. *National policy framework for teacher education and development (NPFTED)*. Pretoria: DoE.

Department of Higher Education and Training (DHET). 2015. National Qualifications Framework Act, 2008 (Act No. 67 of 2008): Revised Policy on the Minimum Requirements for Teacher Education Qualifications. Government Gazette 38487, 19 February. Pretoria: Government Printer.

Fenstermacher, G.D. 1994. The knower and the known: The nature of knowledge in research on teaching. *Review of Research in Education*, 20(1): 3-56. https://doi.org/10.3102/0091732X020001003 & https://doi.org/10.2307/1167381

Fenwick, L. & Cooper, M. 2013. Learning about the effects of context on teaching and learning in pre-service teacher education. *Australian Journal of Teacher Education*, 38(3): 96-110. https://doi.org/10.14221/ajte.2013v38n3.6

Guerriero, S. 2014. Teachers' pedagogical knowledge and the teaching profession: *Background report and project objectives*. Available at: https://www.oecd.org/education/ceri/Background_document_ to_Symposium_ITEL-FINAL.pdf

Hungi, N.; Makuwa, D.; Ross, K.; Saito, M.; Dolata, S.; Van Cappelle, F.; Paviot, L. & Vellien, J. 2010. SACMEQ III project results: Pupil achievement levels in reading and mathematics. Working document, 1. Available at: https://www.sacmeq.org/sites/default/files/sacmeq/reports/sacmeq-iii/working-documents/wd01_sacmeq_iii_results_pupil_achievement.pdf

International Labour Organisation – United Nations Educational, Scientific and Cultural Organisation (ILO-UNESCO). 2003. Joint ILO-UNESCO Committee of Experts on the application of the recommendations concerning teaching personnel. Geneva: ILO and Paris: UNESCO.

Labaree, D.F. 2000. On the nature of teaching and teacher education: Difficult practices that look easy. *Journal of Teacher Education*, 51(3): 228-233. https://doi.org/10.1177/0022487100051003011

Martin, M.O. & Kelly, D.L (eds). 1997. *Third international mathematics and science study: Technical report*. Volume II: Implementation and analysis. Boston College: IEA.

Martin, M.O.; Mullis, I.V.S. & Chrostowski, S.J. 2004. *TIMSS 2003 technical report*. Boston College: IEA.

Mullis, I.V.S.; Martin, M.O.; Gonzalez, E.J.; Gregory, K.D.; Garden, R.A.; O'Connor, K.M.; Chrostowski, S.J. & Smith, T.A. 2000. *TIMSS 1999 international mathematics report*. Boston College: IEA.

National Commission on Teaching & America's Future (NCTAF). 2016. *What matters now: A new compact for teaching and learning*. Arlington: NCTAF. Available at: https://nctaf.org/wp-content/uploads/2016/08/NCTAF_What-Matters-Now_A-Call-to-Action.pdf

Naylor, R. & Sayed, Y. 2014. *Teacher quality: Evidence review*. Canberra: Office of Development Effectiveness.

Organisation for Economic Co-operation and Development (OECD). 2005. *Teachers matter: Attracting, developing and retaining effective teachers – Overview*. Paris: OECD.

Pajares, M. 1992. Teachers' beliefs and educational research: Cleaning up a messy construct. *Review of Educational Research*, 62(3): 307-332. https://doi.org/10.3102/00346543062003307

Reddy, V.; Visser, M.; Winnaar, L.; Arends, F.; Juan, A.; Prinsloo, C.H. & Isdale, K. 2016. *TIMSS 2015: Highlights of mathematics and science achievement of Grade 9 South African learners*. Cape Town: Human Sciences Research Council (HSRC).

Sayed, Y.; Badroodien, A.; McDonald, Z.; Balie, L.; De Kock, T.; Garisch, C. & Foulds, K. (Cape Peninsula University of Technology and University of Sussex Research Consortium: Education and Peacebuilding). 2015. *Teachers and youth as agents of social cohesion in South Africa*. Cape Town: Cape Peninsula University of Technology.

Shulman, L. 1986. Those who understand: Knowledge growth in teaching. *Educational Researcher*, 15(2): 4-14. https://doi.org/10.3102/0013189X015002004

Shulman, L. 1987. Knowledge and teaching: Foundations of the new reform. *Harvard Educational Review*, 57(1): 1-22. https://doi.org/10.17763/haer.57.1.j463w79r56455411

Shulman, L. 1995. Wisdom for practice and wisdom of practice: Two aspects of didactics of substance. In: S. Hopmann & K. Riquarts (eds). *Didaktik and/or curriculum*. Kiel: IPN. 201-204.

Shulman, L. 1997. Professional development: Learning from experience. In: B.S. Kogan (ed.). Common schools: *Uncommon futures: A working consensus for school renewal*. New York: Teachers College Press, 89-106.

Tatto, M.T. 2007. Educational reform and the global regulation of teachers' education, development and work. *International Journal of Educational Research*, 45, 231-241. https://doi.org/10.1016/j.ijer.2007.02.003

Taylor, S.G.S. 2013. Modelling educational achievement. In: N. Taylor, S. van der Berg & T. Mabogoane (eds). *Creating effective schools*. Cape Town: Pearson. 61-99.

Van Fleet, J.W. 2012. *Africa learning barometer*. Washington, D.C.: Centre for Education, Brookings Institution. Available at: https://www.brookings.edu/wp-content/uploads/2012/09/Africa-Learning-BarometerFINAL.pdf

United Nations Association of Greater Philadelphia [UNA-GP]. 2015. *The Sustainable Development Goals 2015-2030*. Available at: https://una-gp.org/the-sustainable-development-goals-2015-2030/.

Chapter 02

Policy & Legislative Context of Initial Teacher Education in South Africa

Yusuf Sayed, Nazir Carrim, Azeem Badroodien, Zahraa McDonald & Marcina Singh

2.1 Introduction

This chapter contextualises ITE programmes in South Africa. By at least the mid-20th century, in South Africa and elsewhere, ITE programmes were chiefly offered in tertiary education institutions. Graduating from such programmes serves as a compulsory catalyst to teachers' careers and professional development. This means that to become a teacher in South Africa (as in most parts of the world), an individual minimally requires an ITE qualification achieved upon successful completion of an accredited ITE programme. An ITE qualification is a requirement for full registration with the South African Council for Educators (SACE), for example. ITE programmes that culminate in such a qualification can be of a variety of types, offered at various tertiary education institutions. A policy and legislative context frames the possibilities and limitations of ITE programmes and consequently how students experience becoming teachers.

This chapter examines what the South African policy and legislative context mean for the types of ITE programmes and the sites where they are offered. The aim of this is to sketch the overall frame within which student teachers are currently experiencing becoming teachers in post-apartheid South Africa.

The chapter starts by first outlining the apartheid policy and legislative framework, because this had specific implications for the type of ITE programmes that existed and sites where they were offered with the advent of democracy in 1994. The historical background of ITE programmes, informed by the legacy of apartheid, casts how the ITE landscape is contoured in post-apartheid South Africa. This is followed by a discussion of the changes in the policy and legislative context that shape the types of ITE programmes and the sites where they are offered in democratic South Africa in the next two sections. Specific attention is paid to changing governance arrangements in the provision of ITE, followed by a discussion of changes in roles and specifications regarding what ITE should seek to achieve in producing future generations of teachers. This chapter then considers the global policy to locate changes in teacher education in post-apartheid South Africa to external factors that influence the direction of policy change. Lastly, the conclusion discusses the implications of the nature and changes of the policy and legislative context – that is, the state of flux in respect of the types of ITE programmes that are offered and the sites where such programmes are offered. Furthermore, the conclusion unpacks what this may mean for student teacher experiences of becoming a teacher in post-apartheid South Africa.

2.2 ITE Under Apartheid

Apartheid is noted for its racist segregationist policies and these impacted ITE programmes too. ITE programmes under apartheid were segregated in terms of race and ethnicity and were unequal in terms of quality. Sayed (2002:381) notes that "the demand and supply of teachers was based on the need to maintain racial and ethnic segregation". Racial inequality was as such shaped by the types of programmes that were offered, as well as the sites where ITE programmes were offered.

Several features describe the type of ITE programme, including entrance requirements and nature (standard) of qualification, under apartheid. Entrance requirements to ITE programmes were not uniform for all race groups during apartheid, resulting in an unequal and differentiated teacher qualification profile. Christie (1996) indicates that by 1988, 62% of African teachers had Standard 10 (equivalent to Grade 12) as their highest qualification level, 32% had a qualification level below Standard 10 and only 5% had a university degree. In comparison, 32% of white teachers had a university degree and none of them were teaching in schools with a qualification below Standard 10.

Unequal entrance requirements were predicated on the assumption that African teachers did not need to be qualified or highly qualified to teach an African child, informed by Hendrik Verwoerd's 1951 Senate speech wherein he made it clear that apartheid education was based on inequality and that the African child did not need an education that was equal to that of a white child.

> There is no place for him [the Bantu] in the European community above the level of certain forms of labour. Within his own community, however, all doors are open. For that reason, it is of no avail for him to receive a training which has as its aim absorption in the European community where he cannot be absorbed. Until now he has been subjected to a school system which drew him away from his own community and misled him in showing the green pastures of European society in which he was not allowed to graze (cited in Rose & Tunmer 1975:120-128).

Verwoerd's pronouncement of Bantu Education as an education for the 'Bantu' is explicit in its racist segregationism and makes it clear that the education of the 'Bantu' could not be the same as that which a 'white' child received. It thus becomes understandable why it was acceptable to have unqualified or underqualified teachers in 'black' schools under apartheid.

Differences in entrance requirements resulted in differing and variable quality programme offerings. Sayed (2002:381) contends that "apartheid policies exacerbated qualification imbalances associated with teacher education".

Racial differentiation in entrance requirements and programme quality was mirrored by institutional and provider segregation:

> [T]he Department of Bantu Education and the Department of Coloured Affairs would, for example, administer teacher colleges designated for each respective apartheid racial category. In other words, the governance of teacher education was deeply fragmented during apartheid rule (Sayed 2002:381).

As a result,
> by the end of the 1980s there were 18 colleges for whites, two colleges for Indians, 16 colleges for coloureds, and 13 colleges for Africans in apartheid South Africa. In addition, there were 78 colleges of teacher education scattered throughout the designated homelands (Council for Higher Education [CHE] 2010:8).

As such, given the framework of apartheid, all ITE programmes under apartheid were offered to different racial groups in teacher training colleges, which were segregated. The chief outcome of the apartheid policy and legislative context for ITE programmes, be it with respect to type or site, was, as Sayed (2002) states, deep fragmentation and an unequal system of teacher education that produced teachers for racially segregated forms of schooling.

The segregated nature of teacher education was mirrored by a spatialised form of governance control in which provinces maintained control of some teacher education colleges. Others were located under racially divided education systems, universities and technicons, as well as under the control of distance providers, religious organisations and private institutions. These differences in control of ITE provisioning were further compounded by the limited access to universities for black, coloured, and Indian students, which meant that they were relegated to the colleges where the disparities in quality between different colleges affected the quality of teachers and their teaching practices.

As a result, by 1994, the teacher education sector had resulted in newly qualified teacher (NQTs) entering the system from different providers, different content and curriculum, as well as with differing qualifications. These differences were racialised in that many black students were qualified as "teachers with Standard 8 leaving certificates" (CHE 2010:8), as opposed to attending a college of teacher education or university. Moreover, the content taught at different institutions did not necessarily include all subjects. Sayed (2002:382) states that "most of the graduates from black teacher training colleges were trained in subjects such as religious studies and history" and were underdeveloped in areas of mathematics, science and technology. African teachers in teacher education colleges were expected to achieve the minimum levels of literacy and numeracy, with low-budget primary schooling provided by African women. In contrast, white teachers were educated in post-secondary school colleges of education and/or universities (Chisholm 2012). The effect of this, according to the CHE (2010:9), is that teachers in "African schools particularly, but also in coloured schools, were poor" and the post-apartheid education system inherited "generations of teachers, of all races, with distorted and deficient understandings of themselves, of each other, and of what was expected of them in a divided society" (Essop 2008; cited in DBE & DHET 2011:19).

2.3 (Re)spatialisation of ITE in Post-apartheid South Africa: Changing the ITE Landscape

This complex terrain inherited by the post-apartheid government resulted in the new government modifying both the governance and curricula of teacher education to shift qualification structures and their requirements (CHE 2010). The governance and curricula of teacher education were considered essential to bring about redress, equity, efficiency and quality in terms of teacher education and preparing teachers to implement the new school curriculum (CHE 2010:9). The reconfiguration of teacher education began with the National Teacher Education Audit of 1995 and later investigations, with the view to making the system more integrated, efficient and transformative.

The spatialised and fragmented system of teacher education was centralised into a unified system of national teacher education provision in post-apartheid South Africa and brought under the ambit of national control by absorbing into universities all teacher education providers (CHE 2010). Thus, many colleges were incorporated into universities and those that were not, were closed or used as premises for FET colleges, teacher development institutes and other provincial offices, with the result that South Africa lost 104 teacher education providers in the six years between 1994 and 2000 (CHE 2010).

The shift in control was motivated on the grounds that the college model of provision "was authoritarian and content centred, with little integration of theory and practice" (CHE 2010:10). Moreover, colleges of education were producing an excess of primary school teachers and were considered inefficient due to their size, low staff-student ratios and high resource wastage resulting from low outputs in terms of qualifying teachers.

Further shifts in governance of teacher education occurred with the merging of HEIs announced in July 1999 by former Minister of Education, Kader Asmal. Higher education mergers between 32 existing universities and technikons resulted in a total of 23 universities, comprehensive universities and universities of technology. As a result, the post-apartheid teacher education landscape now has 21 providers of ITE programmes (DBE & DHET 2011:21) and is from this point on referred to as "teacher education providers". The double governance restructuring of teacher education (from fragmented colleges and other providers to a wholly university-based system and then a university merge process, which further reduced the number of providers) was not without contestation and debate. The resonance of this debate is evident in marked and strident calls for the reopening of colleges and the perception that the university-based models of provision devalued and de-emphasised the practice-based model of college-based training (see Samuel 2002; Sayed 2018).

In summary, the biggest shift in the governance of ITE was the move from provisioning by colleges of education to universities in post-apartheid South Africa (DHET 2013). This relocation of ITE programmes in universities was meant to address the varying and various ITE offerings that occurred under apartheid – to rationalise them, to avoid duplication in the system and to ensure quality and equity. These shifts were accompanied by the creation of a complex set of governance arrangements for assuring teacher quality with contested and contradictory outcomes.

2.4 (Re)curriculation of ITE in Post-apartheid South Africa: Changing Roles and Specifications

Post-apartheid education policymakers sought to transform the content and specifications of what comprised ITE in the context of it being a university-based qualification. Changes to the curriculum of ITE programmes in post-apartheid South Africa were driven by two important and consequential features: creating uniformity in ITE programme curricula and qualifying teachers who would be able to deliver one national school curriculum predicated on equality and democracy. These dual imperatives were marked by two sets of significant policy changes.

First, the NSE policy (DoE 2001), which sought to provide a framework for ITE programmes that would enable them to deliver the required teachers. The NSE was the first major intervention to provide an overarching framework for ITE programmes, as well as articulation of all education-related qualifications to doctoral or National Qualifications Framework (NQF) 10 level.

The NSE lists three applied competencies, namely practical competence, foundational competence and reflexive competence, which are to be developed during the ITE programmes. In terms of the NSE, teachers are conceptualised as fulfilling seven roles. These seven roles are:

1. learning mediator;
2. interpreter and designer of learning programmes and materials;
3. leader, administrator and manager;
4. scholar, researcher and life-long learner;
5. community, citizenship and pastoral role;
6. assessor; and
7. learning area/subject/discipline/phase specialist.

These extended roles of teachers were meant to recognise the different roles teachers are expected to perform in schools – ranging from their transmission of knowledge, preparation of lessons, managing their classrooms, to providing pastoral support to conducting assessments. They also expected teachers to develop themselves in an ongoing way as "life-long learners" and to be "researchers" and "scholars" (DoE 2001:13).

The NSE gave teacher education providers the freedom to decide and design how to integrate the roles and competencies within the modules and programmes they offered (DoE 2001:4). The policy recognises that "these norms and standards, however, do not necessarily reflect or ensure the quality of the qualification or programme" (DoE 2001:30). In other words, in policy terms, the NSE operated as a macro policy vision of what an ideal teacher should be, leaving it to providers to determine how to incorporate these roles into respective programmes. As macro policy vision, the NSE framed the context on teacher education in post-apartheid South Africa in a context of other policy changes, including curricula changes evidenced in Curriculum 2005 (C2005), the National Curriculum Statement (NCS) and the Revised National Curriculum Statement (RNCS). However, this shift in the conceptualisation of teacher roles, while positive, was arguably difficult to implement. Teachers found their extended roles difficult to realise in practice, since they did not have the time to see to all their expected roles and did not feel sufficiently able to conduct such roles, because these roles were not part of their own training (Chisholm et al. 2005). The lack of specifications was also due to ongoing debates and discussion with unions about what teachers are reasonably expected to do in a turbulent and changing policy environment.

As a result, the second big shift in ITE occurred with the release of the NPFTED, aligning policy around the key message that what the system needed was 'more teachers, better teachers'. This was a shift away from what kinds of teachers were required to what was to be the focus and content of their initial preparation. To this end, the second major policy shift about teacher education curricula occurred with the release of the MRTEQ policy in 2011.

The MRTEQ policy was argued to add to the seven roles of the NSE by determining the knowledge that prospective teachers should be equipped with prior to becoming teachers in post-apartheid South Africa. As such, it represented an attempt to begin the dialogue about specifying what ideal teacher education curricula should look like to give expression to the ideal teacher encapsulated in the seven roles specified in the NSE. It was designed to "provide teacher education providers with clear guidelines with regard to the development of HEQF [High Education Qualifications Framework]-aligned qualifications and teacher education programmes" (DHET 2011:9). It thus reflected a shift away from standards and outcomes by specifying teacher roles to giving direction on the inputs needed for achieving these (CHE 2010). A focus on the input, or the black box, of teacher education was also motivated by a review of teacher education programmes by the CHE, which noted concerns about quality in ITE in relation to content, teaching and the types of graduates emerging from ITE programmes (Sayed et al. 2016). It thus significantly began to reconstitute the discourse of teacher education and ITE, especially in ways that privileged what happens within providers rather than about governance or about macro policy vision. In its own words, "addressing the critical challenges facing education in South Africa [...] especially the poor content and conceptual knowledge found amongst teachers, as well as the legacies of apartheid" (DHET 2011:10).

The MRTEQ policy emphasises the development of student teachers' academic skills and knowledge, focusing on the knowledge and learning that all teachers are expected to acquire. As noted in the introduction, the MRTEQ policy speaks about five types of knowledge that are "integrated and applied knowledge" and "should be understood both as being the condition for, and the effect of scrutinising, fusing together and expressing different types of knowing in the moment of practice" (DHET 2011:7). The five kinds of learning that the MRTEQ policy recognises are: "...disciplinary learning, pedagogical learning, practical learning, fundamental learning, and situational learning."

1. "Disciplinary learning" refers to learning of disciplinary or subject knowledge.
2. "Pedagogical learning" refers to "GPK" and "specialised PCK".
3. "Practical learning" refers to "learning in or from practice".
4. "Fundamental learning" refers to "learning to converse in a second official language" and an "ability to use information and communications technologies (ICTs) and the acquisition of academic literacy".
5. "Situational learning" refers to "knowledge of the varied learning situations, contexts, and environments" (DHET 2011:8-9).

The MRTEQ policy thus pays more attention to knowledge and learning, as opposed to the different roles teachers play. It should be noted, however, that MRTEQ policy does not provide teacher education providers with details about what pedagogies or approaches should be taken. Instead, it seeks to establish a basis for a common, accepted curriculum that a programme would cover in terms of knowledge and practice, leaving it up to providers as to how to realise this in programme terms.

The MRTEQ policy was updated in 2015 (DHET 2015). The amendments were mainly technical in nature and thus did not shift the substantive framework related to particular knowledge mixes. Moreover, the emphasis on CK did not shift from 2011 to 2015. In addition, the roles of the NSE are present and defined in exactly the same way in both (DHET 2011:52-53; DHET 2015:60 61). The policy further describes basic competencies teacher education providers should instil in student teachers during the programme (DHET 2011; 2015).

As the content and specifications of ITE shifted, as described above, so did the school curriculum. The curricula as noted (Carrim & Keet 2005) shifted from outcomes-based education (OBE) to NCS to RNCS to CAPS in 2011. The narrowing of the curricula arguably parallels the tighter specification of what happens in ITE in post-apartheid South Africa. As noted above, the shift arguably is a narrowing of the role of the teacher, marked by an increasing emphasis on content and assessment. The shift from C2005 to RNCS to CAPS indicates such differences. C2005 was ideologically much broader in its view of school knowledge and included an emphasis on human rights, inclusivity and equality (see also Carrim & Keet 2005). In CAPS, the emphasis is on subject content, mainly numeracy and literacy, and the nationally standardised assessments of such CK.

In the policy narrative above, the changing of specifications across the policy terrain sketched suggests a process of recurriculation within ITE that is rapid and contradictory. For tertiary institutions that offer ITE programmes, the shifts from the NSE to the MRTEQ policy and the shift from C2005 to RNCS to CAPS had profound implications. Tertiary institutions had to redesign their curricula to align with the MRTEQ policy, after just having redesigned such programmes not so long ago to the NSE and C2005 and then to the RNCS. Tertiary institutions also had to re-register their programmes so that they were legally recognised as being consistent with existing policy. To date (2017), some tertiary institutions are still awaiting such registration and endorsement of their programmes. This means that currently there are tertiary institutions in South Africa offering both the old ITE programme and the new ITE programme. In some cases, tertiary institutions are not offering the new ITE programme in line with the MRTEQ policy and still have the pre-2010 ITE programme in place. The type of ITE programme offered in post-apartheid South Africa has thus not stabilised yet and is not uniform.

Arguably, the piecemeal approach to curricula specification in ITE post-1994 results in a lack of clarity and uniformity about what ITE should comprise. Furthermore, the changes to what ITE should comprise in a context of multiple governance shifts, as noted above, result in the policy being interpreted in different ways.

In the narrative of the shifting governance landscape and the shifting manner of specification regarding what ITE should comprise, is the role of professional bodies with respect to setting standards and additional documents to be used during implementation (DHET 2015:8). Currently, the Teacher Education Programme Evaluation Committee, comprising the DHET, in partnership with three role players namely the DBE, SACE and the Sector Education and Training Authority (SETA), assists in aligning teacher education programmes with policy requirements for teacher education qualifications (Sayed et al. 2016). This process is, however, limited by the fact that there is contestation over which professional body should oversee/monitor/evaluate the quality, standardisation and practice of teacher education (the CHE currently drives the process of accreditation) (Sayed et al. 2016). In addition, the promise that a "process will be put in place to support the development of [...] standards for teacher education" (DHET 2015:8) in the absence of a clear structural framework raises further concerns. Whether a "professional council [...] can take responsibility for the oversights of teacher education programmes as a missing link in the teacher education sector" (Interview with senior civil servant [SCS], cited in Sayed et al. 2016) remains to be seen.

In summary, the changing ITE landscape in post-apartheid teacher education indicates a shift from specifying the ideal teacher as an outcome of ITE to a tighter specification of content. This shift reflects arguably a growing emphasis on looking inside the black box of ITE, as this book seeks to do. Yet, it is done in ways that are contested and contradictory, as it also resonates with a global shift towards a culture of teacher performativity and regulation that signals a trend towards a neo-liberal regulatory framework of teacher governance, as argued by Robinson (2012).

2.5 Global Context of Teachers and Teacher Education

The changing context of ITE in South Africa takes place in a global context where a new global development framework, encompassing new goals, targets and indicators (including for education), was adopted in September 2015 at the UN's General Assembly meeting. This formally marked the ending of the Millennium Development Goals (MDGs) and the Education for All goals adopted in 2000. The SDGs, agreed to in September 2015, lay a foundation for an ambitious plan to eradicate poverty, promote social and economic inclusion, tackle climate change, promote equity and provide access to quality education encompassing both the Global North and the Global South.

Teachers feature prominently in the new education agenda and the McKinsey report (see Barber & Mourshed 2007) goes as far as to state that the quality of an education system cannot exceed the quality of its teachers. The focus on quality in the 2030 Sustainable Development Agenda thus rightly emphasises a concern with teachers, teaching and teacher education (See Sayed & Ahmed 2015, for a more extensive discussion). The specific target in the SDG 4 agenda for teachers is:

> 4.c: By 2030, substantially increase the supply of qualified teachers, including through international cooperation for teacher training in developing countries, especially least developed countries and small island developing states.

This target, which is part of SDG 4 on education, is to be measured by the:

> 4.c.1 [p]roportion of teachers in: (a) pre-primary (b) primary; (c) lower secondary; and (d) upper secondary education who have received at least the minimum organised teacher training (e.g. pedagogical training) pre-service or in-service required for teaching at the relevant level in a given country.

This target and its measurement clearly signal the need for a sufficient supply of teachers but crucially those who are fully trained and qualified. However, an important omission in the construction of the target is the lack of a robust focus on equity. The key issue is not only that all learners should be taught by qualified, professionally trained, motivated and well-supported teachers, but how to get such teachers in hard-to-reach areas. In South Africa, for example, the inequities in education and the existence of two systems of education (Badat & Sayed 2014) can partly be attributed to the fact that good teachers working in an enabling learning environment are clustered in the wealthier school sector which, when added to the cultural capital of learners, creates a double privilege (Sayed & Ahmed 2015). To overcome inequities in South Africa would require positive discrimination in favour of learners in disadvantaged contexts through the distribution and payment of teachers.

Of concern in the discourse of teachers in the post-2015 agenda is: the vast and broad range of expectations and knowledge expected of teachers (similar to the roles specified in the NSE for life skills), citizenship and peace education, moral and ethical education, child protection, human rights, skills for sustainable livelihoods, challenging gender inequalities and practising learner-centredness (Sinclair 2002; Barrett et al. 2015), to name but a few. While these are important concerns, such an ambitious variety of responsibilities, as the South African experience suggests, runs the real risk of overstating the potential of schools and their teachers to effect broad social transformations. Teacher agency, as envisaged in the post-2015 agenda or in South Africa for that matter, is not a realistic possibility, nor is agency easy when faced with multiple and conflicting demands subject to narrow accountability measures. It is therefore necessary to balance teacher agency with appropriate and continuous training to equip teachers to fulfil new roles. Given the experiences of NSE in post-apartheid South Africa, how realistic is it to expect such extended roles of teachers?

Transformation in the professional development discourse of teachers in South Africa (in policy and interventions) has been aimed at ensuring that teachers are prepared to become good-quality teachers with the knowledge, subject expertise and subject PCK (the five knowledge types as indicated earlier), as well as with the dispositions for democracy and social justice. However, while this may be the case officially and systemically, such investments in education do not eradicate the endemic inequalities that persist in school contexts in which teachers are expected to practise.

While the SDGs significantly emphasise the importance of teacher supply and quality, there are also increasing debates about some of the complexities surrounding quality teaching and learning and their implications for ITE. These include recognising teaching as a complex social and cultural practice. For Cochran-Smith et al. (2012), these complex practices include: classroom relations, classroom management and classroom environments; content and curriculum; pedagogy and practice; student learning, opportunities and responsibilities; and professionalism, emotional identities, school context, mission, resilience, hard work and management of curriculum. In this regard, Naylor and Sayed (2014:4) state:

> In summary, there is evidence to suggest that teacher quality is dependent on a combination of different factors such as classroom practices, subject knowledge, professional development, teaching experience and quality of teacher-student relationships, which in turn impact on student outcomes. These findings signal that it cannot be automatically assumed that teacher certificates and qualifications lead to better teaching. Thus, the focus on teacher quality should be on the effects of teachers on learning.

These complexities regarding what impacts teacher quality and the contexts in which teachers practise are remarkably absent from the framing of the SDG teacher target.

In addition, the type of ITE programme or model that should be offered is also not addressed by the SDGs. In this regard, the National Council for the Accreditation of Teacher Education (NCATE 2013) points out that although existing evidence indicates that teacher preparation "does make a difference", some policymakers have recently advocated that a passing score on a test of SMK and a background check are all that is needed to become an effective teacher. Moreover, some policymakers have embraced approaches that permit teachers with no preparation in pedagogy or child/adolescent development to be classified as highly qualified if they pass a test of SMK (usually a licensing exam) (NCATE 2013). This indicates that what teacher preparation should include and what ITE programmes should do is an issue that is debatable. This is also reinforced by the recent development of an 'apprenticeship' model of teacher preparation that is currently being attempted in United Kingdom (UK) schooling contexts. In this apprenticeship model, aspiring teachers are placed with practising teachers as their apprentices and it is assumed that this is all that is needed to become an effective teacher.

As such, although the SDGs' emphasis on teacher supply and quality is welcome, the complexities around models of ITE programmes, the content covered in such programmes and the multiple factors that affect teaching practice also need to be addressed.

2.6 Conclusion

Addressing ITE programmes in post-apartheid South Africa is complex. These complexities stem from the fragmentation in ITE governance and curricula inherited from apartheid, which impacts the reconfiguration of the ITE landscape in post-apartheid South Africa. Persisting inequalities in school contexts where teachers teach also reinforce such complexities. In addition, global developments regarding the SDGs and debates about models of ITE programmes and provisioning, as well as the recognition of the multiple factors which affect quality teaching also impact the complexities surrounding ITE programmes (how they are conceptualised, the sites where they are offered and the school contexts in which prospective teachers are expected to teach). This chapter outlined what these complexities are in the historical legacy of apartheid, how they have developed in post-apartheid South Africa and how they are engaged with in a global context.

Several key issues emerged from the preceding analysis. First, while post-apartheid ITE policies and legislation were aimed at establishing uniformity and equality, inequities persist at the level of school contexts where teachers are expected to practise. It has also been noted that variations in provision exist across HEIs and in how they implement the current MRTEQ ITE policy.

Second, the extended roles of teachers suggested by the SDGs, which mirror (to a large extent) the role of an ideal teacher constructed in the NSE, reveal the problem of teacher ambition and agency rubbing up against the contextual specificities of inequality. Teachers can do much but they are often constrained by the context they find themselves in and the conditions in which they work. To this end, teacher agency as a form of valorising effort must be framed within a broad and systemic approach to improve education quality and recognise the structural and policy context in which teachers work.

Third, post-apartheid ITE policy and legislation specifically and education policy more generally suggest a narrowing of education focus on cognitive content and assessment and consequentially a narrowing of the roles of teachers. The extended roles of teachers, as suggested in the SDGs and the NSE, are not possible in a context where the notion of education quality is reduced to measurable improvements in mathematics/numeracy and languages/literacy hollowing out the concern with the affective domain.

Fourth, there is a clear need to ensure uniformity and consistency in ITE programmes aligned to CAPS and the MRTEQ policy. Such uniformity in terms of these policies will aid in ensuring that aspiring teachers receive the same training across HEIs. However, it has also been indicated that even if such uniformity in terms of CAPS and the MRTEQ policy is achieved in HEIs' ITE programmes, it will not eradicate the inequities which persist in school contexts where aspiring teachers will teach. Moreover, the alignment must not, as argued in this chapter, narrow the focus of teachers' work and reduce their agency to mere literacy/numeracy technicians.

Fifth, the provision of quality teacher education is split across multiple agencies and authorities. These include:

1. the CHE, which is responsible for HEI and programme accreditation;
2. the DHET, responsible for setting teacher employment and professional norms and Education, Training and Development Practices;
3. SETA, supporting work-integrated learning professional development of education; SACE, responsible for teacher registration, professional conduct and more recently overseeing the Continuing Professional Teacher Development System; and
4. the South African Qualifications Authority (SAQA), responsible for the registration of all teacher and education professional qualifications.

In addition, policy decisions in post-apartheid South Africa are determined by the determinations and discussions of the Education Labour Relations Council. What has evolved is a complex governance arrangement which, as argued in this chapter, hinders a clear a focus on teacher quality and increases the burden of bureaucratic regulations, potentially at the expense of teacher agency and professionalism.

In policy terms, ITE policies and programmes need to be in conversation with, if not conjoined with, other policies outside the educational sector so that once qualified, aspiring teachers can experience teaching in school contexts that are relatively equitable. As such, achieving consistency in ITE programmes – how they are governed, the sites where they are offered and the curriculum that is followed – is necessary but not sufficient to ensure that equity in the quality of teachers and teaching is experienced in practice across all schools.

References

Badat, S. & Sayed, Y. 2014. Post-1994 South African education: The challenge of social justice. *The Annals of the American Academy of Political and Social Science*, 652(1): 127-148. https://doi.org/10.1177/0002716213511188

Barber, M. & Mourshed, M. 2007. *How the world's best-performing schools systems come out on top*. Sandton: McKinsey & Company.

Barrett, A.; Sayed, Y.; Scweisfurth, M. & Tikly, L. 2015. Learning, pedagogy and the post-2015 education and development agenda. *International Journal of Educational Development*, 40: 231-236. https://doi.org/10.1016/j.ijedudev.2014.11.003

Carrim, N. & Keet, A. 2005. Infusing human rights into the curriculum: The case of the South African Revised National Curriculum Statement. *Perspectives in Education*,23(2): 99-110.

Chisholm, L. 2012. Apartheid education legacies and new directions in post-apartheid South Africa. *Storia delle Donne*, 8: 81-104.

Chisholm, L.; Hoadley, U.; Kivulu, M.; Brookes, H.; Prinsloo, C.; Kgobe, A.; Mosia, D.; Narsee, H. & Rule, S. 2005. *Educator workload in South Africa*. Pretoria: HSRC Press.

Christie, P. 1996. *The right to learn*. Johannesburg: SACHED Press.

Cochran-Smith, M.; McQuillan, P.; Mitchell, K.; Gahlsdorf-Terrell, D.; Barnatt, J.; D'Souza, L.; Jong, C.; Shakman, K.; Lam, K. & Gleeson, A. 2012. A longitudinal study of teaching practice and early career decisions: A cautionary tale. *American Educational Research Journal*, 49(5): 844-880. https://doi.org/10.3102/0002831211431006

Council on Higher Education (CHE). 2010. *Report on the national review of academic and professional programmes in education*. Pretoria: CHE.

Department of Basic Education (DBE). 2011. *Curriculum and assessment policy statement*. Pretoria: DBE.

Department of Basic Education (DBE). 2012. *Action Plan 2014: Towards the realisation of schooling 2025*. Pretoria: DBE.

Department of Basic Education and Department of Higher Education and Training (DBE & DHET). 2011. *Integrated strategic planning framework for teacher education and development in South Africa, 2011-2025*. Pretoria: Government Printer.

Department of Education (DoE). 1996. *Curriculum 2005: A discussion document*. Pretoria: DoE.

Department of Education (DoE). 2001. *Norms and standards of educators*. Pretoria: DoE.

Department of Education (DoE). 2002. *Revised national curriculum statement (schools)*. Pretoria: DoE.

Department of Higher Education and Training (DHET). 2011. *Minimum requirements for teacher education qualifications policy*. Pretoria: Government Printer.

Department of Higher Education and Training (DHET). 2013. The National Qualifications Framework (2008): Amendment to the determination of the sub-frameworks that comprise the National Qualifications Framework. *Government Gazette 36802*, 30 August. Pretoria: Government Printer.

Department of Higher Education and Training (DHET). 2015. National Qualifications Framework Act, 2008 (Act No. 67 of 2008): Revised Policy on the Minimum Requirements for Teacher Education Qualifications. *Government Gazette 38487*, 19 February. Pretoria: Government Printer.

Hofmeyr, J. & Hall, G. 1995. *The national teacher education audit: Synthesis report*. Johannesburg: Edupol, National Business Initiative. https://doi.org/10.1177/1741143214537227

Howie, S.; Venter, E.; Van Staden, S.; Zimmerman, L.; Long, C.; Scherman, V. & Archer, E. 2007. *PIRLS 2006 summary report: South African children's reading achievement*. Pretoria: Centre for Education Assessment.

Mestry, R. 2014. A critical analysis of the national norms and standards for school funding policy: Implications for social justice and equity in South Africa. *Educational Management Administration and Leadership*, 42(6): 851-867.

Moloi, M.Q. 2000. *Mathematics achievement in South Africa: A comparison of the official curriculum with pupil performance in the SACMEQ (Southern African Consortium for Monitoring Educational Quality) II Project*. Available for download at: https://www.jet.org.za/resources

Morrow, W. & Samuels, M. 2005. *Report of the Ministerial Committee on Teacher Education: A national framework for teacher education in South Africa*. Pretoria: Government Printer.

National Council for the Accreditation of Teacher Education (NCATE). 2013. *What makes an effective teacher?* USA: NCATE.

Naylor, R. & Sayed, Y. 2014. *Teacher quality: Evidence review*. Canberra: Office of Development Effectiveness.

Republic of South Africa (RSA). 1996. National Education Policy Act, no. 27 of 1996. Pretoria: Government Printer.

Robinson, S. 2012. Constructing teacher agency in response to the constraints of education policy: Adoption and adaptation. *Curriculum Journal*, 23(2): 231-245. https://doi.org/10.1080/09585176.2012.678702

Rose, B. & Tunmer, R. 1975. *Documents in South African education*. Johannesburg: Donker.

Samuel, M. 2002. Working in the rain: Pressures and priorities for teacher education curriculum design in South Africa – A case study of the University of Durban-Westville. *International Journal of Educational Development*, 22(3-4): 397-410. https://doi.org/10.1016/S0738-0593(01)00061-X

Sayed, Y. 2002. Changing forms of teacher education in South Africa: A case study of policy change. *International Journal of Education Development*, 22(3-4): 381-395. https://doi.org/10.1016/S0738-0593(01)00062-1

Sayed, Y (ed.). 2018. *Continuing professional teacher development in sub-Saharan Africa: Improving teaching and learning*. London: Bloomsbury Press.

Sayed, Y. & Ahmed, R. 2015. Education quality, and teaching and learning in the post-2015 education agenda. *International Journal of Educational Development (IJED)*, 40: 330-338. https://doi.org/10.1016/j.ijedudev.2014.11.005

Sayed, Y.; Badroodien, A.; McDonald, Z.; Balie, L.; De Kock, T.; Garisch, C. & Foulds, K. (Cape Peninsula University of Technology and University of Sussex Research Consortium: Education and Peace Building). 2015. *Teachers and youth as agents of social cohesion in South Africa.* Cape Town: Cape Peninsula University of Technology.

Sinclair, M. 2002. *Planning education in and after emergencies.* Paris: UNESCO.

United Nations Association of Greater Philadelphia [UNA-GP].2015. *The Sustainable Development Goals 2015-2030.* Available at: https://una-gp.org/the-sustainable-development-goals-2015-2030/.

Chapter 03

Who Becomes a Teacher & Why

Yusuf Sayed, Chiwimbiso Kwenda, Harry Rampa & Thelma Mort

3.1 Introduction

Various international studies highlight the fact that effective schools are those that have good-quality teachers. According to a review by the World Bank (2012:1),

> a number of studies have found that teacher effectiveness is one of the most important school-based predictors of student learning and that several years of teaching by outstanding teachers can offset the learning deficits of disadvantaged students.

Research that explores what makes school systems effective has looked for common characteristics in the top-performing education systems in international achievement tests, with a view to identifying features that account for success (Barber & Mourshed 2007; Mourshed, Chijioke & Barber 2010; OECD 2010; Vegas, Ganimian & Jaimovich 2012). These studies have reached similar conclusions. The key strategies that they identify for improving student outcomes centre around developing a quality teacher workforce, which aims to: attract, recruit and retain high-quality candidates into teacher training;

- ✓ train student teachers with extensive school-based practice;
- ✓ train student teachers with high-level subject specialisation and academic rigour;
- ✓ provide teachers with personalised CPD through mentoring and coaching; and
- ✓ involve teachers in research and education policymaking.

In the South African context, there are systemic concerns about attracting and recruiting the best teachers to redress the legacy of apartheid. Van Broekhuizen (2015) notes several systemic challenges in teacher recruitment. These include balancing supply and demand, attracting the best candidates into teaching, an ageing cohort of teachers which needs replacing, an oversupply in some fields/subjects and undersupply in others – particularly for certain languages, phases and subjects. Furthermore, the well-researched factor of early career teacher attrition is described as a critical factor in the teacher demand-and-supply equation (Gold 1996). In addition, teacher supply is difficult in the rural context (SACE 2010). Another specific problem of teacher supply is in the Foundation Phase, which comprises Grades 1 to 3. A recent estimate using a multivariate model suggested that there will be a negative gap of Foundation Phase teachers of between 15 220 and 42 135 by 2020, accumulating over the years from 2013 to 2019 (Green, Adendorff & Mathebula 2014). The authors indicate that the public higher education system can be expected to produce no more than 3 880 effective new BEd Foundation Phase ITE graduates in total by 2019.

Attracting the best teachers in areas/subjects of need is a priority of policy in South Africa. The DBE (2015) posits that attracting new entrants implies attracting an adequate numbers of new students, attracting sufficient numbers of quality teachers with disciplines aligned to the needs of the education sector and attracting teachers who are able to function effectively as new teachers in diverse contexts. Several specific supply-side interventions, such as the Teacher Rural Incentive Scheme (TRIS), the Funza Lushaka Bursary Programme (FLBP) and the Strengthening Foundation Phase Teacher Education programme, seek to redress this problem.

In this context, this chapter addresses the key questions regarding who becomes a teacher and why, as a way of understanding how quality and supply can be improved in the South African context. The chapter begins by conceptually situating the debate, followed by a brief outline of the methodology. South Africa is still a racialised society more than two decades after democracy and as such race is a salient feature of South African society.[1] Race is not only correlated with the nature and form of education citizens receive (Badat & Sayed 2014) but also with economic opportunities and the nature of economic inequities (Keswell 2004:1). It is for these reasons that the chapter presents and discusses the findings of the study by race (which in this case is also correlated with institutional type to a large extent).[2] This is followed by a conclusion that highlights the findings and contextualises them within larger policy debates.

Addressing the issue of who becomes a teacher and why will shed light on developing a more balanced and equitably deployed teaching corps in which qualified and best-paid educators are not disproportionately located in the former Model C schools (Q5) – and thus the most well-resourced environments – but in those where they are needed most. Understanding why people become teachers is also crucial to unpack the reasons for individuals to remain in the teaching profession. It will add to the research on reasons for studying why individuals choose to become a teacher in South Africa.

3.2 Situating the Debate

Who becomes a teacher and what motivates them to become teachers is a subject of intense discussion and scholarship globally and more recently in South Africa. Literature about teacher motivation argues that reasons to become a teacher are varied and multiple and reflect individual preferences and socio-cultural, political and institutional factors (Tatto 2012; Jungert, Alm & Thornberg 2014). While some regard a broad combination of background factors as meeting in an influential way, like Colley et al. (2003:485), who regard "class stratum, family background and gender" as "combining to predispose young women for caring occupations", Kelleher (2011) and others also note that teaching is a highly feminised profession, particularly at the primary level.

---

1 For this study, we use the racial categories of white, black, coloured, and Indian that our respondents identified themselves with as these are the dominant racial categories that marked apartheid and the inequities that the system engendered. Our usage of these terms does not in any way imply that we endorse racial categorisation and we argue that race is socially constructed and embedded in systems of privilege and inequity.
2 Where appropriate, the categories 'important' and 'high importance' have been collapsed and combined.

Research on motivation to become a teacher has commonly identified three sets of rationales: extrinsic motivation, intrinsic motivation and altruistic reasons – although the distinction between the latter two is not always clear (Richardson & Watt 2010). The factors or reasons that motivate individuals to become teachers have also been divided into a set of push and pull factors.

Push factors are those that explain motivation in relation to extra and contingent factors that draw people into teaching, such as the promise of security, the absence of other career alternatives or teacher education as a route into higher education. Pull factors are those that seek to understand motivation in relation to the desire to do good and contribute to society. Push and pull factors are contextually determined and framed, and shaped by individual biography, positionality, beliefs and histories.

3.3 Extrinsic Motivation to Become a Teacher

In the South African context, the end of apartheid in 1994 afforded new possibilities of changed, improved and different life opportunities or chances (Robinson & McMillan 2006), including going to university and, relevant to this study, new career opportunities, such as considering becoming a teacher for those who previously did not have such opportunities.

Extrinsic motivation emanates from instrumental reasons attached to rewards (Ryan & Deci 2000; Eccles & Wigfield 2002; Lai 2011). For example, prospective teachers may be motivated by what they see as the material benefits or rewards that come from being a teacher, such as salary, vacations or other external rewards.

The security of a future regular income as a state employee is seen as an obvious reason to teach. However, Manuel and Hughes's (2006) study of a cohort of Australian student teachers at the University of Sydney indicated that "salary did not figure in the research as a significant reason for choosing to teach". They noted that the lack of interest paid to salary was not isolated but cited frequently in other similar studies in the late 1980s. A study by Howey and Zimpher (1989) in the USA found that student teachers were "less concerned about material reward and job security" than other university students, despite them articulating an awareness of the difficulties associated with teaching.

Another extrinsic factor is the issue of a bursary or scholarship to study, which offers not only security but a greater likelihood of being able to complete the course owing to having consistent funding. There are also the National Student Financial Aid Scheme (NSFAS) and as previously mentioned, FLBP, which offer incentives to study teaching to those who would never have had that opportunity before. These financial incentive schemes are used to target needy but successful school leavers in priority areas and subjects/phases.

3.4 Intrinsic Motivation to Become a Teacher

Research studies show that student teachers are primarily motivated by intrinsic factors (Howey & Zimpher 1989; Kyriacou & Coulthard 2000) such as: working with young people, the desire to make a difference to children's lives and society more broadly, a desire to maintain engagement with a subject area and an expectation of high levels of job satisfaction, – which figure prominently as motivation to choose to teach (Huberman 1989). For example, the McKinsey reports (Barber & Moursled 2007; Mourshed et al. 2010) found that the most common factor for becoming a teacher was in order to help a new generation succeed. These reasons have been described by some as idealistic, socially motivated or as having "social justice" dimensions, "tacit in statements made by participants such as "making a difference to children's lives" and "helping others"; and these factors may well be implicit in the predominant responses of "personal fulfilment" and "working with young people" (Manuel & Hughes 2006:11).

Furthermore, this high level of intrinsic motivation serves the teaching force well. Baker (2004) found that highly intrinsically motivated people generally outperform less intrinsically motivated people, whereas extrinsic motivation is usually associated with poorer performance and educational outcomes (König & Rothland 2012). Konig and Rothland (2012) also found that "intrinsic motivation is positively correlated with GPK at the first occasion of measurement".

An important predictor of intrinsic career value and perceived teaching ability to be a good teacher is another interpersonal dimension – extraversion – with the defining characteristics of sociability, outgoingness and talkativeness (John, Naumann & Soto 2008). These characteristics are meaningfully related to intrinsic motivation to be a teacher, given that interpersonal contacts with children, parents and other teachers are integral features of the profession. It is also reasonable to assume that persons who are extroverted perceive themselves as suitably skilled for a profession that involves constant interpersonal contact (Jugovic et al. 2012).

3.5 Research Design

The data that this chapter draws on are based on a longitudinal study of ITE conducted by CITE from 2015 (Sayed et al. 2015; Sayed 2017). A mixed-methods approach was used, which included questionnaires and focus group interviews. Typically, mixed-methods studies use both qualitative and quantitative methods and thus collect "two types of data (e.g. numerical and textual), two types of data analysis (statistical and thematic), and two types of conclusions (emic and etic representations, 'objective' and 'subjective')" (Tashakkori & Creswell 2007:4).

There are clear and obvious reasons for using a mixed-methods approach to construct a research output with a stronger validity and a greater research 'yield'. However, it is in the interpretation of the collected data that further strengthening is possible, in that the integration of these research methods is possible on multiple levels; for example in the comparison and discussion of anomalies and similarities in the collected data from different methods.

Focus group interviews were conducted and questionnaires were administered to BEd Foundation Phase and PGCE FET Phase student teachers at four universities, in the Western Cape and Gauteng provinces, offering ITE programmes. These universities are categorised as follows:
- ✓ Institution A – University of Technology
- ✓ Institution B – Traditional University
- ✓ Institution C – University of Technology
- ✓ Institution D – Traditional University

Three questionnaires were administered to student teachers at various stages of the final year of their ITE programme. The first questionnaire focused on teacher motivation and beliefs, the second questionnaire focused on teacher knowledge and the third questionnaire focused on teaching practicum. The data for this chapter are solely focused on the data from the first questionnaire, specifically the section on reasons for becoming a teacher. This section asked student teachers to select their reason for becoming a teacher, which was indicated on a Likert-scale.

The first questionnaire comprised two sections: the first section asked for biographical information and the second section focused on the respondents' reasons for entering the programme and their beliefs about teaching as a career. The respondents were asked to report, on a Likert-scale, how important 16 factors were in influencing them to become a teacher. In addition, the student teachers were asked three open-ended questions that further described their motivation to become teachers. Student teachers were also invited to participate in focus group interviews. The focus group interviews were conducted with selected samples of student teachers from the four universities and probed their reasons for becoming teachers, among other issues.

This study comprised a sample of 323 student teachers. A total of 258 (79,9%) of the students were enrolled in the BEd Foundation Phase programme and a smaller sample of 65 (20,1%) were enrolled in the PGCE FET programmes with a focus on mathematics and languages. The reasoning behind this relates to the chronic shortage of Foundation Phase teachers, as discussed earlier in this chapter. A limitation, however, is that the sizes of samples in certain cohorts were low, such as the PGCE FET cohort.[3] Caution must thus be exercised in interpreting the results presented. Moreover, it must be noted that the respondents were not asked to rank which factor was most important and as such categorical claims cannot be inferred from the data, although they demonstrate important trends and patterns, as the analysis will reveal.

In answering the first research question, which is who becomes a teacher, all the data are analysed in relation to several individual characteristics and background dimensions. The principal axes of this analysis are race and institutional type, although the dataset is more extensive.

---

3   It is important to note that no white students were enrolled in the PGCE FET programme. As a result, no data are compared to the white PGCE FET student teachers, and listed in tables as N/A.

The second research question is why the student teachers are choosing to become teachers and what influenced them. The principal axes of this analysis are race and institutional type, although the dataset is more extensive.

3.6 Findings and Discussion

This section presents and discusses the two main aspects of this study, namely who becomes a teacher and why. It draws on the survey data from four institutions, as well as focus group interviews.

3.6.1 Who Becomes a Teacher in Post-apartheid South Africa?

Table 3.1 provides demographic data on the types of students entering BEd Foundation Phase and PGCE FET teaching. It is important to mention here that the BEd Foundation Phase data were collected from four institutions, as classified in the methodology section of this chapter. The unevenness of the data in this respect is noted but it is important to include the PGCE FET data in this discussion since they illustrate some important differences in reasons to become a teacher, as reported by the participants in the two cohorts.

Table 3.1 reveals that an overwhelming majority of students enrolling for teaching in BEd Foundation Phase were female, with an almost insignificant percentage of males by comparison. Reasons for this disproportionate representation of men may be linked to traditional gender beliefs regarding the roles of men and women in rearing children. The number of men is higher in the PGCE FET cohort, while that of women is lower than in the BEd Foundation Phase. The findings here could be attributed to the fact that in the mathematics PGCE FET cohort there were no women in the class; instead, women were concentrated in the PGCE FET languages cohort.

The table also reveals that 47,5% of those entering teaching in the BEd Foundation Phase at the sample institutions were white, with only 20,8% of the students being black Africans. This raises interesting issues regarding beliefs about which phase is more prestigious to teach in, beliefs which appear to vary by race in the context studied (see interview data). This is closely correlated to home language. In contrast, black African and coloured respondents made up 95,4% of the sample of PGCE FET students. This could be due to the fact that, as discussed below, teaching is regarded as a stable and secure career option.

Regarding involvement in part-time work, three-quarters of the sample of students in both cohorts reported not holding part-time jobs. Since there is a correlation between race and household income, with white households earning more than black families on average (Statistics South Africa [Stats SA] 2017), it can be assumed that most of the BEd Foundation Phase students who worked part-time were black.

With regard to the question of whether BEd Foundation Phase participants in the study were first-generation tertiary education students, 61,6% reported that they were not. They come from educated families and can be assumed to have middle-class parents. The 38,4%

who reported being first-generation students can be assumed to be from working-class families, which are mostly black and coloured. In contrast, 59,1% of PGCE FET students were first generation.

Teaching was the first choice for 51,6% of the sample of BEd Foundation Phase student teachers, compared to only 22,6% of the PGCE FET sample. A total of 48,4% of the BEd Foundation Phase sample reported teaching as not having been their first choice. The figure here is much higher for the PGCE FET cohort at 77,4%. This is an interesting finding since it has implications for the reasons why students enter teaching, in terms of the pull/push factors discussed below.

Table 3.1   Combined Institutional Demographic Profiles of Participants

Variable	Profile	BEd Foundation Phase (FP) %	PGCE FET %
Sex of student	Female	95,8	71,2
	Male	4,2	28,8
Age	17-20	0,4	0
	21-25	78,4	63,6
	26-30	16,6	22,7
	31-35	2,3	4,5
	36-40	1,9	4,5
	Older than 40	0,4	4,5
Race	White	47,5	0
	Coloured	28,2	63,1
	Black	20,8	32,3
	Other	1,9	1,5
	Indian	1,5	3,1
Funding source of student	FLBP	53,3	0
	Family	20,8	19,7
	Other	15,1	6,1
	NSFAS loan/grant	5,8	62,1
	Myself	3,5	9,1
	Student loan	1,5	3
Part-time work	No	74,4	72,7
	Yes	25,6	27,3

Table 3.1 Combined Institutional Demographic Profiles of Participants (*cont*)

Variable	Profile	BEd Foundation Phase (FP) %	PGCE FET %
Home language	Afrikaans	44,4	25,8
	English	34,7	39,4
	Zulu	8,1	1,5
	Sesotho	0	1,5
	isiXhosa	3,1	28,8
	Sepedi	1,5	1,5
	Setswana	0,4	0
	isiNdebele	2,7	0
	siSwati	4,2	0
	Xitsonga	0,8	0
	Other	0	1,5
First-generation student	No	61,6	40,9
	Yes	38,4	59,1
Teaching first choice	Yes	51,6	22,6
	No	48,4	77,4

3.6.2 Motivation for Becoming a Teacher

This section reviews the extrinsic and intrinsic motivation associated with becoming a teacher.[4]

3.6.2.1 Extrinsic Motivation

Table 3.2 lists the variables that relate to extrinsic reasons for becoming a teacher. Key extrinsic variables are discussed in subsequent sub-sections based on this table, as well as other tables that are specific to each item under discussion. The table in general reveals that some extrinsic factors are stronger drivers of motivation to enter teaching than others. In particular, as discussed below, the influences of a school teacher and the family, the importance of teaching for society and teaching as a gateway career option predominated.

---

4 Note that the same respondent can be inspired by a number of the sources included in the question.

Table 3.2   Extrinsic Motivation for Choosing Teaching as a Career

	Programme of study	Scale of Importance			
		No importance	Low importance	Moderate importance	High importance
External motivation for choosing teaching as a career	**A teacher inspired me**				
	BEd FP (n=258)	13,2%	24,8%	31,4%	30,6%
	PGCE FET (n=65)	16,9%	16,9%	44,6%	21,5%
	A family member inspired me				
	BEd FP (n=257)	21,8%	19,8%	29,2%	29,2%
	PGCE FET (n=64)	17,2%	26,6%	29,7%	26,6%
	Someone else inspired me to teach				
	BEd FP (n=257)	36,6%	24,5%	22,6%	16,3%
	PGCE FET (n=65)	40%	15,4%	33,8%	10,8%
	Teaching is an admirable profession				
	BEd FP (n=257)	3,1%	8,6%	31,1%	57,2%
	PGCE FET (n=65)	3,1%	15,4%	27,7%	53,8%
	Teachers are respected in the community				
	BEd FP (n=258)	13,2%	28,7%	34,5%	23,6%
	PGCE FET (n=65)	7,7%	27,7%	40%	24,6%
	Teachers are well paid				
	BEd FP (n=258)	48,1%	35,7%	15,5%	0,8%
	PGCE FET (n=65)	15,4%	44,6%	38,5%	1,5%
	Teachers can find a job				
	BEd FP (n=256)	14,8%	29,3%	37,1%	18,8%

Table 3.2   Extrinsic Motivation for Choosing Teaching as a Career (cont)

External motivation for choosing teaching as a career	PGCE FET (n=65)	1,5%	9,2%	33,8%	55,4%
	There are bursaries				
	BEd FP (n=256)	24,6%	21,5%	28,5%	25,4%
	PGCE FET (n=64)	15,6%	31,3%	28,1%	25%
	Balanced personal and professional life				
	BEd FP (n=256)	11,3%	26,2%	37,9%	24,6%
	PGCE FET (n=65)	9,2%	18,5%	38,5%	33,8%
	Teachers are important for the future				
	BEd FP (n=258)	0,4%	1,9%	12,4%	85,3%
	PGCE FET (n=65)	0%	3,1%	12,3%	84,6%
	Teaching will open up opportunities to other careers				
	BEd FP (n=256)	9,3%	18,2%	28,7%	43,8%
	PGCE FET (n=65)	1,5%	6,2%	36,9%	55,4%

3.6.2.2 Financial Incentives: Bursaries[5]

With regard to funding, Table 3.1 indicated that 53,3% of the BEd Foundation Phase cohort were funded by Funza Lushaka bursaries, compared to 0% of the PGCE FET cohort, which is not covered by this funding source. These BEd Foundation Phase student teachers would mainly be of rural origin. One of the three institutions does not allocate Funza Lushaka bursaries to the PGCE FET students as it is a 'capped' qualification, meaning it is allocated solely to those who did not benefit or who had not obtained any qualification. The FLBP makes those institutions which provide it for both cohorts of candidates very attractive.

Far fewer (5,8%) BEd Foundation Phase participants were funded by NSFAS, compared to 62,1% of their PGCE FET counterparts. A notable difference in the sources of tuition between the BEd Foundation Phase and PGCE FET cohorts is the fact that there were almost 12 times more recipients of the NSFAS in the PGCE FET cohort than in the BEd Foundation Phase cohort.

---

5   While it has not been the focus of the study on which this book and chapter are based, there is a need for further research to examine the policies, procedures, and processes that teacher education providers use in disbursing financial aid.

A total of 20,8% of the BEd Foundation Phase cohort were funded by their families, compared to 19,7% of the PGCE FET sample, while 1,5% of the BEd Foundation Phase student teachers had student loans, and the PGCE FET figure here is 3%. This shows that the BEd Foundation Phase category of student teachers either had family support or access to support structures that would guarantee their loans/stand surety for them.[6]

The breakdown by race in Table 3.3 indicates that 37,8% of the black BEd Foundation Phase participants and 9,5% of the black PGCE FET participants reported the availability of bursaries as being highly important as an extrinsic motivation to enter teaching. The respective figures for the coloured and white respondents are 11,4% BEd Foundation Phase and 7,9% PGCE FET (coloured), and 20% BEd Foundation Phase (white). The figures for the Indian cohort were 0% for both BEd Foundation Phase and PGCE FET. From this data, it can be concluded that bursaries attract more black students to become teachers than any other racial group.[7]

Table 3.3   Perceptions of the Significance of Bursaries by Racial Group

Race of student	No importance		Low importance		Moderate importance		High importance	
	BEd FP	PGCE FET	BEd FP	PGCE FET	BEd FP	PGCE FET	BEd FP	PGCE FET
Black (n=74)	1 (1,4%)	2 (2,7%)	7 (9,5%)	5 (6,8%)	18 (24,3%)	6 (8,1%)	28 (37,8%)	7 (9,5%)
Coloured (n=114)	23 (20,2%)	7 (6,1%)	16 (14%)	13 (11,4%)	21 (18,4%)	12 (10,5%)	13 (11,4%)	9 (7,9%)
Indian (n=6)	2 (33,3%)	1 (16,7%)	1 (16,7%)	1 (16,7%)	1 (16,7%)	0 (0%)	0 (0%)	0 (0%)
White (n=120)	34 (28,3%)	N/A	30 (25%)	N/A	32 (26,7%)	N/A	24 (20%)	N/A
Other (n=6)	3 (50%)	0 (0%)	1 (16,7%)	1 (16,7%)	1 (16,7%)	0 (0%)	0 (0%)	0 (0%)
Total	63	10	55	20	73	18	65	16

---

6   Combining those who selected 'moderate' and 'high' importance in the survey.
7   Combining those who selected 'moderate' and 'high' importance in the survey.

The qualitative data reveal how some student teachers saw the institution as a reason for where to study.[8] One student in this cohort stated:

> The reason I came to [Institution D] was because I got a bursary at [this institution] so I thought okay, I'm going to pursue something in my career because, I mean if its paid for you, you're going to go for it. The reason I didn't choose another institute was because academically I wasn't qualified to be there at UCT or Stellenbosch, so I came to [this institution] for those reasons [PGCE FET Language student explaining why she had not gone to another university] (PGCE, Inst. D).

3.6.2.3 Conditions of Work: Work, Security and Salaries

The literature highlights work security as an important driver to become a teacher. In the data for this study (see Table 3.2) it is noted that 55,9% of the BEd FP cohort, compared to 89,2% of the PGCE FET cohort, are confident that teaching will result in employment.[9]

Variations in the issue of salary as an extrinsic motivator to become a teacher are shown in Table 3.4 by racial group. Across the race groups, teacher salaries were generally perceived to be of low importance in attracting people to enter teaching.

Table 3.4 Perceptions of the Importance of Teacher Salaries as an Extrinsic Motivator (by race)

Race of student	No importance		Low importance		Moderate importance		High importance	
	BEd FP	PGCE FET	BEd FP	PGCE FET	BEd FP	PGCE FET	BEd FP	PGCE FET
Black (n=75)	31 (41,3%)	7 (9,3%)	15 (20%)	8 (10,7%)	7 (9,3%)	5 (6,7%)	1 (1,3%)	1 (1,3%)
Coloured (n=113)	28 (24,8%)	2 (1,8%)	30 (26,5%)	20 (17,7%)	14 (12,4%)	19 (16,8%)	0 (0%)	0 (0%)
Indian (n=6)	0 (0%)	1 (16,7%)	3 (50%)	0 (0%)	1 (16,7%)	1 (16,7%)	0 (0%)	0 (0%)
White (n=123)	63 (51,2%)	N/A	43 (35%)	N/A	16 (13%)	N/A	1 (0,8%)	N/A
Other (n=6)	2 (33,3%)	0 (0%)	1 (16,7%)	1 (16,7%)	2 (33,3%)	0 (0%)	0 (0%)	0 (0%)
Total	124	10	92	29	40	25	2	1

---

8 While it has not been the focus of the study on which this book and chapter are based, there is a need for further research to examine the administration criteria and selection procedures of teacher education providers to better understand how these shape who becomes a teacher.

9 Combining those who selected 'moderate' and 'high' importance in the survey.

The views of participants from the different institutions paint much the same picture as when examined by race. In other words, participants from all categories of institutions did not consider teacher salaries to be important as a reason to enter teaching.

A PGCE FET science student pointed out that he perceived the burgeoning teacher shortages in science and mathematics as a concern:

> I'm from Limpopo. And so another thing, I also heard it last year, that in three years about ten teachers from high school will have resigned. And then a lot of people from home were doing engineering, science, so I don't even know [indistinct], which means there will be gaps (PGCE, Inst. D).

Some black student teachers saw teaching as being 'economically equal' and this correlated with social equality:

> In the apartheid era, the teachers – black and coloured teachers – were treated so badly, but now in the new democratic South Africa, teachers are having the same retirement plans, teachers are earning the same type of salary brackets. Teachers are being respected, let's say from a racial perspective, but teachers are now being respected, as teachers should be (PGCE, Inst. D).

3.6.2.4 Inspiration and Modelling: From Teachers to Family

Three sources of motivation to become a teacher – a teacher, a family member and someone else – were identified from the data. The section below reports on these sources of motivation.

i) Teacher Inspiration

Table 3.2 summarised the BEd Foundation Phase and PGCE FET questionnaire data on extrinsic factors as motivation for entering teaching. A total of 62% of the BEd Foundation Phase cohort and 66,1% of PGCE FET student teachers reported being moderately or highly inspired by practising teachers to enter teaching.[10]

Racial differences on the issue of extrinsic motivation to become teachers are highlighted in Table 3.5. In the table, 48% (BEd Foundation Phase) and 23,7% (PGCE FET) of the black participants reported being moderately or highly inspired by a teacher in their decision to enter teaching. The percentage figures for the coloured sample were 40,4% (BEd Foundation Phase) and 20% (PGCE FET), those of the Indian sample were 50% (BEd Foundation Phase) and 16,7% (PGCE FET), while the figures for the white sample were 58,2% (BEd Foundation Phase) and 0% (PGCE FET). This finding appears to indicate that a sizable number of those entering teaching were inspired by practising teachers to want to become teachers. There tended to be more black and coloured students in the PGCE FET programmes and more white students in the BEd Foundation Phase programmes of ITE institutions. This demographic phenomenon might explain why the percentage is zero for the white cohort in the PGCE FET columns of the table.

---

10 Combining those who selected 'moderate' and 'high' importance in the survey.

Table 3.5   Inspiration to Become Teachers (by race): A Teacher Inspired Me

Race of students	No importance		Low importance		Moderate importance		High importance	
	BEd FP	PGCE FET	BEd FP	PGCE FET	BEd FP	PGCE FET	BEd FP	PGCE FET
Black (n=73)	7 (9,3%)	2 (2,7%)	11 (14,7%)	1 (1,3%)	15 (20%)	11 (14,7%)	21 (28%)	7 (9%)
Coloured (n=113)	15 (13,2%)	8 (7,0%)	12 (10,5%)	10 (8,8%)	19 (16,7%)	16 (14%)	27 (23,7%)	7 (6%)
Indian (n=6)	0 (0%)	1 (16,7%)	1 (16,7%)	0 (0%)	3 (50%)	1 (16,7%)	0 (0%)	0 (0%)
White (n=123)	12 (9,8%)	N/A	39 (32%)	N/A	41 (33,6%)	N/A	30 (24,6%)	N/A
Other (n=6)	0 (0%)	0 (0%)	1 (16,7%)	0 (0%)	3 (50%)	1 (16,7%)	1 (16,7%)	0 (0%)
Total	34	11	64	11	81	29	79	14

ii) Family Inspiration

In general, Table 3.5 shows that family is an important source of motivation to enter teaching and more so when the family member is a teacher. Table 3.2 indicated that family members inspired 58,4% of the BEd Foundation Phase cohort and 56,3% of the PGCE FET cohort.[11]

Table 3.6 shows that 49,3% (BEd Foundation Phase) and 16,5% (PGCE FET) of the black student teachers reported being inspired by a family member to enter teaching. The figures for the coloured sample were 40,7% (BEd Foundation Phase) and 20,4% (PGCE FET), while the figure for the white respondents was 51,3% (BEd Foundation Phase). This seems to indicate that family has a stronger influence on the decision to enter teaching for black and white students enrolled in the BEd Foundation Phase programme.[12]

Table 3.6   Inspiration to Become Teachers (by race): A Family Member Inspired Me

Race of students	No importance		Low importance		Moderate importance		High importance	
	BEd FP	PGCE FET	BEd FP	PGCE FET	BEd FP	PGCE FET	BEd FP	PGCE FET
Black (n=73)	9 (12,3%)	4 (5,5%)	8 (11%)	4 (5,5%)	18 (24,7%)	4 (5,5%)	18 (24,7%)	8 (11%)

---

11 Combining those who selected 'moderate' and 'high' importance in the survey.
12 Combining those who selected 'moderate' and 'high' importance in the survey.

Table 3.6　Inspiration to Become Teachers (by race): A Family Member Inspired Me (cont)

Coloured (n=113)	16 (14,2%)	7 (6,2%)	10 (8,8%)	11 (9,7%)	20 (17,7%)	14 (12,4%)	26 (23%)	9 (8%)
Indian (n=6)	2 (33,3%)	0 (0%)	0 (0%)	1 (16,7%)	2 (33,3%)	1 (16,7%)	0 (0%)	0 (0%)
White (n=123)	28 (22,8%)	N/A	32 (26%)	N/A	35 (28,5%)	N/A	28 (22,8%)	N/A
Other (n=6)	1 (16,7%)	0 (0%)	1 (16,7%)	1 (16,7%)	0 (0%)	0 (0%)	3 (50%)	0 (0%)
Total	56	11	51	17	75	19	75	17

The qualitative data revealed the importance of family, particularly when they were teachers, as a reason for entering teaching. One BEd Foundation Phase student teacher participating in the focus group interview said:

> My teacher also became my parent. So I think the influence my teacher had on me, I wanted to have that effect on other people. So I kind of learned from that experience and saw and thought I want to do that (BEd, FP, Inst. A).

One of the BEd Foundation Phase student teachers had a father who was an oncologist but also a lecturer; it was thus her father who influenced her:

> My dad is a lecturer now and he has always, I don't know, when I was studying he'd always come sit with me and help and teach me things, especially with biology, and I always enjoyed the enthusiasm that my father had with lecturing and teaching (BEd, FP Inst A).

However, family can also be a negative incentive to enter teaching when the parent is a teacher. One BEd Foundation Phase student teacher said:

> I didn't want to do teaching at all, because my mother's a teacher, everyone's a teacher (BEd, FP, Inst. A).

It seems the familiarity with teaching was off-putting to some. The student teachers who had teaching parents were painfully aware of the long hours at meetings, hours of marking, fatigue and the inadequate salaries their parents brought home. Nevertheless, teaching seemed to be a family tradition for participants because, despite their initial dislike for the profession, as the following transcript shows, they ended up becoming teachers:

> My dad is high school, but he's at a special school, and my mom is Foundation Phase, she's Grade 3. But she was high school at some point as well. But when I was small, I used to tell people, they're like, what do you want to become, then I'm like, I don't know. At some point I wanted to become a tennis player, everything but teaching. And I remember like, don't you want to become a teacher? I'm like no, underpaid, sorry, overworked and underpaid [BEd Foundation Phase student teacher] (BEd, FP, Inst. A).

iii) Someone Else Inspired Me

'Someone else' was given as the source of external inspiration by 38,9% of the BEd Foundation Phase cohort and 54,6% of the PGCE FET cohort. [13]

According to Table 3,7, 40,6% (BEd Foundation Phase) and 14,9% (PGCE FET) of the black participants reported someone else as having influenced their decision to become a teacher[14]. The respective percentages for the coloured and white respondents were 18,5% (BEd Foundation Phase) and 15,1% (PGCE FET) and 38,5% (BEd Foundation Phase).

Table 3.7   Inspiration to Become Teachers (by race): Someone Else Inspired Me

Race of student	No importance		Low importance		Moderate importance		High importance	
	BEd FP	PGCE FET	BEd FP	PGCE FET	BEd FP	PGCE FET	BEd FP	PGCE FET
Black (n=74)	15 (20,3%)	6 (8,1%)	8 (10,8%)	4 (5,4%)	15 (20,3%)	7 (9,5%)	15 (20,3%)	4 (5,4%)
Coloured (n=113)	30 (26,5%)	17 (15%)	22 (19,5%)	6 (5,3%)	11 (9,7%)	14 (12,4%)	10 (8,8%)	3 (2,7%)
Indian (n=6)	1 (16,7%)	1 (16,7%)	2 (33,3%)	0 (0%)	0 (0%)	1 (16,7%)	1 (16,7%)	0 (0%)
White (n=122)	46 (37,7%)	N/A	29 (23,8%)	N/A	31 (25,4%)	N/A	16 (13,1%)	N/A
Other (n=6)	2 (33,3%)	1 (16,7%)	2 (33,3%)	0 (0%)	1 (16,7%)	0 (0%)	0 (0%)	0 (0%)
Total	94	25	63	10	58	22	42	7

3.6.2.5 Teaching as a gateway career choice

Across both the Foundation Phase and PGCE FET cohorts, teaching as a gateway career was an important reason for becoming a teacher. A total of 72,5% of Foundation Phase and 92,3% of PGCE FET students respectively identified teaching as opening up opportunities to other careers as an important reason for becoming a teacher (moderate and high importance) (see Table 3.2).

From Table 3.8, when the results are disaggregated by race, if one considers participants who gave 'moderate and high importance' as their response to this item, it can be seen that more black student teachers (48 out of 54 = 89%) appeared to regard entry into teaching as a stepping stone to other careers, compared to the white (84 out of 123 = 68%) and coloured (49 out of 72 = 68%) student teachers. It could be inferred from this finding that more white and coloured students chose teaching as a lifelong career compared to their black counterparts

---

13   Combining those who selected 'moderate' and 'high' importance in the survey.
14   Combining those who selected 'moderate' and 'high' importance in the survey.

in the BEd Foundation Phase cohort. Linked to this issue of entering teaching as a way to access other career paths later on, is the question of the extent to which the participants in the research perceived teaching as offering a balance between career and life generally, as explained below.

Table 3.8 provides a breakdown of the responses to the question regarding the extent to which teaching was perceived by the participants as opening opportunities to enter other careers. The responses are divided by race, where it can be seen that 64% (BEd Foundation Phase) and 26,7% (PGCE FET) black participants in particular rated the statement that teaching opens up opportunities in other careers as moderately and highly important. The percentages for the other racial groups are 43,4% (BEd Foundation Phase) and 32,8% (PGCE FET) for the coloured sample and 68,3% (BEd Foundation Phase) for the white respondents.[15] A significant percentage of all sampled racial groups thus entered teaching with the hope of moving to other careers eventually. When divided by institution, the portrayal of this item appears as in Table 3.8.

Table 3.8   Teaching Will Open Up Opportunities in Other Careers (by race)

Race of Student	No importance		Low importance		Moderate importance		High importance	
	BEd FP	PGCE FET	BEd FP	PGCE FET	BEd FP	PGCE FET	BEd FP	PGCE FET
Black (n=75)	3 (4%)	1 (1,3%)	3 (4%)	0 (0%)	12 (16%)	8 (10,7%)	36 (48%)	12 (16%)
Coloured (n=113)	7 (6,2%)	0 (0%)	16 (14,2%)	4 (3,5%)	22 (19,5%)	14 (12,4%)	27 (23,9%)	23 (20,4%)
Indian (n=6)	0 (0%)	0 (0%)	2 (33,3%)	0 (0%)	2 (33,3%)	2 (33,3%)	0 (0%)	0 (0%)
White (n=123)	14 (11,4%)	N/A	25 (20,3%)	N/A	37 (30,1%)	N/A	47 (38,2%)	N/A
Other (n=6)	0 (0%)	0 (0%)	1 (16,7%)	0 (0%)	1 (16,7%)	0 (0%)	3 (50%)	1 (16,7%)
Total	24	1	47	4	74	24	113	36

A reason for entering teaching was explained by a student teacher from the PGCE FET cohort who noted that teaching offered an entry into other professions. One PGCE FET student teacher, who had finished his BSc degree and was then employed by a school on a temporary status (unqualified teacher), said that he entered teaching because:

> I was drawn in through lack of job opportunities [and] if you are a teacher you've got possibilities of developing yourself in terms of academics; so within teaching I saw a way of developing myself [...] to explore other avenues (PGCE, Inst. D).

---

15 Combining those who selected 'moderate' and 'high' importance in the survey.

3.6.2.6 Teaching as Work-Life Balance

Of the BEd Foundation Phase cohort, 62,5% felt that teaching promised a balanced personal and professional life, compared to 72,3% of the PGCE FET cohort (see Table 3.2).

Variations by race in responses to the question on this item of a balance between work and private life are shown in Table 3.9. From the table it can be seen that marginally more black BEd Foundation Phase students (60%) valued work-life balance than white students (56,1%), when importance and high importance are combined.[16] Generally, this cohort felt that teaching offered work-life balance.

Table 3.9   Balance Between Personal and Professional Life (by race)

Race of student	No importance		Low importance		Moderate importance		High importance	
	BEd FP	PGCE FET	BEd FP	PGCE FET	BEd FP	PGCE FET	BEd FP	PGCE FET
Black (n=75)	0 (0%)	2 (2,7%)	9 (12%)	1 (1,3%)	21 (28%)	8 (10,7%)	24 (32%)	10 (13,3%)
Coloured (n=111)	9 (8,1%)	4 (3,6%)	21 (18,9%)	10 (9%)	24 (21,6%)	15 (13,5%)	16 (14,4%)	12 (10,8%)
Indian (n=6)	0 (0%)	0 (0%)	1 (16,7%)	1 (16,7%)	1 (16,7%)	1 (16,7%)	2 (33,3%)	0 (0%)
White (n=123)	20 (16,3%)	N/A	34 (27,6%)	N/A	49 (39,8%)	N/A	20 (16,3%)	N/A
Other (n=6)	0 (0%)	0 (0%)	2 (33,3%)	0 (0%)	2 (33,3%)	1 (16,7%)	1 (16,7%)	0 (0%)
Total	29	6	67	12	97	25	63	22

The qualitative data revealed how students understood work-life balance. A BSc graduate studying to be a teacher stated that he thought that teaching seemed to offer better work-life balance, as opposed to working in industry, as the quote below shows:

> And then in 2015 I went to work. So as I was working, I noticed how difficult it was out there. Difficult conditions, sometimes [indistinct] from maybe 5 in the morning until 2 am and then sometimes from 5 in the morning until tomorrow at 5 in the morning. And then I didn't have time for myself. I didn't have a life. Like I was always at work; from work I was given work to do at home. Then my two friends who are teachers, at 3 in the afternoon they're already out, they have breaks, they have free periods, they have time to do the things that they want. And then I just said no, even myself, I had [enough] (PGCE, Inst. D).

The sections above focused on the presentation and interpretation of data relating to the extrinsic reasons the participants in this research enrolled for teacher education. The following sections present and discuss findings on the intrinsic reasons of joining teaching. These findings are then disaggregated by race and institution where it is felt necessary to do so for clarity and to aid interpretation.

---

16 Combining those who selected 'moderate' and 'high' importance in the survey.

3.6.2.7 Intrinsic Reasons

The aggregated intrinsic sources of inspiration to enter teaching are summarised in Table 3.10. The table appears to indicate that both the BEd Foundation Phase and PGCE FET cohorts considered intrinsic factors more important than extrinsic ones in making the decision to become a teacher. The findings appear to indicate that most of the student teachers in both the BEd Foundation Phase and PGCE FET cohorts perceived teaching as a civic duty and a commitment to society, which required a sense of selfless service to others. The sub-sections below present extracts from the data to support this suggestion.

Table 3.10   Intrinsic Reasons for Choosing Teaching as a Career

		Scale of importance			
	Programme of study	No importance	Low importance	Moderate importance	High importance
	I can help society				
	BEd FP	0,4%	2,7%	17%	79,9%
	PGCE FET	0%	3,1%	16,9%	80%
	Teaching is a caring profession				
	BEd FP	0,4%	1,6%	13,2%	84,8%
	PGCE FET	0%	1,6%	20,6%	77,8%
	I enjoy working with young children				
	BEd FP	0,4%	0,4%	14,3%	84,9%
	PGCE FET	1,5%	6,2%	32,3%	60%
	To develop young children's cognitive skills				
	BEd FP	0%	0,8%	14,3%	84,9%
	PGCE FET	0%	3,2%	15,9%	81%
	To develop mathematical knowledge				
	BEd FP	0%	6,9%	22,4%	70,7%
	PGCE FET	37,7%	18%	23%	21,3%
	To develop language competency				
	BEd FP	0%	6,9%	22,4%	70,7%
	PGCE FET	37,7%	18%	23%	21,3%

3.6.2.8 Teaching as a Civic Duty/Commitment to Society

A resounding 96,9% of the BEd Foundation Phase respondents perceived teachers as being important for the future and reported their ability to contribute to society as their inspiration to enter the profession. This figure was 96,9% for the PGCE FET cohort (see Table 3.10).[17]

Table 3.11 shows percentages of responses based on the perception that teachers help society, as divided by race. The table shows that 70,6% (BEd Foundation Phase) and 26,7% (PGCE FET) of the black respondents[18] felt that they could help society by becoming teachers. This compares with 64% (BEd Foundation Phase) and 35,9% (PGCE FET) of the coloured sample and 95,2% (BEd Foundation Phase) of the white sample.[19] There seem to be some considerable differences in beliefs about helping society as a reason to become a teacher by race and programme, as the table demonstrates.

Table 3.11   I Can Help Society (by race)

Race of student	No importance		Low importance		Moderate importance		High importance	
	BEd FP	PGCE FET	BEd FP	PGCE FET	BEd FP	PGCE FET	BEd FP	PGCE FET
Black (n=75)	1 (1,3%)	0 (0%)	0 (0%)	1 (1,3%)	4 (5,3%)	3 (4%)	49 (65,3%)	17 (22,7%)
Coloured (n=114)	0 (0%)	0 (0%)	0 (0%)	0 (0%)	11 (9,6%)	7 (6,1%)	62 (54,4%)	34 (29,8%)
Indian (n=6)	0 (0%)	0 (0%)	1 (16,7%)	1 (16,7%)	0 (0%)	1 (16,7%)	3 (50%)	0 (0%)
White (n=123)	0 (0%)	N/A	6 (4,9%)	N/A	28 (22,8%)	N/A	89 (72,4%)	N/A
Other (n=6)	0 (0%)	0 (0%)	0 (0%)	0 (0%)	1 (16,7%)	0 (0%)	4 (66,7%)	1 (16,7%)
Total	1	0	7	2	44	11	207	52
Final total	1		9		55		259	

Extracts from the qualitative data revealed that there was a high sense of civic duty and a desire to serve others. Of particular importance was helping society and the importance of this role in building society through individuals. One participant expressed it as follows:

> The role of a teacher [is] someone to facilitate, someone to be a lifeline, a mentor and, there's so many things, like so many things going on up here but like telling you what it is. But basically it goes beyond the classroom, it's not only what happens in the classroom, it's

---

17   Combining those who selected 'moderate' and 'high' importance in the survey.
18   Combining those who selected 'moderate' and 'high' importance in the survey.
19   Combining those who selected 'moderate' and 'high' importance in the survey.

something that's ongoing as me and my colleagues also mentioned. Something that will resonate with them later on in life as well, whether it's in the workplace, whether it's with their family, that's basically the attitude that they build because I mean, you spend most of your time in school in any case, so the life lessons that are instilled at school, are life issues that will carry you through life like that (PGCE, Inst. D).

Another participant stated:

I started out as [indistinct] accounting, completed degree. I did my honours, completed, and I started working for three years, and then within that three years I discovered that the community in itself is getting behind, and it's not for me to just sit in an office, earning a nice salary, but forgetting about the community outside. Whereas I know the two subjects, the majors that I chose, Accounting and Mathematics, won't be beneficial and help the community itself. That changed my entire perspective of why I wanted to become a teacher; it's because I know I can make a difference, even if it's one child's life, I know it's for the benefit of the community itself (PGCE, Inst. D).

3.6.2.9 Working with Children

Table 3.11 indicated that the majority of the respondents for both the Foundation Phase and the PGCE FET stated that working with young children was a strong motivator to become a teacher. A total of 99,2% of Foundation Phase students and 92,3% of PGCE FET students accorded moderate to high importance to working with young children, with the majority according it high importance[20]. The data in Table 3.11 seemed to be more positive in the case of Foundation Phase student teachers as compared to those studying PGCE FET.

Table 3.12 presents disaggregated data by race to highlight some of these variations. The table shows that 99,1% (BEd Foundation Phase) of the white respondents ascribed 'moderate and high importance' to the item on enjoying working with children. There were no white PGCE FET students enrolled in the programme. The figures for the black sample were 72% (BEd Foundation Phase) and 25,3% (PGCE FET), and those for the coloured sample were 63,2% (BEd Foundation Phase) and 34,2% (PGCE FET).[21] This suggests that a significant portion of all the respondents reported enjoying working with children as being a motivator to become a teacher.

Table 3.12 Enjoy Working with Children (by race)

Race of student	No importance		Low importance		Moderate importance		High importance	
	BEd FP	PGCE FET	BEd FP	PGCE FET	BEd FP	PGCE FET	BEd FP	PGCE FET
Black (n=75)	0 (0%)	0 (0%)	0 (0%)	2 (2,7%)	11 (14,7%)	6 (8%)	43 (57,3%)	13 (17,3%)
Coloured (n=114)	1 (0,9%)	1 (0,9%)	0 (0%)	1 (0,9%)	6 (5,3%)	14 (1,3%)	66 (57,9%)	25 (21,9%)

---

20 Combining those who selected 'moderate' and 'high' importance in the survey.
21 Combining those who selected 'moderate' and 'high' importance in the survey.

Table 3.12   Enjoy Working with Children (by race) (cont)

Race of student	No importance		Low importance		Moderate importance		High importance	
	BEd FP	PGCE FET	BEd FP	PGCE FET	BEd FP	PGCE FET	BEd FP	PGCE FET
Indian (n=6)	0 (0%)	0 (0%)	0 (0%)	0 (0%)	1 (16,7%)	1 (16,7%)	3 (50%)	1 (16,7%)
White (n=123)	0 (0%)	N/A	1 (0,8%)	N/A	19 (15,4%)	N/A	103 (83,7%)	N/A
Other (n=6)	0 (0%)	0 (0%)	0 (0%)	1 (16,7%)	0 (0%)	0 (0%)	5 (83,3%)	0 (0%)
Total	1	1	1	4	37	21	220	39

Enjoying working with children emerged very strongly as an intrinsic motivation for teaching from the qualitative data, as a participant below indicated:

> So teaching is a passion, I love children, I love working with kids, and yeah, it's just who I am, I just I love kids. I volunteer, always busy with, so it's just a passion, I can't really explain it. I'm just, it's just a passion and I'm my happiest when I'm sitting with kids [PGCE FET English student teacher in a focus group] (PGCE, Inst. D).

Yet another PGCE FET student described learning to be a teacher as developing a burgeoning enthusiasm for children:

> ... more and more it became a passion working with people, making a difference, seeing that there's like 30 to 35 learners in the classroom all from different backgrounds [...] But I really, I enjoy working with kids because I have one and it's really to make a difference if I just hope that someday somewhere out there that you can really make a difference in the child's life (PGCE, Inst. D).

Another example of this is that the student teacher cited above tutored in the evenings after work, in response to children's need for extra help in mathematics. Of this experience the student teacher reported:

> I've been a tutor all my life in the community, so I know the need is more in the practice of accounting and maths than in the business world, where I just go in my office, forgetting about everything, forgetting about all the students and the learners, just minding my own business here, which is not beneficial at all (PGCE, Inst. D).

3.6.2.10 Developing Learners' Cognitive Skills

Lortie's (1975) statement that teachers enjoy a prolonged engagement with a subject that they love through the act of teaching is substantiated by the data obtained with regard to reasons for entering teaching. Across both the Foundation Phase and PGCE FET cohorts, the respondents rated the need to develop children's cognitive skills as important – 99,2% and 96,3% respectively (combining moderate and high importance). A similar pattern prevails for developing young children's mathematics and language competencies (93,1% and 44,3%

respectively for mathematics for Foundation Phase and PGCE FET students; and 93,1% and 44,3% respectively for language for Foundation Phase and PGCE FET students) (See Table 3.13).

Table 3.13 provides disaggregated data by race regarding the passion to develop children's cognitive skills. The table notes that regardless of race or programme, developing children's cognitive skills is of high importance to student teachers. The table shows that 64% (BEd Foundation Phase) and 22,7% (PGCE FET) of the black respondents felt developing cognitive skills was of high importance. This compares with 57,1% (BEd Foundation Phase) and 28,6% (PGCE FET) of the coloured sample, and 82,1% (BEd Foundation Phase) of the white sample. A total of 72% of the black Foundation Phase sample reported high importance, compared with 26,7% of the black PGCE sample.[22]

Table 3.13   Developing Children's Cognitive Skills (by race)

Race of students	No importance		Low importance		Moderate importance		High importance	
	BEd FP	PGCE FET	BEd FP	PGCE FET	BEd FP	PGCE FET	BEd FP	PGCE FET
Black (n=75)	0 (0%)	0 (0%)	0 (0%)	1 (1,3%)	6 (8%)	3 (4%)	48 (64%)	17 (22,7%)
Coloured (n=112)	0 (0%)	0 (0%)	1 (0,9%)	1 (0,9%)	8 (7,1%)	6 (5,4%)	64 (57,1%)	32 (28,6%)
Indian n=6)	0 (0%)	0 (0%)	0 (0%)	0 (0%)	0 (0%)	0 (0%)	4 (66,7%)	2 (33,3%)
White (n=123)	0 (0%)	N/A	1 (0,8%)	N/A	21 (17,1%)	N/A	101 (82,1%)	N/A
Other (n=6)	0 (0%)	0 (0%)	0 (0%)	0 (0%)	2 (33,3%)	1 (16,7%)	3 (50%)	0 (0%)
Total	0	0	2	2	37	10	220	51

3.6.2.11 Developing Learners' Cognitive Skills by Mathematics and Languages

Enjoying developing mathematical and literacy skills in young children was, similarly, considered an important reason to enter teaching by many of the respondents (see Table 3.9). Tables 3.14 and 3.15 provide disaggregated data by race regarding developing learners' cognitive skills for languages and mathematics.

Table 3.14 suggests that white BEd Foundation Phase student teachers valued developing children's mathematical abilities (70,7% – high importance). Black BEd students indicated this as of high importance as well (56,8%).[23] For the PGCE FET programme, the majority of

---

22 Combining those who selected 'moderate' and 'high' importance in the survey.
23 Combining those who selected 'moderate' and 'high' importance in the survey.

coloured and Indian students accorded developing mathematics knowledge as high/moderate importance, although it is important to note that this is less than those in the BEd Foundation Phase programme, especially for the coloured sample.

Table 3.14   Developing Children's Mathematical Knowledge Skills (by race)

Race of students	No importance		Low importance		Moderate importance		High importance	
	BEd FP	PGCE FET	BEd FP	PGCE FET	BEd FP	PGCE FET	BEd FP	PGCE FET
Black (n=74)	0 (0%)	2 (2,7%)	2 (2,7%)	2 (2,7%)	10 (13,5%)	6 (8,1%)	42 (56,8%)	10 (13,5%)
Coloured (n=111)	0 (0%)	20 (18%)	5 (4,5%)	8 (7,2%)	19 (17,1%)	7 (6,3%)	49 (44,1%)	3 (2,7%)
Indian (n=6)	0 (0%)	1 (16,7%)	1 (16,7%)	0 (0%)	1 (16,7%)	1 (16,7%)	2 (33,3%)	0 (0%)
White (n=123)	0 (0%)	N/A	10 (8,1%)	N/A	26 (21,1%)	N/A	87 (70,7%)	N/A
Other (n=6)	0 (0%)	0 (0%)	0 (0%)	1 (16,7%)	2 (33,3%)	0 (0%)	3 (50%)	0 (0%)
Total	0	23	18	11	58	14	183	13

Enjoying developing language skills in young children was, similar to developing mathematical skills, considered an important reason to enter teaching by many of the respondents (see Table 3.9). Table 3.15 provides disaggregated data by race regarding developing learners' cognitive skills for languages. It shows that white student teachers (70,7%) in the BEd Foundation Phase program value language skills as highly important as a reason for becoming a teacher. However, for the FET programme, black student teachers (13,5%) ranked language skills of high importance, compared to less than 2,7% of all other races.[24]

Table 3.15   Developing Children's Language Knowledge Skills (by race)

Race of students	No importance		Low importance		Moderate importance		High importance	
	BEd FP	PGCE FET	BEd FP	PGCE FET	BEd FP	PGCE FET	BEd FP	PGCE FET
Black (n=74)	0 (0%)	2 (2,7%)	2 (2,7%)	2 (2,7%)	10 (13,5%)	6 (8,1%)	42 (56,8%)	10 (13,5%)
Coloured (n=111)	0 (0%)	20 (18%)	5 (4,5%)	8 (7,2%)	19 (17,1%)	7 (6,3%)	49 (44,1%)	3 (2,7%)

---

24 Combining those who selected 'moderate' and 'high' importance in the survey.

Table 3.15   Developing Children's Language Knowledge Skills (by race) *(cont)*

Race of students	No importance		Low importance		Moderate importance		High importance	
	BEd FP	PGCE FET	BEd FP	PGCE FET	BEd FP	PGCE FET	BEd FP	PGCE FET
Indian (n=6)	0 (0%)	1 (16,7%)	1 (16,7%)	0 (0%)	1 (16,7%)	1 (16,7%)	2 (33,3%)	0 (0%)
White (n=123)	0 (0%)	N/A	10 (8,1%)	N/A	26 (21,1%)	N/A	87 (70,7%)	N/A
Other (n=6)	0 (0%)	0 (0%)	0 (0%)	1 (16,7%)	2 (33,3%)	0 (0%)	3 (50%)	0 (0%)
Total	0	23	18	11	58	14	183	13

3.7 Conclusion

This chapter provided an empirically grounded account of who becomes a teacher and why, across several teacher education providers. There are several noteworthy patterns of student teacher enrolment and motivation to become a teacher.

First, distinct profiles of Foundation Phase and PGCE FET student teachers emerged from the data. Foundation Phase student teachers in the sample were largely white, female, not the first generation of students and for whom becoming a teacher was the first career option. By contrast, PGCE FET students were largely black, male, the first generation of students and for whom teaching was not the first career option. External funding, the FLBP in the case of BEd Foundation Phase students and NSFAS in the case of PGCE FET students, emerged as core sources of funding. These profiles confirm the findings that at the Foundation Phase, teaching is largely feminised and reflective of traditional gendered beliefs of rearing children. For this group, the choice was also related to the view that teaching in this phase offers work-life balance consistent with the traditional gendered beliefs of women as carers and having the responsibility of taking care of the family. The feminisation of Foundation Phase teaching (although not of leadership) should be a matter of concern as it projects a patriarchal view of teaching in the early years, suggesting that primary school teaching is suitable for women only. Of particular concern is the absence of male and black African teacher role models in the Foundation Phase.

Second, across the sample, financial incentives in the form of the FLBP and NSFAS loans/grants were important sources of funding. This is particularly the case for black, first-generation university students. This suggests that financial incentives are a core motivator to become a teacher and should continue to be a major component of teacher education policy in the future, although it could be targeted much better – for example, by offering enhanced financial incentives for black male students to enrol for teaching in the Foundation Phase.

Third, job security as a motivating factor to become a teacher was important to both groups of students, more so in the case of PGCE FET students than Foundation Phase students. Again, this could be correlated with the demographic intake of the cohort which suggests that for first-generation black (57%) and coloured (56%) university students undertaking PGCE FET, job security and stability remain primary extrinsic drivers of becoming a teacher. Across both groups, not surprisingly, there were concerns regarding their working conditions as future teachers. Future policy needs to be aimed at enhancing the working conditions of teachers to counter attrition and churn.

Fourth, consistent with other research, most entrants chose teaching as a career option due to the influence of others. For both cohorts, their school teachers (average 64%) were significantly the most important source of motivation to become a teacher, consistent with Lortie's (1975) observation of the power of "apprenticeship of observation". Good-quality teaching in school thus matters not just for learners but also for future generations of teachers. Significantly, the family was the second most important source of motivation but this was mainly for black recruits, suggesting some family associations in career decision making.

Fifth, across both the Foundation Phase and PGCE FET cohorts, teaching as a gateway career was an important reason for becoming a teacher. While this has been a perennial problem of teacher supply in most contexts, the high percentages seeing teaching as a gateway to other career options remain a problem in a context where capable NQTs are needed.

Sixth, not surprising for many, teaching is perceived to be a career choice for those seeking work-life balance.

Seventh, and most importantly, across all the cohorts and categories of race (average 96,9%), teaching as a form of civic duty and of helping society emerged as a strong motivator to becoming a teacher, compared to all the other reasons. This certainly contradicts arguments that suggest that prospective teachers and teaching in general are no longer a vocation and a career of service. Yet caution must be exercised in interpreting the data, as it can be plausibly argued that the respondents were merely reflecting what they considered to be positive messaging about becoming teachers as invoked by the institutions and society in general they find themselves in. Nonetheless, this finding offers much hope to policymakers to build upon this positive sense of intrinsic motivation to ensure that such teachers become agents of change and transformation in schools. As one of the first cohorts of post-apartheid graduates, this group's sense of calling and duty provides a beacon of hope to address the systemic and structural inequities in the education system.

Eighth, the analysis of the chapter as to who becomes a teacher has not examined how admissions criteria shape who enters teaching. This is an area of further research as it is likely that the profile of a student teacher is shaped by the admission processes and criteria set and managed by different institutions.

Ninth, the data reported in this chapter suggest that developing disciplinary knowledge, i.e. mathematics and language, is a strong motivator to become a teacher. Thus, student teachers in this research reported a strong disposition towards supporting developing learners' mathematical and language knowledge as key motivating factors for wishing to become a teacher. Whether student teachers are able to do so and how competently, is a concern raised in subsequent chapters and in the conclusion of this book (see Chapter 11).

Finally, and related to the findings above, across the category of race, prospective teachers in the BEd Foundation Phase programme positively (93,1%) indicated that working with young children and supporting their cognitive developing, particularly in mathematics and languages, was a strong reason for choosing teaching as a career option. This positive affirmation of working with learners and developing their learning provides the future education system with well-motivated teachers to teach in priority areas.

The picture that emerges from the data is that motivation to become a teacher is varied and complex, and can be attributed to both extrinsic and intrinsic factors. Dominant extrinsic determinants were on the whole mainly financial: job security and the need to function in a stable work environment. Intrinsic factors such as passion for teaching and supporting and working with young children, as well as doing good for society and the community, suggest that prospective teachers are not without strong altruistic reasons to teach.

In conclusion, future teachers are neither self-seeking individuals nor wholly motivated by intrinsic and altruistic factors, but on balance they exhibit a stronger desire and passion to serve and assist others, particularly young children. To this end, teacher education providers need to nurture and sustain the positive motivation of those choosing teaching as a career option, and develop dispositions that build on the enthusiasm for supporting young children that these cohorts demonstrate. Moreover, both providers and policymakers need to recognise the importance of the teacher in schools as an important role model for prospective teachers. Furthermore, much work needs to be done to ensure that more black and male Foundation Phase teachers join the teaching profession as it will expose young children to a changed and changing South Africa.

References

Alam, M.T. & Farid, S. 2011. Factors affecting teachers motivation. *International Journal of Business and Social Science*, 2(1): 298-304.

Alexander, D.; Chant, D. & Cox, B. 1994. What motivates people to become teachers? *Australian Journal of Teacher Education*, 19(2): 40-49. https://doi.org/10.14221/ajte.1994v19n2.4

Anderson, M.B.G. & Iwanicki, E.F. 1984. Teacher motivation and its relationship to burnout. *Educational Administration Quarterly*, 20(2): 109-132. https://doi.org/10.1177/0013161X84020002007

Badat, S. & Sayed, Y. 2014. Post-1994 South African education: The challenge of social justice. *The Annals of the American Academy of Political and Social Science*, 652(1): 127-148. https://doi.org/10.1177/0002716213511188

Baker, S.R. 2004. Intrinsic, extrinsic and amotivational orientations: Their role in university adjustment, stress, wellbeing, and subsequent academic performance. *Current Psychology*, 23(3): 189-202. https://doi.org/10.1007/s12144-004-1019-9

Barber, M. & Mourshed, M. 2007. *How the world's best-performing schools systems come out on top*. Sandton: McKinsey & Company.

Bennell, P. 2005. *The impact of the Aids epidemic on teachers in South Africa*. Available at: https://www.eldis.org/fulltext/aidssouthafricanote.pdf

Borg, M. 2005. A case study of the development in pedagogic thinking of a pre-service teacher. *TESL/EJ*, 9(2): 1-30.

Cochran-Smith, M. 2004. The problem of teacher education [editorial]. *Journal of Teacher Education*, 55(4): 295-299. https://doi.org/10.1177/0022487104268057

Colley, H. 2006. Learning to labour with feeling: Class, gender and emotion in childcare education and training. *Contemporary Issues in Early Childhood*, 7(1): 15-29. https://doi.org/10.2304/ciec.2006.7.1.15

Colley, H.; James, D.; Tedder, M. & Diment, K. 2003. Learning as becoming in vocational education and training: Class, gender and the role of vocational habitus. *Journal of Vocational Education and Training*, 55(4): 471-497. https://doi.org/10.1080/13636820300200240

DBE (Department of Basic Education). 2015. *Strategy on recruitment and deployment of educators*. Available at: pmg-assets.s3-website-eu-west-1.amazonaws.com/150421Strategy.doc.

Deacon, R. 2012. *The Initial Teacher Education Research Project: The initial professional development of teachers – A literature review*. Johannesburg: JET Education Services. Available at: https://www.jet.org.za/publications/initial-teacher-education-research-project/deacon-initial-professional-development-of-teachers-literature-review-feb15web.pdf

Eccles, J.S. & Wigfield, A. 2002. Motivational beliefs, values, and goals. *Annual Review of Psychology*, 53(1): 109-132. https://doi.org/10.1146/annurev.psych.53.100901.135153

Erasmus, Z. 2008. Race. In: N. Shepherd & S. Robins (eds). *New South African keywords*. Johannesburg: Jacana, 169-181.

Flores, M.A. 2001. Person and context in becoming a new teacher. *Journal of Education for Teaching*, 27(2): 135-148. https://doi.org/10.1080/02607470120067882

Gold, Y. 1996. Beginning teacher support: Attrition, mentoring, and induction. In: J. Sikula (ed.). *Handbook of research on teacher education (2nd ed.)*. New York: Macmillan, 548-594.

Green, W.; Adendorff, M. & Mathebula, B. 2014. Minding the gap? A national Foundation Phase teacher supply and demand analysis: 2012-2020. *South African Journal of Childhood Education* 4(2): 1-23. https://doi.org/10.4102/sajce.v4i3.222

Hayes, D. 2004. Recruitment and retention: Insights into the motivation of primary trainee teachers in England. *Research in Education*, 71(May): 37-49. https://doi.org/10.7227/RIE.71.5

Hayden, S. 2011. *Teacher motivation and student achievement in middle school students*. PhD dissertation. Minneapolis: Walden University.

Hobson, A.J.; Malderez, A.; Tracey, L.; Giannakaki, M.S.; Pell, R.G.; Kerr, K.; Chambers, G.N.; Tomlinson, P.D. & Roper, T. 2006. *Becoming a teacher: Student teachers' experiences of initial teacher training in England*. Research report RR744. United Kingdom: The Department for Education and Skills, University of Nottingham.

Holland, J.L. 1997. *Making vocational choices: A theory of vocational personalities and work environments* (3rd ed.). Florida: Psychological Assessment Resources.

Howey, K.R. & Zimpher, N. 1989. Profiles of pre-service teacher education: Inquiry into the nature of programs. Albany: State University of New York Press.

Huberman, M. 1989. On teachers' careers: Once over lightly with a broad brush. *International Journal of Educational Research*, 13(4): 347-362. https://doi.org/10.1016/0883-0355(89)90033-5

Jessop, T. & Penny, A. 1998. A study of teacher voice and vision in the narratives of rural South African and Gambian primary school teachers. *International Journal of Educational Development*, 18(5): 393-403. https://doi.org/10.1016/S0738-0593(98)00039-X

John, O.P.; Naumann, L.P. & Soto, C.J. 2008. Paradigm shift to the integrative big-five trait taxonomy: History, measurement, and conceptual issues. In: O.P. John, R.W. Robins & L.A. Pervin (eds). *Handbook of personality: Theory and research*. New York: Guilford Press, 114-158.

Jugovic, I.; Marusic, I.; Ivanec, T.P. & Vidovic, V.V. 2012. Motivation and personality of preservice teachers in Croatia. *Asia-Pacific Journal of Teacher Education*, 40(3): 271-287. https://doi.org/10.1080/1359866X.2012.700044

Jungert, T.; Alm, F. & Thornberg, R. 2014. Motives for becoming a teacher and their relations to academic engagement and dropout among student teachers. *Journal of Education for Teaching*, 40(2): 173-185. https://doi.org/10.1080/02607476.2013.869971

Kelleher, F. 2011. *Women and the teaching profession: Exploring the feminisation debate*. Paris: UNESCO. Available at: https://unesdoc.unesco.org/images/0021/002122/212200e.pdf

Keswell, M. 2004. *Education and racial inequality in post-apartheid South Africa*. Working paper no. 2004-02-008. Santa Fe: Santa Fe Institute.

König, J. & Rothland, M. 2012. Motivations for choosing teaching as a career: Effects on general pedagogical knowledge during initial teacher education. *Asia-Pacific Journal of Teacher Education*, 40(3): 289-315. https://doi.org/10.1080/1359866X.2012.700045

Kyriacou, C. & Coulthard, M. 2000. Undergraduates' views of teaching as a career choice. *Journal of Education for Teaching*, 26(2): 117-126. https://doi.org/10.1080/02607470050127036

Lai, E.R. 2011. *Motivation: A literature review*. New York: Pearson. Available at: https://images.pearsonassessments.com/images/tmrs/Motivation_Review_final.pdf

Lortie, D.C. 1975. *School teacher: A sociological study*. Chicago: University of Chicago Press.

Lortie, D.C. 1986. Teacher status in Dade County: A case of structural strain? *The Phi Delta Kappan*, 67(8): 568-575.

Louw, J.; Shisana, O.; Peltzer, K. & Zungu, N. 2009. Examining the impact of HIV and AIDS on South African educators. *South African Journal of Education*, 29(2): 205-217.

Manion, C. 2007. Feeling, thinking, doing: Emotional capital, empowerment, and women's education. In: I. Epstein (ed.). *Recapturing the personal: Essays on education and embodied knowledge in comparative perspective*. Charlotte: Information Age Publishing, 87-109.

Manuel, J. & Hughes, J. 2006. It has always been my dream: Exploring pre-service teachers' motivations for choosing to teach. *Teacher Development*, 10(1): 5-24. https://doi.org/10.1080/13664530600587311

Marsh, S. 2015. Five top reasons people become teachers – and why they quit. *The Guardian*, 27 January. Available at: https://www.theguardian.com/teacher-network/2015/jan/27/five-top-reasons-teachers-join-and-quit

Mourshed, M.; Chijioke, C. & Barber, M. 2010. *How the world's most improved school systems keep getting better*. London: McKinsey & Company.

Organization for Economic Co-operation and Development (OECD). 2010. *PISA 2009 results: What makes a school successful? – Resources, policies and practices* (vol. 6). Paris: OECD. https://doi.org/10.1787/9789264091559-en

Richardson, P.W. & Watt, H.M. 2010. Current and future directions in teacher motivation research. In: *The decade ahead: Applications and contexts of motivation and achievement*. West Yorkshire: Emerald Group Publishing Limited, 139-173. https://doi.org/10.1108/S0749-7423(2010)000016B008

Robinson, M. & McMillan, H. 2006. Who teaches the teachers? Identity, discourse and policy in teacher education. *Teaching and Teacher Education*, 22(3): 327-336. https://doi.org/10.1016/j.tate.2005.11.003

Ryan, R.M. & Deci, E.L. 2000. Self-determination theory and the facilitation of intrinsic motivation, social development, and well-being. *American Psychologist*, 55(1): 68-78. https://doi.org/10.1037/0003-066X.55.1.68

Sayed, Y (ed.). 2017. *Engaging teachers in peacebuilding in post-conflict contexts – Evaluating education interventions in South Africa*. ESRC/DFID research report. UK: University of Sussex & South Africa: Centre for International Teacher Education (CITE).

Sayed, Y.; Badroodien, A.; McDonald, Z.; Balie, L.; De Kock, T.; Garisch, C. & Foulds, K. (Cape Peninsula University of Technology and University of Sussex Research Consortium: Education and Peace building). 2015. *Teachers and youth as agents of social cohesion in South Africa*. Cape Town: Cape Peninsula University of Technology.

Sinclair, C. 2008. Initial and changing student teacher motivation and commitment to teaching. *Asia-Pacific Journal of Teacher Education*, 36(2): 79-104. https://doi.org/10.1080/13598660801971658

South African Council for Educators (SACE). 2010. *A review of teacher supply and demand*. Available at: https://www.sace.org.za/search/index?search=A+review+of+teacher+supply+and+demand

Statistics South Africa (Stats SA). 2017. *Living conditions survey 2014/2015*. Available at: https://www.statssa.gov.za/publications/P0310/P03102014.pdf

Sykes, G. 1983. Contradictions, ironies and promises unfilled: A contemporary account of the status of teaching. *Phi Delta Kappan*, 63(2): 87-93.

Tashakkori, A. & Creswell, J.W. 2007. Editorial: The new era of mixed methods. *Journal of Mixed Methods Research*, 1(1): 3-7. https://doi.org/10.1177/1558689807309913

Tatto, M.T. 2012. *Learning and doing policy analysis in education: Examining diverse approaches to increasing educational access*. Rotterdam: Sense Publishers. https://doi.org/10.1007/978-94-6091-933-6

United Nations International Children's Emergency Fund (UNICEF), World Health Organization (WHO) and World Bank. 2013. *2012 Joint child malnutrition estimates – Levels and trends in child malnutrition*. Available at: https://www.who.int/nutgrowthdb/estimates2012/en/

Van Broekhuizen, H. 2015. *Teacher supply in South Africa: A focus on initial teacher education*. Working paper. Stellenbosch: Stellenbosch University.

Vegas, E., Ganimian, A. & Jaimovich, A. 2012. *Learning from the best: Improving learning through effective teacher policies.* Washington, D.C.: World Bank.

Vegas, E.; Loeb, S.; Romaguera, P.; Paglayan, A.; Goldstein, N.; Ganimian, A.J.; Trembley, A. & Jaimovich, A. 2012. *What matters most in teacher policies? A framework for building a more effective teaching profession.* Washington, D.C.: World Bank.

Virta, A. 2002. Becoming a history teacher: Observations on the beliefs and growth of student teachers. *Teaching and Teacher Education* 18(6): 687-698.
https://doi.org/10.1016/S0742-051X(02)00028-8

Wigfield, A. & Eccles, J.S. 2002. The development of competence beliefs, expectancies for success, and achievement values from childhood through adolescence. In: A. Wigfield & J.S. Eccles (eds). *Development of achievement motivation.* London: Academic Press, 91-120.
https://doi.org/10.1016/B978-012750053-9/50006-1

World Bank. 2012. *What matters most in teacher policies? A framework for building a more effective teaching profession.* Washington, D.C.: World Bank Human Development Network.

Yüksel, H.G. & Kavanoza, S. 2015. Influence of prior experiences on pre-service language teachers' perception of teaching. *Procedia – Social and Behavioural Sciences*, 199: 777-784.
https://doi.org/10.1016/j.sbspro.2015.07.611

Chapter 04

Beliefs about Professional Knowledge

Marcina Singh, Helena Wessels & Anil Kanjee

4.1 Introduction

The aim of this chapter is to discuss, using the data collected for this study, the beliefs that student teachers have about teachers, teaching and their competence and confidence to teach mathematics and language. Pajeres (1992) notes that the beliefs teachers hold, influences their perceptions and judgements, which then goes on to affect their behaviour in the classroom. Therefore, understanding belief structures of teachers and student teachers is essential to improving their professional preparation and teacher practices.

ITE programmes in South Africa have been a key focus area of recent reform initiatives (DBE 2015; Sayed & Badroodien 2016; Taylor 2016) – given its crucial role in the development of teachers' professional knowledge and practice. Within this context, the revised MRTEQ policy (DBE 2015) provides key criteria for the development and recognition of teacher qualifications and learning programmes. Two key issues that have been identified call for:

1. all teacher education programmes to address the critical challenges facing education in South Africa today – especially the poor content and conceptual knowledge found amongst teachers, as well as the legacies of apartheid by incorporating situational and contextual elements that assist teachers in developing competences that enable them to deal with diversity and transformation (DBE 2015:8); and
2. bringing the importance of inter-connections between different types of knowledge and practices into the foreground, as well as the ability of teachers to draw reflexively from integrated and applied knowledge, so as to work flexibly and effectively in a variety of contexts (DBE 2015:9).

Developing such programmes is, however, difficult to achieve given the largely tacit nature of teaching and the intricate knowledge, skills, attitudes and behaviours required for developing quality teachers (Loughran 2010; Winch, Oancea & Orchard, 2013). Specifically, a key challenge is defining what constitutes teacher professional knowledge and how teachers develop this knowledge (Cochran-Smith & Lyttle 1999; Loughran 2010; Tan, Bopry & Libo 2010).

Winch, Oancea and Orchard (2013) note that teacher professional knowledge comprises three interconnected and complementary aspects:

1. situated understanding, technical knowledge and critical reflection. Situated or tacit refers to "that element of 'know-how' which teachers clearly manifest in their practice but which cannot be rendered explicitly in discourse about it" (Winch et al. 2013:3);

2. technical knowledge refers to knowledge that enables teachers "to plan and control a process and also to explain and predict the success or otherwise of an intervention" (Winch et al. 2013:4); and
3. critical reflection refers to teachers' ability to "review seriously what they have done in the past with a view to sustaining or improving their practice in the future" (Winch *et al* 2013:4).

In this context, the development of technical knowledge requires teachers to understand the curriculum and how to deliver it (Ball, Thames & Phelps 2008) – an aspect which is clearly articulated by Shulman (1987) and others who note the following categories of teacher knowledge: GPK, knowledge of students and how they learn, knowledge of the subject matter, PCK, knowledge of other content, knowledge of the curriculum and knowledge of educational aims.

Different domain-specific knowledge frameworks exist for mathematics and languages. Building on Shulman's (1987) knowledge categories, Ball et al. (2008) conceptualised MKT. This knowledge framework consists of two broad domains: SMK and PCK (see Figure 4.1). Each of these domains is subdivided into three categories. SMK comprises general content knowledge, specialised content knowledge (SCK) and knowledge at the mathematical horizon; while PCK consists of knowledge of content and teaching, knowledge of content and learners and knowledge of the curriculum.

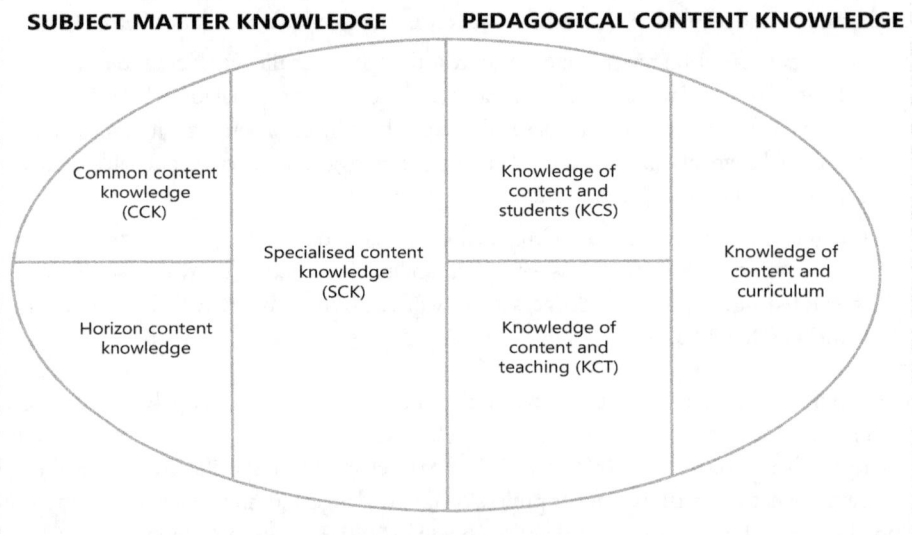

Figure 4.1   Mathematical Knowledge for Teaching (MKT)
Source: Hill, Ball and Schilling (2008:377)

Beliefs about Professional Knowledge

Blömeke et al. (2014:23) point out the reciprocal influence of teacher knowledge and beliefs. A certain level of mathematical CK and mathematical PCK is needed to recognise the dynamic nature of mathematics; however,

> epistemological beliefs [...] probably influence beliefs on the teaching and learning of mathematics. The more a teacher is able to see the dynamic nature of mathematics, the more she may prefer student-oriented teaching methods in which students explore mathematics by themselves rather than just listening to the teacher (Blömeke et al. 2014:23).

The development of CK therefore also influences beliefs, not only the other way around.

In the context of language, similar frameworks are used. Grossman (1990) added two new dimensions to Shulman's (1987) theory of PCK in her framework. These include knowledge of the curriculum and knowledge of the purposes of teaching. According to Fernandez (2014:84), "Grossman was the first to systematise the components of the knowledge base of teachers proposed by Shulman and characterised the concept of PCK in their model of teacher knowledge".

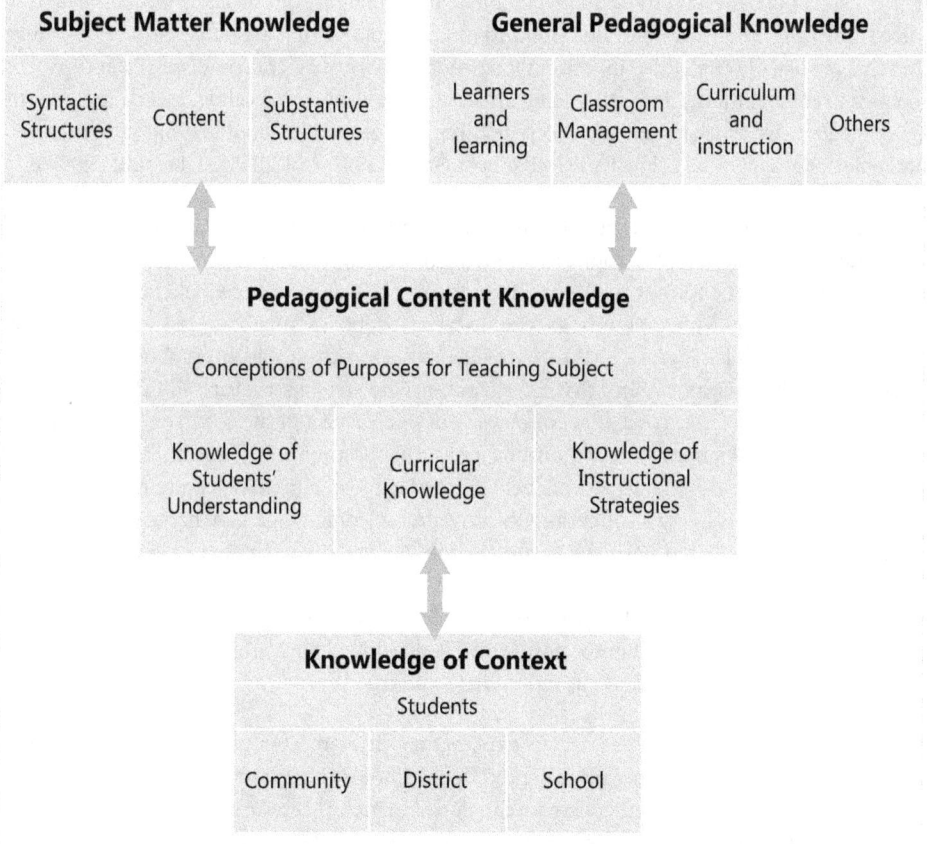

Figure 4.2   Model of Teacher Knowledge
Source: Grossman (1990)

Figure 4.2 demonstrates that SMK, GPK and knowledge of the context all impact PCK. Each of these components also has subcomponents that impact the overall model. What makes this model an improvement on Shulman's (1987) theory is that "the formal and practical character of PCK is explained, since the knowledge and beliefs of teachers are present in the model" (Fernandez 2014:84).

A key factor in how teachers construct and use knowledge in teaching, however, is the beliefs they hold towards teaching and learning (Stipek et al. 2001; Beswick 2008; Anderson 2015). Kuzborska (2011:102) also supports this view by arguing that "understanding this relationship is important for the improvement of teachers' professional preparation and the successful implementation of new curricula". Teachers' beliefs are also recognised as being important for understanding teaching approaches because teachers' beliefs are reflected in how they conceptualise their roles in the classroom, their choice of classroom activities and the instructional strategies they use (Norton et al. 2005). The beliefs teachers hold about teaching and learning are thus extremely important.

The construct of beliefs is often equated to affect, but beliefs are one of four concepts related to affect. The other three are emotions (mild to intense feelings that are subject to rapid change and that are usually embedded in context), attitudes (relatively stable predispositions towards feelings in different situations, balancing affect and cognition) and values, ethics, and morals ('personal truths' that are stable, deeply-held preferences, which could be highly structured and emotional as well as cognitive) (DeBellis & Goldin 1997; Goldin 2002; Hannula 2004).

Definitions of beliefs abound, but despite the important role beliefs play in education and the volume of research on the topic, there seems to be no internationally accepted definition of this construct (Goldin et al. 2016). Richardson (1996:103) defines beliefs in general as "psychologically held understandings, premises, or propositions about the world, that are felt to be true", while Goldin (2002) regards beliefs as mostly stable internal representations of truth, validity or applicability that have a potentially strong structure. Philipp (2007:259) describes beliefs as "lenses that affect one's view of some aspect of the world or as dispositions toward action" and summarises definitions and terms used in beliefs research. He describes emotions as the least cognitive and beliefs as the most cognitive component of affect. Fenstermacher (1994) views beliefs as subjective knowledge, while Northcote (2009) argues that beliefs are associated with the nature of knowledge and learning. Cross (2009:326), in her definition of beliefs, highlights the fact that beliefs can sometimes be less explicit and can even be held unconsciously: "[E]mbodied conscious and unconscious ideas and thoughts about oneself, the world and one's position in it developed through membership in various social groups, and considered by the individual to be true."

Skott (2015:16) refers to beliefs as "an explanatory principle for practice" and points out that although there is no generally accepted definition for the construct of beliefs, sufficient consensus about the core of the construct can be found in the literature. This core exhibits four main features: beliefs are generally used to describe individual (subjective) mental constructs; beliefs have interlinked cognitive and affective aspects; beliefs are usually temporally and contextually stable objectifications that need substantial engagement in relevant social practices to be changed; and beliefs are influential in teachers' sense-making of and engagement in problems of teaching practice (Skott 2015:18,19). Skott (2015:19) summarises the essence of the term "beliefs" as described in the literature as "individual, subjectively true, value-laden mental constructs that are the relatively stable results of substantial social experiences and that have significant impact on one's interpretations of and contributions to classroom practice".

Pajares (1992:316) refers to different beliefs that play a crucial role in the educational context:

> [B]eliefs about confidence to affect students' performance (teacher efficacy), about the nature of knowledge (epistemological beliefs), about causes of teachers' or students' performance (attributions, locus of control, motivation, writing apprehension, mathematics anxiety), about perceptions of self and feelings of self-worth (self-concept, self-esteem), about confidence to perform specific tasks (self-efficacy)

Epistemological beliefs, described by De Corte, Op't Eynde and Verschaffel (2002) as "beliefs about the nature of knowledge and the processes of knowing", play a determining role in the way a teacher conceptualises learning and teaching. Fives, Lacatena and Gerard (2015) caution about taking a one-sided approach and recommend that research on beliefs about teaching should also include research on beliefs about learning, as views about teaching and learning are rooted in epistemological beliefs (Cai & Wang 2010; Cross Francis, Rapacki & Eker 2015). Ernest (1989), for example, distinguishes between three different epistemological views on mathematics, i.e. instrumentalist, Platonist and problem-solving views. Instrumentalist or Platonist views of mathematics can lead to passive, teacher-centred classrooms where the teacher is the authority of knowledge, while a problem-solving view of mathematics can encourage more student-centred classrooms that support mathematical sense-making (Schoenfeld 1992).

Highlighting the value of understanding teacher beliefs, Stipek et al. (2001) and Beswick (2008) argue that the key to changing a teacher's classroom practice lies in changing the teacher's beliefs. However, while supporting this assertion, Mosvold and Fauskanger (2013) highlight the difficulty in distinguishing between beliefs and knowledge, as suggested above, and argue for using the term "teachers' personal epistemology" or "epistemological knowledge", which refers to beliefs teachers have about knowledge needed for teaching. Citing Fives and Buehl (2009), Mosvold and Fauskanger (2013:47) argue that this area constitutes a domain that comprises distinct beliefs about the nature and source of teaching knowledge, as well as the stability, structure and content of teaching knowledge. Charalambous (2015) argues for using the term "pedagogical beliefs" to refer to what teachers believe about teaching and learning.

Beliefs are context specific, whereas values refer to the worth of something and are not as context specific (Philipp 2007:259). The situational nature of beliefs is also highlighted by Skott (2015) and Wong, Ding and Zhang (2016). Schoenfeld (1998) likewise alludes to the fact that an individual's beliefs are context bound and interact with the person's goals and knowledge, influencing decision making in a specific context. Beliefs furthermore do not exist in isolation, but cluster together and function in a belief system that is situational and strongly influences an individual's view of the world and, in the case of this research, the individual's images of practice (Ermeling & Graff-Ermeling 2016).

Felbrich, Kaiser and Schmotz (2014) contend that beliefs constitute an important part of a teacher's professional competence – playing a crucial role in the application of professional knowledge in the classroom. These authors conceptualise beliefs as "a bridge between knowledge and actual teaching" (Felbrich et al. 2014:210). This metaphor of a bridge links with Wilson and Cooney's (2002) assertion that knowledge and beliefs are closely related and that they both contribute to teaching quality. According to Charalambous (2015:427),

> attempts to understand what contributes to teaching quality have been channelled in different directions, with two main research streams focusing on either teacher knowledge or teacher beliefs. Few are the studies that have attended to both the cognitive and affective domain simultaneously, trying to unpack how both jointly contribute to teacher quality.

Knowledge is generally regarded as a social construct (Op 't Eynde et al. 2002), but Liljedahl (2008:2) warns that knowledge is essentially an individual construct and that individuals' actions "are guided by what they believe to be true rather than what may actually be true". The implication is that pre-service teachers' actions and practices will reflect what they believe is true about mathematics and language teaching and learning. Clarifying the distinction between professional knowledge (both CK and PCK) and beliefs in the discourse of teacher training and educational practice is a contentious issue. Leatham (2006:92) argues that

> [o]f all the things we believe, there are some things that we 'just believe' and other things we 'more than believe – we know'. Those things we 'more than believe' we refer to as knowledge and those things we 'just believe' we refer to as beliefs. Thus beliefs and knowledge can profitably be viewed as complementary subsets of the things we believe.

Nespor (1987) provides insight on the issue by applying Abelson's (1979) psychological distinction between knowledge systems and belief systems as a framework with which to understand research conducted in this area. The seven features with which Abelson (1979:356-360, cited in Ashton 2015:36) distinguishes knowledge systems from beliefs systems are the following:

1. The elements (concepts, propositions, rules, etc.) of a belief system are not consensual (they are idiosyncratic and personally derived from experience).
2. Belief systems are in part concerned with existence or nonexistence of certain conceptual entities (e.g. God, extra-sensory perception).
3. Belief systems often include representations of 'alternative worlds', typically the world as it is and the world as it should be.
4. Belief systems rely heavily on evaluative and affective components.
5. Belief systems are likely to include a substantial amount of episodic material from either personal experience or (for cultural belief systems) from folklore or (for political doctrines) from propaganda.
6. The content set to be included in a belief system is usually highly 'open'.
7. Beliefs can be held with varying degrees of certitude.

Contextualising Ernest's (1989) description of the implications of epistemological beliefs in mathematics on teaching and Abelson's (1979) notions of beliefs in terms of its impact on ITE training, it must be acknowledged that student teachers enter the programme with deeply seated beliefs. These inevitably affect their views about teaching, as well as their classroom practices (Ball 1988; Skott 2001; Uusimaki & Nason 2004). These beliefs include: social, political and religious beliefs; general and domain-specific epistemological beliefs; and beliefs about teaching that have evolved through school experiences, observations and exposure to others' ideas (Lasley 1980; Stigler & Hiebert 1998). Gilakjani and Sabouri (2017:80) also highlight the influence of teachers' own school experiences in forming their beliefs: "A lot of teachers know that they were previously learners and how they were taught and these helped them form their beliefs about teaching." A study by Perry et al. (2005:45) on the relationship of student teachers' knowledge and beliefs found that "the stronger the belief in the importance of computation and correct answers, the lower the mathematical content knowledge". This view is in line with a more Platonist view of mathematics.

Teaching languages is not only about relaying content; "teachers need to value students' home languages and cultures and convey that value to the students" (Lucas & Grinberg 2008). Teachers also need to understand that "language, culture, and identity are closely related, and that socio-political factors influence perceptions, uses, and learning of language" (Lucas & Villegas 2011, cited in Lucas, Villegas & Martin 2015:454).

Lasley (1980:38) points to the robustness of beliefs: "[T]hey usually persist, unmodified, unless intentionally or explicitly challenged." This creates extra pressure on ITE programmes, because in order to realise the type of educator envisaged by the institution, student teachers need to be 'convinced' of the merits of the institutional philosophies. Studying and understanding pre-service teachers' beliefs are therefore crucial in course development and improvement (Nespor 1987; Pajares 1992; Schoenfeld 1998).

Beliefs cannot be measured directly, but must be inferred from an individual's words, actions, and intentions (Rokeach 1968; Schoenfeld 1998). Different authors distinguish between espoused or professed beliefs and attributed beliefs; the first being self-reported statements about what they believe as opposed to the latter, which are inferred from observed practice (Calderhead 1996; Putnam & Borko 2000; Bryan 2012). The bulk of research on teacher beliefs focuses on professed beliefs, as is the case in this book.

4.2 Methodology

Using data collected from 259 student teachers completing a BEd in the Foundation Phase and 66 student teachers completing PGCE FET at four universities in South Africa, the aim of this chapter is to gain insight into students' beliefs about professional knowledge. The BEd cohort of student teachers were in their final year of their teaching qualification and would enter the teaching profession in the new academic year. This chapter also aims to understand how beliefs impact student teachers' understanding of professional knowledge, both in terms of CK and PCK.

The data for this chapter were mined from the first set of questionnaires (out of three) administered to the two abovementioned cohorts, as it related specifically to student teachers' beliefs. The participants in the study were from four South African universities that offer ITE programmes. The institutions are classified as follows:

- Institution A: University of Technology
- Institution B: Traditional University
- Institution C: University of Technology
- Institution D: Traditional University

Given the two dominant ITE programmes available to students, this study considered both the four-year BEd programme in the Foundation Phase and the one-year PGCE programme in the FET Phase, referred to as BEd and PGCE respectively in this chapter. Considering that both programmes enable a comprehensive understanding of how the landscape of ITE prepares students to become teachers and what student teachers' experiences of these programmes entail (see Chapter 1), it must be acknowledged that the aim of this research is not to evaluate the ITE programmes but instead to ascertain student teachers' experiences and perceptions of the programme, as well as their beliefs about professional knowledge.

Student teachers' beliefs are discussed according to the following five themes:
1. Beliefs about teaching in general
2. Domain-specific epistemological beliefs
3. Domain-specific beliefs about the teaching of mathematics and language
4. Beliefs about student competence as future teachers
5. Confidence to teach as they reach the end of their ITE programme

Apart from these themes, the data will also be cross-referenced with race to ascertain whether there are any notable differences in how student teachers responded. The rationale for considering race is twofold. First, there is a longstanding relationship between race and education institutions in South Africa. According to Reddy (2004:6), "[t]he intensely differentiated nature of higher education both in the past and present makes it difficult to speak about it as a 'system' having coherence and an undifferentiated identity". Although there has been large-scale transformation in terms of freedom of movement and access to universities in South Africa, behavioural and institutional legacies are still very much evident in the current HEI setting. Second, South Africa is still a racialised society and this is also indicative of the country's previous socialisation process. This means that opportunities (social and economic) were and to a certain extent still are allocated along racial lines. Keswell (2004:1) argues: "Not only does South Africa have among the highest levels of income inequality in the world, but this inequality is strongly racial in nature."

It must also be acknowledged that since 1994, the increase of a non-white middle class impacted greatly on the student demographics of HEIs. However, for this chapter, a discussion relating to class was not investigated. Similarly, gender was not used as a means of stratification as an overwhelming majority of BEd Foundation Phase student teachers who participated in the study were female, thus making any discussion about gender unsubstantial. There were, however, differences in the PGCE cohort but women still dominated the cohort.

The questionnaires were developed using three- to five-point Likert-scales. The quantitative data were analysed using the Statistical Package for the Social Sciences (SPSS) and the qualitative data were analysed using manual coding techniques. The themes for the qualitative data followed the same themes as mentioned above. The percentages included in the discussions are the valid percentage of student teachers who responded to the items and do not include missing data.

4.3 Themes Related to Beliefs about Knowledge: General Beliefs about Teaching

In this section, student teachers were asked non-domain-specific questions relating to instruction, the teaching profession and their views on what constitutes the most powerful determinant of a learner's success. Using a four-point Likert-scale ranging from strongly disagrees to strongly agree, the section on general beliefs yielded the results discussed in this section. The items that were discussed in more detail are emphasised, as they presented a different response to the norm.

4.3.1 Bachelor of Education (BEd)

When student teachers were asked about their general beliefs about teaching, most of the responses across the institutions were similar (see Table 4.1). However, with item G, J and O, student teachers were split in their responses.

Table 4.1 Beliefs about Teaching – Q1 Teacher Motivation and Beliefs (BEd)

Item	Beliefs	Strongly disagree % (n)	Disagree % (n)	Agree % (n)	Strongly agree % (n)
A	Teaching is a calling	1,6 (4)	5 (13)	35,3 (91)	58,1 (150)
B	Teaching should be guided by ethical principles	1,2 (3)	2,3 (6)	46,9 (120)	49,6 (127)
C	Values should be formed during teaching	2 (5)	4,3 (11)	33,6 (86)	60,2 (154)
D	Morality is the foundation of teaching	0 (0)	4,7 (12)	47,7 (122)	47,7 (122)
E	Teaching moulds who learners become	0,4 (1)	2,7 (7)	41 (105)	55,9 (143)
F	All learners are different and should be taught accordingly	0 (0)	0,7 (1)	16 (41)	83,6 (214)
G	Learners are empty vessels to be filled with teaching	37.7 (97)	22,2 (57)	22,6 (58)	17,5 (45)

Table 4.1   Beliefs about Teaching – Q1 Teacher Motivation and Beliefs (BEd) *(cont)*

Item	Beliefs	Strongly disagree % (n)	Disagree % (n)	Agree % (n)	Strongly agree % (n)
H	All children can learn	0 (0)	0,8 (2)	16 (41)	83,2 (213)
I	Teachers are accountable for what learners learn	0,4 (1)	16,5 (41)	54,6 (136)	28,5 (71)
J	Teaching can only occur in a democratic environment	13 (33)	37,4 (95)	34,3 (87)	15,4 (39)
K	Teaching should be fun	0 (0)	0,8 (2)	21,2 (54)	78 (199)
L	Teaching should be underpinned by assessment	5,2 (13)	22,6 (56)	54 (134)	18,1 (45)
M	Praise is important during teaching	0,8 (2)	5,1 (13)	33,9 (87)	60,3 (155)
N	Teaching is stressful	2,3 (6)	16,8 (43)	55,1 (141)	25,8 (66)
O	It is impractical to tailor teaching to individual needs	20,5 (52)	39,4 (100)	29,1 (74)	11 (28)

Item G asked about the relationship between learners and teaching. Although more student teachers disagreed, an overwhelming 40% of the respondents agreed that learners are empty vessels to be filled with teaching. When this item was stratified according to race, most black, coloured and Indian teachers disagreed, whereas more white student teachers agreed.

With Item J, which asked about the teaching environment, the respondents were equally divided between disagree and agree, 50% and 49,7% respectively. When this item was stratified according to race, black, coloured and Indian student teachers disagreed and white student teachers agreed.

Item O stated that it is impractical to tailor lessons to individual needs. Only 59,9% of pre-service teachers disagreed, and 40,1% agreed. When this item was stratified according to race, white, coloured and Indian student teachers disagreed and black students agreed with this statement.

4.3.2 Postgraduate Certificate in Education (PGCE)

The results from the PGCE cohort followed the same response patterns as the BEd student teachers' (see Table 4.2).

Table 4.2 Beliefs about Teaching – Q1 Teacher Motivation and Beliefs (PGCE)

Item	Beliefs	Strongly disagree % (n)	Disagree % (n)	Agree % (n)	Strongly agree % (n)
A	Teaching is a calling	7,6 (5)	15,2 (10)	54,5 (36)	22,7 (15)
B	Teaching should be guided by ethical principles	0 (0)	1,5 (1)	43,9 (29)	54,5 (36)
C	Values should be formed during teaching	0 (0)	4,5 (3)	53 (35)	42,4 (28)
D	Morality is the foundation of teaching	0 (0)	4,5 (3)	50 (33)	45,5 (30)
E	Teaching moulds who learners become	0 (0)	6,2 (4)	41,5 (27)	52,3 (34)
F	All learners are different and should be taught accordingly	0 (0)	3 (2)	27,3 (18)	69,7 (46)
G	Learners are empty vessels to be filled with teaching	31,8 (21)	33,3 (22)	21,2 (14)	13,6 (9)
H	All children can learn	0 (0)	3 (2)	28,8 (19)	68,2 (45)
I	Teachers are accountable for what learners learn	1,5 (1)	28,8 (19)	54,5 (36)	15,2 (10)
J	Teaching can only occur in a democratic environment	15,2 (10)	39,4 (26)	34,8 (23)	10,6 (7)
K	Teaching should be fun	1,5 (1)	1,5 (1)	24,2 (16)	72,7 (48)
L	Teaching should be underpinned by assessment	1,5 (1)	15,4 (10)	63,1 (41)	20 (13)
M	Praise is important during teaching	6,2 (4)	4,6 (3)	38,5 (25)	50,8 (33)
N	Teaching is stressful	9,1 (6)	15,2 (10)	42,4 (28)	33,3 (22)
O	It is impractical to tailor teaching to individual needs	16,7 (11)	45,5 (30)	25,8 (17)	12,1 (8)

Similarly, Items G, J and O were contested items, with the rest of the items having a clear positive or negative trajectory. Looking at these bold items from a race perspective, Indians agreed more than their black and coloured counterparts. There were no white students in this cohort.

Table 4.3 indicates what student teachers thought were the most powerful determinants of a learner's success. The respondents were asked to choose one option they considered the most powerful.

4.3.3 BEd and PGCE

The student teachers from the BEd cohort listed parental support as the most powerful determinant in a learner's success at the Foundation Phase level (see Table 4.3). This was followed by learner perseverance and home background. When these results were stratified according to institution and race, all races equally agreed that parental support was the most important determinant, but they differed on other items on the list.

Table 4.3 Most Powerful Determinant of a Learner's Success – Q1 Teacher Motivation and Beliefs (BEd)

Item	Most powerful determinant of a learner's success	BEd % (n)	PGCE % (n)
A	Home background	14,6 (37)	6,1 (4)
B	Intellectual ability	3,5 (9)	4,5 (3)
C	Learner enthusiasm	13 (33)	9,1 (6)
D	Learner perseverance	14,2 (36)	28,8 (19)
E	**Parental support**	24,4 (62)	27,3 (18)
F	Teacher attention to learner interest	7,9 (20)	4,5 (3)
G	Teacher use of teaching methods	11,8 (30)	6,1 (4)
H	Teacher enthusiasm	3,1 (8)	3 (2)
I	Teacher perseverance	4,7 (12)	7,6 (5)
J	Other (Please specify)	2,8 (7)	3 (2)

The PGCE respondents chose learner perseverance as the most powerful determinant of a learner's success, with parental support second and learner enthusiasm third. The two cohorts both listed learner perseverance and parental support as important determinants. When the data were stratified according to race, all student teachers s agreed that learner perseverance was the most important.

4.3.4 Qualitative Data

After the questionnaires were administered, student teachers also had the opportunity to participate in focus groups to provide further insight into their beliefs about teaching and learning and knowledge in general. Volunteers from both cohorts were asked whether their beliefs about teaching changed over the course of the programme. The student teachers gave the following responses:

4.3.4.1 BEd

There were changes in how student teachers understood what the teaching profession entails:

> A lot, ma'am, like I said before that I just came here, I just kept enrolling. I didn't love kids so now I love kids now, so I've changed. So I thought teaching it was just teaching, going there and teach but now I get to understand that teaching, it's not about teaching, it's all about different strategies to use as a teacher. So that you can make sure that each and every learner there in class is covered… like teaching is not about teaching that I will go there and teach, but you must have an idea on how are you going to teach (BEd, FP, Institution [Inst.] C 2016).

Teaching is not only seen as a profession, but as a way to give back to the local community:

> My belief about teaching… before I come to teaching I wanted to be a nurse but since I've been here I enjoy being a teacher because I felt teaching was for old, like for women around 50s and above. So now I've seen that teaching is not about that, so being there for those kids made me realise that I can do it and I want to do it. So to be around those kids, to help them in whatever they are facing, it's like something that I want to do not because I'm forced or because I'm going to get paid or just that I want to do it with my heart, with my mind and, yes. Yes, I do want to be a teacher, the teacher who's going to give everything in teaching a kid, to be there for those who don't have parents or who are facing anything. Learners, they should trust me with whatever they are facing. So I want to be a teacher and I hope and I believe that I'm going to be that teacher, yes (BEd FP, Inst. C).

The requirements to teach learners basic literacy and numeracy are more complex than anticipated:

> I didn't think it would be difficult, I actually thought it would be easy but I thought it can be teaching Foundation Phase could like one plus one, you know, how difficult can it be; A-B-C. But I didn't think it would be as involved as it is, I didn't think there was so much to it, there were so many layers to attention, and like, in coming in I realised that it's not just curriculum, it's emotional, it's everything. You set into the context of the school you have; like, how you feel in the morning when you wake up, how do you feel during the day, what happens if you don't like the teacher in the classroom and you have to work with them, like, is everything, and I actually thought about that before because as a child you see your teachers, okay, they work together, you don't care as a kid, you don't pay so much attention to that. And yeah, it definitely changed my perception of teaching, but I think in a good way, yeah (BEd FP, Inst. C).

> So it's very difficult but… this course has absolutely changed my view of teaching… I had a completely different, like, image of what it's actually going to be like. And I think [it] has changed my view a little bit more (BEd FP, Inst. A).

Challenged traditional methods of teaching and learning:

> Yeah, I think also, obviously, when you've just started to do teaching, you think about the types that you use in school, like how you refer to your teachers and what they did. And it was very like the teacher is the teacher, she does all of the talking at the school I went to, so you kind of imagine it the way you have been taught and, yeah, through practicals... That whole idea has totally changed, we're all learner centred, you know, you're the teacher that facilitates and not sort of the leader, which is a huge change because I always thought of teaching and all of our friends, still, you don't study teaching you think of... like so traditional way like where the teachers kind of control everything where actually now it's moved to the learners are more in control and you just kind of guide, yeah, you facilitate (BEd FP, Inst. B).

Although teaching is a practical endeavour, it is rooted in theoretical constructs that need to be understood in order to grasp the process of how learners learn and develop their cognitive abilities:

> I think my whole view changed as well, like it's [initially I] just thought you just walk into the class, you teach, you do your thing, and that's it. But now I see there's a lot more, there's a lot of theory that actually backs up what they're doing in class and we learned a lot about the child development in psychology, which, like, helped a lot because we learned about all the differences that the child might have and how to teach diverse classrooms (BEd FP, Inst. B).

4.4 Beliefs about Domain-Specific Subject Knowledge (Language and Mathematics)

In this section, student teachers were asked questions regarding their beliefs about teaching language and mathematics. The questionnaires also probed items such as views about specific concepts relating to mathematics and language learning and teaching, as well as the importance of specific concepts relating to how language and mathematics should be taught.

4.4.1 BEd: Language

Table 4.4 Beliefs about Language as a Subject – Q1 Teacher Motivation and Beliefs (BEd)

Item	Beliefs about language as a subject	Strongly disagree % (n)	Disagree % (n)	Agree % (n)	Strongly agree % (n)
A	Language is a tool for thought	0 (0)	1,2 (3)	49,6 (127)	49,2 (126)
B	Language is a tool for communication	0,4 (1)	0,4 (1)	23 (59)	79,3 (196)
C	Language is a shared means to make better sense of the world we live in	0,4 (1)	0,8 (2)	39,8 (102)	59 (151)
D	Language is important for one's identity	0,8 (2)	12,9 (33)	50,6 (129)	35,7 (91)

Beliefs about Professional Knowledge

Table 4.4 Beliefs about Language as a Subject – Q1 Teacher Motivation and Beliefs (BEd) (cont)

Item	Beliefs about language as a subject	Strongly disagree % (n)	Disagree % (n)	Agree % (n)	Strongly agree % (n)
E	Language is the most important subject taught at school	2 (5)	30,6 (78)	47,8 (122)	19,6 (50)
F	Language assists learners to listen, speak, read, and write	0 (0)	0 (0)	26,1 (67)	73,9 (190)
G	Language facilitates understanding across the curriculum	0 (0)	1,2 (3)	42,6 (109)	56,3 (144)

All student teacher responses for Table 4.4 were distributed between agree and strongly agree, except for Items D and E, where a large percentage of student teachers (12,9% and 30,6% respectively) disagreed with the statements "Language is the most important subject taught at school" and "Language is important for one's identity". Examining this from a race perspective, more white student teachers agreed with this statement than black, coloured and Indian respondents.

Table 4.5 Views about Teaching Language – Q1 Teacher Motivation and Beliefs (BEd)

Item	Views about teaching language	Strongly disagree % (n)	Disagree % (n)	Agree % (n)	Strongly agree % (n)
A	There is a correlation between a child's speed of reading and his/her reading comprehension	3,6 (9)	22,2 (56)	56,3 (142)	17,9 (45)
B	There is a correlation between reading and writing, and understanding languages	0,4 (1)	6,7 (17)	65,5 (165)	27,4 (69)
C	Teaching in a learner's home language helps with their cognitive development	0 (0)	2,8 (7)	48 (122)	49,2 (125)
D	Teaching in the learner's home language helps in learning an additional language	2,8 (7)	17 (43)	48,6 (123)	31,6 (80)
E	Verbal interactions develop vocabulary and comprehension	0,4 (1)	0,8 (2)	36 (91)	62,8 (159)
F	Prescribed language textbooks are the most important resources a teacher has	22,2 (56)	42,5 (107)	26,6 (67)	8,7 (22)
G	Exposure to different types of texts is useful for learning a language	0,4 (1)	0,4 (1)	46,7 (119)	52,5 (134)
H	Parents should be involved in teaching languages at home	0 (0)	1,6 (4)	29,8 (76)	68,6 (175)

Most items in Table 4.5 are evenly distributed towards positive or negative, except for Items A, D and F, where quite a number of respondents went against this trend. These items related to how learners learn language, as well as the resources to teach languages. When examining this item from a race perspective, more black student teachers agreed than the rest of the racial groups.

Table 4.6 Importance of Developing Language Skills – Q1 Teacher Motivation and Beliefs (BEd)

Item	Importance of developing the following skills	Not at all % (n)	Somewhat important % (n)	Important % (n)	Very important % (n)
A	Learning to speak	0 (0)	3,9 (10)	20,1 (52)	76,1 (197)
B	Learning to listen with comprehension	0 (0)	1,2 (3)	15,4 (40)	83,4 (216)
C	Learning to recognise sounds	0,4 (1)	2,3 (6)	26,6 (69)	70,7 (183)
D	Learning to read	0,4 (1)	1,2 (3)	19,7 (51)	78,8 (204)
E	Learning to write	0 (0)	3,5 (9)	21,2 (55)	75,3 (195)

All the items in Table 4.6 were relatively evenly distributed, with no significant differences in relation to race. It is also interesting to note that, generally, student teachers did not answer all of the items. However, for this section, all items were completed.

For this cohort, all the respondents were in agreement that it is important to develop basic language skills. Table 4.4 showed that although the majority agreed that language was the most important skill learned in schools, more than 30% of student teachers disagreed. Unfortunately, due to the nature of the data-collection instrument, a further probe into what these student teachers who disagreed considered to be the most important learning area was not investigated. This is a crucial finding as it indicates the level of emphasis a teacher may put on language as a learning area. Lack of emphasis due to the belief that it is not the most important learning area can impact student teachers' beliefs and impressions about the learning area and even discourage participation.

In Table 4.6, more than 25% of the respondents disagreed or strongly disagreed about the causal link between reading speed and comprehension. It is also interesting to note that the majority of student teachers assumed that if a learner reads fast, that they understand what they are reading, which is not necessarily the case. This table also indicated that the majority of student teachers found using learners' home language a useful tool to teach additional languages. More than 66% of student teachers disagreed that textbooks were the most important resource for learning language. This could be due to the fact that other easy-to-obtain material such as newspapers, magazines, and in certain contexts, technology, may aid in teaching language skills rather than the traditional textbook-only method.

4.4.2 PGCE: Language

Table 4.7   Beliefs about Language as a Subject – Q1 Teacher Motivation and Beliefs (PGCE)

Item	Beliefs about language as a subject	Strongly disagree % (n)	Disagree % (n)	Agree % (n)	Strongly agree % (n)
A	Language is tool for thought	0 (0)	0 (0)	40,4 (23)	59,6 (34)
B	Language is a tool for communication	0 (0)	0 (0)	24,1 (14)	75,9 (44)
C	Language is a shared means to make better sense of the world we live in	0 (0)	0 (0)	37,9 (22)	62,1 (36)
D	Language is important for one's identity	0 (0)	0 (0)	51,7 (30)	48,3 (28)
E	Language is the most important subject taught at school	0 (0)	8,6 (5)	44,8 (26)	46,6 (27)
F	Language assists learners to listen, speak, read and write	0 (0)	0 (0)	19 (11)	81 (47)
G	Language facilitates understanding across the curriculum	0 (0)	0 (0)	24,1 (14)	75,9 (44)

No significant differences were found between the items and the items stratified by race (Table 4.7).

Table 4.8   Views about Teaching Language – Q1 Teacher Motivation and Beliefs (PGCE)

Item	Views about teaching language	Strongly disagree % (n)	Disagree % (n)	Agree % (n)	Strongly agree % (n)
A	The goal of teaching language is to help learners think and reason	1,7 (1)	5,2 (3)	48,3 (28)	44,8 (26)
B	There is a correlation between reading and writing, and understanding languages	0 (0)	3,4 (2)	39,7 (23)	56,9 (33)
C	Teaching literature is about expecting the right answer	32,8 (19)	62,1 (36)	5,2 (3)	0 (0)
D	Classroom discussion is useful	0 (0)	0 (0)	37,9 (22)	62,1 (36)
E	Language is a tool for thought and communication	0 (0)	0 (0)	36,8 (21)	63,2 (36)

Table 4.8 Views about Teaching Language – Q1 Teacher Motivation and Beliefs (PGCE) *(cont)*

Item	Views about teaching language	Strongly disagree % (n)	Disagree % (n)	Agree % (n)	Strongly agree % (n)
F	Prescribed language textbooks are the most important resources a teacher has	5,2 (3)	50 (29)	41,4 (24)	3,4 (2)
G	Exposure to different types of texts is useful for learning a language	0 (0)	0 (0)	36,2 (21)	63,8 (37)
H	Parents should be involved in teaching languages at home	0 (0)	0 (0)	22,4 (13)	77,6 (45)

The responses for items in Table 4.8 were either positive or negative, expect for Item F. Student teachers seemed divided about the merits of the statement in Item F. When examining this item from a race perspective, coloured and Indian student teachers disagreed and black student teachers agreed with this statement.

Table 4.9 Importance of Developing Language Skills – Q1 Teacher Motivation and Beliefs (PGCE)

Item	Importance of developing the following skills	Not at all % (n)	Somewhat important (% (n)	Important % (n)	Very important % (n)
A	Learning to speak	0 (0)	1,7 (1)	22,4 (14)	75,9 (44)
B	Learning to listen with comprehension	0 (0)	0 (0)	14 (8)	86 (49)
C	Learning grammatical structures	0 (0)	8,6 (5)	32,8 (19)	58,6 (34)
D	Learning to read with comprehension	0 (0)	0 (0)	10,5 (6)	89,5 (51)
E	Learning to write	0 (0)	0 (0)	20,7 (12)	79,3 (46)

According to Table 4.9, student teachers responded in a relatively uniform manner. No significant changes were found when the data were stratified according to race.

Student teachers in the PGCE programme responded more consistently than those in the BEd programme. Table 4.8 showed a disagreement within the cohort regarding whether textbooks were the most important resource in the language class. This could be indicative of the varied schooling landscape that exists in South Africa.

4.4.3 BEd: Mathematics

Table 4.10 Beliefs about Mathematics as a Subject – Q1 Teacher Motivation and Beliefs (BEd)

Item	Beliefs about mathematics as a subject	Strongly disagree % (n)	Disagree % (n)	Agree % (n)	Strongly agree % (n)
A	It is a language that makes use of symbols and notations	0,8 (2)	8,7 (22)	66,9 (170)	23,6 (60)
B	It is a language that is used to describe numerical, geometric and graphical relationships	0,4 (1)	3,1 (8)	69,8 (178)	26,7 (68)
C	It is about solving problems and testing understanding through examples	0,4 (1)	3,1 (8)	49,2 (127)	47,3 (122)
D	It is a human activity that involves observing, representing, and investigating patterns and quantitative relationships in physical and social phenomena	0 (0)	1,9 (5)	59,5 (153)	38,5 (99)
E	It is a set of formulas and rules that have been worked out by experts	3,5 (9)	27,7 (71)	51,6 (132)	17,2 (44)
F	It is a human activity that involves observing relationships between mathematical objects	0 (0)	5,1 (13)	70,3 (180)	24,6 (63)
G	It is the one subject that intimidates more learners than any other subject	1,9 (5)	8,9 (23)	40,1 (103)	49 (126)
H	It is a subject that predicts later academic achievement	7,1 (18)	41,6 (106)	32,5 (83)	18,8 (48)
I	It helps to develop mental processes that enhance logical and critical thinking, accuracy and problem solving	0,4 (1)	1,5 (4)	44,4 (115)	53,7 (139)
J	Foundation Phase mathematics is only about getting the correct answer	53,1 (137)	33,7 (87)	9,3 (24)	3,9 (10)
K	To excel in mathematics, it is important to understand what you have done, as well as why you have done it	0 (0)	2,3 (6)	40,1 (103)	57,6 (148)

According to Table 4.10, the respondents answered similarly, with interesting responses to Items E and H. When examining Item E in terms of race, black and coloured student teachers agreed and Indian and white student teachers were ambivalent in their responses between agree and disagree. The majority of the black student teachers agreed with Item H.

Table 4.11 Beliefs about the Goals of Mathematics – Q1 Teacher Motivation and Beliefs (BEd)

Item	Beliefs about the goals of mathematics	Strongly disagree % (n)	Disagree % (n)	Agree % (n)	Strongly agree % (n)
A	To help develop mathematical thinking and understanding	0 (0)	0,4 (1)	41,1 (106)	58,8 (151)
B	To understand the structure of the number system	0 (0)	3,9 (10)	56,4 (145)	39,7 (102)
C	To assist learners in solving real-world problems	0 (1)	1,9 (5)	29,6 (76)	68,1 (175)
D	To develop learners' ability to communicate mathematically	0 (1)	3,5 (9)	48,8 (126)	47,3 (122)
E	To make connections between different aspects of mathematics	0 (0)	2 (5)	63,4 (161)	34,6 (88)

All the respondents answered these items in a consistent manner (see Table 4.11). No significant differences were found when the data were stratified according to race.

Table 4.12 Views about Mathematics Teaching – Q1 Teacher Motivation and Beliefs (BEd)

Item	Views about mathematics teaching	Strongly disagree % (n)	Disagree % (n)	Agree % (n)	Strongly agree % (n)
A	Explaining why an answer is correct is just as important as getting a correct answer	0,8 (2)	10,1 (26)	38,9 (100)	50,2 (129)
B	Even with the availability of calculators and computers, learners need to learn to make use of mental calculation to do mathematics	0 (0)	0 (0)	32,8 (85)	67,2 (174)
C	Learners should be able to figure out for themselves whether they have solved a mathematical problem correctly	0 (0)	10,9 (28)	48,4 (125)	40,7 (105)
D	Learners should learn basic skills before being asked to solve complex mathematical problems	1,6 (4)	8,2 (21)	43,2 (111)	47,1 (121)
E	Asking learners to solve difficult problems in class helps them become good problem solvers	1,6 (4)	11,6 (30)	51,9 (134)	34,9 (90)
F	Learners should solve a few complex problems rather than many relatively easy ones	1,2 (3)	14,8 (38)	49,4 (127)	34,6 (89)

Beliefs about Professional Knowledge

Table 4.12 Views about Mathematics Teaching – Q1 Teacher Motivation and Beliefs (BEd) *(cont)*

Item	Views about mathematics teaching	Strongly disagree % (n)	Disagree % (n)	Agree % (n)	Strongly agree % (n)
G	Doing mathematics requires hypothesising, estimating and creative thinking	0,4 (1)	5,1 (13)	55,3 (140)	39,1 (99)
H	Most things a learner needs to know in mathematics can be learned through memorisation	29,6 (76)	40,5 (104)	20,2 (52)	9,7 (25)
I	There is usually a best method for solving a mathematical problem and my job is to make sure learners learn that method	26,4 (68)	27,5 (71)	29,1 (75)	17,1 (44)

According to Table 4.12, most of the items received a similar response, i.e. either agreeing or strongly agreeing with the items, except Items H and I. In Item H, 70,1% of the student teachers disagreed and 30,2% agreed. When examining this item in terms of race, white, coloured and Indian student teachers mostly disagreed and black student teachers mostly agreed. In Item I there was a relative even spread across three options; strongly disagree (26,4%), disagree 27,5%), and agree (29,1%), with strongly agree (17,1%) not too far behind.

Table 4.13 Importance of Developing Mathematical Knowledge – Q1 Teacher Motivation and Beliefs (BEd)

Item	Importance of developing mathematical knowledge	Not at all % (n)	Somewhat important % (n)	Important % (n)	Very important % (n)
A	Developing the correct use of terminology	0,4 (1)	14 (36)	53,3 (137)	32,3 (83)
B	Learning to investigate, analyse, represent and interpret mathematical information	0 (0)	4,6 (12)	46,7 (121)	48,6 (126)
C	Developing number concept, calculation and application skills	0 (0)	1,9 (5)	41,9 (108)	56,2 (145)
D	Recognising and using properties of operations	0,8 (2)	8,1 (21)	54,3 (140)	36,8 (95)
E	Learning rules and how to apply them	3,9 (10)	15,9 (41)	45,3 (117)	34,9 (90)
F	Developing mathematical communication skills	0 (0)	5,4 (14)	47,7 (123)	46,9 (121)
G	Developing problem-solving ability	0 (0)	0 (0)	29,8 (77)	70,2 (181)

The student teachers responded to items in Table 4.13 in a similar fashion, with no significant differences found when stratifying the data according to race.

4.4.4 PGCE: Mathematics

Table 4.14 Beliefs about Mathematics as a Subject – Q1 Teacher Motivation and Belief (PGCE)

Item	Beliefs about mathematics as a subject	Strongly disagree % (n)	Disagree % (n)	Agree % (n)	Strongly agree % (n)
A	It is a language that makes use of symbols and notations	0 (0)	0 (0)	66,7 (8)	33 (4)
B	It is a language that is used to describe numerical, geometric and graphical relationships	0 (0)	0 (0)	33 (4)	66,7 (8)
C	It is about solving problems and testing understanding through examples	0 (0)	0 (0)	25 (3)	75 (9)
D	It is a human activity that involves observing, representing, and investigating patterns and quantitative relationships in physical and social phenomena	0 (0)	0 (0)	50 (6)	50 (6)
E	It is a set of formulas and rules that have been worked out by experts	8,3 (1)	25 (3)	25 (3)	41,7 (5)
F	It is a human activity that involves observing relationships between mathematical objects	0 (0)	0 (0)	75 (9)	25 (3)
G	It is the one subject that intimidates more learners than any other subject	8,3 (1)	25 (3)	25 (3)	41,7 (5)
H	It is a subject that predicts later academic achievement	16,7 (2)	25 (3)	33,3 (4)	25 (3)
I	It helps to develop mental processes that enhance logical and critical thinking, accuracy and problem solving	0 (0)	0 (0)	25 (3)	75 (9)
J	It is about formulas and cranking out computations	0 (0)	50 (6)	33,3 (4)	16,7 (2)
K	To excel in mathematics, it is important to understand what you have done, as well as why you have done it	0 (0)	0 (0)	36,4 (4)	63,6 (7)

According to Table 4.14, students generally responded the same, except for Item H. No Indian and white student teachers responded to this item and the coloured and black student teachers who did answer, responded quite ambivalently. Half of the coloured student teachers either agreed or disagreed, with a slight variation towards agree for black student teachers.

Beliefs about Professional Knowledge

Table 4.15 Beliefs about Goals for Mathematics Teaching – Q1 Teacher Motivation and Beliefs (PGCE)

Item	Beliefs about goals for mathematics teaching	Strongly disagree % (n)	Disagree % (n)	Agree % (n)	Strongly agree % (n)
A	To help develop mathematical thinking and understanding	0 (0)	0 (0)	25 (3)	75 (9)
B	To understand the structure of the number system	0 (0)	0 (0)	41,7 (5)	58,3 (7)
C	To assist learners in solving real-world problems	0 (0)	8,3 (1)	25 (3)	66,7 (8)
D	To develop learners' ability to communicate mathematically	0 (0)	0 (0)	41,7 (5)	58,3 (7)
E	To make connections between different aspects of mathematics	0 (0)	0 (0)	75 (9)	25 (3)

According to Table 4.15, the student teachers responded in a similar fashion, with no significant differences found between races. It is also crucial to note that there were no white or Indian students in the mathematics cohort.

Table 4.16 Views about Teaching Mathematics – Q1 Teacher Motivation and Beliefs (PGCE)

Item	Views about teaching mathematics	Strongly disagree % (n)	Disagree % (n)	Agree % (n)	Strongly agree % (n)
A	Explaining why an answer is correct is just as important as getting a correct answer	0 (0)	8,3 (1)	50 (6)	41,7 (5)
B	Even with the availability of calculators and computers, learners need to learn to make use of mental calculation to do mathematics	0 (0)	0 (0)	16,7 (2)	83,3 (10)
C	Learners should be able to figure out for themselves whether they have solved a mathematical problem correctly	8,3 (1)	16,7 (2)	41,7 (5)	33,3 (4)
D	Learners should learn basic skills before being asked to solve complex mathematical problems	0 (0)	0 (0)	25 (3)	75 (9)
E	Asking learners to solve difficult problems in class helps them become good problem solvers	0 (0)	16,7 (2)	50 (6)	33,3 (4)

Table 4.16 Views about Teaching Mathematics – Q1 Teacher Motivation and Beliefs (PGCE) (*cont*)

Item	Views about teaching mathematics	Strongly disagree % (n)	Disagree % (n)	Agree % (n)	Strongly agree % (n)
F	Learners should solve a few complex problems, rather than many relatively easy ones	8,3 (1)	25 (3)	50 (6)	16,7 (2)
G	Doing mathematics requires hypothesising, estimating, and creative thinking	0 (0)	8,3 (1)	50 (6)	41,7 (5)
H	Most things a learner needs to know in mathematics can be learned through memorisation	33,3 (4)	41,7 (5)	16,7 (2)	8,3 (1)
I	There is usually a best method for solving a mathematical problem and my job is to make sure learners learn that method	0 (0)	25 (3)	33,3 (4)	41,7 (5)

While most student teachers responded similarly, Items C, F, and H were not as clear cut (see Table 4.16). For Item C, some student teachers believed that learners should be able to figure out correct answers for themselves. For Item F, over 30% disagreed that it is okay for learners to solve a few complex problems as opposed to many easy ones. For Item H, more that 20% of the student teachers agreed that most things a learner needs to know in mathematics can be learned through memorisation. No significant differences were found when stratifying these data according to race. Institutional comparisons were not applicable in this case.

Table 4.17 Importance of Developing Mathematical Knowledge – Q1 Teacher Motivation and Beliefs (PGCE)

Item	Importance of developing mathematical knowledge	Not at all % (n)	Somewhat important % (n)	Important % (n)	Very important % (n)
A	Developing the correct use of terminology	0 (0)	0 (0)	58,3 (7)	41,7 (5)
B	Learning to investigate, analyse, represent and interpret mathematical information	0 (0)	8,3 (1)	41,7 (5)	50 (6)
C	Developing number concept, calculation and application skills	0 (0)	8,3 (1)	33,3 (4)	58,3 (7)
D	Recognising and using properties of operations	0 (0)	8,3 (1)	50 (6)	41,7 (5)

Table 4.17 Importance of Developing Mathematical Knowledge – Q1 Teacher Motivation and Beliefs (PGCE) (*cont*)

Item	Importance of developing mathematical knowledge	Not at all % (n)	Somewhat important % (n)	Important % (n)	Very important % (n)
E	Learning rules and how to apply them	0 (0)	0 (0)	16,7 (2)	83,3 (10)
F	Developing mathematical communication skills	0 (0)	0 (0)	33,3 (4)	66,7 (8)
G	Developing problem solving ability	0 (0)	0 (0)	16,7 (2)	83,3 (10)

No significant differences were found when the data were stratified between the races that responded to the items (see Table 4.17).

4.4.5 Analysis

The analysis for this theme is divided into the two learning areas of language and mathematics.

Considering student teachers' beliefs about learners and their dispositions in relation to language, in both BEd and PGCE programmes, most student teachers agreed that there is a correlation between learners' linguistic ability and their performance. The nature of this correlation, however, whether strong or weak, was not further investigated in this study.

With reference to student teachers' beliefs about the act and activities of teaching language, more than 30% of the BEd cohort disagreed that language is the most important subject taught at school (Item E, Table 4.4), despite being the conduit through which other subjects are taught. The student teachers did, however, agree that language facilitates understanding across the curriculum (Item G, Table 4.4). More black students agreed that the prescribed language textbook was the most important resource that a teacher has (Item F, Table 4.5). A similar trend can be observed among students in the PGCE programme (Item F, Table 4.8), as well as for students in the BEd programme (Item F, Table 4.5). This could be indicative of the nature of resources encountered by these students, who may have more experience in poor schools. Alternative explanations for this view could be, firstly, that textbooks have always been promoted as the most important resource for teaching and learning, and teachers who adopted this view may have transmitted this belief to their learners. Secondly, novice teachers would initially have an overreliance on textbooks in order to develop their experience and knowledge. This is part of the on-site self-development of NQTs.

The student teachers in both programmes were ambivalent about the relationship between mathematics and learners' academic achievement. The responses were more or less equal between agree and disagree. Mostly black student teachers agreed with this statement, however. This response tends to mirror the higher education landscape whereby it is still mostly white and Indian students who gain university access to highly skilled programmes, which often require high levels of mathematical competency.

More than 30% of the student teachers in the BEd programme agreed that most things learners need to know about mathematics can be learned through memorisation (Table 4.12, Item H).

A similar pattern was found in the PGCE programme (Table 4.16, Item H). This view could have problematic implications for how the subject is taught; whereby learners are taught to memorise as opposed to understand. Almost 50% of the student teachers in the BEd programme (mostly black student teachers) agreed that there is a best method for solving mathematical problems and it is the teacher's function to teach this specific method (Table 4.12, Item I). This view may be associated with a lack of creativity in the mathematics classroom and could prevent learners from taking opportunities to explore other ways of problem solving.

The student teachers in the BEd programme agreed that they needed to expose learners to a wide range of texts as a pedagogical tool to improve language learning and understanding (Table 4.5, Item G). The student teachers in the PGCE programme also completely agreed or strongly agreed with this statement.

The student teachers in both programmes agreed that developing specific skills in learners is important, which indicates a common understanding between the cohorts of the kinds of skills that are required in the mathematics classroom. Learners may thus be exposed to a similar approach to mathematics when they enter, as well as when they leave, school.

4.5 Competence to Teach (Language and Mathematics)

The following tables demonstrate student teachers' beliefs regarding their competence to teach language and mathematics. These questions were only administered to student teachers in the BEd programme.

4.5.1 BEd: Language

Table 4.18 Competence to Teach Language Skills – Q1 Teacher Motivation and Beliefs (BEd)

Item	Competence to teach the following language skills	Not at all % (n)	Somewhat competent % (n)	Competent % (n)	Very competent % (n)
A	Speaking	0 (0)	8,5 (22)	48,8 (126)	42,6 (110)
B	Listening with comprehension	0 (0)	10,9 (28)	49,6 (128)	39,5 (102)
C	Sound recognition	0 (0)	9,3 (24)	48,1 (124)	42,6 (110)
D	Reading	0 (0)	10,1 (26)	51,2 (132)	38,8 (100)
E	Writing	0,4 (1)	10,5 (27)	49,2 (127)	39,9 (103)

Only one student teacher out of the total cohort who responded did not feel competent in writing (see Table 4.18). In all other items, the student teachers felt a certain degree of competency, although 49.3% noted 'somewhat competent' across all the language skills listed. No significant differences were found when examining race.

PGCE: This question was not asked to the PGCE student teachers because the programme is only one year.

4.5.2 BEd: Mathematics

Table 4.19 Competence to Teach Mathematical Skills – Q1 Teacher Motivation and Beliefs (BEd)

Item	Competence to teach the following mathematical skills	Not at all % (n)	Somewhat competent % (n)	Competent % (n)	Very competent % (n)
A	Developing the correct use of basic terminology	0 (0)	10,9 (28)	59 (151)	30,1 (77)
B	Learning to investigate, analyse, represent and interpret information	0,4 (1)	12,9 (33)	62,1 (159)	24,6 (63)
C	Developing number concept, calculation and application skills	0,8 (2)	9,7 (25)	58,4 (150)	31,1 (80)
D	Recognising and using properties of operations	0,8 (2)	17,8 (46)	58,9 (152)	22,5 (58)
E	Learning rules and how to apply them	2,7 (7)	17,1 (44)	52,5 (135)	27,6 (71)
F	Developing mathematical communication skills	0,4 (1)	16,7 (43)	54,9 (141)	28 (72)
G	Developing problem-solving abilities	0 (0)	9 (23)	53,5 (137)	37,5 (96)

Most items, apart from Items E and F, received a uniform response from the student teachers (see Table 4.19). Thirteen student teachers did not feel competent in teaching one or more items. For Item E, when examining the data from a race perspective, no black student teachers felt incompetent to teach learners rules and how to apply them, as opposed to the other racial categories. From an institutional standpoint, it was mostly student teachers from Institution B who did not feel competent to teach this.

For Item F, only one Indian student teacher from Institution A did not feel competent to teach this.

PGCE: This question was not asked in the questionnaire administered to PGCE students because they were at the beginning of the programme.

Most student teachers felt competent to teach various language skills. For mathematics, teaching learners rules and how to apply them was the most problematic item to teach. Although very few student teachers did not feel competent to teach certain skills, most pedagogical techniques improve with practice and student teachers' competence tends to increase once they have been exposed to teaching these skills more regularly.

4.6 Confidence to Teach (Language and Mathematics)

The items in this section asked student teachers about their confidence to teach various language and mathematical skills. Both cohorts responded to these questions.

4.6.1 BEd: Language

Table 4.20 Confidence to Teach Language Skills – Q1 Teacher Motivation and Beliefs (BEd)

Item	Confidence to teach language	Not at all % (n)	Somewhat confident % (n)	Confident % (n)	Very confident % (n)
A	Speaking	0,4 (1)	9,3 (24)	45,7 (118)	44,6 (115)
B	Listening with comprehension	0 (0)	12,8 (33)	49,2 (127)	38 (98)
C	Sound recognition	0,4 (1)	9,3 (24)	45,3 (117)	45 (116)
D	Reading	0 (0)	13,7 (35)	47,3 (121)	39,1 (100)
E	Writing	0 (0)	12,5 (32)	48,6 (125)	38,9 (100)

Only two student teachers in the BEd cohort did not feel confident to teach a language skill (speaking and sound recognition) (Table 4.20, Items A and C). All the other respondents felt some level of confidence. No significant differences were found when stratifying these items according to race.

Beliefs about Professional Knowledge

Table 4.21   Confidence to Teach Mathematics – Q1 Teacher Motivation and Beliefs (BEd)

Item	Confidence to teach mathematics	Not at all % (n)	Somewhat confident % (n)	Confident % (n)	Very confident % (n)
A	Developing the correct use of basic terminology	0,4 (1)	13,2 (34)	60,3 (155)	26,1 (67)
B	Learning to investigate, analyse, represent and interpret mathematical information	0,8 (2)	16,7 (43)	61,1 (157)	21,4 (55)
C	Developing number concept, calculation and application skills	0,8 (2)	13,6 (35)	58 (149)	27,6 (71)
D	Recognising and using properties of operations	0,8 (2)	21,4 (55)	54,5 (140)	23,3 (60)
E	Learning rules and how to apply them	2,3 (6)	21,1 (54)	48,4 (124)	28,1 (72)
F	Developing mathematical communication skills	0,8 (2)	19,8 (51)	51,9 (134)	27,5 (71)
G	Developing problem-solving ability	0,8 (2)	14,8 (38)	50,6 (130)	33,9 (87)

All the items, except for Item E, received a similar response. From a race perspective, black and coloured student teachers felt confident to teach this item, as opposed to 2% of white and 0.4% of Indian student teachers.

4.6.2   PGCE: Language

Table 4.22   Confidence to Teach Language – Q1 Teacher Motivation and Beliefs (PGCE)

Item	Confidence to teach language	Not at all % (n)	Somewhat confident % (n)	Confident % (n)	Very confident % (n)
A	Speaking	0 (0)	10,7 (6)	53,6 (30)	35,7 (20)
B	Listening with comprehension	0 (0)	14,5 (8)	41,8 (23)	43,6 (24)
C	Grammatical structures	0 (0)	19,6 (11)	44,6 (25)	35,7 (20)
D	Reading with comprehension	0 (0)	10,7 (6)	39,3 (22)	50 (28)
E	Writing	0 (0)	10,7 (6)	41,1 (23)	48,2 (27)

All the respondents felt a certain degree of confidence to teach all the language skills (see Table 4.22). No significant differences were found when stratifying these items according to race. An institutional comparison is not applicable as the questionnaire was administered at one institution only.

Table 4.23   Confidence to Teach Mathematics – Q1 Teacher Motivation and Beliefs (PGCE)

Item	Confidence to teach mathematics	Not at all % (n)	Somewhat confident % (n)	Confident % (n)	Very confident % (n)
A	Developing the correct use of basic terminology	0 (0)	0 (0)	66,7 (8)	33,3 (4)
B	Learning to investigate, analyse, represent and interpret mathematical information	0 (0)	8,3 (1)	50 (6)	41,7 (5)
C	Developing number concept, calculation and application skills	0 (0)	16,7 (2)	41,7 (5)	41,7 (5)
D	Recognising and using properties of operations	0 (0)	8,3 (1)	33,3 (4)	58,3 (7)
E	Learning rules and how to apply them	0 (0)	0 (0)	33,3 (4)	66,7 (8)
F	Developing mathematical communication skills	0 (0)	8,3 (1)	41,7 (5)	50 (6)
G	Developing problem-solving ability	0 (0)	0 (0)	33,3 (4)	66,7 (8)

Most respondents felt confident or very confident about developing the language skills (see Table 4.23). No significant differences were found when stratifying these items according to race. An institutional comparison is not applicable as only one institution was investigated.

4.7   Discussion

Teacher education in South Africa is a particularly challenging discursive space due to the pre-1994 political context (see Chapter 2). Segregation was enforced to such a degree that 24 years after democratisation, the conscious and unconscious prejudices that people hold remain evident in their ritualistic actions based on how they understand and interact with the world. Dewey (1916, cited by Dadvand 2015:77) regards schools as microcosms where the democratic ideals of society are reflected. The student teachers in both programmes agreed or strongly agreed (95% for both cohorts) that morality is the foundation of teaching (see Tables 4.1 and 4.2, Item D). Student teachers' views about whether teaching can only occur in a democratic environment were, however, more evenly spread. In the BEd programme, more white student teachers agreed with this statement than black, coloured and Indian student teachers. Student teachers from the two universities of technology tended to agree more with this statement than those from the traditional universities (see Table 4.1, Item J). Dadvand (2015:88) recorded similar contrasting findings with two student teachers who had different views from other participants, defining teaching as "a value-laden activity with political significance" and leaning towards beliefs favouring more democratic classroom environments through deliberation and power sharing. The responses to the prompt about teaching occurring only in democratic environments is also as a result how teaching and learning occurred in non-white spaces prior to 1994. Black, coloured, and Indian teachers and learners taught and learned in non-democratic spaces and although the environment was not ideal, acceptable levels of teaching and learning did occur. It is also important to note that the latter comment makes reference to context and not content.

The student teachers' beliefs about learners and their dispositions showed a difference, albeit small, in what student teachers from the BEd and PGCE programmes believed. BEd students, who were preparing to teach six- to nine-year-old children, believed that for these young children parental support was the most powerful determinant of a learner's success. PGCE students, who were preparing to teach learners older than 14, believed that a learner's success is attributed to learner perseverance.

With regard to teacher values, including reference to teacher competence and confidence, none of the student teachers listed teachers as important determinants of a learner's success. This could mean either that they do not see teachers as having agency to do so, or they believe teachers are there to facilitate what learners should know, but that the parents and the learners themselves are ultimately responsible for the learner's success.

With regard to beliefs about the act and activities of teaching, the two cohorts were divided on the statement that learners are empty vessels to be filled with teaching. In the BEd programme, black, coloured and Indian student teachers disagreed with the banking model,[1] whereas white student teachers agreed. In the PGCE programme, black and coloured student teachers disagreed, whereas Indian student teachers agreed more. A possible explanation could be the passive manner in which learners of colour were taught. The pre-1994 curriculum was much more prescriptive, with teacher-centred classroom environments. One of the huge developments made since 1994 in the curriculum discourse was to create learner-centred classrooms, which enabled a voice being given to a previously silenced cohort.

The qualitative responses in the interviews demonstrated that the ITE programmes at all the institutions have changed, and in some instances challenged student teachers' beliefs about teaching and becoming a teacher. This means that these programmes have the ability to shape and reshape student teachers' thinking, beliefs, and attitudes. The qualitative responses, moreover, suggested that in the absence of ITE interventions, student teachers may revert to traditional pedagogical practices that could or could not benefit learners.

---

1   The banking model is a term coined by Paulo Freire in *Pedagogy of the Oppressed* (1970). This model of education is a process where teachers 'deposit' information into students. Emphasis is on memorisation, as opposed to understanding. Teachers are the active drivers in the classroom and learners are passive.

In both programmes, student teachers' beliefs about mathematics very strongly supported problem-solving views of mathematics (see Table 4.10, Items D, F, I, and K). Ernest (1989) regards a problem-solving view of mathematics as the highest of three hierarchical levels of the three philosophies of mathematics as psychological systems of belief. Of concern, however, is that about two-thirds (68.8%) of the student teachers agreed or strongly agreed with an instrumental view of mathematics as a set of rules that have been worked out by experts (see Table 4.10, Item E) – a view contradictory to a problem-solving view and on the lowest hierarchical level. The questionnaire, however, did not require the student teachers to choose between the three views, but rather placed them alongside each other in separate items. The results may have been different if the student teachers were required to choose between the three views. Contradictory expressed beliefs were also reported in other studies (Verjovsky & Waldegg 2005; Snider & Roehl 2007; Cheng et al. 2009). The concern is that "these teachers may be learning the appropriate language of educational contexts and appropriating it without actually committing to these beliefs" (Fives et al. 2015:256). Fives et al (2015:262) state the necessity of helping teachers to understand their multiple and possibly contrasting beliefs, as well as the triggers "that evoke one belief or set of beliefs over another".

The student teachers in the PGCE programme felt much more confident to develop the specified mathematical skills in learners than the fourth-year BEd student teachers. This can possibly be attributed to PGCE student teachers having had more exposure to working through content, in a context where knowing content well is the requirement for successful completion of the qualification. The BEd programme focuses equally on education theories, PCK and CK – leaving less time to work through subject content. However, for the development of skills in languages there seems to be almost no difference in confidence between these two cohorts. Other researchers have also observed this kind of dichotomy between beliefs in different learning areas. Louca et al. (2004) noted that student teachers' general epistemological beliefs are different in structure and function from domain-specific beliefs about knowledge and knowing, while Buehl, Alexander and Murphy (2002) found that student teachers' beliefs about knowledge and knowing differ between domains.

With regard to beliefs about their own competence and confidence, the student teachers in the PGCE programme appeared more confident than those in the BEd programme. This can be attributed to the fact that PGCE student teachers have had more exposure to subject content when they specialised in a specific academic learning area prior to joining the ITE programme.

4.8 Limitations

The questionnaire administered to the participants prompted a wealth of items relating to student teachers' beliefs about teaching in general, about teaching mathematics and language, as well as their competence and confidence to teach. Although much more could have been said and more analyses could have been provided, this output has its limitations. It should also be noted that a different analytical mechanism could have added a different dimension to the data. However, given the large dataset, the analytical tools were sufficient to enrich the body of knowledge concerning beliefs about professional knowledge.

The assessment of teaching and learning beliefs through Likert-scales might not have been ideal. Fives et al. (2015:254) contend that teaching and learning beliefs in Likert-scale research "may collapse into a hierarchy of shared philosophies", which can cause the theoretical distinctions among beliefs within a single paradigm to not be well discernible and difficult to tease apart. However, semi-structured group interviews, which included open-ended questions, complemented the student teachers' self-reported beliefs and mitigated this problem.

It must also be mentioned that uneven race distribution between institutions and programmes also had an effect on the results that are presented here. In South Africa, there is a long-standing relationship between race and institution, and hopefully these themes will be discussed in follow-up publications and outputs relating to the data collected for this project.

4.9 Conclusion

The dynamic and complex relationship between student teachers' knowledge and beliefs complicates the conceptualisation and planning of ITE programmes. The development of knowledge and beliefs cannot be addressed in isolation, as Charalambous (2015:443) points out: "Knowledge and beliefs interact in informing teachers' behaviours, and therefore, both need to be targeted to equip teachers with the inclination and the toolkit needed for structuring mathematically rich environments." Borg and Al-Busaidi (2012:6) state that "teachers' beliefs can powerfully shape both what teachers do and consequently, the learning opportunity learners receive". Research-based teacher education programmes built on an understanding of where beliefs about teaching originate and how they can be intentionally challenged are therefore crucial to positively influence their practices. Mirroring this sentiment, if teachers' beliefs influence their teaching, and therefore their learners' opportunities to learn, then beliefs should be of fundamental concern for teaching and teacher education (Ammon & Levin 1993; Kagan 1992; Shulman 1986, cited in Levin 2015:49).

References

Abdi, H. & Asadi, B. 2015. A synopsis of researches on teachers' and students' beliefs about language learning. *International Journal on Studies in English Language and Literature*, 3(4): 104-114.

Abelson, R. 1979. Differences between belief systems and knowledge systems. *Cognitive Science*, 3(4): 355-366. https://doi.org/10.1207/s15516709cog0304_4

Ambrose, R. 2004. Initiating change in prospective elementary school teachers' orientations to mathematics teaching by building on beliefs. *Journal of Mathematics Teacher Education*, 7(2): 91-119. https://doi.org/10.1023/B:JMTE.0000021879.74957.63

Anderson, D. 2015. The nature and influence of teacher beliefs and knowledge on the science teaching practice of three generalist New Zealand primary teachers. *Research in Science Education*, 45(3): 395-423. https://doi.org/10.1007/s11165-014-9428-8

Ashton, P. 2015. Historical overview and theoretical perspectives of research on teachers' beliefs. In: H. Fives & M. Gill (eds). *International handbook of research on teacher beliefs*. New York: Routledge, 31-46.

Ball, D.L. 1988. Unlearning to teach mathematics. *For the Learning of Mathematics*, 8(1): 40-48.

Ball, D.L.; Thames, M.H. & Phelps, G. 2008. Content knowledge for teaching: What makes it special? *Journal of Teacher Education*, 59(5): 398-407.

Beswick, K. 2008. Influencing teachers' beliefs about teaching mathematics for numeracy to students with mathematics learning difficulties. *Mathematics Teacher Education and Development*, 9: 3-20.

Blömeke, S.; Hsieh, F-J.; Kaiser, G. & Schmidt, W. 2014. *International perspectives on teacher knowledge, beliefs and opportunities to learn: TEDS-M Results*. New York, NY: Springer. https://doi.org/10.1007/978-94-007-6437-8

Borg, S. & Al-Busaidi. 2012. *Learner Autonomy: English Language Teachers Beliefs and Practices*. British Council ELT Research Paper 12-07.

Bryan, L. 2012. Research on science teacher beliefs. In: B. Fraser, K. Tobin & C. McRobbie (eds). *Second international handbook of science education*. Dordrecht: Springer, 477-495. https://doi.org/10.1007/978-1-4020-9041-7_33

Buehl, M.; Alexander, P. & Murphy, P. 2002. Beliefs about schooled knowledge: Domain specific or domain general? *Contemporary Educational Psychology*, 27: 415-449. https://doi.org/10.1006/ceps.2001.1103

Cai, J. & Wang, T. 2010. Conceptions of effective mathematics teaching within a cultural context: Perspectives of teachers from China and the United States. *Journal of Mathematics Teacher Education*, 13(3): 265-287. https://doi.org/10.1007/s10857-009-9132-1

Calderhead, J. 1996. Teachers: Beliefs and knowledge. In: D. Berliner & R. Calfee (eds). *Handbook of educational psychology*. New York: Simon & Shuster, 709-725.

Carney, M.; Brendefur, J.; Hughes, G. & Thiede, K. 2015. Developing a mathematics instruction practice survey: Considerations and evidence. *Mathematics Teacher Educator*, 4(1): 93-118. https://doi.org/10.5951/mathteaceduc.4.1.0093

Carney, M.; Brendefur, J.L.; Thiede, K.; Hughes, G. & Sutton, J. 2016. Statewide mathematics professional development teacher knowledge, self-efficacy, and beliefs. *Educational Policy*, 30(4): 539-572. https://doi.org/10.1177/0895904814550075

Charalambous, C. 2015. Working at the intersection of teacher knowledge, teacher beliefs, and teaching practice: A multiple-case study. *Mathematics Teacher Education*, 18(5): 427-445. https://doi.org/10.1007/s10857-015-9318-7

Cheng, M.; Chan, K.; Tang, S. & Cheng, A. 2009. Pre-service teacher education students' epistemological beliefs and their conceptions of teaching. *Teaching and Teacher Education*, 25(2): 319-327. https://doi.org/10.1016/j.tate.2008.09.018

Cochran-Smith, M. & Lytle, S.L. 1999. Relationships of knowledge and practice: Teacher learning in communities. *Review of Research in Education*, 24: 249-305. https://doi.org/10.2307/1167272

Cross, D. 2009. Alignment, cohesion and change: Examining mathematics teachers' belief structure and its influence on instructional practice. *Journal of Mathematics Teacher Education*, 12(5): 325-346. https://doi.org/10.1007/s10857-009-9120-5

Cross Francis, D.; Rapacki, L. & Eker, A. 2015. The individual, the context, and practice: A review of the research on teachers' beliefs related to mathematics. In: H. Fives & M. Gill (eds). *International handbook of research on teacher beliefs*. New York: Routledge, 336-352.

Dadvand, B. 2015. Teaching for democracy: Towards an ecological understanding of pre-service teachers' beliefs. *Australian Journal of Teacher Education*, 40(5): 77-93. https://doi.org/10.14221/ajte.2015v40n2.6

DeBellis, V. & Goldin, G. 1997. The affective domain in mathematical problem solving. In: E. Pehkonen (ed.). *Proceedings of the 21st Annual Meeting of Psychology of Mathematics Education (PME)* (vol. 2). Lahti, Finland: University of Helsinki, 209-216.

De Corte, E.; Op't Eynde, P. & Verschaffel, L. 2002. Knowing what to believe: The relevance of students' mathematical beliefs for mathematics education. In: B. Hofer & P. Pintrich (eds). *Personal epistemology: The psychology of beliefs about knowledge and knowing*. Mahwah, NJ: Erlbaum, 297-320.

Department of Basic Education (DBE). 2015. *Minimum requirements for teacher education qualifications policy*. Pretoria: DBE.

Ermeling, B. & Graff-Ermeling, G. 2016. *Teaching better: Igniting and sustaining instructional improvement*. Thousand Oaks, CA: Sage Publications.

Ernest, P. 1989. The impact of beliefs on the teaching of mathematics. In: P. Ernest (ed.). *Mathematics teaching: The state of the art*. London: Falmer Press, 249-254.

Felbrich, A.; Kaiser, G. & Schmotz, C. 2014. The cultural dimension of beliefs: An investigation of future primary teachers' epistemological beliefs concerning the nature of mathematics in 15 countries: TEDS-M results. In: S. Blömeke, F. Hsieh, G. Kaiser & W. Schmidt (eds). *International perspectives on teacher knowledge, beliefs and opportunities to learn*. Dordrecht: Springer, 209-230. https://doi.org/10.1007/978-94-007-6437-8_10

Fenstermacher, G.D. 1994. The knower and the known: The nature of knowledge in research on teaching. *Review of Research in Education*, 20(1): 3-56. https://doi.org/10.3102/0091732X020001003

Fernandez, C. 2014. Knowledge base for teaching and pedagogical content knowledge (PCK): Some useful models and implications for teachers training. *Problems of Education in the 21st Century*, 60: 79-99.

Fives, H. & Buehl, M. 2010. Examining the factor structure of the teachers' sense of efficacy scale. *The Journal of Experimental Education*, 78(1): 118-134. https://doi.org/10.1080/00220970903224461

Fives, H. & Gill, M. 2015. Introduction. In: H. Fives & M. Gill (eds). *International handbook of research on teacher beliefs*. New York: Routledge, 1-10.

Fives, H.; Lacatena, N. & Gerard, L. 2015. Teachers' beliefs about teaching (and learning). In: H. Fives & M. Gill (eds). *International handbook of research on teacher beliefs*. New York: Routledge, 249-265.

Freire, P. 1970. *Pedagogy of the oppressed*. New York: Seabury Press. https://doi.org/10.5539/elt.v10n4p78

Gilakjani, A. & Sabouri, N. 2017. Teachers' beliefs in English language teaching and learning: A review of the literature. *English Language Teaching*, 10(4): 78-86.

Glass, M.; Kim, J.; Evens, M. & Michael, J. 1999. Novice vs. expert tutors: A comparison of style. In: *Proceedings of the Midwest Artificial Intelligence and Cognitive Science Conference 99*. Menlo Park: AAAI Press, 43-49.

Goldin, G. 2002. Affect, meta-affect, and mathematical belief structures. In: G. Leder, E. Phekonen & G. Törner (eds). *Beliefs: A hidden variable in mathematics education.* Dordrecht, The Netherlands: Kluwer, 59-72.

Goldin, G.; Hannula, M.S.; Heyd-Metzuyanim, E.; Jansen, A.; Kaasila, R.; Lutovac, S.; Di Martino, P.; Morselli, F.; Middleton, J.A.; Pantziara, M. & Zhang, Q. 2016. *Attitudes, beliefs, motivation and identity in mathematics education: An overview of the field and future directions.* New York: Springer Open.

Grossman, P.L. 1990. *The making of a teacher: Teacher knowledge and teacher education.* New York: Teachers College Press.

Hannula, M. 2004. *Affect in mathematical thinking and learning.* Finland: University of Turku.

Hativa, N.; Barak, R. & Simhi, E. 2001. Exemplary university teachers: Knowledge and beliefs regarding effective teaching dimensions and strategies. *Journal of Higher Education,* 72(6): 699-729. https://doi.org/10.2307/2672900

Hill, H.; Ball, D.L. & Schilling, S. 2008. Unpacking pedagogical content knowledge: Conceptualising and measuring teachers' topic-specific knowledge of students. *Journal for Research in Mathematics Education,* 39(4): 372-400.

Hodgen, J. & Askew, M. 2007. Emotion, identity and teacher learning: Becoming a primary mathematics teacher. *Oxford Review of Education,* 33(4): 469-487. https://doi.org/10.1080/03054980701451090

Kagan, D. 1992. Professional growth among pre-service and beginning teachers. *Review of Educational Research,* 62(2): 129-169. https://doi.org/10.3102/00346543062002129

Kassim, A. 2016. Perceptions of pre-service teachers in Foundation Phase mathematics about their professional development. PhD dissertation. Stellenbosch: Stellenbosch University.

Keswell, M. 2004. Education and racial inequality in post-apartheid South Africa. Working paper no. 2004-02-008. Santa Fe: Santa Fe Institute.

Kindsvatter, R.; Willen, W. & Isher, M. 1988. *Dynamics of effective teaching.* New York: Longman.

Kuzborska, I. 2011. Links between teachers' beliefs and practices and research on reading. *Reading in a Foreign Language,* 23(1): 102-128.

Lasley, T. 1980. Pre-service teacher beliefs about teaching. *Journal of Teacher Education,* 31(4): 38-41. https://doi.org/10.1177/002248718003100410

Leatham, K. 2006. Viewing mathematics teachers' beliefs as sensible systems. *Journal of Mathematics Teacher Education,* 9(2): 91-102. https://doi.org/10.1007/s10857-006-9006-8

Leder, G.; Pehkonen, E. & Törner, G. (eds). 2002. *Beliefs: A hidden variable in mathematics education.* Dordrecht: Kluwer. https://doi.org/10.1007/0-306-47958-3

Levin, B. 2015. The development of teachers' beliefs. In: H. Fives & M. Gill (eds). *International handbook of research on teacher beliefs.* New York: Routledge, 48-65.

Liljedahl, P. 2008. *Teachers' beliefs as teachers' knowledge.* Available at: https://www.unige.ch/math/EnsMath/Rome2008/WG2/Papers/LILJED.pdf

Llinares, S. 2002. Participation and reification in learning to teach: The role of knowledge and beliefs. In: G. Leder, E. Pehkonen & G. Törner (eds) *Beliefs: A hidden variable in mathematics education?* Dordrecht: Kluwer, 195-209.

Louca, L.; Elby, A.; Hammer, D. & Kagey, T. 2004. Epistemological resources: Applying a new epistemological framework to science instruction. *Educational Psychologist*, 39(1): 57-68. https://doi.org/10.1207/s15326985ep3901_6

Loughran, J. 2010. *What expert teachers do: Enhancing professional knowledge for classroom practice.* London: Routledge.

Lucas, T. & Grinberg, J. 2008. Responding to the linguistic reality of mainstream classrooms: Preparing all teachers to teach English language learners. In: M. Cochran-Smith, S. Feiman-Nemser & J. McIntyre (eds). *Handbook of research on teacher education: Enduring issues in changing contexts* (3rd ed.). Mahwah, NJ: Lawrence Erlbaum, 606-636.

Lucas, T. & Villegas, A.M. 2011. A framework for preparing linguistically responsive teachers. In: T. Lucas (ed.). *Teacher preparation for linguistically diverse classrooms: A resource for teacher educators.* New York, NY: Taylor & Francis, 55-72.

Lucas, T.; Villegas, A.M. & Martin, A.D. 2015. Teachers' beliefs about English language learners. In: H. Fives & M. Gregorie Gill (eds). *International handbook of research on teachers' beliefs.* New York, NY: Routledge, 453-474.

MacLeod, G. & Cebula, K.R. 2009. Experiences of disabled students in initial teacher education. *Cambridge Journal of Education*, 39(4): 457-472. https://doi.org/10.1080/03057640903352465

MacNab, D. & Payne, F. 2003. Beliefs, attitudes and practices in mathematics teaching: Perceptions of Scottish primary school student teachers. *Journal of Education for Teaching*, 29(1): 55-68. https://doi.org/10.1080/0260747022000057927

Millsaps, G. 2000. Secondary mathematics teachers' mathematics autobiographies: Definitions of mathematics and beliefs about mathematics instructional practice. *Focus on Learning Problems in Mathematics*, 22(1): 45-67.

Mosvold, R. & Fauskanger, J. 2013. Teachers' beliefs about mathematical knowledge for teaching definitions. *International Electronic Journal of Mathematics Education*, 8(2-3): 43-61.

Nespor, J. 1987. The role of beliefs in the practice of teaching. *Journal of Curriculum Studies*, 19(4): 317-328. https://doi.org/10.1080/0022027870190403

Nicholas, H.; Ng, W. & Williams, A. 2010. School experience influences on pre-service teachers' evolving beliefs about effective teaching. *Teaching and Teacher Education*, 26(2): 278-289. https://doi.org/10.1016/j.tate.2009.03.010

Northcote, M. 2009. Educational beliefs of higher education teachers and students: Implications for teacher education. *Australian Journal of Teacher Education*, 34(3). Available at: https://ro.ecu.edu.au/ajte/vol34/iss3/3/ https://doi.org/10.14221/ajte.2009v34n3.3

Norton, L.; Richardson, T.; Hartley, J.; Newstead, S. & Mayes, J. 2005. Teachers' beliefs and intentions concerning teaching in higher education. *Higher Education*, 50(4): 537-571. https://doi.org/10.1007/s10734-004-6363-z

Op't Eynde, P.; De Corte, E. & Verschaffel, L. 2002. Framing students' mathematics related beliefs: A quest for conceptual clarity and a comprehensive categorization. In: G. Leder, E. Pehkonen & G. Törner (eds). *Beliefs: A hidden variable in mathematics education.* Boston, MA: Kluwer Academic Publishing, 13-38. https://doi.org/10.1007/0-306-47958-3_2

Pajares, M. 1992. Teachers' beliefs and educational research: Cleaning up a messy construct. *Review of Educational Research*, 62(3): 307-332. https://doi.org/10.3102/00346543062003307

Perry, B.; Way, J.; Southwell, B.; White, A. & Pattison, J. 2005. Mathematical beliefs and achievement of pre-service primary teachers. In: P. Clarkson, A. Downton, D. Gronn, M. Horne, A. McDonough, R. Pierce, & A. Roche (eds). *Building connections: Research, theory and practice – Proceedings of the 28th annual conference of the Mathematics Education Research Group of Australasia* (vol. 2). Sydney: MERGA, 625-632.

Philipp, R. 2007. Mathematics teachers' beliefs and affect. In: F. Lester (ed.). *Second handbook of research on mathematics teaching and learning*. Charlotte: Information Age Publishing, 257-315.

Putnam, R. & Borko, H. 2000. What do new views of knowledge and thinking have to say about research on teacher learning? *Educational Researcher*, 29(1): 4-15. https://doi.org/10.3102/0013189X029001004

Reddy, T. 2004. *Higher education and social transformation: South Africa case study*. Pretoria: Council on Higher Education (CHE).

Richardson, V. 1996. The role of attitudes and beliefs in learning to teach. In: J. Sikula (ed.). *Handbook of research on teacher education* (2nd ed.). New York: Macmillan, 102-119.

Rokeach, M. 1968. *Beliefs, attitudes, and values: A theory of organization and change*. San Francisco: Jossey-Bass.

Sanger, M. & Osguthorpe, R. 2011. Teacher education, pre-service teacher beliefs and the moral work of teaching. *Teaching and Teacher Education*, 27(3): 569-578. https://doi.org/10.1016/j.tate.2010.10.011

Sayed, Y. & Badroodien, A. 2016. Teachers and social cohesion in diverse contexts in the Global South. *Education as Change*, 20(3): 15-37. https://doi.org/10.17159/1947-9417/2016/1975

Schoenfeld, A. 1992. Learning to think mathematically: Problem solving, metacognition, and sense making in mathematics. In: D. Grouws (ed.). *Handbook for research on mathematics teaching and learning*. New York: Macmillan, 334-370.

Schoenfeld, A. 1998. Toward a theory of teaching-in-context. *Issues in Education*, 4(1): 1-94. https://doi.org/10.1016/S1080-9724(99)80076-7

Schommer-Aikins, M.; Duell, O. & Hutter, R. 2005. Epistemological beliefs, mathematical problem-solving beliefs, and academic performance of middle school students. *The Elementary School Journal*, 105(3): 289-304. https://doi.org/10.1086/428745

Shulman, L. 1986. Those who understand: Knowledge growth in teaching. *Educational Researcher*, Vol 15(2): 4-14. https://doi.org/10.3102/0013189X015002004

Shulman, L. 1987. Knowledge and teaching: Foundations of the new reform. *Harvard Educational Review*, 57(1): 1-22. https://doi.org/10.17763/haer.57.1.j463w79r56455411

Skott, J. 2001. The emerging practices of novice teachers: The roles of his school mathematics images. *Journal of Mathematics Teacher Education*, 4(1): 3-28. https://doi.org/10.1023/A:1009978831627

Skott, J. 2015. The promises, problems and prospects of research on teachers' beliefs. In: H. Fives & M. Gill (eds). *International handbook of research on teacher beliefs*. New York: Routledge, 13-30.

Snider, V. & Roehl, R. 2007. Teachers' beliefs about pedagogy and related issues. *Psychology in the Schools*, 44(8): 873-886. https://doi.org/10.1002/pits.20272

Speer, N. 2005. Issues of methods and theory in the study of mathematics teachers' professed and attributed beliefs. *Educational Studies in Mathematics*, 58: 361-391. https://doi.org/10.1007/s10649-005-2745-0

Stigler, J. & Hiebert, J. 1998. Teaching is a cultural activity. *American Educator*, 22(4): 4-11.

Stipek, D.; Givvin, K.; Salmon, J. & MacGyvers, V. 2001. Teacher's beliefs and practices related to mathematics instruction. *Teaching and Teacher Education*, 17(2): 213-226. https://doi.org/10.1016/S0742-051X(00)00052-4

Tan, L.; Bopry, J. & Libo, G. 2010. Portraits of new literacies in two Singapore classrooms. *RELC Journal*, 41(1): 5-17. https://doi.org/10.1177/0033688210343864

Taylor, N. 2016. Thinking, language and learning in initial teacher education. *Perspectives in Education*, 34(1): 10-26. https://doi.org/10.18820/2519593X/pie.v34i1.2

Uusimaki, L. & Nason, R. 2004. Causes underlying pre-service teachers' negative beliefs and anxieties about mathematics. In: M.J. Hoines & A.B. Fuglestad (eds). *Proceedings of the 28th Annual Conference for the Psychology of Mathematics Education (PME)*. Cape Town: International Group for the Psychology of Mathematics Education, 369-376. Available at: https://eric.ed.gov/?id=ED489178.

Verjovsky, J. & Waldegg, G. 2005. Analyzing beliefs and practices of a Mexican high school biology teacher. *Journal of Research in Science Teaching*, 42(4): 465-491. https://doi.org/10.1002/tea.20059

Wilcox, S.; Lanier, P.; Schram, P. & Lappan, G. 1992. *Influencing beginning teachers' practice in mathematics education: Confronting constraints of knowledge, beliefs, and context*. East Lansing, East Michigan: Ericson Flail.

Wilson, M. & Cooney, T. 2002. Mathematics teacher change and development: The role of beliefs. In: G. Leder, E. Pehkonen & G. Törner (eds). *Beliefs: A hidden variable in mathematics education?* Dordrecht: Kluwer, 127-147.

Winch, C.; Oancea, A.E. & Orchard, J. 2013. *The contribution of educational research to teachers' professional learning – Philosophical understandings*. London: BERA.

Wong, N.; Ding, R. & Zhang, Q. 2016. From classroom environment to conception of mathematics. In: R. King & A. Bernardo (eds). *The psychology of Asian learners*. Singapore: Springer, 541-557. https://doi.org/10.1007/978-981-287-576-1_33

Woolfolk-Hoy, A.; Davis, H. & Pape, S. 2006. Teacher knowledge and beliefs. In: P. Alexander & P. Winne (eds). *Handbook of educational psychology* (2nd ed.). New York: Routledge, 715-737.

Zheng, H. 2015. *Teacher beliefs as a complex system: English language teachers in China*. New York: Springer. https://doi.org/10.1007/978-3-319-23009-2

Chapter 05

Ways of Knowing: Developing Professional Knowledge of Foundation Phase Student Teachers

Rada Jancic Mogliacci, Maureen Robinson & Nicoline Rousseau

5.1   Introduction

This chapter explores the perceptions of BEd Foundation Phase student teachers of the 'professional knowledge for teaching' that they gained in their ITE programmes. The Foundation Phase programme prepares student teachers to teach Grades R-3 at schools. The chapter draws on data from three Foundation Phase teacher education programmes in South Africa, referred to in the chapter as Institutions A, B and C. It explores the experiences of student teachers of the content of their programmes and the extent to which they believe this content aids them in their teaching experiences. Epistemological issues related to what constitutes professional knowledge and what kind of knowledge is needed for professional teaching practice, are also addressed.

The starting premise of the chapter is that teacher professional knowledge is a complex construction (Adoniou 2014), with many understandings of what constitutes teacher professional knowledge. These include PCK (Shulman 1987), tacit pedagogical knowledge (Toom 2006), SMK (Shulman 1987) and personal practical knowledge (Clandinin 2013). This chapter asserts that one way of understanding teacher knowledge is through the formation of a didactic triangle between teacher, learner and content (Kansenen & Meri 1999); a triangle that pulls together various forms of knowledge, which include (i) knowledge of the content (subject matter and the curriculum), (ii) knowledge about the learners, (iii) pedagogical approaches, (iv) knowledge about teaching and learning and (v) knowledge about the professional self (teaching profession). These are similarly outlined in the MRTEQ policy (DHET 2015), which emphasises some of the key complexities tied to teacher professional knowledge (cf. Chapter 2).

This chapter works from the premise that teacher professional agency (Toom, Pietarinen, Soini & Pyhältö 2017) is an important condition for the ongoing development of teacher professional knowledge. Agency, we argue, contributes to how teacher professional knowledge is developed and deployed. In light of the many concerns that have been expressed about the quality of teaching and teacher education in South Africa (Sayed & Ahmed 2011; Gravett 2012; Schäfer & Wilmot 2012), new teachers and their knowledge are essential in building an improved state of education in the country. We argue that it is in the capacity of teachers to recognise themselves as initiators of – or responsible for – action (or non-action) within the education system that teacher professional knowledge can best be developed.

This expected responsibility to act as agents of change is foregrounded in national policy for the MRTEQ policy, which argues that a key function of teacher education programmes is to address the challenges of education in South Africa by focusing on

> the poor content and conceptual knowledge found among teachers as well as the legacies of apartheid by incorporating situational and contextual elements that assist teachers in developing competences that enable them to deal with diversity and transformation (DHET 2015:8).

In the framework described in Chapter 1, an integration of the three knowledge sets would translate into professional knowledge for teaching.

In this chapter we tease out teacher professional knowledge along the above lines, exploring how different aspects of teacher professional knowledge are expressed within the views of student teachers. The chapter concludes with a discussion of key findings from the study, as well as their implications for teacher education programmes.

5.2 Debates in the Literature

This section explores conceptions of student teachers' professional knowledge for teaching. The section considers what professional knowledge for teaching might entail, as well as the role of teacher education in the development of such knowledge. The framework developed in this section is drawn on in later sections to analyse student teachers' views of their professional knowledge gained at university and in schools during teaching practice.

ITE internationally and in South Africa, aims to equip student teachers with sufficient knowledge that will enable them to provide high-quality teaching. Studies demonstrate, however, that student teachers develop understanding of teachers' work and what knowledge teachers should acquire, from previous teachers, teaching and learning experience (Lortie 1975), personal biographies (see e.g. Miller & Shifflet 2016) and beliefs about knowledge, teaching and learning (Brownlee et al. 1998). Here the main focus is on student teachers' experience of developing teacher professional knowledge with specific regard to teacher education programmes. Further research might explore how previous teachers, personal biographies and/or beliefs about knowledge have influenced the development of their views on teacher professional knowledge.

Various categorisations of professional knowledge for teaching have been put forward in the literature (Fenstermacher 1994; Cochran-Smith & Lytle 1999; Wilson & Berne 1999; Beijaard, Verloop & Vermunt 2000; Dickson 2007). A useful overview, as provided by Capel, Leask and Turner (2013:15), was given in the introductory chapter of this book. It is mainly an adaptation of Shulman's (1987) description of forms of professional knowledge for teaching.

The complexity of teacher professional knowledge is recognised in the MRTEQ policy, which identifies different types of knowledge associated with the acquisition, integration, and application of knowledge for teaching purposes. For the prospective teacher, the MRTEQ policy thus promotes disciplinary learning, pedagogical learning, practical learning, fundamental learning and situational learning (DHET 2015).

Adoniou (2014) suggests the analytic categories of "knowing what, knowing why, and knowing how" as an overlay to the categorisations of teacher professional knowledge. For every aspect of teaching, teachers would need to ask questions about what they are doing, why they doing what they are doing, and how they might carry out the work of teaching. Each of these knowledge discourses (knowing what, how, and why), Adoniou (2014:113) argues, is important: "Combined, they contribute to deep understanding, with the intersection of the three representing the optimum teacher knowledge". The challenge for those who prepare and support prospective teachers, she continues, "is how to develop all three 'ways of knowing' across the multiple knowledge domains" (Adoniou 2014:113).

How prospective teachers' experiences relate to the three ways of knowing is thus commensurate to gaining an understanding of the development of their teacher professional knowledge.

This chapter draws on these intersecting ways on knowing to analyse the questionnaires and focus group discussions with student teachers in the BEd Foundation Phase at the selected universities.

It considers if and how student teachers identify the various ways of knowing associated with teacher professional knowledge.

In doing so, the focus is on three aspects of the teacher education programme: the teaching of mathematics, the teaching of language and the school-based practicum, with the emphasis on the latter. In our own experience as teacher educators and as evidenced from the data of this study, the practicum is often referred to by student teachers as the most influential aspect of their teacher preparation. It is here, they say, that they have the opportunity to learn about 'reality', where they gain 'experience', and where they move away from 'theory' to finally understand 'practice'. This may also be articulated where they move from 'knowing what to knowing how'. It is this tension that has influenced teacher education policy in, for example the UK, where schools have been given a more extended role in teacher education (McNamara, Murray & Phillips 2017).

Despite the strong arguments for more school-based work in teacher education, authors like Russell (1993:207) contest the assumption that learning from experience is simple or straightforward. Rather, he argues, "experience often leads to ritual knowledge rather than the desired understanding of principles", thus undermining the kind of deep learning that can endure over time and in different scenarios. As he puts it:

> The issue is not whether teacher education is better situated in universities or in schools. Both settings are rich in pedagogical practices rooted in ritual rather than principle. The challenge is to develop strategies for learning from experience and developing principled understanding of the phenomena of teaching. Then theory and research could contribute to practice rather than provide further criticism of practice, criticism that easily leads not to improvements but to maintaining society's undervaluing of the professional knowledge of teachers and teacher educators (Russell 1993:214).

This chapter highlights the ways in which student teachers in this study talk about the practicum, showing how, in their view, the practicum contributes to their own professional learning. We consider the extent to which student teachers feel that their experience in schools complements or contradicts the 'theoretical' learning at the university, and explore what tensions, if any, they experience as they move between university and school. In particular, we are interested in how the development of their professional knowledge is supported or constrained by the school-based experience.

Thus far we have outlined various ways in which professional knowledge is explored in the teacher education literature, as well as in South African policy. We introduce here a further important concept, namely that of 'professional agency'. We argue that a sense of agency is needed if new teachers are to actively locate themselves at the centre of improving the quality of education in the country.

South Africa displays high levels of inequality in the conditions of schooling for learners across the social spectrum and teachers are often expected to compensate for poor family and community support systems for children. Under such circumstances, teachers need more than knowledge of their subject or knowledge of their learners – rather they need to develop the capacity to actively engage in improving the life chances of these learners. This is where the notion of professional agency becomes relevant. As Toom et al. (2017:126) explain: "[P]rofessional agency is an integrated concept comprising teacher's cognitive, motivational, and attitudinal resources as well as skills and abilities to promote and manage learning in multiple professional contexts."

Our interest in the notion of professional agency arises from the view that "self-knowledge and a sense of agency with the intent of purposefully negotiating personal and professional contexts may be as important, if not more important, than the more traditional conceptions of professional knowledge" (Fairbanks, Duffy, Faircloth, He, Levin, Rohr & Stein 2010:167). Fairbanks et al. argue that there are many new teachers who, even when technically competent, are "not particularly responsive to students or situations, despite our best intentions and our belief that it is such responsiveness that constitutes thoughtful teaching and lies at the centre of teacher effectiveness" (2010:161). According to Fairbanks et al. (2010), self-knowledge and agency are critical factors for thoughtful teaching beyond other forms of professional knowledge. These terms imply

> awareness of one's beliefs and theories about teaching and learning, a vision to guide practice, a sense of belonging to and a stake in the professional community, and ways of imagining and enacting identities consistent with the visions and beliefs they have constructed from knowledge and experience (Fairbanks et al. 2010:167).

For teacher education, this implies a pedagogy that promotes – in various ways – a thoughtful relationship between knowledge domains and practical experience, with critical reflection as a means towards developing professional agency. Examples here include helping student teachers to appreciate the difference between ritual and principled knowledge, learning to work with diversity as a norm and understanding (as the student teachers in this study seemed to do) that there are multiple influences that impact teaching and learning. In pedagogical terms, this can take the form of guided reflection, where concrete examples from the real classroom serve as a basis for student teachers to explore their personal theories of learning, as well as to extract core ideas and principles of teaching and learning (Gravett 2012). A coherent vision and collaborative energy among teacher educators themselves are important underpinning elements of developing the kind of knowledge mix that can advance a responsive teacher education curriculum (Rousseau 2014). The conceptual framework developed in this chapter adds to the third knowledge set described in Chapter 1. Professional agency is critical to forging the affective dimensions for a social justice agenda within education as teacher education articulates a coherent vision and collaborative energy so they could imbibe in student teachers a collective professional agency that could transform education to engender social justice.

Our interest is thus also to explore how student teachers in this study talk about their opportunities to deploy and develop agency, both during the university-based and school-based components of their training. We identify how student teachers experience the pedagogical practices of the teacher education programme, as well as the affordances and constraints offered by the school during the practicum We also seek to understand the ways in which these interrelate with the development of their professional knowledge as prospective Foundation Phase teachers in South African schools.

5.3 Methodology

> How teachers think about their work and how teachers develop personal and practical knowledge in their professional activities can be studied in many ways (Russell 1993:206).

The data for this chapter were obtained from the fourth-year students of the BEd Foundation Phase programmes at four sites of teacher education in South Africa. Eleven focus group interviews of seven to nine participants each were conducted; six in May 2016 and five in November 2016.

The focus group interviews explored student teachers' views of their preparation for teaching and the strengths, gaps and challenges of their programme, particularly in relation to the teaching of Foundation Phase mathematics and language.

Three sets of questionnaires were administered to student teachers in the Foundation Phase programme as well. The first questionnaire explored student teachers' motivation and beliefs (completed by 259 respondents). The second questionnaire explored perceptions of knowledge and PCK development (completed by 224 respondents). The third questionnaire explored experiences of the teaching practicum (completed by 243 respondents). This chapter presents findings from Sections 4 and 5 of the first questionnaire (student teachers' beliefs about language and teaching language in the Foundation Phase, and beliefs about mathematics and teaching mathematics in the Foundation Phase), as well as the full set of responses to the second and third questionnaires. Thematic analysis was used to categorise the main findings of both the focus group interviews and the questionnaires.

5.4 Analysis of Findings

Although the focus groups and questionnaires represented four different campuses and three different BEd Foundation Phase programmes, the perceptions and beliefs of student teachers about the professional knowledge gained through their programmes, were remarkably similar. The data are thus presented according to the main thematic trends. A summary of the findings is as follows:

- ✓ Student teachers' sense of their preparedness to teach was reflected through their perception of their: (i) CK, (ii) ability to teach in multilingual and multicultural environments, (iii) assessment techniques and skills, and (iv) knowledge gained through participation in extra classroom activities during teaching practice.
- ✓ The participants provided somewhat of a mixed message regarding their readiness to teach. On the one hand, they indicated that they were confident about their preparedness to teach, particularly regarding CK. On the other hand, they indicated a lack of confidence arising from perceived gaps between teacher education programmes and the realities of the school context (a gap between what and how).
- ✓ Assessment techniques and skills and working with diversity (in particular with multilingualism in the classroom) were highlighted as areas of concern.
- ✓ Student teachers displayed a growing awareness that teaching and learning are more complex than they had initially thought.
- ✓ There was a growing frustration with what they perceived as the potential of schools to stifle innovation.
- ✓ They did not have a strong sense of professional agency and perceived a range of factors other than the teacher as contributing to learner success.

The general finding was that the participants believed their programmes to have prepared them well. In a focus group at Institution A, one of the student teachers expressed the belief that since they specialised in Foundation Phase, "I believe I can teach whatever" (FG, BEd, Inst. A 2016). The other student teachers in this group confirmed this perception when they indicated that they can assist student teachers who did a more general course since they specialised in Foundation Phase. Their confidence in their programme was further confirmed:

> I think I will be able to know everything [....] Schools suppose we know everything (FG, BEd, Inst. A 2016).

The questionnaires showed that the student teachers agreed and disagreed in all the "right" places regarding the teaching of CK and felt rather well prepared to teach all aspects of the content and develop the relevant skills. Even though student teachers expressed that they felt prepared to teach many aspects of the (pedagogical) content knowledge, they still stated that they require some additional development in order to be able to teach those aspects of (pedagogical) content knowledge that were identified as taught. For example, 88,6% of the student teachers indicated that they were taught how to develop the correct use of basic terminology in teaching mathematics (see Table 5.1), yet 64,8% of them thought that they needed additional knowledge in teaching the use of basic terminology (see Table 5.2).

Table 5.1 Do You Develop The Following Mathematical Knowledge and Skill in Learners: The Correct use of Basic Terminology

	Response	Frequency	Percentage (%)
Valid	Not at all	3	1,4
	Somewhat	22	10
	Moderately	97	44,3
	Totally	97	44,3

Q2 = Teacher Knowledge
N = 224; missing = 5; % = percentage of total valid responses

Table 5.2 Do You Require Additional Development to Teach the Following Mathematical Knowledge Skills to Learners: The Correct Use of Basic Terminology

	Response	Frequency	Percentage (%)
Valid	Not at all	29	13,4
	Somewhat	47	21,8
	Moderately	80	37
	Totally	60	27,8

Q2 = Teacher knowledge
N=224; missing = 8; % = percentage of total valid responses

The focus groups in Institution B referred to their training as more 'hands-on' and therefore better than, for example, the BEd Intermediate Phase programme, which prepares students for Grades 4 to 7 (FG, BEd, Inst. B 2016). They claimed that their programme has a good reputation and one of the student teachers in this group declared, "I have all the theoretical knowledge behind me" (FG, BEd, Inst. B 2016). A focus group respondent in Institution C expressed a similar view when stating that they can prepare their own lessons, "control" learners and can manage time and the classroom as a whole (FG, BEd, Inst. C 2016). Their confidence seemed to be predominantly based on knowing 'what' and 'how' to teach.

There was a perception that Foundation Phase teacher education is in some ways 'superior' to programmes for other phases of schooling:

> [I] think compared to the Intermediate and Senior phases, I think if they – no offence but – if you just look at the Foundation Phase [...] it is really good (FG, BEd, Inst. A 2016).

The interviews held later in the year, however, reflected a slight shift with regard to the participants' confidence in their preparedness to teach. It is significant that these interviews followed a second extended period of teaching experience in schools and also took them closer to graduation.

Assessment seemed to be the most challenging aspect that student teachers encountered during their practicum. Even though in Questionnaire 2, three-quarters of student teachers (75,9%) agreed that learning about assessment was useful (see Table 5.3), in Questionnaire 3, which explored their experience of the teaching practicum, assessment was identified as a problematic area. Similarly, a quarter of the participants said that they did not learn how to use or report assessment results.

In addition, more than a half of the student teachers only partially, if at all, learned how to train learners to conduct self-assessment (see Table 5.4). As a consequence, in teaching language, 21,3% claimed not to have knowledge and skills to develop assessment (see Table 5.5). Similar results were obtained for teaching mathematics. Almost a quarter of the student teachers (22,1%) indicated not learning at all how to develop assessment (see Table 5.6). Nevertheless, in the self-rating, the student teachers claimed that they were able to assess learners in reliable and varied ways (85,5%), displaying a confidence that was reiterated in the focus groups.

On the one hand, it appeared that student teachers felt very confident about learning to identify learners' strengths and weakness and provide feedback. On the other hand, they identified some of its constituents as problematic, such as 'learning to develop assessments', which was identified as weak in their knowledge (52,3%).

Table 5.3   Learners' Assessment

	Response	Frequency	Percentage (%)
	Not at all	6	3
Valid	Somewhat useful	26	12,9
	Useful	71	35,1
	Very useful	99	49

Q2 – Teaching knowledge
N=224; Missing = 22; % = percentage of total valid responses

Table 5.4   To What Extent Have You Learned about the Following during Teaching Practice: Learned to Train Learners to Conduct Self-assessment

	Response	Frequency	Percentage (%)
	Not at all	49	20,6
Valid	To some extent	85	35,7
	To a large extent	79	33,2
	Completely	25	10,5

Q3 – Teaching practice
N=243; Missing = 5; % = % of total valid responses

Table 5.5   Knowledge and Skills in Assessing Language: Learned to Develop Assessments

	Response	Frequency	Percentage (%)
Valid	Not at all	51	21,3
	To some extent	93	38,9
	To a large extent	73	30,5
	Completely	22	9,2

Q3 – Teaching practice
N=243; Missing = 4; % = percentage of total valid responses

Table 5.6   Knowledge and Skills Gained in Assessing Mathematics: Learned to Develop Assessments

	Response	Frequency	Percentage (%)
Valid	Not at all	52	22,1
	To some extent	85	36,2
	To a large extent	77	32,8
	Completely	21	8,9

Q3 – Teaching practice
N=243; Missing = 8; % = percentage of total valid responses

The lack of confidence expressed during the focus group interviews later in the year seemed to have been caused predominantly by a growing frustration about what the student teachers perceived as the gaps between university training and school reality. The student teachers, however, were not consistent in where they placed the blame for their uncertainty. Students of Institution C mentioned their need for more "how" and complained about "too much theory", while other students in the same programme and focus group blamed teachers for "teaching for assessment" and "to keep the [provincial] Department [of Education] happy" (FG, BEd, Inst. C 2016).

The perception that school contexts represented the 'real world' was a recurring theme in the various focus groups. In Institution B, the focus group referred to "real work experience" while indicating that they now (in their final year) felt they "can face the real world" (FG, BEd, Inst. B 2016). This 'real world' was seen as practical in comparison to the 'theoretical world' of university. As one student put it: "Theoretical things can be found in books but practical things you have to practise" (FG, BEd, Inst. A 2016). A student teacher from Institution A admitted in the final interview to not knowing that there was "so much theory". She further said: "If university did not teach it, we wouldn't know since teachers just do" (FG, BEd, Inst. A 2016). At Institution B, a student teacher in the focus group felt that "lecturers do not see what actually happens in classrooms – it keeps us away from practical and the outside world" (FG, BEd, Inst. B 2016). The "real world", a student teacher from Institution B indicated in a focus group, is "faster" and "more challenging" – presumably a reference to the image of schooling as experienced within teacher education programme (FG, BEd, Inst. B 2016).

When the focus groups referred to the types of knowledge they felt they needed most, the discourse revolved in the main around procedural, everyday knowledge needed 'for' (what) and 'in' (how) practice. Issues mentioned in this regard included discipline, lesson plans, resources, preparing assessment reports, parent evenings, registers, how to administer Ritalin and step-by-step instructions to teach reading. Interestingly, despite this desire for more 'extra-classroom' experience, the questionnaires revealed that a fairly large percentage of the participants (36,4%) did not have an opportunity to participate in general administrative work during teaching practice (see Table 5.7).

Table 5.7   Activities Able to Participate in during Teaching Practice: General Administrative Work

	Response	Frequency	Percentage (%)
Valid	Yes	150	63,6
	No	86	36,4

Q3 = Teaching practice
N=243; missing = 7; % = percentage of total valid responses

The impression created was that participants seemed to long for a type of packaged ritual knowledge (Edwards & Mercer 1987) that would allow them to operationalise procedural knowledge in such a way that success is guaranteed in the diverse contexts of schooling. A focus group from Institution C indicated that they wanted more 'how'; one student added that she wants all her learners to pass with 100% in all their subjects (FG, BEd, Inst. C 2016). This might be a somewhat unrealistic expectation, although it does reflect a perceived emphasis on learners' results linked to teachers' accountability. In Institution E, the student teacher focus group agreed that even novice teachers teach for assessment since they fear weak results and therefore "trouble with the HoD" or they might "fall behind other teachers" (FG, BEd, Inst. C 2016). In Institution A, a student reiterated that they need more "how to", while doubting that the reading of academic articles can assist them at all: "You can't give a child an article" (FG, BEd, Inst. A 2016).

Despite the evidence that the student teachers in the focus groups were predominantly interested in short-term solutions for the practical problems they might encounter in the schools, there were also signs of a growing awareness that teaching and learning represent a complexity beyond the practical and procedural. Participants from Institution B regretted the time spent on subjects they "won't even be teaching in Foundation Phase"; they also indicated that they were learning "to broaden [their] thinking" (FG, BEd, Inst. B 2016). While they might understand mathematics, some students were uncertain how to transfer it to their learners and how to establish whether their learners would be able to retain the knowledge (FG, BEd, Inst. B 2016). Yet there was an awareness that some knowledge can only be gained through practice. A student teacher from Institution B mentioned that sometimes they got contradictory approaches from their lecturers but that they realised they could not just rely on "the one lecturer's way of doing" (FG, BEd, Inst. B 2016). While they believed they have "the right backing" (presumably their university training), they realised they also needed to do their own research and develop their own views through the course of their teaching careers (FG, BEd Inst. B 2016).

Careful guidance and reflection on practice would be an important way for a student teacher to develop his or her own views of teaching. However, during teaching practice, 82,7% of all the participants substituted for a teacher that was other than their mentor teacher (see Table 5.8). This may raise many issues about teaching practice as a systematic and thoughtful activity supported by mentor teachers.

Table 5.8   Activities Able to Participate in during Teaching Practice: Substituting for a Teacher Other Than My Mentor Teacher

	Response	Frequency	Percentage (%)
Valid	Yes	196	82,7
	No	41	17,3

Q3 = Teaching practice
N=243; missing = 6; % = percentage of total valid responses

Another recurring theme was the participants' lack of confidence with regard to issues of diversity in schools. This is not surprising since diversity is a characteristic of many South African classrooms and the challenges it poses are well documented. In the first set of interviews, the participants referred to the difficulty of dealing with learners who are challenged in various ways and some teachers' inability to cope with this. A student from Institution C reported that she did not know how to cater for [name of learner] and continued: "If I had a broader knowledge of inclusive education and the skills and maybe the resources to be able to help..." (FG, BEd, Inst. C 2016). This perception became more pronounced in the second set of interviews towards the end of the year and after more time spent in schools. The student teachers in Institution C reported that they needed different strategies to cope with the diversity in the classrooms (FG, BEd, Inst. C 2016). A participant from Institution A confided that they have "files and files on language teaching strategies but each child is different" (FG, BEd, Inst. A 2016). The main areas of concern in this regard seemed to be mathematics and having learners in the classroom with languages other than the language of learning and teaching (LoLT) as their mother tongue.

When asked in the questionnaire to what extent they had learned about teaching in multilingual classrooms during their school-based teaching practice, the results are not clear. Although 60% of the student teachers claimed to have learned about teaching in multilingual classrooms to a large extent or completely, 38,9% of the respondents still indicated that they had not learned at all about teaching in multilingual classrooms or only to some extent (see Table 5.9).

Table 5.9   To What Extent Have You Learned about the Following during Teaching Practice?: Learned to Teach in Multilingual Classrooms

	Response	Frequency	Percentage (%)
Valid	Not at all	32	13,4
	To some extent	61	25,5
	To a large extent	94	39,3
	Completely	52	21,8

Q3 = Teaching practice
N=243; missing = 4; % = percentage of total valid responses

The uncertainty about how to cope with diversity contributed to previously indicated increasing realisation that education is more complex than originally thought. A participant from Institution A commented that her view of teaching has changed: "I thought it was simple but it is more complicated, especially with diversity" (FG, BEd, Inst. A 2016). Along with this insight came the realisation that a certain flexibility is necessary. The participants from Institution B came to the conclusion that the school curriculum (CAPS) itself needs to be more flexible. They pointed out that it needs to be more flexible in terms of cultural needs and that the time indications are not realistic.

The data seemed to suggest a shift in emphasis among the participants from perceiving the professional knowledge offered by university as 'not real enough' to a growing frustration with the realities of the school context. Some examples given were: Teachers were reported to leave because of pressure; teachers suppress creativity; there are too many administrative duties; teachers teach the curriculum instead of according to the needs of the learners; and children in top groups are not challenged. While student teachers know "the university way" can work, teachers are not willing for learners to try new things (FG, BEd, Inst. B 2016).

The participants indicated that they not only needed theory and practice and the strategies and methods, "but also how the brain works, how language is acquired, also the emotional side; we learn steps but not how learners learn language" (FG, BEd, Inst. A 2016). A participant in Institution A commented: "BEd has changed our beliefs – [it is] more complex than we thought; we thought it is about what you teach but now I know it is about the why you have to do things" (FG, BEd, Inst. A 2016). The participant further stated that they now look differently at children – not just superficially at their appearance. They have been taught about constructivism, learner-centredness and that learning can be fun. Some of the older teachers "don't understand why we're trying to do certain things and they can't understand me when I talk to them about constructivism" (FG, BEd, Inst. A 2016). Another participant summed up the problematics of the situation: "I feel prepared but uncertain if [I] can deal with all the challenges in school and if there will be support" (FG, BEd, Inst. A 2016).

We argued earlier that teacher professional agency is an essential element of teacher professional knowledge. The responses in the questionnaires, however, indicated that the participants in this study did not seem to recognise themselves as the most responsible agent for student learning. A large majority of the participants (79,9%) claimed that teachers are accountable for 'what' learners learn (see Table 5.10), yet the success of learning was ascribed to parental support (24,4%), home background (14,6%) and learner perseverance (14,2%). On the other hand, teacher-related items scored low; 7,9% of the student teachers ascribed the success of learners to teacher attention to learners' interests and 11,8% believed that teachers' use of teaching methods determined the success of learning. Teacher enthusiasm and perseverance each scored under 5% (see Table 5.11).

Table 5.10   Teachers are accountable for what learners learn

	Response	Frequency	Percentage (%)
Valid	Strongly disagree	1	0,4
	Disagree	41	16,5
	Agree	136	540,6
	Strongly agree	71	28,5

Q1 = Teaching motivation and beliefs
N=259; missing = 10; % = percentage of total valid responses

Table 5.11   Determinants of Learner Success

	Response	Frequency	Percentage (%)
Valid	Home background	37	14,6
	Intellectual ability	9	3,5
	Learner enthusiasm	33	13
	Learner perseverance	36	14,2
	Parental support	62	24,4
	Teacher attention to learner interest	20	7,9
	Teacher use of teaching methods	30	11,8
	Teacher enthusiasm	8	3,1
	Teacher perseverance	12	4,7
	Other	7	2,8

Q1 = Teaching motivation and beliefs
N=259; missing = 5; % = percentage of total valid responses

One interpretation of the responses is that how and why learners at school learn lies outside of the 'power' of teachers. The impression that learning was seen as something that happens because of the 'other' (learners' dispositions, parental involvement and socio-economic background). A clear notion of how transformation of 'what knowledge' happens in order to bring about learning, or the specific role of teachers in that process, is not strong. However, the respondents have not had the experience of teaching on a full-time basis. This may reflect their own experience of learning more than their experience of teaching. This perception could still affect the professional agency they bring to bear on the development of their professional knowledge.

5.5 Conclusion

This chapter sought to explore the perceptions of BEd Foundation Phase student teachers of the professional knowledge for teaching gained in their ITE programmes. Adoniou's (2014) analytical lens, which proposes three prongs of "knowing what, knowing why, and knowing how" for understanding professional development, was drawn on in the chapter to analyse student experiences. The three ways of knowing are not divorced from the many conceptualisations of teacher knowledge (Shulman 1987 and Capel et al. 2013); rather they seek to encapsulate them.

Data were drawn from three questionnaires and focus group interviews with BEd Foundation Phase student teachers at three HEIs in South Africa. The data presented indicated that the Foundation Phase student teachers expressed confidence that they had developed teacher professional knowledge during the teacher education programmes. At the same time, they recognised that their teacher professional knowledge was still evolving. In particular, the challenging context of the school environment seemed to present limits to the development of their professional knowledge.

Various examples of perceived constraints in the school setting were mentioned: the challenges of teaching a diversity of learners, the prescriptive nature of the school curriculum that is too focused on assessment and not sufficiently sensitive to cultural differences, the lack of support from mentors and the time spent on administrative and other extra-classroom duties. While the teacher education programmes encouraged a flexible approach focusing on the needs of the learners, the school context was seen to be more tightly structured and controlling. To the extent that teaching practice is embedded within teacher education programmes, the school experience frames student teachers' professional knowledge development and constrains their development of professional agency towards social justice. Data presented in this chapter thus suggest that schools are a barrier to the development of the third knowledge set, as sketched in Chapter 1. As such, schools appear to impede developing professional knowledge for teaching. What the data point to is that for teacher education programmes to improve, schools need to be adapted to professional knowledge funds (see Robinson 2014, 2015).

It would appear that the Foundation Phase student teachers in this study had mixed views about their sense of preparedness for teaching and learning in terms of professional knowledge gained in ITE programmes. The participants felt confident in the knowledge domains of SCK and general PCK, which they tended to see as 'given knowledge'. On the one hand, they indicated feeling mastery of certain aspects of professional knowledge, eliciting their ability to handle subject matter, manage the classroom, respond to individual learners' needs and transfer the knowledge to learners.

On the other hand, they also voiced doubt about handling surprising pedagogical moments in everyday teaching practice. It was in the application of knowledge in variable contexts that they hesitated and became overwhelmed. The conclusion can be drawn that, although the student teachers may feel confident with regard to their 'knowing what, why, and how', their experience of 'knowing how' is situation specific. As recourse, student teachers expected teacher education programmes to equip them better with ready-made, applicable and practical skills, and recipe-like pieces of advice to be used in classroom teaching. A desire for a more comprehensive professional knowledge repertoire is thus evident.

The participants realised towards the end of their teacher education programme that teaching and learning are complex issues. In doing so, Adoniou's (2014) comment that professional knowledge is a complex construction is confirmed. As such, the prospective teachers demonstrated professional agency in the development of their professional knowledge. The development of professional agency, we argue, does not lie only in the mastering of the different knowledge domains (although this aspect of learning to be a teacher is essential), but also in the development of an understanding of the dynamic relationship between knowledge domains, school contexts and the teacher's own sense of agency to act.

In their final interview, one of the participants in Institution A expressed a need for more focus on personal development and possible counselling support for students who are not coping. This suggestion may reflect an awareness of a reciprocal relationship between professional agency and context – a context in which the university, school, community and education department are recognised as equal partners. Such a relationship may assist in steering clear of unproductive dualities such as seeing theory and practice as opposing forces, thereby encouraging prospective and new teachers to see practical experience and ritual knowledge as safe options towards survival in the 'real world'. Furthermore, this relationship can establish a better understanding that practical experience is not simply an implementation of students' 'theoretical' knowledge where they test 'what works', but that school-based and university-based preparations are part of the comprehensive development of student teachers' professional knowledge. Finally, the comment also reflects a growing awareness that there is a need to take personal and collaborative responsibility', and to become active participants in the ongoing process of teacher professional knowledge development.

At the same time that the context of schooling is seen as a stumbling block in prospective teachers' minds, new teachers, who have so much to offer the country, may become disillusioned and demotivated if they are unable to develop the professional knowledge related to 'knowing how' in all situations. The long-term challenge for Foundation Phase teacher education is thus to identify the affordances of the learning environment at both school and university that promote or hinder the development of professional knowledge, which builds a personal vision of teaching that is not frustrated by the work environment, and in so doing, addressing all four contexts of learning to be a teacher (Adoniou 2013): the personal beliefs, university-based coursework, the practicum experiences and the first employment context.

References

Adoniou, M. 2013. Preparing teachers: The importance of connecting contexts in teacher education. *Australian Journal of Teacher Education*, 38(8): 46-60. https://doi.org/10.14221/ajte.2013v38n8.7

Adoniou, M. 2014. Teacher knowledge: A complex tapestry. *Asia-Pacific Journal of Teacher Education*, 43(2): 99-116. https://doi.org/10.1080/1359866X.2014.932330

Beijaard, D.; Verloop, N. & Vermunt, J.D. 2000. Teachers' perceptions of professional identity: An exploratory study from a personal knowledge perspective. *Teaching and Teacher Education*, 16(7): 749-764. https://doi.org/10.1016/S0742-051X(00)00023-8

Brownlee, J.; Dart, B.; Boulton-Lewis, G. & McCrindle, A. 1998. The integration of pre-service teachers' naive and informed beliefs about learning and teaching. *Asia-Pacific Journal of Teacher Education*, 26(2): 107-120. https://doi.org/10.1080/1359866980260203

Capel, S.A.; Leask, M. & Turner, T. (eds). 2013. *Learning to teach in the secondary school: A companion to school experience (6th ed.)*. Milton Park, Abingdon, Oxon: Routledge.

Clandinin, D.J. 2013. Personal practical knowledge: A study of teachers' classroom images. In: C.J. Craig, P.C. Meijer & J. Broeckmans (eds). *From teacher thinking to teachers and teaching: The evolution of a research community. (Advances in Research on Teaching Series, vol. 19)*. West Yorkshire: Emerald Group Publishing Limited, 67-95.

Cochran-Smith, M. & Lytle, S.L. 1999. Relationships of knowledge and practice: Teacher learning in communities. *Review of Research in Education*, 24: 249-305. https://doi.org/10.2307/1167272

Department of Higher Education and Training (DHET). 2015. National Qualifications Framework Act, 2008 (Act No. 67 of 2008): Revised Policy on the Minimum Requirements for Teacher Education Qualifications. *Government Gazette*, 38487, 19 February. Pretoria: Government Printer.

Dickson, B. 2007. Defining and interpreting professional knowledge in an age of performativity: A Scottish case study. *Australian Journal of Teacher Education*, 32(4): 1-15. https://doi.org/10.14221/ajte.2007v32n4.2

Edwards, D. & Mercer, N. 1987. *Common knowledge: The development of understanding in the classroom*. London: Methuen/Routledge.

Fairbanks, C.M.; Duffy, G.G.; Faircloth, B.S.; He, Y.; Levin, B.; Rohr, J. & Stein, C. 2010. Beyond knowledge: Exploring why some teachers are more thoughtfully adaptive than others. *Journal of Teacher Education*, 61(1-2): 161-171. https://doi.org/10.1177/0022487109347874

Fenstermacher, G.D. 1994. The place of practical argument in the education of teachers. In: V. Richardson (ed.). *Teacher change and the staff development process. A case in reading instruction*. New York: Teachers College Press, 23-42.

Gravett, S. 2012. Crossing the "theory-practice divide": Learning to be(come) a teacher. *South African Journal of Childhood Education*, 2(2):1-14. https://doi.org/10.4102/sajce.v2i2.9

Kansenen, P. & Meri, M. 1999. The didactic relation in the teaching-studying-learning process. *Didaktik/Fachdidaktik as Science(-s) of the Teaching Profession*, 2(1): 107-116.

Lortie, D.C. 1975. *School teacher: A sociological study*. Chicago: University of Chicago Press.

McNamara, O.; Murray, J. & Phillips, R. 2017. *Policy and research evidence in the 'reform' of primary initial teacher education in England*. York: Cambridge Primary Review Trust. Available at: https://cprtrust.org.uk/wp-content/uploads/2017/01/McNamara-report-170127.pdf

Miller, K. & Shifflet, R. 2016. How memories of school inform pre-service teachers' feared and desired selves as teachers. *Teaching and Teacher Education*, 53: 20-29. https://doi.org/10.1016/j.tate.2015.10.002

Robinson, M. 2014. Selecting teaching practice schools across social contexts: Conceptual and policy challenges. *South Africa Journal of Education for Teaching: International Research and Pedagogy*, 40(2): 114-127. https://doi.org/10.4102/sajce.v4i1.182

Robinson, M. 2015. *Teaching and learning together: The establishment of professional practice schools in South Africa*. A research report for the Department of Higher Education and Training. Stellenbosch: Stellenbosch University.

Rousseau, N. 2014. Integrating different forms of knowledge in the teaching qualification Diploma in Grade R Teaching. *South African Journal of Childhood Education*, 4(1): 167-186.

Russell, T. 1993. Teachers' professional knowledge and the future of teacher education. *Journal of Education for Teaching*, 19(4): 205-215. https://doi.org/10.1080/0260747930190418

Sayed, Y. & Ahmed, R. 2011. Education quality in post-apartheid South African policy: Balancing equity, diversity, rights and participation. *Comparative Education*, 47(1): 103-118. https://doi.org/10.1080/03050068.2011.541680

Schäfer, M. & Wilmot, D. 2012. Teacher education in post-apartheid South Africa: Navigating a way through competing state and global imperatives for change. *Prospects*, 42(1): 41-54. https://doi.org/10.1007/s11125-012-9220-3

Shulman, L. 1987. Knowledge and teaching: Foundations of the new reform. *Harvard Educational Review*, 57(1): 1-22. https://doi.org/10.17763/haer.57.1.j463w79r56455411

Toom, A. 2006. *Tacit pedagogical knowing at the core of teacher's professionality*. Research report 276. Finland: Faculty of Behavioural Sciences, University of Helsinki.

Toom, A.; Pietarinen, J.; Soini, T. & Pyhältö, K. 2017. How does the learning environment in teacher education cultivate first-year student teachers' sense of professional agency in the professional community? *Teaching and Teacher Education*, 63: 126-136. https://doi.org/10.1016/j.tate.2016.12.013

Wilson, S.M. & Berne, J. 1999. Teacher learning and the acquisition of professional knowledge: An examination of research on contemporary professional development. *Review of Research in Education*, 24: 173-209. https://doi.org/10.2307/1167270

Chapter 06

Developing Student Teachers' Professional Knowledge (Including Teaching Practice) in the Further Education & Training Phase

Trevor Moodley, Melanie Sadeck & Melanie Luckay

6.1 Introduction

Teacher professional knowledge is a complex construction, because teachers must know a great deal in multiple areas and in multiple ways (Adoniou 2014:99). Many have described the concept (Shulman 1987; Toom 2006; Gess-Newsome 2015) and have shown that there are many understandings of what teacher professional knowledge entails. ITE programmes at HEIs prepare pre-service teachers to develop professional knowledge at various levels, with the ultimate goal of preparing them to gain sufficient knowledge to enact high-quality teaching practice at schools.

This chapter discusses the perceptions of pre-service teachers in the Grades 10-12 PGCE FET programme at one HEI.

The PGCE FET programme trains subject specialists for Grades 8-10 teaching (CHE 2010). These students (ought to) have gained strong disciplinary and subject knowledge via their first degree – either through a BA, BSc or BCom degree – and are then expected to convert this knowledge to teaching capital (Verbeek 2014:40). Students are generally academically equipped with a deep disciplinary knowledge in at least one field of study through their first degree (Verbeek 2014:40). Moreover, it is assumed that the PGCE students have gained critical skills in their undergraduate degree; that is, they have learned to think critically, to find and access information and to study independently (Griesel & Parker 2009).

The focus of this chapter is to examine the development of professional knowledge of a group of PGCE FET pre-service teachers at one HEI. The student teachers, who have specialist disciplinary knowledge in two areas, namely English and Mathematics, were administered selected and structured survey questionnaires and focus group interviews were conducted with them.

The survey questions and focus group interviews investigated these PGCE students' perceptions of the content of the PGCE programme and whether it enhanced their professional knowledge development. Whether such professional knowledge development was reinforced in their teaching practice experiences was also investigated.

The sections that follow outline the theoretical position used in this chapter, which is an adapted version of Shulman's (1987; 1992) model for teacher professional knowledge. This is followed by a description of the mixed-methods approach used in the research with this group of PGCE student teachers, in which we describe the background of the student teachers and the context that influences their learning and teaching experiences. In the discussion, we draw on the data, both quantitative and qualitative, to analyse the student teachers' responses to the survey and their reflections in the interviews. In the conclusion, we discuss the implications of the data for the PGCE FET programme.

6.2 The PGCE Programme

The professional knowledge of the prospective teachers within the PGCE programme is developed through a structured teaching programme consisting of a variety of modules, some are compulsory core modules and others are elective modules. The compulsory modules are Education Theory, Language Communication (English, Afrikaans and African languages) and Education Practice modules. The PGCE students are offered two subject method specialisations. In order to qualify for admission to a subject method specialisation, the student must have successfully completed at least a second-year university-level course in that subject. Student teachers choose their subject method specialisations from selected teaching subjects that align with the MRTEQ policy and university list of approved subjects.

A core course within the one-year PGCE programme is the teaching practice component. Teaching practice is designed within a conceptually coherent and contextually responsive curriculum. Therefore the student teachers develop a theoretical lens through which to understand the ways in which structural and classroom practice may constrain as well as enhance learning (Rusznyak 2015:8). Within the course, knowledge is specifically selected to focus on theoretical, disciplinary and practical knowledge in order to give student teachers the conceptual tools to analyse the assumptions that constitute effective teaching and learning. Many student teachers enter the tertiary programme from largely dysfunctional schooling systems, where pervasive practices like insufficient engagement with conceptual knowledge and the use of corporal punishment could be considered normal in their practice (Fleisch 2007; Taylor, Van der Berg & Mabogoane 2013). The programme attempts to distantiate the student teachers from such practices.

The structure of the course allows the PGCE student teachers to spend a total of nine weeks at two schools (School A and School B). The student teachers complete a week of school and classroom observation during March and April (one week each) – two weeks in total. During the March teaching practice period, students will experience teaching practice at School A and during April they will experience teaching practice at School B for one week. From July to September, students spend seven weeks in School B. Students spend a longer period at School B to familiarise themselves with the school and to build relationships with both the learners and teachers during this time.

PGCE students are assessed four times during the teaching practice period. The university assigns a teaching practice supervisor and the school assigns a teaching practice mentor (one in each subject area). The teaching practice supervisor visits the student teachers and supports their development throughout the teaching practice period. After the assessment, the supervisor and mentor give the student teachers feedback on their teaching based on criteria set out by the university. Student teachers are familiarised with the assessment criteria during the Education Practice module lectures and the supervisors brief the student teachers on their school experience before they go to schools.

The aim of ITE is to extend the knowledge and experiences of the prospective teachers and to expand their repertoire of teaching-related skills. In order to effectively prepare pre-service teachers to teach, the ITE curriculum should ideally include experiences in all the domains. The extent of inclusion, although somewhat prescribed in policy (MRTEQ 2015), is largely determined by the individual Teacher Education Institutions. Hofmeyer and Hall (1995:15) propose that all teacher education qualifications should comprise four essential elements, i.e. subject study, educational studies, teaching methodology/didactics and practice, which "need to interact with each other in a dynamic way, while at the same time ensuring that their appropriate balance is achieved". The Higher Education Quality Committee's (2010) Report on the National Review of Academic and Professional Programmes in Education review of 22 PGCE programmes in South Africa found problems with assessment practices, as well as the time allocated to various components of the ITE courses and teaching practicum (CHE 2010:31).

Generally, school-based practicum provides prospective teachers with the opportunity to observe practice, to practise their classroom management and teaching skills and to implement what they have learned in the academy in a real setting. It also provides them with a chance to reflect on and evaluate their own skills and knowledge and to examine the applicability and relevance of the theoretical preparation in their ITE programme for practice (Gujjar et al. 2010; Hamaidi, Al-Shara, Arouri & Awwad 2014).

Practical learning is regarded as "an important condition for the development of tacit knowledge, which is an essential component of learning to teach that should be undertaken by the student teachers" (DHET 2015:10). Many teacher educators and researchers believe that teaching practice is one of the most important components of an ITE programme (Ngidi & Sibaya 2003; Kiggundu 2007; Hamaidi et al. 2014). Hamaidi et al. (2014:191) describe it as "the core and the central element of teacher professional training programmes". Teaching practice can also be seen as the transition between professional preparation in the university and practice in authentic classroom settings (Dicko 2010:38).

The 1995 National Teacher Education Audit Synthesis Report noted challenges with regard to the teaching practice component of ITE programmes. Most notably, it was found to be an adjunct to the ITE formal curriculum, as opposed to being an integral and central part of it (Hofmeyer & Hall 1995:92). The 2014 Jet Education Services Report also found variations across programmes/institutions in terms of quantity (length of time spent in schools) and the quality of the provision and consequent experience (Taylor 2014:10).

6.3 Theoretical Framework

This chapter draws on the theoretical framework used in this book. Regarding teacher professional knowledge, an adopted model of Shulman's (1987) model of teacher professional knowledge is used. In this model, Shulman distinguishes between SCK and PCK.

Munby and Russel (1996:1) describe such SCK and PCK as propositional knowledge, which they assert is "typically conveyed in teacher education courses and texts" and the non-propositional or 'knowing-in-action' knowledge which comes into play when teachers are "performing the activities of teaching". Essentially, this covers the 'what' and 'how' to teach.

Gitomer and Zisk (2015:7) also indicate that what teachers need to know and how they can use this knowledge to teach are related to underlying conceptions of the role of the teacher and the profession. Clandinin and Connelly (1996:24) linked teacher professional knowledge to context and proposed that teacher knowledge is shaped by the professional knowledge context in which teachers work. They conceptualise the professional knowledge context as "an intellectual and a moral landscape" that is composed of people, places and things, and the relationships between them (Clandinin & Connelly 1996:25). Clandinin and Connelly (1996) further argue that teachers will bring their professional knowledge of what and how to teach, as well as their beliefs about teaching and learning, to bear when confronted with particular situations in the classroom.

As such, the theoretical framework used in this chapter, which draws on the theoretical framework in the book, views SCK and PCK as important influences in teachers' and prospective teachers' conceptions of teaching and learning. It also views SCK and PCK as being influenced by the context within which teaching and learning occurs.

6.4 Methodology

This chapter is based on both quantitative and qualitative data collected at one institution. Quantitative and qualitative data were analysed separately, then compared and synthesised to provide a nuanced perspective of the respondents' views regarding their professional knowledge development. Data were collected using survey questionnaires and focus group interviews. Data were collected from student teachers enrolled for the PGCE programme. This programme prepares students for the FET phase. Convenience sampling was used to survey a sample of 45 students (33 women and 12 men) to gauge their views of the PGCE programme. Most of the survey respondents (80%) fell in the age range of 21 to 30 years. In terms of racial grouping, most respondents were coloured (64%), followed by black Africans (23%). English was the home language of about 47% of the survey respondents, followed by Afrikaans (31%), isiXhosa (18%) and other languages (4%). Most of the respondents (80%) were specialising in English as a teaching subject, followed by Mathematics (18%) and a small percentage of respondents were specialising in other subjects (2%).

The quantitative data from the survey questionnaire were analysed using simple descriptive statistics such as frequencies. Four focus group interviews collected qualitative data. The number of respondents in each focus group ranged from seven to nine PGCE students. The interviews were conducted in English, as the language of teaching and learning at the HEI concerned. The interviews were audio-recorded and transcribed. The usual ethical protocols were followed prior to the commencement of the data collection (see introduction for details).

6.5 Findings and Discussion

PGCE student teachers shared their views about different aspects of their experiences of the PGCE programme. These views provided insight into student teachers' professional knowledge, as well as their experiences of the PGCE programme in preparing them professionally as teachers.

Table 6.1   Professional Knowledge Components Covered in the Course (N=45)

Aspects of professional knowledge	A Yes, we covered this aspect Frequency (%)	B Useful to very useful Frequency (%)
a) CK	35 (78)	30 (75)
b) PCK	38 (84)	30 (70)
c) Knowledge of the FET CAPS curriculum	30 (78)	26 (67)
d) Child development	36 (87)	35 (83)
e) Learner assessment	36 (87)	32 (76)
f) ICT skills	18 (40)	11 (41)
g) Classroom management	34 (76)	24 (63)
h) Teaching for inclusive education	37 (82)	31 (74)
i) Teaching in a multilingual setting	31 (69)	22 (61)
j) Managing diverse learner needs in the classroom	37 (82)	31 (74)
k) Integrated teaching and learning	31 (69)	24 (65)
l) Knowledge of the Constitution	29 (64)	18 (59)
m) Teaching democratic values and practices	30 (67)	22 (64)
n) Managing relationships with parents	23 (51)	13 (6)

Table 6.1 indicates the frequency and percentage of responses to each of the items in the questionnaire that was administered to the PGCE student teachers. Although the total number of respondents was 45, it should be noted that not all student teachers responded to all the questions in the questionnaire. The percentages indicated in Table 6.1 should thus be viewed in relation to the frequency of responses to the item in the questionnaire and not in relation to the total number of respondents (N=45).

It is important to note that the survey data suggest that most respondents found the PGCE programme to be an effective programme (see Tables 6.1 and 6.2), and, in the main, were happy with the programme. The focus group interviews provided more depth and diversity in terms of PGCE student teachers' views and experiences of the programme. Therefore, the diverse views provided by the qualitative data do not contradict the quantitative findings. Rather, the data provide a nuanced account of the respondents' views, which are complex and multi-layered. A discussion of the different themes that emerged from these analysis of data follows.

6.5.1   The Role of a Teacher

The focus group respondents mentioned different roles that a teacher fulfils, which were broader in scope than just ensuring that learners gained academic knowledge. The following teacher roles were identified: being a role model, facilitating learning, providing holistic education, teaching life skills that could be useful beyond the classroom, inspiring and guiding learners, developing in learners an eagerness to want to learn, being a substitute parent (*loco parentis*), enforcing discipline and developing a positive attitude towards the role of being teacher. One respondent mentioned that his/her prior experiences of teachers at school contributed to his/her understanding of the roles that he/she ought to play as a teacher. Another respondent mentioned that the role of the teacher is so broad that it was difficult to define. This view reflects the complexity of 'playing' teacher. The view that a teacher is a facilitator of learning, suggests the active role that learners need to play in their own learning in line with a constructivist approach to teaching and learning. In terms of holistic education, the teacher must consider developing the whole learner in terms of the different domains (e.g. cognitive, emotional and spiritual). The *loco parentis* role of a teacher suggests that teachers have a nurturing 'protective' role to play with regard to their learners. The teacher's attitude was considered a prerequisite for successful learning and was deemed more important than teacher knowledge and skills. The following responses reflect respondents' perceptions of the different roles of a teacher:

> Giving them the things that maybe they didn't know that they need, but they can use in their life, not just like, you know, formulas and, you know, different learning areas, but things that can help them to just empower them, things like that, so that they can make something of themselves (FG, PGCE, Inst. D 2016).

> So, I think a teacher's role is not just educating; you are like another parent to that child and sometimes that's the only smile or the only positive regard the child gets is at school with you. So, I think that we can't really define the role of the teacher (FG, PGCE, Inst. D 2016).

> You might get your knowledge and your skills 100% but if the attitude is zero, everything falls (FG, PGCE, Inst. D 2016).

> They aren't there just to educate, but to guide and inspire as well because at the end of the day that's what you remember after school (FG, PGCE, Inst. D 2016).

> So, if the student is lying, they [DBE] would investigate and they would find the teacher not guilty ... The department deals with the issue and the principals' rights are diminished, and they fear to be victimised (FG, PGCE, Inst. D 2016).

PGCE had given me the opportunity for me to view a teacher as a real teacher, whereas I was also a student, a learner, viewing a teacher as just being there... A teacher had most of the time teaching a whole day, like maybe one period off. Whereas when you get the teacher, you only think that you are the only students getting the teaching but now the ball game changes. Now you will have different classes... sometimes different subjects to teach in that same school... I've more intense, more respect for teachers than I used to have, when I didn't do the teaching programme or I didn't start in teaching... And now I really seen the admins work, the amount of work that teachers really have to give and give back and do. It made me feel okay, so yes, PGCE had showed me the real teacher, as opposed to what I initially thought what a teacher was (FG, PGCE, Inst. D 2016).

6.5.2 Perceptions of the PGCE Programme in Preparing Students for the Teaching Profession (Theory/Practice Praxis)

The survey data in Table 6.1 indicated the respondents' perceptions of different aspects of professional knowledge in relation to their experiences of the PGCE programme. Column A of the table indicated the frequency and percentage of responses and those who indicated that the particular professional knowledge components were covered in the PGCE programme. Column B indicated the frequency and percentage of the respondents who indicated that the particular professional knowledge component was found useful. An analysis of Table 6.1 suggests that for most of the identified professional knowledge components, the majority of the respondents (64% or more for each item) acknowledged covering them in the PGCE programme and finding them very useful. However, a minority of respondents (40%) indicated that they did not learn ICT skills in the PGCE programme. This is a concerning finding, considering the increasing focus on integrating ICT into curriculum delivery, given that learners in contemporary society are digital natives (Prensky 2001:30).

Table 6.2 Perceptions of Experiences of Learning in the PGCE Programme (N=45)

Perceptions of the PGCE programme	Agree & strongly agree Frequency (%)
a) I am happy that I chose to do this programme.	42 (93)
b) Having already completed a degree, I find the programme quite easy.	33 (73)
c) I feel overwhelmed by all the reading I have to do.	20 (44)
d) I do not want to continue this programme.	2 (5)
e) I enjoy the varied reading texts we engage with during the programme.	33 (73)
f) I find this programme difficult.	4 (9)
g) I find the programme too theoretical.	23 (52)
h) There are too many assignments.	17 (40)
i) The readings for the programme are not relevant.	8 (19)

The data in Table 6.2 indicate the respondents' views about their experiences of learning in the PGCE programme. A large majority of the respondents (93%) were happy that they had chosen the PGCE programme. The majority of the respondents (73%) found the PGCE programme to be relatively easy since they had already attained a degree prior to their current study and also found the varied reading material enjoyable (73%). However, 44% found the volume of reading in the PGCE programme overwhelming and 52% found it too theoretical. Only 5% of the respondents did not want to continue with the PGCE programme.

The focus group discussions identified the following factors related to the theory/practice divide: university preparation to teach in relation to real classroom experiences, the PGCE programme in relation to education policy, the role of teaching practice in the PGCE programme, and mentor teacher contributions to student teachers' development and agency.

The respondents shared different views with regard to university preparation to teach in real classroom contexts. Some respondents felt that the PGCE programme provided a foundation for teaching, with theory informing their approaches to teaching and learning. Others supported this view but highlighted certain shortcomings, such as the programme being too short (one year) and too congested for adequate preparation as a teacher. Moreover, the respondents also mentioned that there was a divide between what was taught at university (theory) and the reality of classroom teaching (practice). For instance, one respondent mentioned that a well-prepared lesson on paper does not necessarily prepare one for the delivery of the lesson when the contextual realities take place in the classroom setting. Some student teachers, especially those in specialised fields like mathematics and science, mentioned initial surprise in realising that the PGCE programme included theoretical input 'outside' their specialist subjects, such as learning educational psychology. They also acknowledged how such input had contributed to the development of professional knowledge.

Another challenge mentioned was the gaps they experienced in terms of their knowledge and skills during teaching practice because the practice teaching period occurred within and not at the end of the academic year. An example of the latter challenge was their 'un(der) preparedness' with regard to classroom management – an aspect that was only formally covered by the curriculum after teaching practice had been completed. Some respondents felt that the programme should include more practical experience. Practical experience, in this instance, referred to actual teaching practice periods at schools rather than the university-based micro-teaching component. Mention was made that the PGCE programme made student teachers aware of the policy framework governing education but that teaching experience provided practical training in the profession. Some respondents expressed the view that mentor teachers made a bigger impact on their development than the university programme. Other respondents mentioned the need for student teachers to take initiative (agency) in applying skills and knowledge gained at university in the practice of teaching. The following responses indicate these views, as expressed by respondents in the interviews:

> In all honesty, I believe that PGCE it was a nice course, it facilitated many things with regards to make me aware personally of ... theory and you know all these other things. But from a practical aspect, you need to bring a lot of yourself into it, so you need to sort of build yourself, start with yourself (FG, PGCE, Inst. D 2016).

> I don't think anything can prepare you for what happens in the classroom setting, so you need to be out there in the field to really experience, you know, sort of feel your way around it, what works and what doesn't work. They can advise you and textbooks can say this, like it all goes out to a particular experience (FG, PGCE, Inst. D 2016).

> I started attending lectures and seeing how things are, the educational [part], the theoretical part, the psychological part, I didn't do any of those things in my undergrad. So, for me that was helpful because when I stood in front of the class or when I was in a classroom setting, I could see some of the kids, some the things that the lecturers said they actually were playing out in front of me (FG, PGCE, Inst. D 2016).

> So, I've enjoyed PGCE. It's been really nice with regards to policies and how things work and all of that, ... the practical ways you gain all of that while we are teaching (FG, PGCE, Inst. D 2016).

> So, I'm not saying that PGCE didn't help me in terms of my teaching, it did help me but it was a bit limiting, it did help me (FG, PGCE, Inst. D 2016).

6.5.3 Teaching Practice Experiences

As expected, teaching practice offered student teachers a range of experiences in their development as teachers. Table 6.3 includes some of these diverse experiences and indicates that most students (over 50%) benefit from their teaching practice experiences. Only the management of learner conflict seemed to be challenging, with only 38% of the participants indicating that they had successfully learned how to manage learner conflict. This statistic is unsurprising given the widespread challenge of learner indiscipline in many South African schools (Joubert, De Waal & Rossouw 2004:84). According to Burton (2008:1), violence is quite common in South African schools; with a likely negative impact on learners in different ways.

Table 6.3 Teaching Practice Experiences (N=45)

Teaching practice experience	Agree & strongly agree Frequency (%)
I learned to manage the classroom.	29 (64)
I learned to build a pedagogical relationship with learners.	30 (67)
I learned to teach in classrooms with learners from diverse backgrounds.	34 (76)
I learned to teach large classes.	29 (64)
I learned to teach in multilingual classrooms.	24 (53)
I learned to manage conflict among learners.	17 (38)
I learned to discipline learners.	24 (53)
I learned about being a professional.	39 (87)

Table 6.3   Teaching Practice Experiences (N=45) *(cont)*

Teaching practice experience	Agree & strongly agree Frequency (%)
I learned to develop assessments (e.g. tests, assignments, etc.).	28 (62)
I learned to develop assessment memoranda (e.g. for tests, assignments, etc.).	26 (58)
I learned to ask higher-order thinking questions.	28 (62)
I learned to identify learners' strengths and weaknesses	30 (67)

6.5.3.1 Experiences of Teacher Mentors

The data in Table 6.3 suggest an overwhelming positive experience with mentors, where mentors were described as being happy with student teachers' work, eager to advise and provide feedback, as well as attentive, accessible, empathetic, fair and inspirational. The focus group respondents reported varied experiences of their respective mentor teachers. Many of the respondents who had a positive experience with the mentors claimed that it was because they had a good relationship of support and trust, while those who were negative had the opposite experience. However, there were positive as well as negative experiences of mentors, and in some instances, there were both positive and negative experiences of a specific mentor. A few PGCE student teachers, however, reported that their mentors were not available or were absent and did not provide guidance or feedback.

(i)   Positive Experiences of Teacher Mentors

Positive experiences of mentor teachers included providing guidance with regard to lesson planning and delivery, being good role models, having a nurturing disposition in their mentorship roles, encouraging autonomy and the mentor teacher being willing to learn from the student teacher. The support with lesson planning and delivery included the mentor teachers sharing their experience and expertise in relation to PCK, providing learning and teaching support materials and providing valuable feedback to student teachers after lessons were taught. Good role modelling was evident in the mentor teachers' willingness to assist the student teachers with any challenges they were experiencing and student teachers observing the mentor teacher delivering lessons. There were also reports of some mentors encouraging student teachers by praising them when they had performed well in class. In some instances, student teachers were encouraged to develop autonomy as teachers-in-the-making by being allowed to choose what lessons they wanted to teach. One respondent commented that the mentor teacher identified that he/she was more knowledgeable in a certain topic and asked him/her to teach the topic. This experience also suggests good role modelling on the part of the teacher, who demonstrated willingness to learn from another, even when the other party occupied a relatively junior status at school. Positive experiences of mentor teachers are reflected in the following responses:

> So, uhm, very helpful like little hints like that and they are teaching for many, many years and also like to guide you in terms of how to teach you, the learners, to learn that part (FG, PGCE, Inst. D 2016).

Yeah, so she knows my weaknesses and my strengths and I know her weaknesses and strengths. We have a great relationship like where I can...I can go in wherever whenever I want. I asked her advice according to the lesson according to whatever I've prepared. We had this bond where I first prepare something she will check, moderate it, as she is the HoD as well. So she will go through the work and give me advice (FG, PGCE, Inst. D 2016).

They would sit me down in the staffroom, give me some feedback, give me some good pointers and stuff which actually helped me quite a bit (FG, PGCE, Inst. D 2016).

(ii) Negative Experiences of Teacher Mentors

Negative experiences encountered by student teachers in relation to some of their mentor teachers included mentor teachers providing inadequate mentoring, being reticent about student teachers observing their lessons and student teachers delivering lessons, exploiting student teachers, student teachers being unable to develop relationships with their mentor and possibly breaching ethical boundaries. Inadequate mentoring included the mentor teacher expecting the student teacher to plan work such as lessons and assessment tasks without giving any support and guidance. Some mentor teachers also did not observe the student teacher delivering lessons, so no effective feedback was provided as to how they had fared in their delivery of lessons. Mentor teachers' reticence to allow students to observe their lessons was interpreted as the mentor teacher fearing appearing incompetent in the delivery of lessons.

Some respondents reported that they had felt exploited because some mentor teachers expected them to teach while the mentor teacher left the classroom to take breaks. One respondent reported that the mentor teacher seemed to overly share with learners his sexual experiences. The student felt that the mentor teacher had breached ethical boundaries by sharing such intimate experiences during lessons. The following responses reflect some of the negative experiences student teachers had with mentor teachers:

... certain teachers don't want you there because they don't want you see what it is they're doing right, or what it is they're not doing right (FG PGCE D 2016).

But then that's just one issue that I had because I remember I was doing a lesson to Grade 11 on teenage pregnancy and then I was telling the functions of a condom, that it protects sperm from entering the vagina and he [mentor teacher] stood up and said, 'No, miss, you are being sexist. It has to do [with] vagina slash anus.' I said, 'But sir, we are dealing with teenage pregnancy and I don't see how teenagers can fall pregnant from the anus' (FG, PGCE, Inst. D 2016).

The accounting mentor, I didn't bond so well with as the maths she felt almost like, yah, I'm just doing the accounting because we need to do two modules because she knew already my focus is going to the maths teacher (FG, PGCE, Inst. D 2016).

6.5.3.2 Demonstrating Agency During Teaching Practice

The notion of agency arose from the student teachers' responses to what initially appeared to be negative (deficient) teaching and learning contexts. The respondents' reports suggest that they demonstrated agency during their teaching practice in different ways. According to Keogh et al. (2012), teachers can address and overcome many challenges through agency.

For example, some participants responded to inadequate or reluctant mentoring by seizing the opportunity to prepare and deliver lessons using own initiative and trying out different teaching methods. One respondent related that the experience of classroom supervision was an opportunity to really get to know the learners and build a relationship with them. Teacher absence from school was also viewed by another respondent as an opportunity to teach as much as possible, thereby gaining experience. Another respondent took the opportunity during teaching practice to learn more about the broader school context, not just limiting his/her learning to teaching and learning. Agency was expressed as follows:

> So I sort of, I grabbed that opportunity [referring to teacher reluctance to mentor] to get the exposure to teaching and in that way I could make my mistakes, I could learn, I could try different methods with discipline and I could learn, see what works, what doesn't work (FG, PGCE, Inst. D 2016).

> It was bad and good because I learned how to do it on my own, but it was, no one used to help me to do it also, it was okay to learn that. And the tests also, I had to make up my own tests (FG, PGCE, Inst. D 2016).

> So, I think that was most important the fact that I put myself out there to get to know the learners and to, like, to get to know how the school works, besides standing in front and teaching whatever things that needed to be taught (FG, PGCE, Inst. D 2016).

6.5.3.3 Reflections of Lesson Planning and Delivery During Teaching Practice

The data indicated generally positive responses related to student teachers' preparation for teaching practice in the university. About 70% agreed/strongly agreed that their lecturers prepared them sufficiently for teaching practice and that the lesson planning-related documents were useful.

The focus group respondents' reflections about their experiences in the planning and delivery of lessons during teaching practice suggested that these were rich learning experiences. These reflections included the application of knowledge from different sources, considerations about how to make lessons interesting, connecting new knowledge to learners' prior knowledge, optimally managing time during lesson delivery, presumptions about learners' abilities and the evaluation of their performances during the delivery of lessons.

Some respondents mentioned that they could employ theories taught in the theory modules (non-methods modules) during their teaching practice stints in both classroom management and in the planning and delivery of lessons. Another source of knowledge that was mentioned by one respondent was the knowledge gained as a scholar at high school, which was used to plan lessons for a subject that was not part of the student's specialisation in the PGCE programme.

This application of knowledge from different sources resonates with one of Feuerstein's (1980 cited in Green 2014:182) principles of transcendence or bridging, which is reflected in the following respondent's view:

> ... because now you tend to understand learners' way of understanding things from different types of fields, you are able to like other psychological theories, encouraging that you should learn, you should know your learners individually so that you understand their barriers, individually. You don't use the one-glove-fits-all approach (FG, PGCE, Inst. D 2016).

The respondents reported that during the planning of lessons, they considered making lessons interesting by making them relevant, enhancing lesson delivery with audio-visual resources (e.g. video clips), using a variety of teaching methods, presenting content by employing a contemporary orientation and considering learner diversity. The following captures these PGCE student teachers' aspirations in making lessons interesting:

> So I learned in teaching language is that you cannot use the same method, you must always be considerate of different types of learners, you must always mix and match different methods. Your video clips, your cartoons, I used a lot of cartoons because they are here, they are tangible and they are fun, and they can be interpreted differently, you give them same cartoon to different learners they will always come up with different words of interpreting. And that works for me and I think I will carry on mixing and matching different types of methods (FG, PGCE, Inst. D 2016).

One of the challenges mentioned in the delivery of lessons was attempting to bridge the gap between learners' prior knowledge and the grade level of knowledge that needed to be taught. The student teachers acknowledged that although CK was important, delivering the content through well-prepared lesson plans was pivotal to learning. Another challenge was time management in the delivery of lessons so that the time allocated was optimally used in terms of setting the pace of lessons. The following excerpts reflect these challenges:

> For me the most challenging part of teaching language was the fact that with each lesson, say, for example, maybe I did something on grammar where they'd be... and I'm talking about Grade 11s. I would always have to go back to the things I can't... I would have to go back to parts of speech, I would have to explain to them with each lesson. I would use, our periods were 60 minutes long, at least I had the time, I would have to take the first 15 minutes of my lesson and go through the basic things that kids are taught on primary school level, intermediate level (FG, PGCE, Inst. D 2016).

> So I found that was one of the biggest barriers and also time management in class. Sometimes I'd find myself having too little time, and sometimes I'd find myself having too much time to spare (FG, PGCE, Inst. D 2016).

> ... the issue of a lesson plan. You know, I always believed that all the topics that we've encountered in maths ... I do have so much content, far greater the level in Grade 10, Grade 11, but then even so you still need to prepare how you're going to deliver. It's not an issue of knowing the content but the delivering part. It becomes challenging (FG, PGCE, Inst. D 2016).

It was encouraging that the respondents reflected on their expectations of learners' abilities. For example, some respondents reported that the cognitive levels at which they had pitched their lessons were too low for different reasons. One reason for pitching lessons too low was PGCE student teachers' inexperience. Another reason was the underestimation of the abilities of learners attending schools located in a low socio-economic status (SES) neighbourhood. Consequently, the respondents reported that the teaching practice experience had taught them to expect more of learners coming from low SES backgrounds. This reflection suggests that the PGCE student teachers in question were willing to confront the stereotypical beliefs they had held of learners from low SES contexts. There were also lessons learned about learners' ability generally and that children had the potential to be the agents of their own learning instead of being 'saved' by the teacher as the fountain of knowledge through transmission teaching. Therefore, the respondents also mentioned that they had learned to be patient during lessons and to give learners more time to think. The following responses succinctly capture the respondents' reflections of learners' [in]abilities:

> So some of the questions that I asked didn't challenge them, so I discovered that I must stop undermining these learners because of the situation and the social conditions that they come from (FG, PGCE, Inst. D 2016).

> So when I do go in front of a classroom next year when I'm teaching, I will always remember that learners are at a level where they are able to think out of the box and the teacher doesn't need to give everything to them (FG, PGCE, Inst. D 2016).

> Because, if the learners took too long to answer, I would get worried like am I doing something wrong, what's going on, but then the skill that I learned was I need to give myself a chance and I need to give them also a chance to give the work back to me. Because they do know what is going in, they just need time (FG, PGCE, Inst. D 2016).

> The teaching method, sometimes you need to feel examples that will feed the students' questions and the background of the student. If the student can relate to what you are trying to explain at a certain way or the background they are growing at. You need to be able to accommodate the background of that student in order to make the student understand what you are trying to say in the position of the student (FG, PGCE, Inst. D 2016).

The respondents also evaluated their own performances during the delivery of lessons. For example, one respondent realised that he/she was speaking too fast during lessons, possibly due to anxiety, which had a negative impact on lesson delivery. Another respondent reported feeling embarrassed when he/she could not define a word during a lesson. There was the realisation that thorough planning of lessons was important, but that teachers could also learn from learners. Feedback from learners was another source of evaluating how they fared during lesson delivery. One respondent was reminded by learners to contain his/her excitement when teaching and to minimise his/her verbal input during lessons. However, reports from the respondents included the realisation that they had the potential to be good at teaching and just needed to calm down when delivering lessons. The following reflects evaluations of respondents' performances in the delivery of lessons:

> When I stand in front of a classroom I get so enthusiastic, I just speak so fast. With regards to the language barrier, I was causing the barrier most of the time because I couldn't see like that, perhaps it's the nerves or I don't know what it was but I was just so enthusiastic all of the time (FG, PGCE, Inst. D 2016).

> Some of the learners actually came to me and said, 'Miss, please breathe, you need to breathe because you just speaking and speaking and you're not breathing. Are you okay?' and then I said, 'No, its fine, I'm fine' (FG, PGCE, Inst. D 2016).

> So, then I had to learn to compose myself because I know what I'm doing, I know the content, I'm not scared of learners asking me difficult questions and stuff like that, so I just needed to tone myself down (FG, PGCE, Inst. D 2016).

6.5.3.4 Experiences of Classroom Management

The survey revealed that about 90% of the student teachers reported that they had learned to discipline and manage conflict among learners during their teaching practice. The issue of discipline was raised again in the focus groups. Many of the respondents felt that they were not adequately prepared to deal with the level of ill-discipline and seemed surprised at the extent of the problem. Many, however, appreciated the opportunity to develop their own strategies to deal with behaviour-related issues. They expressed empathy for the challenges that teachers face in managing learner discipline since it seemed as if contemporary strategies in the absence of corporal punishment were ineffective. In fact, as time progressed during the teaching practice period, it was evident that their respect for teachers and teaching increased. They also reported that they learned much from observing how the teachers managed the class, which allowed them to reflect on and think about their own methods. However, the respondents expressed tension in attempting to understand their role in enforcing discipline, because many felt that the learners were given more rights in the classroom and this mandate, in their view, was supported by the DBE. Consequently, the student teachers questioned the power relations between themselves and the learners.

The student teachers reported that on occasion there would be no mentor teacher in the classroom assisting them with classroom discipline. In fact, some had to manage discipline in violent classroom situations on their own. Discipline is indicated as one of the major challenges of becoming teachers, particularly in the South African context (see also Marais & Meier 2004).

The respondents mentioned that classroom management was the basis of successful lessons; yet it was a very challenging aspect of a teacher's role. One respondent mentioned that the biggest contribution that teaching practice had made to his/her development as a teacher was in learning strategies to effectively manage learners. Another respondent mentioned that he/she learned to tailor-make classroom management strategies for different classroom contexts. Mention was also made of developing a teacher persona, to project an image of oneself other than one's natural disposition; for example, being strict and not too friendly so that learners do not take advantage of one as the teacher. This suggested that teaching as an art form also includes acting, and yet it also suggests some incongruence between one's natural disposition and one's projected image as a teacher.

There was also mention of how learners could entice teachers into reacting inappropriately to learner indiscipline and then reporting the teacher for unprofessional conduct. However, the respondents realised that learner indiscipline was at times a foil for personal challenges that learners faced and that teachers needed to make efforts to really connect with difficult learners in an attempt to understand their lives. The respondents also realised the positive influence they could have on learners who were considered ill-disciplined. The following responses reflect the respondents' opinions of classroom management:

> I think the most important that they can take or that I've taken with me from my practical was classroom management. You see, as I said earlier on, you can prepare yourself for the best lesson in the world, but if you cannot manage those learners, no learning is going to take place (FG, PGCE, Inst. D 2016).

So I now understand the frustration of corporal punishment not being used anymore that was my biggest challenge (FG, PGCE, Inst. D 2016).

So if you need to be cold, ice cold, for them to actually, you have to, you have to put up that persona to get them in line, because without discipline nobody is going to learn. You understand what I'm saying? (FG, PGCE, Inst. D 2016).

But I was able to sort of work out little strategies of getting them; an example would be I have a very loud voice, I can project my voice well. But during specific lessons, with specific classes, I would speak very softly and they would have to listen to me, so they wanted to hear what I want to say, they would actually have to be quiet and listen. And that worked here and there, I would adjust it, obviously according to classes (FG, PGCE, Inst. D 2016).

… when you're in the classroom setting, you become a different person. I found myself being an adult quite a bit. I consider myself to be quite a kid at heart, so I found myself, I had to be this person, the person that's in charge, the person that needs to be there. So yeah, it taught me quite a bit, it really did (FG, PGCE, Inst. D 2016).

And they frustrated the teacher to a point where she lost her cool, and they recorded her very nicely and took the recording to the WC [WCED – Western Cape Education Department] where they laid a charge against the teacher. And I'm making this example, that's just an example of one of the many pitfalls waiting for us next year as teachers; we need to be prepared for this. You can't go in there blind sided because these are things that happen and that is what I learned during my practical (FG, PGCE, Inst. D 2016).

6.6 Conclusion

This chapter focused on the professional development experiences of prospective PGCE teachers at one HEI. A mixed-methods research approach was employed. The study findings suggest that student teachers were generally satisfied with the content and delivery of the programme, as reported by the quantitative data. Qualitative findings via focus group interviews highlighted multiple perceptions and experiences related by PGCE student teachers. The main themes that emerged from the data were student teachers' views about the role of a teacher, their perceptions of the PGCE programme in preparing them for the teaching profession (theory/practice praxis) and their teaching practice experiences. The teaching practice experiences seemed to have played a major role in introducing these aspiring teachers to the 'real world' of teaching as a profession and they had experienced much learning during the teaching practice, which enhanced their levels of professional knowledge.

Based on the research conducted with these prospective teachers in a PGCE programme at one HEI, it can be said that the programme provides important exposure for the development of teacher professional knowledge and practice. Unlike the 1995 National Teacher Education Audit Synthesis Report's finding, the teacher education component in this PGCE programme was not an adjunct to the programme but an integral part of it and experienced as such by the student teachers reached in this study. Clandinin and Connelly's (1996) point that teacher professional knowledge is also influenced by the contexts in which teaching occurs was also shown to be significant in this study. The teaching contexts these PGCE prospective teachers found themselves teaching in, seem to have impacted most on the challenges they faced in managing their classrooms and dealing with discipline. Training to become a teacher was found in this study to be crucial for the development of teacher professional knowledge and practice through the programme and the supervisors the university provided and the inclusion of teacher mentors in the programme.

References

Adoniou, M. 2014. Teacher knowledge: A complex tapestry. *Asia-Pacific Journal of Teacher Education*, 43(2): 99-116. https://doi.org/10.1080/1359866X.2014.932330

Anderson, D. & Clark, M. 2012. Development of syntactic subject matter knowledge and pedagogical content knowledge for science by a generalist elementary teacher. *Teachers and Teaching: Theory and Practice*, 18(3): 315-330. https://doi.org/10.1080/13540602.2012.629838

Bertram, C. 2011. What does research say about teacher learning and teacher knowledge? Implications for professional development in South Africa. *Journal of Education*, 52: 3-26.

Burton, P. 2008. Dealing with school violence in South Africa. *Centre for Justice and Crime Prevention (CJCP)*, Issue Paper, 4, April: 1-16.

Clandinin, D.J. & Connelly, F.M. 1996. Teachers' professional knowledge landscapes: Teacher stories – stories of teachers – school stories – stories of schools 1. *Educational Researcher*, 25(3): 24-30. https://doi.org/10.2307/1176665

Council on Higher Education (CHE). 2010. *Report on the national review of academic and professional programmes in education*. Pretoria: CHE. https://www.che.ac.za/sites/default/files/publications/Higher_Education_Monitor_11.pdf

Department of Higher Education and Training (DHET). 2011. The minimum requirements for teacher education qualifications (MRTEQ). *Government Gazette*, 553(34467). Pretoria.

Department of Higher Education and Training (DHET). 2015. National Qualifications Framework Act, 2008 (Act No. 67 of 2008): Revised Policy on the Minimum Requirements for Teacher Education Qualifications. *Government Gazette*, 38487, 19 February. Pretoria: Government Printer.

Dicko, A. 2010. Multicultural education in USA: Place of ethnic minorities. *Asian Social Science*, 6(12): 36.

Fleisch, B. 2007. *Primary education in crisis: Why South African schoolchildren underachieve in reading and mathematics*. Cape Town: Juta.

Gess-Newsome, J. 2015. A model of teacher professional knowledge and skill, including PCK: Results of the thinking from the PCK summit. In: A. Berry, P. Friedrichsen & J. Loughran (eds). *Re-examining pedagogical content knowledge in science education*. New York, NY: Routledge, 28-42.

Gitomer, D.H. & Zisk, R.C. 2015. Knowing what teachers know. *Review of Research in Education*, 39(1): 1-53. https://doi.org/10.3102/0091732X14557001

Green, L. (ed.). 2014. *Schools as thinking communities*. Pretoria: Van Schaik Publishers.

Griesel, H. & Parker, B. 2009. *Graduate attributes: A baseline study on South African graduates from the perspective of employers*. Pretoria: Higher Education South Africa (HESA) & the South African Qualifications Authority (SAQA).

Gujjar, A.A.; Naoreen, B.; Saifi, S. & Bajwa, M.J. 2010. Teaching practice: Problems and issues in Pakistan. *International Online Journal of Educational Sciences*, 2(2): 339-361.

Hamaidi, D.; Al-Shara, I.; Arouri, Y. & Awwad, F. 2014. A student-teachers' perspectives of practicum practices and challenges. *European Scientific Journal*, 10(13): 191-214.

Hofmeyer, J. & Hall, G. 1995. *The national teacher education audit: Synthesis report*. Johannesburg: Edupol, National Business Initiative.

Joubert, R.; De Waal, E. & Rossouw, J.P. 2004. Discipline: Impact on access to equal educational opportunities. *Perspectives in Education*, 22(3): 77-87.

Keogh, J.; Garvis, S.; Pendergast, D. & Diamond, P. 2012. Self-determination: Using agency, efficacy and resilience (AER) to counter novice teachers' experiences of intensification. *Australian Journal of Teacher Education*, 37(8): 46-65. https://doi.org/10.14221/ajte.2012v37n8.3

Kiggundu, E. 2007. Teaching practice in the Greater Vaal Triangle area: The student teachers' experience. *Journal of College Teaching & Learning (TLC)*, 4(6): 25-36.

Marais, P. & Meier, C. 2004. Hear our voices: Student teachers' experiences during practical teaching. *Africa Education Review*, 1(2): 220-233. https://doi.org/10.1080/18146620408566281

Munby, H. & Russell, T. 1996. *Theory follows practice in learning to teach and in research on teaching*. New York: American Educational Research Association.

Ngidi, D.P. & Sibaya, P.T. 2013. Student teacher anxieties related to practice teaching. *South African Journal of Education*, 23(1): 18-22.

Prensky, M. 2001. Digital natives, digital immigrants (part 1). *On the Horizon*, 9(5): 1-6. https://doi.org/10.1108/10748120110424843

Rusznyak, L. 2015. Knowledge selection in initial teacher education programmes and its implications for curricular coherence. *Journal of Education*, 60(1): 7-30.

Shulman, L. 1986. Those who understand: Knowledge growth in teaching. *Educational Researcher*, 15(2): 4-14. https://doi.org/10.3102/0013189X015002004

Shulman, L. 1987. Knowledge and teaching: Foundations of the new reform. *Harvard Educational Review*, 57(1): 1-22. https://doi.org/10.17763/haer.57.1.j463w79r56455411

Shulman, L. 1992. Ways of seeing, ways of knowing, ways of teaching, ways of learning about teaching. *Journal of Curriculum Studies*, 28: 393-396.

Taylor, N. 2014. *Initial Teacher Education Research Project: An examination of aspects of initial teacher education curricula at five higher education institutions*. Summary report. Johannesburg: JET Education Services.

Taylor, N.; Van der Berg, S. & Mabogoane, T. (eds). 2013. *Creating effective schools*. Cape Town: Pearson Education.

Toom, A. 2006. *Tacit pedagogical knowing at the core of teacher's professionality*. Research report 276. Finland: Faculty of Behavioural Sciences, University of Helsinki.

Verbeek, C. 2014. Critical reflections on the PGCE (Foundation Phase) qualification in South Africa. *South African Journal of Childhood Education*, 4(3): 37-51. https://doi.org/10.4102/sajce.v4i3.225

Chapter 07

Teaching & Learning Foundation Phase Mathematics

Sharon McAuliffe, Hamsa Venkatakrishnan & Jeanette Ramollo

7.1 Introduction

Ongoing concerns about learning outcomes in mathematics at all levels have led to increasing questions about the role and effectiveness of ITE in South Africa. The focus in this chapter is on Foundation Phase ITE. The specific disciplinary focus is on mathematics teacher education, and an exploration, through a small selection of student teacher interviews, of outcomes in terms of the way exiting ITE students understand and work with important parts of the mathematics curriculum that they will teach as Foundation Phase teachers.

This focus needs justification. Liping Ma, who wrote a highly influential book on the fundamental differences between American and Chinese primary teachers' ways of working with the mathematics that they taught, provides a very useful concept for this chapter, namely the "profound understanding of fundamental mathematics" (PUFM). This entails being "not only aware of the conceptual structure and basic attitudes of mathematics inherent in elementary mathematics" but also being "able to teach them to students" (Ma 1999:xxiv), and is underpinned by four principles, namely:

- ✓ connectedness – between the concepts and procedures within tasks and between topics and sub-domains;
- ✓ multiple perspectives – understanding different facets of mathematical ideas and different approaches to problem solving, while also appreciating that some approaches may be more efficient and/or more powerful than others;
- ✓ basic ideas – awareness and revisiting of basic ideas and principles in mathematics across work on different topics; and
- ✓ longitudinal coherence – awareness of the span of topics across the primary grades, rather than a narrower focus on the mathematics to be dealt with in particular grades (Ma 1999:xxiv).

For this chapter, the interest is more specifically on Ma's (1999) focus on 'how' mathematics is known and worked with, which is in stark contrast to approaches that test teachers' mathematical knowledge or that focus on their generic pedagogical orientations and practices. In South Africa, several larger-scale national and regional studies (Carnoy, Chisholm & Chilisa 2012; Taylor & Taylor 2013; Venkat & Spaull 2015) have given similar attention to primary school teachers' mathematical knowledge. However, more data are available on the Intermediate Phase level than the Foundation Phase, with findings pointing to gaps in important areas, such as in proportional reasoning and in PCK.

Other more classroom-based studies in South Africa have focused on generic pedagogical features, which have shown a prevalence of chorused oral responses, weak pacing, and limited individuated feedback, alongside subject-specific concerns about the nature of the mathematical knowledge presented in instruction (Hoadley 2012). These classroom-based studies identified key concerns, related to connections and coherence in the mathematics presented and, with regard to Foundation Phase, an apprehension about concrete orientations to mathematics involving counting-based strategies without progression towards more abstract symbolic orientations.

It is the latter concern, namely issues relating to connections and coherence in how mathematics is presented in instruction, which is primarily foregrounded in this chapter. These incorporate:

1. concerns with instructional talk that moves between colloquial to mathematical naming, rather than remaining entrenched in colloquial registers (Adler & Ronda 2015);
2. slippages between the tasks, examples, and selections of artefacts, inscriptions and the kinds of talk and gestures that teachers use to solve problems; to respond to what learners offer (Venkat & Askew 2012; Mathews 2016); and
3. working with examples in highly 'separate' ways with little emphasis on relationships between them (Venkat & Naidoo 2012).

What is interesting across this body of work that observes mathematics teaching in the Foundation Phase is that teachers are seen to very rarely offer incorrect answers to problems in their lessons, instead exhibiting more alarming problems with their assembly of the problem-solving process. This suggests a serious dichotomy between 'doing mathematics for oneself' and 'mediating mathematics in teaching' and points to the usefulness of investigating teachers' ways of working with problems for themselves (relating to the first issue) and their ways of working with, and connecting, problems in the context of instruction (relating to the second issue).

It is the above dichotomy with which this chapter mainly grapples. It does so in the context of Ma's (1999) key observation that ITE is crucial in changing the status quo of teachers in contexts where there are concerns about the quality of teacher knowledge and instruction. Ma (1999:149) observes that "[i]n the vicious circle formed by low-quality mathematics education and low-quality teacher knowledge of school mathematics, a third party – teacher preparation – may serve as the force to break the circle".

Notably, the sets of questionnaires that were collected as part of this book and overall study on the ITE experiences of Foundation Phase student teachers at three participating HEIs recorded broad satisfaction with mathematical learning and preparedness to teach mathematics. Over 75% of all responses in the questionnaires indicated student teachers being either 'confident' or 'very confident' across mathematical topic areas, both in developing learner thinking and in using a range of resources and representations (across more concrete and more symbolic mathematics). Twenty-six percent of the respondents indicated, for example, that they were 'very confident' about developing learner skills related to number concepts, calculation and application skills, while 58% indicated being 'confident'. Similarly, 20% of the respondents stated being 'very confident' about developing learner skills related to recognising and using properties of operations and a further 58% indicated being 'confident'. In terms of whole-class teaching of mathematical concepts, 86% of all the responses indicated the respondents being 'very confident' or 'confident' about this enterprise.

However, we were particularly aware in working with the above data that evidence from other studies presented a far less rosy picture of student teacher confidence in teaching mathematics. As such, we decided to design and conduct further exploratory task-based interviews with four exit-level pre-service Foundation Phase students drawn from two institutions that were part of the broader project as a way of understanding student teachers' ways of knowing mathematics for themselves and for teaching. We sought to appreciate their ways of knowing and working with mathematics and the ways in which they worked through two pairs of linked problems (one pair focused on additive relations and the other on division).

More specifically, we were interested in:
- ✓ their ways of solving the problems for themselves, including whether they recognised and worked with the problem pairs in linked or separate ways, and
- ✓ their ways of representing and explaining problem-solving processes for the purposes of instruction.

The sections that follow briefly outline the literature dealing with the ways in which 'maths for oneself' and 'maths for the learning of others' potentially overlap and differ. Our theoretical position is grounded in a socio-cultural view of mathematical activity as goal-directed towards increasingly powerful, general and flexible domain-related competences, and mediated through a range of semiotic forms. This is followed by an explanation of our methodological choices and some background on the student teachers who agreed to participate in the study in informal one-to-one task-based interviews, as well as detail on the tasks used with them. Thereafter follows an analysis of their responses and some of their commentary and reflections on their working, locating the findings in relation to the broader study's questionnaire-based dataset on the broader experiences of pre-service mathematics education programmes. The conclusion reflects on what the findings point to in the context of Foundation Phase ITE, related to ways of working with mathematics for oneself and mathematics for instruction.

7.2 Literature Review: Student Teacher Knowledge Perspectives in Mathematics Education

Interest in the types of subject-related knowledge unique to teaching originates from Shulman's (1986, 1987) studies on the work of secondary teachers and the development of teachers' SMK. While it is widely accepted that teachers need to know the content they are teaching (SMK), Shulman identified the need for a knowledge base related to how to teach the subject matter. This way of thinking about knowledge for teaching moved beyond disciplinary CK and is referred to as PCK.

This study focuses on the development of both SMK and PCK in the teaching of mathematics, with the former linked to the notion of 'maths for oneself' and the latter linked to 'maths for the learning of others'. We approach SMK as incorporating, as noted by Shulman (1986:9), "the amount and the organisation of knowledge per se in the mind of the teacher" – meaning that the teacher must not only understand 'that' something is so but further understand 'why' it is so. This comprises the theories, concepts, principles and approaches to generating and verifying mathematical ideas. PCK is approached as the knowledge that is particular to the work of teaching and includes ways of representing the content to make it comprehensible to others and "understanding what makes the learning of specific topics easy or difficult" (Shulman 1986:9). It includes the knowledge of the most useful forms of representations: "illustrations, examples, explanations and demonstrations, knowledge of learner conceptions, and preconceptions" (Shulman 1986:9).

This chapter mainly utilises the work of Deborah Ball and her colleagues on teacher knowledge. Their contribution elaborates on Shulman's work and uses detailed analyses of the actual work of mathematics teaching in primary schools (Ball, Hill & Bass 2004). The value of their practice-based theory model on MKT is that "it provides a professional knowledge of mathematics that is different from that demanded by other mathematically intensive occupations", such as engineering and carpentry and constitutes the mathematical knowledge needed to carry out the work of teaching mathematics at the primary school level (Ball, Hill & Bass 2005; Ball et al. 2008).

Notably, their MKT model separates SMK and PCK into further sub-classifications, as shown below.

Table 7.1   Comparison of the Shulman and Ball Models

Shulman (1987)	Ball et al. 2005; Ball et al. 2008
SMK	Common content knowledge (CCK)
	Specialised content knowledge (SCK)
	Horizon knowledge (HK)
PCK	Knowledge of content and teaching (KCT)
	Knowledge of content and students (KCS)
Curricular knowledge	Knowledge of content and curriculum (KCC)

For this chapter, the analysis is limited to Ball et al. 2005 and Ball et al. 2008, which are sub-category of CCK and SCK. We feel these allow us to more usefully engage with teachers' ways of knowing mathematics for themselves and for teaching. Ball et al. (2008) note that their categories provide a different orientation that allows for an 'unpacked' rather than a 'compressed' approach to mathematics; something that is crucial in teaching others.

Definitionally, CCK is the mathematical knowledge and skill used in settings other than teaching and involves correctly solving mathematical problems. It requires that teachers know the work they must teach, recognise incorrect answers, correctly use mathematical terms and notations, and have knowledge of the school mathematics curriculum to be able to design, plan and execute lessons. SCK, on the other hand, is defined as the mathematical knowledge and skill that are unique to teaching mathematics and involves unique mathematical understanding and reasoning. SCK requires knowledge beyond that which is taught to learners, where teachers need to understand different interpretations of mathematical problems and solutions and thereby help learners to make sense of their work and that of others. SCK involves making features of particular content visible to and learnable by learners and explaining how mathematical language is used, with teachers being able to choose, make and use effective mathematical representations that help learners to explain and justify their mathematical ideas.

7.3 Methodology

As noted in the introduction, this is a qualitative study that utilised interviews and questionnaires and incorporates the views of four student teachers as case studies. Methodologically, four student teachers who had exited an ITE programme were invited to interviews and their responses to a set of tasks were then analysed. The four students were from Institution A (a historically disadvantaged institution: three students); and Institution B (a historically advantaged institution: one student). All were fourth-year student teachers who had just completed their degree, including the relevant teaching practice experience. The three students at Institution A had practicum experience across Grades R-3, while the student at Institution B had taught predominately in Grade R and Grade 1 across her practicum experiences. All these student teachers had completed the required 32 weeks of teaching practice and had taught quite a bit of mathematics.

The focus in analysing the interview data was to record and understand their 'doing' of mathematics and their delineations of how they would go about teaching the mathematical ideas related to tasks aimed at Foundation Phase children. In this regard, the CCK/SCK distinction was particularly helpful since the respondents' CCK responses (how they solved the tasks for themselves) frequently differed from how they described working with these tasks with learners.

We selected two pairs of problems (on additive relations and on multiplicative relations) that each of the respondents were asked to solve. Both pairs were central to the Foundation Phase mathematics curriculum:

- ✓ A 1. 48 + 37
- ✓ A 2. 85 - 48
- ✓ M 1. 112 apples are put into packets containing 8 apples each. How many packets are needed?
- ✓ M 2. 112 apples are shared equally between 8 families. How many apples should each family receive?

Problems A 1 and A 2 are linked by the inverse relationship between addition and subtraction. Working with the link between the two problems required them to be mindful that the second problem could be answered without a separate calculation. Problems M 1 and M 2 are linked by the same quantities being used in two different kinds of division situations; M 1 is a 'grouping' situation, in which the size of a group is known and the number of groups must be calculated; M 2 is a 'sharing' situation involving distributing actions, in which the size of each group must be calculated. The student teachers were given time to solve each problem and to explain their strategies and were then asked to explain how they would go about teaching children how to solve the problems. We were also interested in whether the respondents saw connections between the problem pairs and probed for this if they did not notice connections spontaneously. The interviews were video recorded and transcribed to provide written evidence of their thinking and explanations.

The overall analysis included engaging with responses in the questionnaires completed by final-year student teachers related to teaching mathematics in the Foundation Phase, as well as selected questions related to CCK and SCK in the interviews.

7.4   Data Analysis

As mentioned previously, the analysis focused on the definitions provided within the MKT model for CCK and SCK as it related to student teachers' ways of working with problems for themselves and ways of representing and explaining problem-solving processes for the purpose of teaching. We first looked at their use of CCK: how they solved various problems and the explanations they gave based on their solutions, along with the mathematical terms and notation used and their knowledge of school mathematics.

Secondly, we analysed student teachers' SCK by focusing on their knowledge and their use of explanations, representations, and tasks to help children make sense of the mathematics and to develop their thinking. Their knowledge of explanation descriptors included being able to unpack the mathematics in order to provide meaning for children, and then further involved their presentation of ideas and the explanations and justifications of mathematical ideas – which included being able to make connections between ideas and knowledge of alternative algorithms for calculating. Knowledge of **representations** included knowing how to represent mathematical ideas, being able to map between different representations:

1. enactive; iconic and symbolic (Bruner 1974);
2. being able to connect and link representations; recognise what is involved in using a particular representation;
3. selecting and making use of representations for particular purposes; and
4. identifying and distinguishing between the range of different situations that can be modelled, e.g. subtraction, division, etc. (Ball et al. 2004, Ball et al. 2008).

The knowledge of **tasks** involved making judgments about the mathematical quality of instructional materials and being able to modify as necessary, selecting appropriate mathematical examples, appraising and adapting content, and modifying tasks to make them easier or more difficult (Ball et al. 2004, Ball et al. 2008).

7.5 Results

This section starts with excerpts from student teachers' responses to the pairs of problems presented to them with specific regard to CCK and SCK issues. Providing an analysis of their CCK and SCK offers brief introductions to each of the respondents.

We then discuss patterns emerging from these responses in relation to the MKT literature. We argue that the responses provide useful insights into thinking about mathematics education-oriented courses for Foundation Phase ITE students.

7.5.1 Case Study 1

Ms L is a mature student with a son in primary school who helps her when she prepares her mathematics homework. She says the mathematics courses she took at university were important, relevant and useful, and offered her an alternative experience of learning mathematics.

> The training I got is very important, it is very relevant, it helped me to understand the learners better. It helped me understand and I've gained insight into how the little ones deal with problems… We need to probe and ask questions: How did you get this answer?

Not having experienced this during her own schooling, she felt that children needed to have a well-established number sense.

Common Content Knowledge (CCK)

Across all four tasks, Ms L's responses suggested a flexible and fluent approach to solving the problems for herself. With the two additive tasks and the additional additive tasks used to probe the nature of Ms L's approaches, she presented a range of efficient mental calculation strategies where she used combinations of rounding, compensating and place value, decomposing of numbers (Delaney 2008). She used a flexible range of strategies that reflected an awareness of number relationships and properties, which is a key marker of having "number sense" (MacIntosh, Reys & Reys 1992). Similarly, on the two division tasks, Ms L was able to efficiently solve both division tasks, although the first 'grouping' of apples-based task she initially solved with a 'sharing'-based diagram, which she subsequently changed to a grouping-based diagram.

Specialised Content Knowledge (SCK)

With regard to Ms L's own problem solving, there were contrasts between her fluency and flexibility and her discourse around how she would go about teaching the ideas related to these tasks. On the additive relations, her initial explanations for her selected strategies for solving the different tasks were poorly articulated and imprecise. For example, in her own solution of $18 + 17$, Ms L used a rounding and compensating method that she described in the following terms:

> [L]ook at what is the nearest 10 to round it off, which gives me 20, and I have added 2 there, plus 17 to the nearest 10, would give me 20, added 3 there. Then 20 plus 20 is 40, and then minus 2 plus 3 is five, which would give me a total of 35.

When asked if she would use this method in teaching, she commented that for struggling children, she would use prompts like:

> What next biggest number is closest to 18? And closest to 17?

When we suggested that children might respond with "19" to this question, she then amended her initial response with a follow-up question:

> Yes, 19. But is 19 to the nearest 10?

In other instances she displayed similar imprecisions related to teaching, but with further follow-up probing, she was able to recognise her errors and self-corrected them.

Furthermore, while Ms L was able to flexibly change her strategy for efficient working related to the set problems, these changes often relied on tacit understandings and she was not able to make the changes explicit in her explanatory talk. As before, when probed, her initial explanations contained imprecisions. However, with further questioning, she was able to clarify and correct her answers. She explained this flexible orientation as important to building number sense and as something that she encouraged within her teaching:

> No, I wasn't looking for a particular method, I looked at what they can do first and I decided okay, I can see that you are struggling then I would ask them (12 + 17), what about turning the numbers around and counting on from there… [I]t is not a particular method that I am looking for but how they lead me.

While the above suggested a flexible repertoire of strategies, it was in her verbalised rationale for flexibly shifting to a different approach that key gaps appeared. Overall, her explications of when and why shifts were made, were largely of tacit nature.

7.5.2 Case Study 2

Ms Y is a young teacher who entered the Foundation Phase ITE programme straight from school. While she enjoys mathematics, she does not feel confident about teaching the subject to younger children.

CCK

In completing the tasks, Ms Y had no difficulty in providing solutions for all four tasks using a variety of strategies. These included number decomposition, compensation, column subtraction and division as a mental calculation. She experienced no difficulties in completing the tasks, although her range of strategies was not as flexible as Ms L's. Her CCK indicated understanding of the problems and her solutions were not restricted to standard algorithms. She noted that she felt comfortable to teach mathematics but not in all topics:

> I feel comfortable with data handing, with space and shape, because you can explore a lot with those things. Division and multiplication, I would say that I would be a lot more nervous with fractions as well.

SCK

When asked how she would help children operating at the more concrete level to solve an additive problem such as 48 + 37, Ms Y offered a range of approaches such as using resources like place value cards, number charts, counters and unifix blocks. She suggested that these were more useful for children struggling to work with large numbers:

> Sometimes they are not quite ready to use these kind of big numbers; they still need to see it and feel it.

However, although she demonstrated a good understanding of how to use different resources to develop mathematical thinking, when probed she showed less of a sense of how to appropriately use them. For example, when asked to explain how she would work with the place value cards to solve 8 + 7, she quickly abandoned this resource and switched to using a number line. In other instances she would often start with a particular explanation, realise it was not helpful for children, and then provide a self-corrected method. A key concern was her tendency to default to concrete/pictorial representations to meet lower attainers where they were rather focusing on how these children might be supported to move on from such representations:

> We do something like this as a word sum or word problem so that children can visualise and are able to draw it. Because when they see this, they feel like it is calculating.

A key problem for Ms Y in the above regard was that she could not always coherently explain her use of different representations/resources when teaching children various problems, especially with an eye on them successfully completing their tasks. While able to solve all the problems, she displayed a limited range of strategies to do so, or how to help children make connections and link representations (Ball et al. 2008) to solve problems.

7.5.3 Case Study 3

Ms M only engaged with Grade R and Grade 1 classrooms in her practicum experience. She had not had any opportunities during her teaching practicums to apply her knowledge and skills to Grade 2 and Grade 3 children, although she did share key theories of how to teach older children. This background shaped her responses to the questions on SCK.

CCK

Ms M made use of a variety of strategies to solve addition and subtraction problems, including place value, decomposition and building to ten.

> A1: I would add the 10s and the units. 40 + 30 = 70, then 8 + 7 = 8 + 2 + 5 so that is another 10 and then I have the 5: 48 + 37 = (40 + 30) + (8 + 7) = 70 + (8 + 2) + 5 = 70 + 10 + 5 = 85.

She also recognised that the above strategies would not work for a subtraction problem such as 94 - 37, and was able to suggest alternative solution strategies such as breaking the numbers into easy parts, i.e. 94 - 37 = 94 - 4 - 30 - 3, using the number line to track back from 94. In her interview, Ms M shared a range of appropriate representations for addition and subtraction problems and for solving the division problems. She was also able to identify different types of problems (sharing and grouping) and their links to division.

SCK

Ms M expressed commitment to the 'problem-solving method' in teaching mathematics, as promoted during her ITE course. This involved the teacher working with the whole class and/or smaller ability groups, presenting problems in context and giving children time to think about solutions using different manipulatives. Children are encouraged to move between enactive, iconic and symbolic representations (Bruner 1974). She noted that this included no prescriptions being given for solving problems and all solution offers being shared and discussed with children. Ms M also showed an awareness of a range of modes of representational thought.

A key concern was that she associated these with different learner abilities, rather than seeing them as progressively possible:

> The least developed will concentrate more on the drawings than the actual representation of the number and if you've got a top group learner, then they most likely do it without any drawing at all.

While she was aware of the need for oral and written communication in explanations, she did not mention the need for justification, nor of teacher modelling of different and more advanced strategies. There was pedagogical awareness, however, of early number strategies involving counting all and counting on and a strong commitment to non-directive teaching. When explaining how different children might solve the $18 + 7$ problem, she suggested the following:

> The more developed would probably break it up. They would use the numerals. So they would probably go, they'll know there's 10 and probably do the, probably fill up the 8 or the 7.

Interviewer: So how does that work? Show us.

> Okay, so they've got the $10 + 8 + 2 + 5$. That's just an option because we are told they can all come up with their own way.

When prompted, she was reluctant to actively engage in developing more advanced strategies, either through questioning or modelling alternatives for children's productions. She also displayed some difficulty with the selection and sequencing of tasks. When asked to provide a follow-up problem for $15 - 8$, she suggested $13 - 9$ and used the same strategy to solve the problem, which she wrote as follows:

> $13 - 9 = (10 + 3) - (3 + 6)$, so the 3s cancel one another and I am left with $10 - 6 = 4$.

The above responses indicate a good awareness of progression and different solution strategies, but worryingly, Ms M was not able to provide alternative strategies for teaching this problem. Thus, while she could solve the given problems for herself with various flexible solution strategies and using different representations, she displayed a general reluctance to develop strategies that provided more explicit explanations and alternative representations.

7.5.4 Case Study 4

Ms T is an older student. She was confident about where she has problems in solving problems and providing explanations, and generally about her mathematical knowledge:

> No topic is a problem, as far as I know I have been equipped with brilliant skills.

CCK

Ms T successfully completed all four tasks. She quickly recognised and calculated the answers but was unable in some cases to provide alternate ways for completing them. She used place value decomposition to solve the addition problem and the standard subtraction algorithm for 85 - 48 but without linking the two. The division problems were explained using groupings of eights, building up to 112, with some confusion about sharing and grouping. Her CCK was limited in terms of using different strategies to solve problems and extended to a lack of confidence in checking her answers.

When asked to comment on the mathematics content part of the course, she could not see the relevance of revisiting school mathematics for herself:

> If you have been through school to get to tertiary, you know your basics. For me, personally, Pythagoras does not have any dealings in my Foundation Phase classroom... For me I felt that [mathematics content] was a bit of a waste somewhat.

She expressed a preference for ITE programmes to give more time to the teaching of mathematics to better equip her for the classroom and saw no connection between higher levels of school mathematics and mathematics content in the Foundation Phase.

SCK

Ms T's explanations and representations of mathematical ideas related to addition included references to different strategies such as place value decomposition, grouping, place value cards, number charts with counting on, and counters. She described three different strategies that she could use with children, but could not explain how these strategies connected to one another.

She was able to solve the subtraction problem using the standard algorithm, but was unclear on what methods were appropriate to use to help children solve problems such as 85 - 48:

> That's like a trick question, cause in my numeracy [class], I've been asking how to teach taking away. The best that I would be able to do, would probably work with my tens and my units. How, I'm not quite sure just yet. I think maybe halving, that's even if they are on that level. So half of 80 would be 40, I don't know. First work out my groupings; actually I don't know how I'd work it out with them if I was given something like this.

The above showed that while Ms T had some knowledge of different representations and resources, she had a very limited sense of how resources and models could be used to develop children's understanding. When asked, for example, to modify the addition task, 18 + 17, to make it harder and to challenge children, she included an additional number and suggested the use of colour-coded place value cards and counters. Ms T was also happy for children to use whatever method they chose, with little mention of appraising and adapting content to make it easier or more difficult for them (Ball et al. 2008).

In the interview, Ms T displayed a limited repertoire of how to help children make meaning and could not easily build connections or develop strategies to improve their mathematical proficiency. While she mentioned different resources and methods, she could not easily identify or distinguish between the range or sequence of solutions that could be modelled for addition, subtraction and division.

7.6 Discussion

This section discusses some key issues that arose in the results section above, with a special focus on how the orchestration of tasks, resources, talk and children's offers in class are supported, as well as understandings of progression.

7.6.1 Supporting the Orchestration of Tasks, Resources, Talk and Children's Offers

Overall, the literature on the quality of primary mathematics instruction observes significant levels of imprecision and ambiguity in instructional talk (Hill et al. 2008). This was particularly evident in the case of Ms L, who exhibited important strengths in her CCK but displayed significant 'lags' in her SCK discourse. The latter, Ball et al. (2008) argue, is more important for teaching.

However, the problem becomes somewhat more acute when, as in the cases of Ms Y and Ms T, weaknesses were seen at the level of the CCK of teachers. When teachers lack flexibility in their own mathematical problem solving and are generally unable to provide or explain any alternative solutions beyond their own algorithm use, this does not bode well for how they would go about teaching those problems.

Ms L and Ms T, on the other hand, were able to improve or self-correct during the interviews when they were probed. They could think through what their responses implied and provide alternative answers. With regard to Foundation Phase mathematics, their approaches suggest the need to create opportunities within ITE programmes for greater practising of the coherent, connected and progression-oriented assembly of talk, resources, and inscriptions in the context of tasks (see Venkat & Askew 2017). In current iterations, this assembly tends to fall outside the gaze of traditional lesson plans, which generally focus on 'what' needs be covered in lessons and the resources needed to support this coverage, with much less explicit attention given to 'how' these forms should be orchestrated in concert with one another.

This was especially evident in the responses of Ms T and Ms Y, who mentioned a range of commonly used resources and models but showed very limited sense of how these resources should be used to teach specific tasks and ideas. For them, the resources seemed to be 'stand-alones', with them not taking into account what needed to be said alongside these resources and examples. Furthermore, Ms T named different resources and methods in ways that were largely dissociated from considerations of what children were likely offered. For example, with number chart working, she was aware that 'plus 10' involved moving down a square, but this was linked more to her own method and thinking and did not take into account how a child would respond. Overall, across the four case studies, there was pedagogical evidence of 'knowledge-in-pieces' in relation to the resources and models used, teacher talk and children's responses.

7.6.2 Understanding of Progression

In the four case studies there was evidence of significant limitations among the respondents in distinguishing elements of mathematical progression and providing tasks of greater difficulty. For example, Ms M described 13 - 9 as another example of 15 - 8, yet 13 - 9 could quite efficiently be solved mathematically by using a counting on from 9 (or a counting back to 9), while the same approach would be less appropriate for 15 - 8. Another example was evident in the case of Ms Y, who was asked to provide varied examples to cater for different ability levels on addition. She offered 25 + 11, 43 + 27, and 74 + 32, with her notion of progression explicitly focused on larger numbers but making no reference to the strategic sophistication that would be needed in developing early number learning. Ms Y's second and third examples involved 'carrying' but she made no reference to this in her explanation. Ms T also offered larger numbers (or increasing numbers) as the key mechanism to make examples more difficult.

7.7 Conclusion

According to Ball et al.'s (2008) contributions, the findings in the above case studies suggest that, overall, the respondents displayed strengths in CCK – they could mainly solve problems correctly in the context of the work that they needed to teach. Most of the respondents could also produce a variety of solution strategies for each of the problems provided and could identify artefacts/resources and representations that would assist in the formulation of answers.

However, in each of the case studies there was clear evidence of significant challenges in the respondents' specialised knowledge for teaching. They displayed limited mathematical understanding and reasoning needed for teaching, especially when it came to helping children make meaningful connections between number operations. Furthermore, and importantly, the questionnaire responses overviewed earlier in this chapter and that are presented in other chapters of this book, suggest that exiting ITE students are largely unaware of what the literature suggests are important parts of the professional knowledge base for mathematics teaching. Thus, a key value of the four case studies explored in the chapter was that it also raised serious methodological questions about the value of using questionnaire data when grappling with some fundamental questions in Foundation Phase teaching and learning.

In that respect, the findings and analysis provided in this chapter point to the need for ITE programmes to provide greater opportunities in their student teaching scenarios (in Foundation Phase mathematics) for mediation and the bringing together of different number forms. While all the student teachers were able to answer questions for themselves, their attempts to tailor their tasks/examples/resources and explanations for a range of children were much less fluent and flexible. The above analysis also suggests that the high levels of confidence encountered in the questionnaire data were probably tied to a notion of being able to do the mathematics 'for oneself' rather than 'for teaching'. While the 'dynamic situation of teaching' entails SMK, PCK and curricular knowledge needing to come together, this chapter illustrates the importance of being able to teach mathematics and being able to understand mathematical knowledge in ways that facilitate its teaching.

References

Adler, J. & Ronda, E. 2015. A framework for describing mathematics discourse in instruction and interpreting differences in teaching. *African Journal of Research in Mathematics, Science and Technology Education*, 19(3): 237-254. https://doi.org/10.1080/10288457.2015.1089677

Ball, D.L.; Bass, H. & Hill, H.C. 2004. Knowing and using mathematical knowledge in teaching: Learning what matters. In: A. Buffler, & R.C. Laugksch (eds). *Proceedings of the 12th Annual Conference of the Southern African Association for Research in Mathematics, Science and Technology Education (SAARMSTE)*. Durban: SAARMSTE, 51-65.

Ball, D.L.; Hill, H.C. & Bass, H. 2005. Knowing mathematics for teaching: Who knows mathematics well enough to teach third grade, and how can we decide? *American Educator*, 29(3): 14-46.

Ball, D.L.; Thames, M.H. & Phelps, G. 2008. Content knowledge for teaching: What makes it special? *Journal of Teacher Education*, 59(5): 398-407.

Bowie, L. & Reed, Y. 2016. How much of what? An analysis of the espoused and enacted mathematics and English curricula for Intermediate Phase student teachers at five South African universities. *Perspectives in Education*, 34(1): 102-119. https://doi.org/10.18820/2519593X/pie.v34i1.8

Bruner, J.C. 1974. *Beyond the information given: Studies in the psychology of knowing*. London: George Allan and Unwin.

Carnoy, M.; Chisholm, L. & Chilisa, B. (eds). 2012. *The low achievement trap: Comparing schools in Botswana and South Africa*. Cape Town: HSRC Press.

Delaney, S.F. 2008. *Adapting and using US measures to study Irish teachers' mathematical knowledge for teaching*. PhD dissertation. Ann Arbor: University of Michigan.

Hill, H.; Blunk, M.; Charalambos, Y.; Lewis, J.; Phelps, G.; Sleep, L. & Ball, D.L. 2008. Mathematical knowledge for teaching and the mathematical quality of instruction: An exploratory study. *Cognition and Instruction*, 26(4): 430-511. https://doi.org/10.1080/07370000802177235

Hoadley, U. 2012. What do we know about teaching and learning in South African primary schools? *Education as Change*, 16(2): 187-202. https://doi.org/10.1080/16823206.2012.745725

Ma, L.P. 1999. *Knowing and teaching elementary mathematics*. Mahwah, NJ: Lawrence Erlbaum.

Mathews, C. 2016. *Division means less: Chains of signification in a South African classroom*. Extended paper presented at the 13th International Congress on Mathematical Education. Hamburg, Germany, 24-31 July.

McIntosh, A.; Reys, B.J. & Reys, R.E. 1992. A proposed framework for examining basic number sense. *For the Learning of Mathematics*, 12(3): 2-44.

Rowland, T.; Turner, F.; Thwaites, A. & Huckstep, P. 2009. *Developing primary mathematics teaching*. London: Sage Publications.

Shulman, L. 1986. Those who understand: Knowledge growth in teaching. *Educational Researcher*, 15(2): 4-14. https://doi.org/10.3102/0013189X015002004

Shulman, L. 1987. Knowledge and teaching: Foundations of the new reform. *Harvard Educational Review*, 57(1): 1-22. https://doi.org/10.17763/haer.57.1.j463w79r56455411

Taylor, N. & Taylor, S. 2013. Teacher knowledge and professional habitus. In: N. Taylor, S. van der Berg & T. Mabogoane (eds). *Creating effective schools*. Johannesburg: Pearson Education, 202-232.

Venkat, H. & Askew, M. 2012. Mediating early number learning: Specialising across teacher talk and tools? *Journal of Education*, 56: 67-90.

Venkat, H. & Askew, M. 2017. *Focusing on the 'middle ground' of example spaces in primary mathematics teaching development in South Africa*. Paper presented at the Congress of European Research in Mathematics Education (CERME) 10 Conference. Dublin, 1-5 February.

Venkat, H. & Naidoo, D. 2012. Analyzing coherence for conceptual learning in a Grade 2 numeracy lesson. *Education as Change*, 16(1): 21-33. https://doi.org/10.1080/16823206.2012.691686

Venkat, H. & Spaull, N. 2015. What do we know about primary teachers' mathematical content knowledge in South Africa? An analysis of the SACMEQ 2007. *International Journal of Educational Development*, 41: 121-130. https://doi.org/10.1016/j.ijedudev.2015.02.002

Chapter 08

Learning to Teach Language in the Foundation Phase

Zelda Barends & Shelley Aronstam

8.1 Introduction

Teaching and learning language in the Foundation Phase in South Africa are complex. Prospective teachers' experiences of learning to teach languages are circumscribed by education language policy on the one hand and the diverse language situations in classrooms on the other. South Africa is a multilingual country, a fact which prompted the DoE to direct that learners are proficient and are able to communicate in at least two of the 11 official languages (DoE 2002:20). The DoE follows "an additive or incremental approach to multilingualism" (DoE 2002:20); that is, learning language in the Foundation Phase is divided into learning home language and one first additional language. This means that the Foundation Phase curriculum makes provision for language to be taught at the level of home language and one additional official language. Moreover, the curriculum makes provision for the languages to be taught discretely on the assumption that the home language is their mother tongue and the additional language is acquired at school.

The Foundation Phase curriculum makes provision for language to be taught via literacy (DoE 2002:15). Literacy or being literate refers to the ability to read and write well enough to enable functioning in society. Literacy rests on skills that enable one to solve problems, learn new information and find pleasure in written words (Brewer 2014:296). Within literacy, the focus is on the development of particular skills, namely listening and speaking, reading and phonics, writing and handwriting, thinking and reasoning, and language structure and use (DBE 2011:8). The CAPS encapsulates teaching of listening and speaking, phonics, reading and viewing, and writing as knowledge Foundation Phase learners ought to acquire in the process of learning language (DBE 2011:23-30), which would enable learners to be literate (i.e. listen, speak, spell, read and write).

With this in mind, this chapter asks what the experiences of Foundation Phase student teachers are regarding learning to teach language. In keeping with the theoretical framework provided in Chapter 1, knowledge sets relevant to teaching and developing language among Foundation Phase learners are discussed in this chapter. The chapter then presents data from BEd Foundation Phase student teachers relating to their perceived experiences of learning to teach language with respect to the knowledge sets.

8.2 Language and Literacy in the Foundation Phase

Shulman's (1986) conception of CK for teacher preparation is used in this chapter (together with Moats 1999 and Brewer 2014) as a framework to explore what the perceived experiences of student teachers are regarding learning to teach language. Shulman (1986), Moats (1999) and Brewer's (2014) conceptions of knowledge may be located in the first knowledge set of Chapter 1. A consequence of Shulman's conception of CK for teaching is that teacher preparation must take cognisance of context. Shulman's (1986, cf. introduction of the book) theoretical framework for teacher CK for teaching consists of SMK, PCK and curricular knowledge. Adopting this framework within ITE programmes will not only allow teachers to have knowledge of content but they will also understand the nature of knowledge and inquiry, as well as know their subjects from a pedagogical perspective (Barends 2015:40).

Young et al. (2001:1) state that the expectations for teachers are high in today's educational reform and policy agendas. Especially in the Foundation Phase, teachers need to be experts in one or more specific subjects, namely mathematics, languages (literacy) and life skills as Foundation Phase demands an integrated knowledge base. They must also be prepared to effectively handle the challenges of a growing diverse population of students with diverse needs and who are multicultural and multilinguistic (National Association for the Education of Young Children [NAEYC] 1995:2). Under these conditions, PCK and curricular knowledge are not static elements of knowledge development in the same way that CK or SMK is.

In South Africa, children are exposed to different languages in the home, at school and in their communities. South Africa's Language-in-Education Policy (LiEP) (DoE 1997) encourages that in the Foundation Phase, learners' LoLT should be their home language, while they should also acquire an additional language (DBE 2010:6). The LiEP states that all children have the right to learn in the language of their choice, usually their home language. The underlying principle of the LiEP is to maintain the use of home language as the LoLT, especially in the Foundation Phase.

Although South Africa has this LiEP that promotes additive multilingualism, many children are taught in a language other than their home language at school. The implementation of the LiEP in the diverse South African context is complicated by various socio-economic, political and social factors. The difficulties faced by schools in implementing LiEP fall into three categories: a mismatch between LoLT in the Foundation Phase and the home language of most learners, the dialectisation of African languages and the problem of terminology in mathematics (National Education Evaluation and Development Unit [NEEDU] 2012:3). English is considered to provide better social, economic and educational opportunities (Alexander 2010). This encourages English as a preferred language of instruction, rather than mother-tongue instruction (De Wet 2002), which contributes to the mismatch between the LoLT and the home language of learners.

The mismatch between LoLT and home language means that a large number of learners are schooled in a language that differs from the one spoken in their homes. The diversity of languages in the schools intensifies the multiplicity of teaching reading and writing. A common problem in the schools is that the African language spoken by many township children is seldom the standard form of that language. This phenomenon is known as the 'dialectisation' of a language. Dialect usually relates to a language spoken in a specific area or region. The NEEDU (2012) report also maintains that if learners do not attain language proficiency in the Foundation Phase, they will continue to face difficulties as they move into the Intermediate Phase.

A notable contribution to low academic results in South Africa is learners' poor language abilities. Many learners are often labelled 'slow learners' because of their limited language proficiency in the LoLT (Nel, Nel & Hugo 2016:93). Fleisch and Shoer (2014) and Spaull (2015) claim that this is evident in the ANA and PIRLS results in South Africa. Since language is the basis for all learning, it is vital that it receives proper attention in the classrooms. "All learning is based on a language system" (Choate 2004:152) and knowledge is presented by means of language (Raymond 2008).

As a consequence, home language can more accurately be regarded as the home language offered by the school and not necessarily the mother tongue of all learners in that school. Moreover, there is unequal access and differential exposure to the first additional language offered at schools.

The PCK to deliver language SMK to learners with a diverse range of language (and related literacy) proficiencies within a standardised curricula context is, at best, complex.

The LiEP promotes additive multilingualism so that learners in the Foundation Phase learn and develop their home language and a first additional language at the same time (DoE 2003:21). Additive multilingualism allows learners to acquire complex skills such as reading and writing in their home language and then transfer these skills to their additional language. This is considered integral in that learners learn how to listen, speak, read, write, think and reason in the Foundation Phase (DoE 2003:21-22). The CAPS curriculum condenses these skills into listening and speaking, phonics, reading and viewing, and handwriting and writing. It further acknowledges that in the Foundation Phase, a thematic approach is used for learners to acquire knowledge and the languages programme is integrated into all other subject areas as language is used across the curriculum in all oral work, reading and writing (DBE 2011:8).

Combined, the acquisition of these skills will enable Foundation Phase learners to be literate. That is, to repeat the ability to read and write in a language that they will use to function in society (Brewer 2014:296). Therefore, in the Foundation Phase, learners learn language through the acquisition of literacy and the skills associated with its development (DoE 2003; DBE 2011). In order to do this, teachers are expected to teach two languages at varying levels. Consequently, integrating SMK, PCK and curricular knowledge is an intricate task. From the perspective of student teachers, this means they would have experienced learning to teach a home language and first additional language during their initial teacher training before entering their own classrooms.

The debates about LiEP, the implementation thereof and the context of language and literacy in the Foundation Phase, highlight the intricacy of teaching and learning language in this phase. Considering this, ITE programmes have a pivotal role to play in preparing teachers to teach language in the Foundation Phase. Prospective teachers should acquire knowledge that will equip them to be able to promote multilingualism in a diverse South Africa. In addition, prospective teachers need preparation to provide all learners with equal learning opportunities in their own language. Moreover, prospective teachers must acquire skills to promote learners' literacy abilities as well as promote learners' English literacy abilities, considering the implementation of the LiEP.

8.3 Literacy in the Foundation Phase

The history of South Africa has filtered into the education system and has left classrooms with complex issues that challenge teaching and learning. Current South African classrooms are confronted with circumstances where teachers and learners do not share the same common language or cultural background. Multilingualism is a functional reality in society and it challenges traditional visions of language education (Ziegler 2013:2). Teachers need to embrace diversity but handle situations which lean towards uniformity and conformity (Bloch 1999:40). Irrespective of the language permutations in a classroom and between the mother tongue of learners and the LoLT, teachers are expected to follow a standardised curriculum and learners are expected to write similar, standardised tests. This has major implications for teaching literacy (the ability to read and write), which is a central concern of Foundation Phase teaching and learning (DBE 2011:8).

Hannon (1995:5-6) describes literacy as the key to the rest of the curriculum as the school curriculum requires learners to be literate to progress through it. This is so because learners are expected to work independently, read, write and follow directions and instructions. It is for this reason that learners' language proficiency plays a pivotal role in the development of literacy.

Language is an integral part of literacy in the Foundation Phase curriculum (Motshekga 2010). The DoE (2002) integrates the four language systems into the school curriculum that learners need to acquire (see Table 8.1).

Table 8.1   The Four Language Systems which Learners Must Acquire

Aural language	Oral language	Print system	Written language
(Language heard)	(Language spoken)	(Language seen)	(Language used)
This refers to receptive language, which is language that is heard.	This refers to expressive language, which is language that is spoken.	This refers to receptive language, which includes printed words.	This refers to expressive language, which is written language.

Embedded in the language systems are the literacy skills (stipulated by the DBE in the CAPS curriculum) that learners must acquire. It can thus be seen that the knowledge required to teach literacy is embedded in language and this is confirmed by Moats and Tolman (2009:9), who state that language proficiency and literacy (reading, spelling and writing achievement) are strongly related to each other. It is expected that Foundation Phase student teachers would be exposed to elements of literacy in the process of learning language.

Language is essential in the acquisition of literacy as it is the foundation of listening, speaking, spelling, reading and writing. Furthermore, language is a system of communication used by humans; it is either produced orally or by sign and can be extended into written form (Brewer 2014:258). Also, it is important to note that language is rule-governed and thus has a set of systems that depicts its structure. Language is a code or system used to represent concepts, while words are the symbols of the code (Nel 2015:3). Each language has its own rules and sets of sound combinations. The systems of language include phonology, morphology, syntax, semantics and pragmatics (Brewer 2014).

In addition, the knowledge of systems of language enables users of language to read and write, which embodies literacy. It can thus be concluded that the systems of language should be embedded in the disciplinary knowledge for literacy teaching courses in ITE programmes (Van der Merwe & Nel 2012). It can be interpreted that language is a necessary prerequisite for literacy, even though having the knowledge of language does not necessarily mean one is fully literate. The two are in a complex symbiotic relationship.

Acknowledging that teaching is a complicated task due to the learning environment and its demands, prospective teachers require the necessary knowledge that will equip them to teach. Considering how language and literacy are dependent on each other highlights the difficulty language teachers experience as they have to understand their subject matter (CK) deeply and flexibly in order to help learners in their classroom, but they also have to understand how concepts connect in and to everyday life (Shulman 1987:7). Thus, language teachers ought to understand how the structure of language contributes to their SMK so that they are able to teach literacy and produce literate learners. In practice, according to Shulman's conception, this means that each student teacher would require the CK or SMK of two languages in order to be prepared to deliver the Foundation Phase curriculum in full with regard to language teaching (HL and FAL). Moreover, student teachers ought to be able to draw on PCK, which will enable them to deliver SMK to learners with diverse competencies in each language in order to reach the aims of a standard curriculum. Bloch (1999:55-56) states that teachers' acquisition of the teaching skills necessary to teach language and literacy are critical, especially in South Africa as there is much uncertainty about how to teach literacy, as well as which language to use.

8.4 Content or Subject Matter Knowledge for Literacy

According to the DoE (2008:12), teachers responsible for teaching literacy in the Foundation Phase must have knowledge of the five components of reading, namely phonemic awareness, word recognition, vocabulary, fluency and comprehension. In 1997, the National Reading Panel (NRP) assessed the status of research-based knowledge as well as the effectiveness of various approaches to teaching children to read in English (NRP 2000:1-1) and found, like the DoE, that the inclusion of these five components in the teaching of literacy should form an integral part of Foundation Phase teacher preparation programmes. Moats et al. (2010:1) maintain that teaching literacy and reading requires specialised knowledge about language and how children learn and acquire literacy skills and instructional strategies. Moats (1999:14) established a core curriculum for literacy and reading teacher preparation and its goal is to bring continuity, consistency and comprehensiveness to ITE. This particular curriculum is divided into four areas:

- ✓ Understanding knowledge of reading psychology and development.
- ✓ Understanding knowledge of language structure, which is the content of instruction.
- ✓ Applying best practices in all aspects of reading instruction.
- ✓ Using validated, reliable and efficient assessments to inform classroom teaching.

Research indicates that teachers' knowledge of language structure contributes to teaching literacy and reading effectively and to differentiate instruction for diverse learners. This component of the curriculum proposed by Moats is what Shulman refers to as content or subject matter knowledge for teaching. Van der Merwe and Nel (2012:145-146) found that language structure should form the bedrock of literacy training so that pre-service teachers can be equipped to teach phonemic awareness, phonics, fluency, vocabulary and reading comprehension. Not only do these components form part of the scientifically based reading instruction programme, but inherently forms the CK (or SMK) that Shulman (1986) refers to. Moreover, the CAPS expects both to be covered in HL as well as FAL teaching in the Foundation Phase. Table 8.2 indicates how the aspects of language structure that form the disciplinary knowledge base can be incorporated into literacy modules so that student teachers can teach the reading literacy components.

Table 8.2   The Disciplinary Knowledge Base Required to Teach the Reading Literacy Component

Aspect of language structure	Reading literacy component
Phonology	Phonemic awareness
Phonology Morphology Etymology Orthography	Phonics
Morphology Etymology Orthography Semantics	Vocabulary
Syntax Pragmatics	Reading comprehension
Fluency is tied to all of the aspects of language structure and the integration of the instruction of phonology, morphology, etymology, orthography, semantics, syntax, and pragmatics will develop fluency.	Fluency

Source: Van der Merwe and Nel (2012:146)

8.4.1 Pedagogical Content Knowledge (PCK)

PCK refers to knowing how to deliver subject matter in the classroom. Put simply, it refers to the knowledge for teaching and captures the complex yet necessary relationship between SMK and professional knowledge or teaching ability. This complex relationship is illustrated by Snow, Burns and Griffin (1998:279), who state that

> teachers must understand a great deal about how children develop and learn, what they know, and what they can do. Teachers must know and be able to apply a variety of teaching techniques to meet the individual needs of learners. They must be able to identify learners' strengths and weaknesses and plan instructional programmes that help make learner's progress.

Knowing the subject matter is necessary for PCK, but not sufficient. Barends (2015:56) found that knowledge for teaching requires that teachers take complex CK, break it down into understandable entities and use that in their teaching. For example, for reading literacy, teachers' knowledge of morphology enables teaching vocabulary; and teachers' ability to unpack morphology into its most basic form such as suffixes, prefixes, compounds and roots contributes to teaching learners vocabulary. In addition, knowledge for teaching or PCK comprises knowledge of which methods and activities to draw on, as well as considering ways to represent and formulate the content so that it is understandable to learners (Ball 2000:245). This means that when teaching reading literacy, for example, a repertoire of knowledge and skills to teach morphology and develop vocabulary is required for a diverse group of learners from different backgrounds with varying competencies and experiences. The capacity to mediate learning requires that teachers have a firm grasp of particular content or subject matter, as well as the manner in which learners learn and know that content or subject matter.

Grossman, Schoenfeld and Lee (2005:205) state that effective teachers need subject matter competence, they need to know how to solve problems that they pose to learners and know that there are multiple approaches to solving many problems; however, this is not enough. Teachers need to make the right choices. Therefore, they need to know what kinds of mistakes learners are likely to make and they must be prepared to address the sources of learners' errors in a way that will contribute to their learning. Effective teachers know much more than their subjects and good pedagogy; "they know how students tend to understand (and misunderstand) their subjects, they know how to anticipate and diagnose such misunderstandings, and they know how to deal with them when they arise" (Grossman et al. 2005:205) and this knowledge is known as PCK.

A teacher education programme that carefully constructs student teacher experiences of learning to teach, as described by Darling-Hammond (2009), would allow PCK to be developed. Careful construction involves integration and an ongoing loop between formal lectures, practical teaching opportunities and guided reflection (Darling-Hammond 2009). In South Africa, teaching practice forms a critical component of teacher education programmes, thus providing ample opportunity for such integration. The Integrated Strategic Planning Framework for Teacher Education and Development in South Africa: 2011-2025 notes that the teaching practice component of teacher education programmes can be strengthened (DBE & DHET 2011). A study related to reading literacy and teaching practice drawing on data from teacher educators found that enhanced integration between various stakeholders is required (Barends 2015). This study could not, however, locate research that gathered data from the perspective of student teachers, specifically with regard to learning to teach language. The data presented in this chapter make a contribution in this regard, although further research in this area is required, as will be argued in the conclusion.

8.5 Methodology

The data for this chapter were obtained from fourth-year BEd Foundation Phase student teachers at three institutions offering teacher education in South Africa. This chapter draws on data from three questionnaires and focus group interviews conducted with student teachers.

The questionnaires focused on generating information about students' motivation for becoming a teacher and their experiences related to their academic programme and teaching practice. The data for this chapter draw on Section 4 of Questionnaire 1; being the beliefs and language and teaching language(s) in the Foundation Phase, and Section C of Questionnaire 2, being about learning about language and teaching language(s) in the Foundation Phase. Questionnaires were selected as a source of data collection because more responses can be obtained in a shorter time period than qualitative methods like interviews or observation. Questionnaires are, however, limited in their ability to tease out content or subject matter, as well as the pedagogic subject matter of more than one language. Moreover, questionnaire data are limited to the extent that they can capture integration between formal lectures, teaching practice and guided reflection.

The focus group interviews were conducted to elicit student teachers' perceptions and views of their ITE programme in a narrative form. The focus group interviews were conducted on four different campuses of three institutions from three different BEd Foundation Phase programmes. Themes that were extracted from responses to the focus group interview questions are discussed. The focus group interviews provide additional insight into student teachers' experiences regarding learning to teach language in the Foundation Phase.

8.6 Student Teachers' Experiences in Learning to Teach Languages in the Foundation Phase

8.6.1 Student Teachers' Language Demographics

Student teachers' experience of learning to teach language is framed by their personal language biographies. In other words, the language competencies student teachers arrive at teacher education providers with shape their engagement with language in the programme. This section presents the data that describe the language demographics of the student teachers who completed the questionnaires. Table 8.3 describes the primary home language of student teachers who responded to Questionnaire 2. Table 8.4 illustrates their home language in Grade 12.

Table 8.3 Primary Home Language of Student Teachers

Primary home language	N (%)
isiXhosa	8 (3,3)
Afrikaans	130 (53,7)
English	70 (28,9)
isiZulu	20 (8,3)
Sesotho	0 (0)
Setswana	1 (0,4)
Sepedi	1 (0,4)
isiNdebele	6 (2,5)
Tshivenda	0 (0)
Xitsonga	1 (0,4)
siSwati	5 (2,1)
Q3 Teaching practice (BEd): N=243 (missing = 1)	

Table 8.4 Home Language in Grade 12

Home language in Grade 12	N (%)
isiXhosa	8 (3,3)
Afrikaans	131 (53,9)
English	71 (29,2)
isiZulu	19 (7,8)
Sesotho	0 (0)
Setswana	1 (0,4)
Sepedi	1 (,4)
isiNdebele	6 (2,5)
Tshivenda	0 (0)
Xitsonga	1 (0,4)
siSwati	5 (2,1)
Q3 Teaching practice (BEd): N=243	

Most student teachers who responded to the questionnaire reported Afrikaans or English as their primary home language and Grade 12 home language. African languages were reported as the primary home language and Grade 12 home language of 24% and 22% of the student teachers respectively. Table 8.5 shows the student teachers' FAL in Grade 12.

Table 8.5   First Additional Language (FAL) in Grade 12

FAL in Grade 12	N (%)
isiXhosa	2 (0,8)
Afrikaans	69 (28,6)
English	169 (70,1)
isiZulu	0 (0)
Sesotho	0 (0)
Setswana	0 (0)
Sepedi	0 (0)
isiNdebele	0 (0)
Tshivenda	0 (0)
Xitsonga	0 (0)
siSwati	0 (0)
Q3 Teaching practice (BEd): N=243 (missing = 3)	

The majority of the student teachers did English (71,1%) or Afrikaans (27,9%) as their FAL in Grade 12. This means that just less than one quarter of the student teachers who responded to the questionnaires had prior knowledge of an African language when entering the teacher education programme.

8.6.2   Student Teachers' Exposure to Language in the BEd Programmes

Exposure to language, and hence the experience of learning to teach language in BEd programmes, takes on various forms. Programme courses are offered in a particular language, language courses are offered, language method courses are offered and teaching practice is conducted in classrooms with particular LoLTs. This section first presents data related to programme courses and then data related to teaching practice.

The language of instruction in the BEd programmes varies between English and Afrikaans, depending on the institution; Institutions A and B offer lectures in English and Afrikaans, while Institution C offers lectures in English. Institutions A and B also offer English, Afrikaans and isiXhosa language courses. Institution C offers English, Afrikaans and Sesotho language courses. Institutions A and B offer English and Afrikaans language method or language in education courses. Institution C offers English, Afrikaans and Sesotho language method courses. In language courses, knowledge of the subject content language is taught, while in language method or language in education courses, SCK and PCK are presented.

All three questionnaires asked student teachers to report on knowledge they had gained during their programme relating to the following literacy skills: speaking, listening and comprehension, and reading and writing. Due to the diverse range of language course offerings and the nature of a questionnaire as a data-collection tool, it was not possible to ask questions that relate to every language permutation. The choice to focus on literacy skills was guided by the CAPS language documents. This limitation of the study requires more extensive engagement in future research.

The first questionnaire asked student teachers about their motivations and beliefs related to language teaching, as well as their competence and confidence to develop these skills in Foundation Phase learners. The findings from these questionnaires are presented below according to items asked and do not necessarily follow the order of the questionnaires or questions. The findings are presented in order to demonstrate how student teachers perceive what they know about teaching languages in the Foundation Phase, as an essential element of their experience of learning to teach language.

The findings presented here describe student teachers' perceived experience of knowledge of language and literacy as elicited from the questionnaires. Responses to qualitative questions in the questionnaires as well as focus group interviews are integrated where relevant. Table 8.6 indicates that student teachers clearly acknowledged the symbiotic relationship discussed above between language and literacy. Not one student teacher who responded to this item about beliefs regarding language either strongly disagreed or disagreed that language assists learners to listen, speak, read and write.

Table 8.6   Beliefs about Language

Item	Strongly disagree N (%)	Disagree N (%)	Agree N (%)	Strongly agree N (%)
Language assists learners to listen, speak, read and write.	0 (0)	0 (0)	67 (26,1)	190 (73,9)
Q1 Teacher motivation and beliefs (BEd): N=259 (missing = 2)				

Student teachers reported that it is important to develop literacy skills – including speaking, listening with comprehension, reading and writing – during language teaching. In all cases, more than 75% of the respondents indicated that these were very important. Table 8.7 is an indication of responses regarding how important developing reading is in language teaching.

Table 8.7   How Important is Developing These Skills during Language Teaching?

Item	Not at all N (%)	Somewhat important N (%)	Important N (%)	Very important N (%)
Learning to read	1 (0,4)	3 (1,2)	51 (19,7)	204 (78,8)
Q1 Teacher motivation and beliefs (BEd): N=259				

The data suggest that student teachers' experiences encompassed SMK and PCK associated with learning to teach language in the Foundation Phase. In the second questionnaire administered to the student teachers, they were asked three general questions related to whether their programmes covered the CK, PCK and curricula knowledge of Foundation Phase subjects. In all cases, 100% of the total valid responses were that the student teachers' programmes had covered it. In addition, over 85% of the respondents indicated that the coverage was either useful (over 35%) or very useful (over 44%). The majority of the student teachers (54,1%) indicated that the curricula content was very useful for their development as a teacher. Table 8.8 indicates the student teachers' responses to how useful the coverage of knowledge of the CAPS curriculum in their academic programme was to their development as a teacher.

Table 8.8   How Useful was the Coverage of Knowledge of the CAPS Curriculum in the Programme

Item	Not at all N (%)	Somewhat useful N (%)	Useful N (%)	Very useful N (%)
Knowledge of the CAPS curriculum	1 (0,4)	3 (1,2)	51 (19,7)	204 (78,8)
Q2 Teacher knowledge (BEd): N=224 (missing = 19)				

Similarly, in the third questionnaire, student teachers agreed (77,5%) to having sound subject knowledge, as well as knowing how to teach their subject (73,2%). In addition, student teachers agreed (64%) and strongly agreed (32,5%) that they were knowledgeable about the curriculum. The answers to these questions reveal that student teachers have experienced SCK associated with language.

Student teachers were asked to report on the extent to which they had been taught to develop literacy skills (speaking, listening and comprehension, reading aloud and writing) in language teaching on a scale of 'not at all', 'somewhat', 'moderately' and 'totally'. The responses to 'totally' ranged between 49,3% (speaking) and 54,8% (reading aloud). The responses to 'moderately' ranged between 38,9% (reading aloud) and 43,9% (speaking). In all cases the combined total of 'moderately' and 'totally' amounted to over 93%. Notwithstanding these responses, over 60% reported that they required additional development either moderately or totally with regard to the same literacy skills. Similarly, in the third questionnaire, the majority (over 55%) indicated they would like to receive substantial CPD in literacy skills. The responses to these prompts reveal that student teachers have experienced SCK associated with learning to teach language. At the same time, student teachers' experiences seem to have brought awareness that their knowledge is not absolute and that their development in this regard ought to continue.

Student teachers were asked how competent they felt to develop the skills during language teaching as a feature of their perceived PCK. In all cases – in speaking, listening and comprehension, reading, and writing – the responses to 'competent' and 'very competent' totalled over 85%, equally split between the two (competent and very competent). The only diversion from this was reading, where, although the combined percentage also totalled over 85%, the split was less equal. Table 8.9 presents the student teachers' responses to how competent they reported being to develop reading during language teaching.

Table 8.9 Competence in Developing Reading Skills in Learners during Language Teaching

Item	Not at all N (%)	Somewhat competent N (%)	Competent N (%)	Very competent N (%)
Reading	0 (0)	26 (10,1)	132 (51,2)	100 (38,8)
Q1 Teacher motivation and beliefs (BEd): N=259 (missing = 1)				

Student teachers were asked how confident they felt to develop the skills during language teaching, as another feature of their perceived PCK. Similar to the responses to how competent they felt, in all cases – in speaking, listening and comprehension, reading and writing – the responses 'confident' and 'very confident' totalled over 85%, equally split between the two (confident and very confident). In this case, reading did not present a diversion; it was also split equally. The combined total of confidence to develop reading during language teaching was, however, the least, at 86,4%. Table 8.10 indicates the student teachers' responses to how confident they reported being to develop reading during language teaching.

Table 8.10 Confidence in Developing Reading Skills in Learners during Language Teaching (Q1)

Item	Not at all N (%)	Somewhat confident N (%)	Confident N (%)	Very confident N (%)
Reading	0 (0)	35 (13,7)	121 (47,3)	100 (39,1)
Q1 Teacher motivation and beliefs (BEd): N = 259 (missing = 3)				

When responding to the third questionnaire, the student teachers' combined responses to 'confident' and 'very confident' to indicate that reading development went up to 93,8% (see Table 8.11).

Table 8.11 Confidence in Developing Reading Skills in Learners during Language Teaching (Q3)

Item	Not at all N (%)	Somewhat confident N (%)	Confident N (%)	Very confident N (%)
Reading	0 (0)	15 (6,3)	111 (46,3)	114 (47,5)
Q3 Teaching practice (BEd): N=243 (missing = 3)				

Student teachers were asked to indicate whether a number of teaching strategies had been taught to them by their lecturers with specific regard to teaching language in the Foundation Phase. These questions were regarded as further features of their perceived pedagogical and pedagogical content knowledge. Most student teachers responded that they had been taught these moderately or totally on a scale of not at all, somewhat, moderately and totally – to all the teaching strategies:

- ✓ Explicitly state learning goals
- ✓ Start from learners' prior knowledge
- ✓ Group learners according to their ability
- ✓ Read for enjoyment
- ✓ Use language to develop concepts
- ✓ Storytelling
- ✓ Allow learners to follow their own interests and ideas
- ✓ Allow for interpretations and comments from learners themselves

Table 8.12 presents the student teachers' responses to being prepared to use the teaching strategy of 'start from learners' prior knowledge'. Student teachers reported being especially well prepared in this regard.

Table 8.12 Extent to which You have been Prepared to use the 'Start from Learners' Prior Knowledge' Teaching Strategy

Item	Not at all N (%)	Somewhat N (%)	Moderately N (%)	Totally N (%)
Start from learners' prior knowledge	1 (0,5)	4 (1,8)	55 (24,9)	161 (72,9)
Q2 Teacher knowledge (BEd): N = 224 (missing = 3)				

In addition, student teachers were asked to indicate whether a number of lesson strategies had been taught to them by their lecturers with specific regard to reading and writing, as well as listening and comprehension. Most student teachers responded in the affirmative to all the lesson strategies:

- ✓ Whole-class teaching.
- ✓ Group learners according to their ability.
- ✓ Use of multimodal and visual texts.
- ✓ Use of drama and role play.
- ✓ Use of the chalkboard.
- ✓ Use of the whiteboard.
- ✓ Have learners work individually.
- ✓ Have learners work in pairs.
- ✓ Have learners work in groups.
- ✓ Use of worksheets.
- ✓ Use of prescribed textbooks.
- ✓ Use of educational technology.
- ✓ Facilitate a class discussion.

For both reading and writing, as well as listening and comprehension, 100% of the student teachers responded that they had been taught these lesson strategies by their lecturers.

The teaching and lesson strategies demonstrate aspects of student teachers' experience of pedagogical knowledge and pedagogical content knowledge. The questionnaires are, however, not helpful in understanding exactly how student teachers experienced and perceived the integration between the content or SMK, PCK and curricula knowledge. These strategies are established during teaching practice. One participant indicated:

> [M]ost of the time we do our things in practicals. Like today, we were learning about group reading. We ended up doing it practically, and we will present it. We presented it... and now we know how to do it (FG, BEd, Inst. A 2016).

In the focus group interviews, the student teachers provided narrative responses of their experiences in learning to teach language. In one focus group interview, the respondents reported that they were very well prepared to teach learners to read and write in Afrikaans, but not for any other language, including English.

One participant indicated:

> [T]he nitty-gritty things about the reading and writing, like for English. I am going to teach in English obviously because I am English but I don't feel like I am prepared. I am more prepared to teach reading and writing in Afrikaans than I am able to teach it in English (FG, BEd, Inst. B 2016).

Another participant stated:

> I would use my Afrikaans lesson plan to teach English (FG, BEd, Inst. B 2016).

This is a concern as it emphasises that the student teachers' experiences of learning to teach all languages are not similar. The data from the focus group interviews indicate that the respondents may regard the nature of learning to teach a language as didactic. One participant indicated:

> Because technically, what you learn in Afrikaans, you learn in English, even if it's a different language. We didn't have a textbook to guide us... I bought our Afrikaans book in English... It wasn't recommended by the lecturer or anything, literally our Afrikaans textbook in English (FG, BEd, Inst. B 2016).

The focus group responses suggest that PCK is experienced by the student teachers as interchangeable. Moreover, from the focus group interviews it appears that the student teachers did not experience a uniform approach to PCK in their courses. As such, while the quantitative data indicate that the student teachers had certainly experienced SMK and PCK in their BEd programmes, the qualitative data draw attention to a possible lack of integration in their overall experience. Data are not presented related to the student teachers' teaching practice experience.

The following four tables (Tables 8.13 to 8.16) contain student teachers' responses to the medium of instruction of the classroom in which they taught during teaching practice. The medium of instruction of the classrooms in which the student teachers taught during teaching practice somewhat mirrors the primary medium home language and Grade 12 home language of the respondents. Between 10% and 15% fewer student teachers have, however, taught in Afrikaans classrooms during teaching practice than those whose home language is Afrikaans. Student teachers taught in classrooms where an African language is the medium of instruction in between 12% (in second to fourth year) and 18% (first year) of cases.

Table 8.13   Medium of Instruction Year 1[1]

Medium of instruction Year 1	N (%)
isiXhosa	3 (1,8)
Afrikaans	67 (40,1)
English	63 (37,7)
isiZulu	17 (10,2)
Sesotho	0 (0)
Setswana	1 (0,6)
Sepedi	2 (1,2)
isiNdebele	3 (1,8)
Tshivenda	0 (0)
Xitsonga	0 (0)

1   Missing in this table is high because the students from one institution do not go on teaching practice in the first year.

Table 8.13   Medium of Instruction Year 1 *(cont)*

Medium of instruction Year 1	N (%)
siSwati	4 (2,4)
Q3 Teaching practice (BEd): N=243 (missing = 76)	

Table 8.14   Medium of Instruction Year 2

Medium of instruction Year 2	N (%)
isiXhosa	2 (0,8)
Afrikaans	69 (28,6)
English	169 (70,1)
isiZulu	0 (0)
Sesotho	0 (0)
Setswana	0 (0)
Sepedi	0 (0)
isiNdebele	0 (0)
Tshivenda	0 (0)
Xitsonga	0 (0)
siSwati	0 (0)
Q3 Teaching practice (BEd): N=243 (missing = 31)	

Table 8.15   Medium of Instruction Year 3

Medium of instruction Year 3	N (%)
isiXhosa	3 (1,4)
Afrikaans	92 (43,4)
English	80 (37,7)
isiZulu	14 (6,6)
Sesotho	0 (0)
Setswana	1 (0,5)
Sepedi	0 (0)
isiNdebele	4 (1,9)
Tshivenda	0 (0)
Xitsonga	0 (0)
siSwati	4 (1,9)
Q3 Teaching practice (BEd): N=243 (missing = 31)	

Table 8.16   Medium of Instruction Year 4

Medium of instruction Year 4	N (%)
isiXhosa	3 (1,4)
Afrikaans	95 (45)
English	76 (36)
isiZulu	13 (6,2)
Sesotho	0 (0)
Setswana	0 (0)
Sepedi	2 (0,9)
isiNdebele	3 (1,4)
Ishivenda	0 (0)
Xitsonga	1 (0,5)
siSwati	4 (1,9)
Q3 Teaching practice (BEd): N=243 (missing = 32)	

Of the African languages, isiXhosa and Sesotho are offered in the BEd programmes. Not one student teacher taught in a Sesotho classroom during teaching practice and only three student teachers taught in an isiXhosa classroom in each year of teaching practice. Student teachers noted there is a need for programmes to address the inclusion of African languages into Foundation Phase ITE programmes (FG, BEd, Inst. C 2016).

A participant stated:

> I think they should also include, in terms of language, we do Afrikaans and Sotho. And I'm from a Zulu-speaking family and a Zulu-speaking background, so I have not been offered those languages, yet I'm going to teach in those places. So I don't have so much knowledge about those languages that I'm going there to teach (FG, BEd, Inst. C 2016).

From these focus group interviews it appears that although the quantitative data indicated that SMK had been experienced by the student teachers, it does not mean that this is adequate in all respects. This student teacher could have reported that SMK related to language was covered in the programme, even though it did not include isiZulu.

In the third questionnaire, the student teachers were asked about language teaching during teaching practice and how confident they felt at the end of their teacher education programme. Table 8.17 indicates the student teachers' responses to the extent to which they learned to teach languages during teaching practice.

Learning to Teach Language in the Foundation Phase

Table 8.17   To What Extent Have You Learned to Teach Languages in Teaching Practice?

Item	Not at all N (%)	To some extent N (%)	To a large extent N (%)	Completely N (%)
Learned to teach languages	5 (2,1)	25 (10,4)	118 (49,2)	92 (38,3)
Q3 Teaching practice (BEd): N=243 (missing = 3)				

The majority (61,5%) of the student teachers agreed that mentor teachers helped them understand the language curricula (see Table 8.18).

Table 8.18   Learning Experiences Facilitated by Mentor

Item	Strongly disagree N (%)	Disagree N (%)	Agree N (%)	Strongly agree N (%)
Mentor helped me understand the language curriculum.	7 (2,9)	30 (12,6)	147 (61,5)	55 (23,0)
Q3 Teaching practice (BEd): N=243 (missing = 4)				

The items in the questionnaires did not probe what the mentor teachers helped the student teachers understand specifically. The responses, however, demonstrated that teaching practice contributed to their experience of learning to teach language. The respondents confirmed the value of mentor teachers within their experience of learning to teach language and were more specific in the focus groups.

A participant indicated:

> So die juffrou het my ook baie gehelp, want sy is ook eintlik Afrikaans, maar sy is eintlik sterk tweetalig so sy het nou baie vir my baie gehelp met die Engels, so toe het ek 'n bietjie Engelse kennis agtergrond gekry.
>
> (So the [mentor] teacher also helped me a lot; because she is actually Afrikaans, but she is also fully bilingual. So she helped me a lot with English, so I obtained a little bit of background on English knowledge) (FG, BEd, Inst. B 2016).

The data from the questionnaires and focus group interviews presented here provide a sense of student teachers' experiences of learning to teach language in BEd Foundation Phase programmes. The data show that the student teachers experienced elements of both subject content, pedagogical, and pedagogical content knowledge related to language and literacy as related to language teaching in South Africa. The data further suggest awareness among the student teachers that inasmuch as their experiences were useful, they were not adequate or sufficient. In particular, the student teachers' experiences of learning to teach language revealed inconsistencies in PCK between languages, as well as absences of other languages. Much more attention ought to be paid to student teachers' experiences of learning to teach language in the Foundation Phase, including how it relates to their NQT experience.

8.7 Conclusion

The aim of this chapter was to contribute to what is known about student teacher experiences of learning to teach languages in the Foundation Phase. As a measure thereof, this chapter explored the experiences of BEd Foundation Phase student teachers in this regard at three institutions. Data drawn from three questionnaires and focus group interviews – exploring student teachers' experiences regarding knowledge of literacy with regard to teaching and developing language among Foundation Phase learners – were presented in the chapter.

Conceptually, the chapter drew on Shulman's (1986, 1987) conception of CK or SMK, PCK and curricula knowledge as general concepts. In addition, the work of Moats (1999), Brewer (2014) and others was drawn on for particular knowledge or SMK relevant to language teaching. To this end, the chapter extended the first knowledge set conceptualised in Chapter 1 with respect to teaching language in the Foundation Phase.

The chapter depicted language as a necessary prerequisite for literacy. Knowledge of language is essential for literacy but knowledge of language does not mean one is literate. This relationship between language and literacy can thus be understood as a complex symbiosis. Indeed, this is how language teaching is constituted in language curricula in the Foundation Phase in South Africa.

Adding to this complex symbiosis, education language policy in South Africa requires that two languages, one a home language and another a first additional language, be taught, via literacy skills, in the Foundation Phase classroom. This means that teachers require CK or SMK, PCK and curricula knowledge of two languages in order to teach in a Foundation Phase classroom.

The data indicated that the student teachers' experience of Foundation Phase ITE programmes is that it provides them with CK or SMK, PCK and curricula knowledge related to literacy skills. However, evidence from the qualitative data suggests that the knowledge or SMK and PCK were not adequate or sufficient. This inadequacy was deduced from student teachers' revealing inconsistencies in their experiences of learning to teach language with regard to PCK between languages. Insufficiency is drawn from evidence of student teachers' experiences related to absences of African languages in the teacher education programmes.

Inadequacies in PCK and insufficiencies in SMK of Foundation Phase language teacher education programmes stand in contrast to a social justice model of teacher education, as well as a democratic public good approach to teacher education. Problems associated with monolingual ideologies, despite multilingualism that pervades the formal educational discourse, according to McKinney (2017), appear to be evident in teacher education programmes as well. Much more attention ought to be paid to student teachers' experiences of learning to teach language in the Foundation Phase, including how it relates to their NQT experience and how multiple literacies may be incorporated in learning languages.

References

Alexander, N. 2010. Schooling in and for the new South Africa. Focus: *The Journal of the Helen Suzman Foundation*, 56: 7-13.

Ball, D.L. 2000. Bridging practices: Intertwining content and pedagogy in teaching and learning to read. *Journal of Teacher Education*, 51(3): 241-247. https://doi.org/10.1177/0022487100051003013

Barends, Z. 2015. *Foundation Phase BEd Teacher Education: Bridging the theory-practice divide in reading literacy teacher preparation through work-integrated learning*. PhD dissertation. North-West University, Potchefstroom.

Bloch, C. 1999. Literacy in the early years: Teaching and learning in multilingual early childhood classrooms. *International Journal of Early Years Education*, 7(1): 39-59. https://doi.org/10.1080/0966976990070104

Brewer, J. 2014. *Introduction to early childhood education: Pre-school through primary grades (6th ed.)*. Boston: Pearson Education.

Choate, J. 2004. *Successful inclusive teaching*. Boston: Pearson Education.

Department of Basic Education (DBE). 2010. *The status of the language of learning and teaching (LoLT) in South African public schools: A quantitative overview*. Pretoria: DBE.

Department of Basic Education (DBE). 2011. *Curriculum and assessment policy statement*. Pretoria: DBE.

Department of Education (DoE). 1997. Language in Education Policy. *Government Gazette*, 17997(383), 9 May 1997. Pretoria: Government Printer.

Department of Education (DoE). 2002. *Revised national curriculum statement (schools)*. Pretoria: DoE.

Department of Education (DoE). 2003. *Revised national curriculum statement for Grades R-9 (schools): Teacher's guide for the development of learning programmes: Mathematics*. Pretoria: DoE.

Department of Education (DoE). 2008. *Teaching reading in the early grades: A teachers' handbook*. Pretoria: DoE.

Department of Higher Education and Training (DHET). 2011. *Minimum requirements for teacher education qualifications policy*. Pretoria: Government Printer.

De Wet, C. 2002. Factors influencing the choice of English as language of learning and teaching (LoLT): A South African perspective. *South African Journal of Education*, 22(2): 119-124.

Dyers, C. 2003. Intervention and language attitudes: The effects of one development programme on the language attitudes of primary school educators. *Journal of Language Teaching*, 37(1): 60-73. https://doi.org/10.4314/jlt.v37i1.5980

Fleisch, B. & Schoer, V. 2014. Large-scale instructional reform in the Global South: Insights from the mid-point evaluation of the Gauteng Primary Language and Mathematics Strategy. *South African Journal of Education*, 34(3): 1-12. https://doi.org/10.15700/201409161040

Grossman, P.; Schoenfeld, A. & Lee, C. 2005. Teaching subject matter. In: L. Darling-Hammond & J. Bransford (eds). *Preparing teachers for a changing world: What teachers should learn and be able to do*. San Francisco: Jossey-Bass, 201-231.

Hannon, P. 1995. *Literacy, home and school.* London: Falmer Press.

McKinney, C. 2017. *Language and Power in Postcolonial Schooling: Ideologies in Practice.* New York: Routledge.

Moats, L.C. 1999. *Teaching reading is rocket science: What expert teachers of reading should know and be able to do.* Washington, D.C.: American Federation of Teachers.

Moats, L.C.; Carreker, S.; Davis, R.; Meisel, P.; Spear-Swerling, L. & Wilson, B. 2010. *Knowledge and practice standards for teachers of reading.* Baltimore: The International Dyslexia Association Professional Standards and Practices Committee. Available at: https://www.wabida.org/kps/ KPSforEducators.pdf

Moats, L.C. & Tolman, C. 2009. *Language essentials for teacher of reading and spelling (LETRS). Module 1: The challenge of learning to read.* Boston, MA: Sopris West Educational Services.

Motshekga, A. 2010. Statement by the Minister of Basic Education, Mrs Angie Motshekga, MP, on the progress of the review of the National Curriculum Statement. Available at: https://www.education.gov.za

National Association for the Education of Young Children (NAEYC). 1995. *Responding to linguistic and cultural diversity recommendations for effective early childhood education: A position paper of the National Association for the Education of Young Children.* Washington, D.C.: NAEYC. Available at: https://www.naeyc.org/files/naeyc/file/positions/PSDIV98.pdf

National Education Evaluation & Development Unit (NEEDU). 2012. *National Report 2012.* Pretoria: NEEDU.

National Reading Panel (NRP). 2000. *Teaching children to read: An evidence-based assessment of the scientific research literature on reading and its implications for reading instruction: Reports of the subgroups.* Washington, D.C.: U.S. Government Printing Office. Available at: https://nationalreadingpanel.org

Neaum, S. 2012. *Language and literacy for the early years.* Thousand Oaks, CA: Sage Publications.

Nel, M. (ed.). 2015. *How to support English second language learners.* Pretoria: Van Schaik Publishers.

Nel, M.; Nel, N. & Hugo, A (eds). 2016. *Learner support in a diverse classroom: A guide for Foundation, Intermediate and Senior Phase teachers in Language and Mathematics (2nd ed.).* Pretoria: Van Schaik Publishers.

Owens, R.E. 2004. *Language disorders: A functional approach to assessment.* Boston, MA: Allyn & Bacon.

Pretorius, E.J. 2002. Reading ability and academic performance in South Africa: Are we fiddling while Rome is burning? *Language Matters,* 33(1): 169-196. https://doi.org/10.1080/10228190208566183

Raymond, E.B. 2008. *Learners with mild disabilities: A characteristics approach (3rd ed.).* Boston: Pearson Education.

Seligman, J. 2012. *Academic literacy for education students.* Cape Town: Oxford University Press.

Shulman, L. 1986. Those who understand: Knowledge growth in teaching. *Educational Researcher,* 15(2): 4-14. https://doi.org/10.3102/0013189X015002004

Shulman, L. 1987. Knowledge and teaching: Foundations of the new reform. *Harvard Educational Review,* 57(1): 1-22. https://doi.org/10.17763/haer.57.1.j463w79r56455411

Snow, C.E.; Burns, S.M. & Griffin, P. (eds). 1998. *Preventing reading difficulties in young children.* Washington, D.C.: National Research Council.

Spaull, N. 2013. Poverty and privilege: Primary school inequality in South Africa. *International Journal of Educational Development,* 33(5): 436-447.https://doi.org/10.1016/j.ijedudev.2012.09.009

Spaull, N. 2015. Accountability and capacity in South African education. *Education as Change,* 19(3): 113-142. https://doi.org/10.1080/16823206.2015.1056199

Van der Merwe, Z. & Nel, C. 2012. Reading literacy within a teacher preparation programme: What we know and what we should know. *South African Journal of Childhood Education,* 2(2): 137-157. https://doi.org/10.4102/sajce.v2i2.16

Young, E.; Grant, P.; Montbriand, C. & Therriault, D. 2001. *Education pre-service teachers: The state of affairs.* Naperville, IL: North Central Regional Educational Laboratory.

Ziegler, G. 2013. Multilingualism and the language education landscape: Challenges for teacher training in Europe. *Multilingual Education,* 3(1): 2-23. https://doi.org/10.1186/2191-5059-3-1

Chapter 09

Engaging Further Education & Training Mathematics Student Teachers' Knowledge

Rajendran Govender, Conrad Potberg & Jacques Verster

9.1 Introduction

The revised MRTEQ policy's (DHET 2015) stipulations regarding the acquisition of mathematical knowledge outline the kinds of knowledge '*mixes*' that are required from ITE programmes. These knowledge mixes are discussed in the first part of this chapter, in relation to types of knowledge. The second part of this chapter focuses on the qualitative study that was conducted to actively engage mathematics pre-service teachers (MPTs) in processes associated with developing particular SMK and PCK; that is, generalising via a problem requiring the use of technology such as *Geometer's Sketchpad* (*GSP*). The focus was on creating a space for pre-service mathematics teachers to experience the process of developing a generalisation in a non-deductive manner; through experimentation and the use of counter-examples. By using *Geometer's Sketchpad*, student teachers were confronted with TPACK. While the MRTEQ policy (DHET 2015) considers knowledge of ICTs to be part of the fundamental learning embedded in ITE programmes, very little is known of student teachers' experiences thereof in South Africa.

Two important points emerge from the study reported in this chapter. Firstly, advanced mathematical teaching and learning, which is stipulated in the MRTEQ policy (DHET 2015), requires actively working with mathematical objects. Such active engagement with mathematical objects enables teaching and learning of mathematics to lead to generalisations, thus developing what Chapter 1 defined as the first knowledge set. Secondly, the study also shows that the use of technology, in this case *GSP*, may assist in enabling advanced mathematical learning. This suggests that ITE for mathematics teachers could be enhanced through creating necessary and sufficient spaces for MPTs to experience ICTs, such as dynamically 'dragging' mathematical objects within a *GSP* environment using systematically designed mathematical activities.

9.2 Mathematical Learning in Policy Context

The MRTEQ policy (DHET 2015) uses the idea of knowledge 'mixes' to indicate the different kinds of knowledge, skills, and competencies prospective teachers ought to possess when they enter the teaching profession. These knowledge 'mixes' work with the understanding that there are different types of knowledge in teaching, and that such types of knowledge indicate how 'complex' teaching is.

The knowledge mix is a consequence of five types of learning (see Appendix C) (DHET 2015:10-11). These five types of learning are to be experienced as "integrated and applied knowledge" to assist in the process of making sense of teaching as "a complex activity" (DHET 2015:9). The policy guidelines are applicable to all subject and phase specialisations. Focusing specifically on requirements for MPTs, types of understanding of the knowledge necessary for mathematics teaching were extracted from the literature.

Four teacher knowledge categories specific to mathematics teachers were identified by Ball, Thames and Phelps (2008:393-397):

- ✓ CCK involves the ability to do mathematics, including the school mathematics curriculum (Ball et al. 2008:394);
- ✓ SCK involves the holding of advanced mathematical understanding beyond that included in the school curriculum, which allows an individual to be called a mathematician (Ball et al. 2008:397);
- ✓ KCS involves deep understanding of how to retain learners' interest and keeping learners motivated until they can master the presented mathematical content included in the school curriculum (Ball et al. 2008:397); and
- ✓ KCT involves deep understanding of different teaching approaches and learning-teaching resources to best transfer specific mathematical content included in the school curriculum.

In addition to the above four knowledge categories, a fifth teacher knowledge category identified by Mishra and Koehler (2006:1030) is presented, namely TPACK. TPACK serves as an all-encompassing knowledge category as it merges the other categories. To clarify, TPACK involves a deep understanding of:

- ✓ how to present concepts by using the most appropriate and available standard technologies (books, chalkboard/whiteboard, etc.) and/or more advanced technologies (Internet, digital videos and software programs);
- ✓ the most appropriate pedagogy to gain maximum benefit from available technology (standard or more advanced);
- ✓ how technology (standard and more advanced) can assist learners to overcome specific challenges relating to mastering specific content; and
- ✓ how technology can identify and build upon existing knowledge held by learners (Mishra & Koehler 2006:1028-1029).

The key variable from the knowledge categories presented above (and in the policy guidelines) is understanding the process in mastering mathematical content, as indicated in Table 9.1.

Table 9.1   Five Kinds of Mathematical Competencies or 'Strands'

Competency or 'strand'	Brief explanation
Conceptual understanding	Comprehension of mathematical concepts, operations, and relations.
Procedural fluency	Skill in carrying out procedures flexibly, accurately, efficiently, and appropriately.
Strategic competence	Ability to formulate, represent, and solve mathematical problems.
Adaptive reasoning	Capacity for logical thought, reflection, explanation, and justification.
Productive disposition	Habitual inclination to see mathematics as sensible, useful, and worthwhile, coupled with a belief in one's own efficacy.

Source: Kilpatrick, Swafford and Findell (2001:116)

Concerning the process of mastering such content, Kilpatrick et al. (2001:116) argue that "mathematical proficiency" requires the simultaneous and integrated acquisition of five competencies or strands, as presented in Table 9.1. This means that proficiency is required "along each of the five strands, rather than by completely mastering any one individual strand" (Hiebert, Morris & Glass 2003:204). A mathematics teacher therefore needs to be proficient in mathematics across all five strands and understand how a learner needs to be guided across the five strands to become proficient.

Mathematics, including Mathematical Literacy, is deemed "compulsory for all learners" (November 2010:195). This creates an increasing demand for mathematics teachers. Unfortunately, 'low' numbers of students are selecting (or potentially qualifying for) mathematics as a major when pursuing ITE (DBE-DHET 2011:68; Jansen 2013:91; Taylor 2014:19). There is also no 'guarantee' that the 'low' number will receive the 'right' quality of university education (Taylor 2014:19,23). Enhancing our understanding with respect to engaging mathematics student teachers' knowledge continues to be critical.

A graduate holding an academic degree (like a BSc, BA, or Bachelor of Commerce [BCom]) pursues a PGCE qualification, which is one year long (28 academic weeks), to qualify as a beginner teacher. To qualify for PGCE in mathematics, the subject would have to be passed at second-year level in a bachelor's degree. Out of the 28 weeks, the students are expected to spend about 10 weeks at schools for the purpose of work-integrated learning and about four weeks are taken up by university-wide summative assessments. Consequently, only about 42 periods of one hour each remain to teach pedagogical and assessment practices. The time available in PGCE programmes poses a challenge in terms of upholding the quality of learning to teach (Hobson et al. 2006:266; Robinson & Lomofsky 2010:32). A second challenge, related to time and lack of resources, is linking theory with practice and vice versa (O'Connell 2013:142; MacBeath 2012:17).

In order to examine mathematics student teachers' knowledge, a qualitative study with eight PGCE FET MPTs was conducted. These eight MPTs are not from the cohort of PGCE students that was part of the designed ITE research project. All eight PGCE students completed Grade 12 at urban schools and obtained good passes in higher-grade mathematics. They completed pure mathematics courses up to at least second-year university level, which included modules like differential and integral calculus, linear algebra, differential equations and statistics. All eight MPTs were registered for a PGCE mathematics methods course, and participating in micro-teaching and school-based teaching practice activities.

As will be seen below, the study indicates the importance of recognising mathematics teaching and learning as a complex activity. It also shows that for effective mathematics learning and teaching to occur, working with mathematical objects is important. The study also demonstrates how TPACK can be a valuable tool in developing advanced mathematical knowledge (particularly as defined in the first knowledge set in Chapter 1).

9.2.1 Research Question

Can MPTs construct an inductive generalisation, which says that the sum of the distances from a point inside an equilateral triangle to its sides is constant? If so, how do they accomplish this generalisation?

9.2.2 Conceptual Framework for the Study with FET MPTs: Generalisation

Carraher, Martinez and Schliemann (2008:3) explain:

> Mathematical generalization involves a claim that some property or technique holds for a large set of mathematical objects or conditions. The scope of the claim is always larger than the set of individually verified cases; typically, it involves an infinite number of cases (e.g. 'for all integers').

For example, at primary school, learners might have done activities that required them to count the number of unit squares that cover the area of specific rectangles. At the end of such a series of activities, they might have been able to generalise their experiences by saying area of a rectangle = length x width. Such a generalisation "applies even when the length and width are not integers but any real numbers" (Mason 1999:11). In analytical geometry, the rule $(x;y) \rightarrow (x \cos\theta - y \sin\theta; x \sin\theta + y \cos\theta)$ serves as a general way of describing the effect of rotating any point $P(x;y)$ in the plane about the origin through any angle θ in an anti-clockwise direction (Mason 1999:11; Carter, Govender & Heany 2007:251-252).

Mason (1999:9) states: "Generalizing has to do with noticing patterns and properties common to several situations", and asserts that a generalisation is regarded as an expression or statement that can be specialised. This means as one uses/examines particular cases to recognise a pattern or regularity to provoke the formulation of a generalisation (Njisane 1992:61), one should also be able to use such a formulated generalisation in turn to produce particular cases or examples which it can characteristically generalise (compare Mason 1999:10). For example, consider a point $P(2;3)$ on a circle O, whose centre is at the origin. One can determine the coordinates

of the image of the point P(2;3) after it has been rotated about the origin through each of the angles 60° and 330° by using the generalised rule: $(x;y) \rightarrow (x\cos\theta - y\sin\theta; x\sin\theta + y\cos\theta)$. The particular cases will then be as follows:

Particular case 1:
$(2;3) \rightarrow (2\cos 60° - 3\sin 60°; 2\sin 60° + 3\cos 60°) \equiv (1 - (3\sqrt{3})/2; \sqrt{3} + 3/2)$

Therefore the coordinates of P are: $\left(\dfrac{1 - 3\sqrt{3}}{2}; \dfrac{\sqrt{3} + 3}{2} \right)$

Particular case 2:
$(2;3) \rightarrow (2\cos 330° - 3\sin 330°; 2\sin 330° + 3\cos 330°) \equiv \left(\dfrac{\sqrt{3} + 3}{2}; -1 + \dfrac{3\sqrt{3}}{2} \right)$

Therefore the coordinates of P are: $\left(\dfrac{\sqrt{3} + 3}{2}; -1 + \dfrac{3\sqrt{3}}{2} \right)$

The processes of specialising and generalising are intrinsically intertwined. In light of this, Tall (1988:2) asserts that "generalization and the complementary process of specialization is common to both elementary and advanced mathematical thinking". Picking up on this, Mason (1999:33) similarly emphasises this complementarity as follows: "Specializing can provide fodder for generalisation, and generalisations must be checked to see that they do specialise back to the particular cases which spawned them."

9.2.3 Inductive Generalisations

Inductive generalisation means that a generalisation is initially made on quasi-empirical grounds without necessarily any deductive thought involved, for example observing and formulating generalisations from the consideration of some particular cases (De Villiers 1996:86). Similarly, Yerushalmy (1993:247, citing Chi & Bassok 1989) states:

> Induction is a well-known process to reach generalizations by examination of instances or examples. An instance or a set of instances is examined, certain properties are identified. The given example is then taken as a member of a larger set and its properties are put into a larger set. Such generalization from multiple examples is developed on a similarity-based approach.

As alluded to earlier, the development of an inductive generalisation is facilitated by the process of inductive reasoning. Inductive reasoning is a process of observing data, recognising or abstracting patterns/common features/qualities across a set of objects under consideration and then making a statement that one thinks may be true for all the given objects (cases) under consideration, as well as other objects (cases) of the same type or class; although at the time of making the statement one does not really know for sure that it is generally valid (see Polya 1954; De Villiers 1992). Such a statement is called 'conjecture' and is described by Mason, Burton and Stacey (1982:72) as follows:

> A conjecture is a statement which appears reasonable, but whose truth has not been established. In other words, it has not been convincingly justified and yet it is not known to be contradicted by any examples, nor is it known to have any consequences which are false.

Polya (1967) and Reid (2002) (cited in Cañadas & Castro 2005:402) suggest that the process of developing an inductive generalisation (i.e. a conjecture generalisation) via inductive reasoning occurs in the following ways:

- ✓ **Observation of particular cases:** Students experiment with particular cases of the problem posed and then try to note a pattern or observe regularity.
- ✓ **Conjecture formulation:** Students then formulate a conjecture, by making a statement about all possible cases, but with an element of doubt.
- ✓ **Conjecture validation:** At this stage, students attempt to experiment with further new particular cases, but not general cases, to see if the conjecture still holds true for the new particular cases.
- ✓ **Conjecture generalisation:** On seeing that a conjecture is true for some particular cases, and having experimented to see that it holds for further new particular cases (conjecture validation), students might hypothesise that the conjecture is generally true.

Similarly, James (1992:160) describes the various processes, specialising, abstracting, generalising and testing, which work in a harmonious way to build an inductive generalisation. These processes can be itemised as follows:

- ✓ **Specialising:** Students examine particular cases and become familiar with the details of each case.
- ✓ **Seeing generality:** As the students move through particular cases, they begin to see some regularity across the cases. This awareness of the abstracted regularity or underlying sameness becomes more and more prominent as the students pass from one particular case to the next, and consequently boosts their sense of confidence in their observed degree of sameness across the special (or particular) cases.
- ✓ **Expressing the generality:** As soon as the student is quite confident with the underlying sameness that he/she has increasingly seen across the particular cases, he/she then begins to articulate the sameness in his/her own words and also comes to grips with concepts that underpin it.

9.2.4 Counter-Examples

According to Hummel (2000) and Bolt and Hobbs (2004), a counter-example is a particular case (or example) which disproves a conjecture. Similarly, Klymchuk (2008:1) states that "a counter-example is an example that shows that a given statement (conjecture, hypothesis, proposition, rule) is false". According to Houston (2009:92), "the 'counter' part of the word (counter-example) comes from the fact that we are countering, in the sense of rejecting or rebutting, the truth of a statement".

For example, consider the conjecture: "$f(n) = n^2 - n + 41$" is a prime number for every natural number n" (Hummel 2000). If a student attempted to establish the truth of this conjecture by cases (or a case-based approach), he/she may proceed as follows (cited in Hummel 2000:61):

If $n = 1$, then $n^2 - n + 41 = 41$ is a prime number.

If $n = 2$, then $n^2 - n + 41 = 43$ is a prime number.

If $n = 3$, then $n^2 - n + 41 = 47$ is a prime number.

If $n = 4$, then $n^2 - n + 41 = 53$ is a prime number.

If $n = 5$, then $n^2 - n + 41 = 61$ is a prime number.

If $n = 10$, then $n^2 - n + 41 = 131$ is a prime number.

If $n = 20$, then $n^2 - n + 41 = 421$ is a prime number.

If $n = 39$, then $n^2 - n + 41 = 1\,523$ is a prime number.

If $n = 40$, then $n^2 - n + 41 = 1\,601$ is a prime number.

Having found that the result for all 40 cases is always a prime number, the student may attempt to say that the conjecture must be true. However, not every case was considered and the conjecture explicitly states that $n^2 - n + 41$ is a prime for 'every' natural number n. Hence, to make such a conclusion (i.e. $n^2 - n + 41$ is a prime for 'every' natural number n) is deemed to be fallacious in nature, particularly because not all cases have been considered. For example, for the case $n = 41$, we get $n^2 - n + 41 = (41)^2 - 41 + 41 = (41)^2 = 1\,681$, which is not a prime number. This kind of example leads us to say that the number 41 (or case $n = 41$) is a counter-example to the statement, "If n is any natural number, then $f(n)=n^2 - n + 41$ is a prime", primarily because it makes $f(41)$ a composite number rather than a prime number. In fact, in terms of logic and propositional calculus, the number 41 makes the antecedent true and the consequent false, and therefore we regard the number 41 as a counter-example to the given conjecture (Hummel 2000). In equivalent terms, we say that a counter-example is "an example that satisfies all the conditions of a statement but not the conclusion" (Education Development Centre Inc. 2002:15).

9.2.5 Conjecturing, Generalising, and Justifying within a Dynamic Geometry Context

9.2.5.1 The Geometer's Sketchpad (GSP): What it is and What Can You Do With it

The development and introduction of dynamic geometry software (DGS), such as the *GSP*, *Cabri* and *Cinderella*, into the fields of mathematics and mathematics education have created a classroom atmosphere wherein students' learning can go well beyond standard traditional mathematics content and practices. For example, in geometry there are now more opportunities than before for students to: construct figures (or engage with ready-made figures); explore, make and test conjectures; justify and refute their generalisations; pose and solve significant problems; and devise original proofs (Schwartz & Yerushalmy 1986; Battista & Clements 1995; Jackie 1995; Scher 2002). In addition, the advent of DGS has sparked the development of research in new fields, for example chaos theory and fractal geometry, and rejuvenated existing areas of research (De Villiers 2007).

De Villiers (2007), however, cautions that there are some pitfalls associated with DGS, like "painless learning", "visualization made easier" and "dynamic experimentation as sufficient verification".

Since *GSP* is the software that the participants in this study used during their one-to-one task-based activities, the ensuing discussions relate mainly to this software. *GSP* affords students opportunities to engage with already constructed dynamic figures or to actually construct dynamic figures on their own (with guidance if necessary) in terms of given mathematical relationships (or properties) using the relevant construction tools such as line segment, point, circle, etc. The aforementioned *GSP* constructions (figures) can "always be dragged, squeezed, stretched, or otherwise changed while keeping all mathematical properties interact" (Jackie 1991:2). For example, Figure 9.1, called a sketch, contains a cyclic quadrilateral *ABCD*, which has been constructed by combining the following objects: points, circle and line segments.

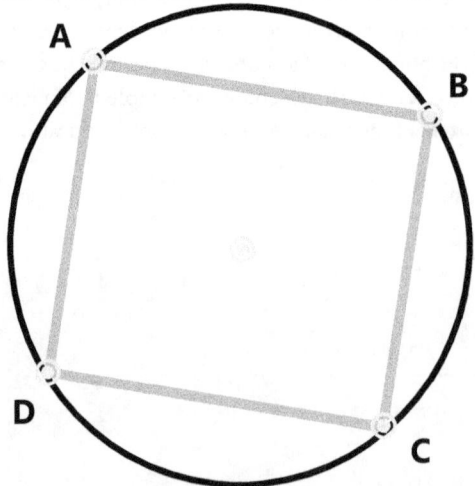

Figure 9.1   Dynamic Sketch

The 'drag' mode makes it possible for students to experiment with the afore constructed cyclic quadrilateral (which is called a mathematical object) in such a way that the relationship among points (A, B, C, D), line segments (AB, BC, CD, and DB) and circle ABCD with centre O, which has been defined by the construction itself, is preserved at all times either when the figure is manipulated or when one of the basic components of the construction is dragged (see Hoyles & Noss 1994:716).

For example, if point B is dragged in any direction, one would always obtain quadrilateral A'B'C'D' such that points A',B',C',D' are concyclic (i.e. A'B'C'D' will still remain a cyclic quadrilateral). According to Driscoll et al. (2009:162), "an invariant is something about a situation that stays the same, even as parts of the situation vary". We may therefore regard the vertices of quadrilateral ABCD always being concyclic points, as an invariant property of figure ABCD.

In the main, one can distinguish between random dragging (i.e. wandering dragging) and directed dragging. Wandering dragging is done without any particular goal in mind or intent about what is being looked for and directed dragging occurs when a student has an intention to move something or create some alternative experience. Generally, when students engage in random dragging, their opportunities to discover are compromised and they often become distracted from lesson activities and do not achieve the intended outcomes of the task/lesson (compare Gray 2008). However, students will often do random dragging, then pause to think, and then do directed dragging when conducting investigative activities using *GSP*.

In general, when a dynamic *GSP* figure is dragged, the relationships defined by the construction will always be maintained, but the properties that are not defined by the construction could change or vary. Therefore, in effect, by manipulating a figure, for example through the drag mode, one could explore a range of possible figures that are governed by the set of construction constraints. According to Jackie (1991:2), this feature of *GSP* "makes it easy to distinguish between those properties that are sometimes true, and those that are always true for a given situation". In addition, *GSP* makes provision for students to record the instructional steps for their geometric constructions as scripts, thus making it possible for students to play back a script in order to either construct or re-construct the desired figure in a sketch. The latest version of *GSP* (version 5) uses scripts in the form of a 'Create Tool' button. Being able to replay a script provides students with the added opportunity of being able to retrace the process (or the path that was followed) in the construction of a particular dynamic figure. Giamati (1995:456) explains: "The most useful aspect of scripting one's constructions is that students can test whether their constructions work in general or whether they have discovered a special case."

In particular, the drag effect made possible by the tools embedded in *GSP*, can create opportunities for one to see many empirical examples quickly and thereby construct plausible inductive generalisations (conjectures). By dragging, students can alter the size and orientation of constructions and notice that a specific conjecture they produced always remains true and therefore become quite convinced of the truth of their conjecture – such that it may result in them wanting to know why their conjecture is always true (see Mudaly & De Villiers 2002). Students in such circumstances quite often feel no need for deductive justification, as reported by Mariotti (2001). A downside to the drag effect is that students operating under an empirical proof scheme (Sowder & Harel 1998) may mistakenly take the array of supporting empirical examples produced through dragging as a means of proving (in the deductive sense) (see Izen 1998:719). With regard to the latter, De Villiers (1998) reports that in such instances he managed to encourage a deductive explanation by explicitly asking the students to determine why their results, which they have obtained through the use of interactive software, were true.

GSP, regarded by many as a dynamic chalkboard, is a powerful tool for visualisation. For example, Whiteley (2000:2) writes:

> The programs (Cabri and Sketchpad) expand the role of precise visual and diagrammatic reasoning in all stages of our work: posing questions, making conjectures, creating counter-examples, seeking and recognising connections. The change is dramatic and we leave a session with the program with more refined information, connections, and images. These refined images then run our heads as we work with problems and the solutions, both mentally and with words and pictures on paper, guided by these dynamic visual processes. These diagrams become part of our internal vocabulary and our ongoing mental processes. We also see unexpected events: an extra coincidence of lines or points in the construction; a transformation; or a mental association with some pattern in some previous geometric study.

Furthermore, Scher (2002:60) has shown that "the mathematical insights that students derived from dynamic geometry software were not always those intended by the interviewers". In other words, through using DGS, students were able to make constructions that would not have been realisable in a paper, pencil and straight edge context, and therefore managed to assimilate mathematical discoveries that were not within the range of results the facilitator expected. This kind of enactment demonstrates that GSP, when used diligently, can push the boundaries of knowledge production to an extent that new results can surprisingly be discovered.

9.2.5.2 Research Related to Conjecturing, Generalising, and Justifying in a GSP Context

Being able to construct dynamic figures or use ready-made sketches, which can be manipulated, particularly through dragging, has made the processes of conjecturing, validating and generalising much more accessible to both students and teachers across mathematics classrooms at both school and tertiary levels. In light of this, the focus shifts to research pertaining to the learning and/or teaching of geometry within a *GSP* context.

In a study involving university students, Giamati (1995), who views *GSP* as an exploratory tool that enables students to investigate and hence uncover invariants, formulated, tested and refined conjectures. She then presented her students, who were exploring rotations and their centres, the following question, which was suitable for exploration within a *GSP* environment: "If $\Delta A'B'C' = R_{\beta/D}(\Delta ABC)$, how can we locate D and find β, where D is the centre of rotation and β is the angle of rotation?"

To facilitate the exploration, students were given several ready-made sketches of triangles and their images under rotation about point D. The students discovered that they needed to construct the following line segments: $\overline{AA'}$, $\overline{BB'}$ and $\overline{CC'}$ and did so accordingly. Some students proceeded to construct the perpendicular bisectors of the aforementioned segments, with points E, F and G being their respective midpoints. In most instances students got into the habit of recording all their constructions as scripts of a rotation of a triangle about a given point and this enabled the them to quickly observe that the bisectors appeared to be concurrent at a point. Figure 9.2 illustrates a successful conjecture that students made, namely: "D is the centre of rotation for mapping onto" (Giamati 1995:456).

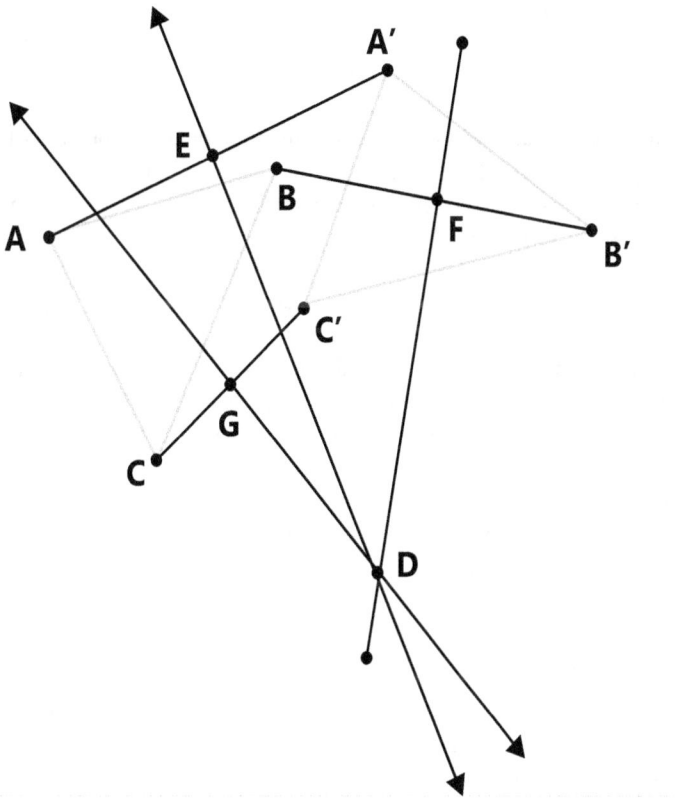

Figure 9.2   An Illustration of a Successful Conjecture. *Source:* Giamati (1995:456)

With regard to the aforementioned task being foregrounded in a *GSP* environment, Giamati (1995:458) maintains it was an invaluable experience for the students and accordingly comments:

> The students gained a deeper understanding of the problem by using their scripts to explore it and make conjectures than they would have if the results had merely been explained to them. Naturally, the exploration did not replace the proof, but it became a solid foundation on which to build the proof. The students were able to construct various examples quickly enough to recognise that certain conjectures were unreasonable [...] In this example, the students found it satisfying to see the proof of their conjecture [...] The power of the Geometer's Sketchpad combined with the power of proof gave a complete illustration of the theorem and the aspects of 'doing' Mathematics.

In a paradigm similar to that of Giamati (1995), Izen (1998) asserts that software such as *GSP* makes the construction of both simple and complex figures much easier for students as compared to pencil and paper; allows students to measure distances between points, lengths of segments, angles, gradients (slopes), perimeters and areas; and makes it possible for students to set up formulas that could support their conjectures. In particular, Izen (1998:718) reaffirms that the move of selecting a vertex of a figure and dragging it is equivalent to the actual construction of many figures – satisfying the same given information in a conjecture. These series of constructed figures thus make it possible for students to see that their established conjecture continues to be true. Hence, in this sense Izen (1998) holds the view that inductive reasoning can be utilised to "demonstrate the likelihood that a theorem is true", and that both the process of inductive reasoning and deductive reasoning can be used to complement each other to such an extent that students can gain a full understanding of and insight into a given theorem. Furthermore, Izen (1998) firmly asserts that although working in a DGS environment can enable one to generate compelling empirical evidence to justify the truth of a theorem, it is certainly not a mathematical proof.

Izen (1998) believes that his approach to the teaching and learning of geometry embraces the involvement of his students in dynamic geometry tasks that encourage them to discover geometric relationships. This is done to establish the extent of the validity of their conjecture through experimentation and to construct the conclusions as theorems before getting the students to construct a justification via deductive proof for the stated theorem or established conjecture. For example, in retrospect, the construction of the following theorem, "The angle bisector of an angle of a triangle divides the opposite sides into two segments that are proportional to the other two sides" (Izen 1998:719), the activity, which had to be done using *GSP*, was initially given by Izen to his students.

9.3 Methodology

A qualitative research approach allows researchers – through the use of task-based activities, interviews and recordings – to observe, interpret, or make sense of participants' engagement/ response/behaviour towards a phenomenon (or phenomena) under consideration in a given natural setting (Hitchcock & Hughes 1995; Denzin & Lincoln 2005), like a typical mathematics classroom.

In this research, the phenomenon of inductive generalisation through experimentation, conjecturing, validation and generalising was explored. Through conducting one-to-one task-based interviews with MPTs within a dynamic geometric context, the research attempted to construct a holistic, detailed account of the generalising experience of MPTs. This was accentuated by recording verbal responses, collecting worksheet responses, capturing onscreen 'drag moves' within a *GSP* context; then analysing, interpreting and making sense of the MPTs' interactions, communications, worksheet responses and onscreen drag moves. The goal was to capture the complexity of the world as it appeared to the subjects in the study and to report the events related to their processes of generalising. Hence, through using a qualitative approach via a case-based strategy of inquiry that is located within the interpretive paradigm, the research attempted to capture, account and give meaning to the MPTs' experiences. This is done with construction of an inductive generalisation, in anticipation that readers who have not experienced the process of generalising should then be able to make sense of it after reading the in-depth experiences of the subjects who participated in the study.

This study, which bears some commonalities with Giamati's (1995) and Izen's (1998) studies in respect of the didactical approaches employed to conjecturing and generalising, utilised a scaffolded worksheet selected from De Villiers's (1999) curriculum material – as a tool to facilitate meaningful learning within a dynamic geometry context. The design of the material afforded the MPTs the necessary opportunities to explore, make observations and conjecture (or discover) a plausible solution to the "given shipwreck" problem (see Contreras & Martinez Cruz 2009:246).

The problem given to the MPTs to solve within a dynamic geometric context was structured as follows:

> Sarah, a shipwreck survivor, manages to swim to a deserted island. As it happens, the island closely approximates the shape of an equilateral triangle. She soon discovers that the surfing is outstanding on all three of the island's coasts and crafts a surfboard from a fallen tree and surfs every day. Where should Sarah build her house so that the total sum of the distances from the house to all three beaches is a minimum? (She visits them with equal frequency) (see De Villiers 2003a:23).

In task 1(a) Appendix A, mathematics pre-service teachers were first asked to locate a point in the given equilateral triangle where Sarah should build her house, while not using technology (like *GSP*), and then explain why they chose the particular point.

To kick-start the inductive processes of exploration and conjecture, a ready-made dynamic sketch of an equilateral triangle containing the elements described in the shipwreck problem was made available to the MPTs in a *GSP* context. The MPTs were then requested to proceed with the set of activities as outlined in Task 1(b) in Appendix A. Subsequently, the MPTS proceeded to Task 1(c) as described in Appendix A.

9.4 Results and Discussion

This section presents the data and findings related to the MPTs making an initial conjecture in a non-*GSP* context and then a conjecture generalisation by empirical induction from dynamic cases. This is then followed by the presentation of the data and findings in relation to:

- ✓ the MPTs' certainty of their conjecture generalisations; and
- ✓ the MPTs' heuristic counter-example experience and their search for counter-examples.

9.4.1   Making an Initial Conjecture in a Non-*Geometer Sketchpad (GSP)* Context

Although the focus of the study is on the development of conjecture generalisation through the process of generalising, the study was also an opportunity for MPTs to develop a conjecture without any specific restriction on the process. This means that each MPT was given an opportunity to develop an initial conjecture before engaging with *GSP* – either through explanation, belief, experience, deductive proof or generalisation.

Hence, the following question was initially posed to each MPT after each one read the Viviani problem: "Before you proceed further, locate a point in the triangle at the point where you think Sarah should build her house."

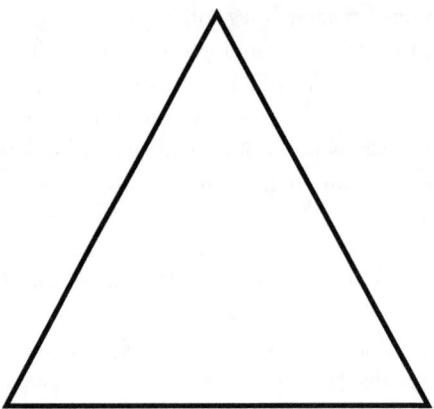

Figure 9.3   Equilateral Triangle

All eight of the MPTs located a point in the centre of the triangle, but provided no explanation or reasoned argument for their choice, as illustrated by the response of Victor.

Case: Victor

Researcher	Read the question, Task 1(a)(i), and do the first part of the activity.
Victor	Okay, there [points to centre of triangle].

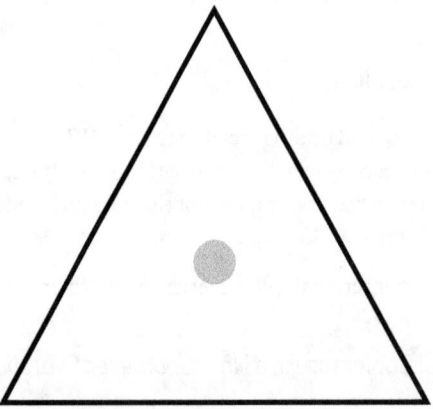

Figure 9.4   Victor's Initial Response to the Shipwreck Problem

The MPTs' unanimous choice of the centre of the equilateral triangle as the position where Sarah should build her house is indeed one of the correct positions; among many others.

After each of the MPTs located a common position, the centre, where Sarah should build her house, the following question was posed (see Task1(a)(ii) of the Viviani worksheet in Appendix A: "Why did you choose that position? Explain or justify your choice."

Three of the eight MPTs (Logan, Victor and Renny) seemed to come up with the incorrect argument that the distances to the sides should be equal to minimise the sum, but it is likely some of the others intuitively were thinking along similar lines. However, Victor confused sides with vertices – he was looking at the distances to the vertices instead of the sides.

The following two excerpts are representative of the MPTs' attempted justifications that display the misconception that the three distances to the sides must be equal in order to minimise the sum.

Case: Logan

Logan	I think it should be there. Almost in the middle of the triangle ... because she has to move equal distances to all this. If she wants to go to beach A or beach B or C, it will almost be the same.
Researcher	Is that your reason for choosing the middle?
Logan	Yes, that is my reason, because they ask where Sarah should build her house so that the total sum of the distances from the house to all the beaches is a minimum.

Case: Victor

Researcher	... in the middle. Okay ... alright. Now why did you place it there?
Victor	I just wanted it to be in the middle – in order for the lines from A to B, okay, from A to the point C, from C to the point B – I wanted all those lines to be equal so that this can be in the middle so that I can get the minimum distance from all the points of the triangle.

The remaining five MPTs offered no reason why they chose the centre. Two of the five remaining MPTs, Shannon and Tony, did not answer the question and just attempted to explain where the centre was (or how it could be located) by utilising their knowledge associated with the concurrency theorems that they learned at high school. However, Shannon and Tony did not say why they thought the minimum would be at the centre. For example, Shannon responded as follows:

Case: Shannon

Shannon	But I don't need to do any calculations?
Researcher	I don't know.
Shannon	I don't think so. I think it would be more or less here.
Researcher	More or less where?
Shannon	You draw a line from here to there … from halfway between the two sides – between the sides – and where the point meets.
Researcher	So are you saying that you found the midpoint of BC?
Shannon	Yes.
Researcher	And then what did you do?
Shannon	The midpoint of BC, the midpoint of AB and the midpoint of AC.
Researcher	And then what did you do?
Shannon	And then construct a line towards … so that it meets angle, or point B, and until it meets all the angles.
Researcher	So are you saying that you drew BC – you drew this line from the midpoint of BC to the vertex A?
Shannon	Yes, from the midpoint of AC to vertex B and the midpoint of AB to vertex C. And then where all three lines meet, that would be the equal distance.

On reflecting on Shannon's response of drawing the median to locate the required centre, one can conjecture from her mentioning the "equal distance" that it is the 'equality' (or symmetry) misconception that was at play here.

In general, an argument from symmetry would suggest that if there is a minimum, the points holding this minimum should have the symmetries of the equilateral triangle (three-fold rotation and mirrors). Therefore, if there is only one point, there are good general principles suggesting this is the centroid. However, none of the MPTs offered symmetry as a reason for their initial choices.

9.4.1.1 Findings Based on Making an Initial Conjecture

1. All the MPTs located an optimal solution at the centre (or middle), which indeed is one of the correct positions – among many others. Only three MPTs voiced reasons why they chose the centre and displayed a misconception that the distances have to be equal in order to minimise the sum.
2. Five MPTs offered no reasons why they chose the centre, but two of these five MPTs explained how it could be located using their previous knowledge about the concurrency of the medians of the triangle.
3. In the main, none of the MPTs offered symmetry as a reason for their initial choices.

9.4.2 Making a conjecture by empirical induction from dynamic cases in a GSP context

This section first discusses the MPTs' construction of their conjecture by empirical induction from dynamic cases. The section then discusses the validation of their conjecture for new, particular cases and the formulations of their conjecture generalisations.

The MPTs were each asked to open the sketch *Distances.gsp*, which was a ready-made sketch containing an equilateral triangle with a point P inside the triangle, representing a possible position of the house. In addition, the sketch included a button which showed the distance sum from point P to the sides of the given equilateral triangle. Each student was asked to drag point P to experiment with their sketch (see Task 1(b) in Appendix A for details).

In particular, each MPT was asked to solve the following problem:
> Press the button to show the distance sum. Drag point P around the interior of the triangle. What do you notice about the sum of the distances?

By dragging point P around the interior of the equilateral triangle predominantly through directed dragging, each MPT essentially constructed a visual continuum of cases, but with each having a different location of point P. This provided an opportunity for each MPT to observe a continuity of visual cases and identify the invariant property in the dynamic situation. The MPTs were quite surprised to find that the total sum of the distances from point P, which represented Sarah's house, to all three sides of the equilateral triangle, which represented all three beaches, remained constant irrespective of the position where point P was dragged to. This surprising result and new experience, which were made possible through experimental exploration in a dynamic geometry context, contradicted the MPTs' assumption in their initial conjecture (which was made in a non-GSP context). Their initial conjecture was that the centre point (midpoint or centroid) of the equilateral triangle was the only possible point creating the minimum distance and not that this centre point (midpoint or centroid) failed to produce the minimum distance. This in a sense means that the MPTs' limited choice of the centre as the only possible position was contradicted and not what they actually claimed as a conjecture.

This new dynamic result seemed to create some cognitive conflict within their cognitive structures and therefore disturbed their cognitive equilibrium – their state of mental balance (Berger 2004; Piaget 1978, 1985). This in turn means that through the process of accommodation (Berger 2004; Piaget 1978, 1985) the MPTs' existing schema could be reconstructed and reorganised to accommodate the new idea and thereby achieve the necessary cognitive equilibrium.

Although all the MPTs were surprised by their observations, namely the sum of the distances from point P remains constant irrespective of the position of point P within the triangle, they appeared to have achieved this 'cognitive equilibrium' as they were now able to improve (modify) their initial correct conjecture to embrace any point within the equilateral triangle, and be convinced about it, as shown in the following representative excerpt from the one-to-one task-based interviews with the MPTs.

Case: Shannon

Researcher	Okay. Alright. So I want you to … uhm … now open this. So if you read the first question there, it says: Press the button to show the distance sum and drag point P around the interior of the triangle. What do you notice about the sum of the distances?
Shannon	It always stays the same [with a very surprised expression on her face].
Researcher	What stays the same?
Shannon	The sum of the distances is constant from all the points.
Researcher	When you say all the points, you mean from …?
Shannon	The sum of the distances of a point inside the equilateral triangle is always the same.
Researcher	So the sum of the distances from point P to the sides will always be the same?
Shannon	Yes, so it doesn't matter where she builds her house.

The drag effect allowed the MPTs to see many empirical examples in a short space of time and notice that the sum of the distances h1, h2 and h3 always remains the same, while the individual distances h1, h2 and h3 vary. Furthermore, it appears that the carefully designed empirical investigative task – which provided opportunities for dynamic visualisation, as well as the necessary facilitation by the researcher – assisted the MPTs to discover that Sarah could build her house anywhere inside the equilateral triangle since the total sum of the distances from the house to all three beaches is a constant.

9.4.2.1 Validating the Conjecture for New Particular Cases

In the next task (see Task 1(b)(ii) in Appendix A, which required the MPTs to test whether their conjecture was valid for new particular cases, each MPT was asked to do the following: "Drag a vertex of the triangle to change the triangle's size. Again, drag point P around the interior of the triangle. What do you notice?"

When the MPTs enlarged the size of the equilateral triangle, they were quick to notice that the sum of the distances from point P to the sides increased or decreased in correspondence with the size of the triangle. However, when they again dragged point P inside the already enlarged or decreased figure, they noticed with great satisfaction that the sum of distances from point P to the sides remained unchanged or constant. Moreover, the MPTs' observations remained consistent for a wide range of equilateral triangles created by the drag effect, which means they had succeeded in validating their observations for more new particular cases. The following two task-based interview excerpts are representative of the MPTs' moves and observations.

Case: Shannon

Researcher	Now look at Question (ii). It says: Drag the vertex of the triangle to change the triangle's size. Again drag point P around the interior of the triangle – and what do you notice?
Shannon	I'm dragging point P to change the size of the triangle. It could be any size. Okay, and then the distance …
Researcher	What happens to the sum there?
Shannon	The distance sum will increase if I increase the size of the triangle. But when I drag point P around the interior of a triangle, the sum still stays constant.
Researcher	The sum of the distances from point P to the sides remains constant. So you increased the size of the triangle, okay. Now I want you to decrease the size of the triangle […] Now, what happened to the total sum?
Shannon	It's also changing. It's getting less. It's decreasing.
Researcher	But now investigate what happens to the sum when you drag point P inside this smaller-size triangle.
Shannon	It still stays constant. The sum of the distances from point P to the sides of a triangle [referring to an equilateral triangle] still stays constant.

9.4.2.2 Mathematics Pre-Service Teachers (MPTs)' Formulations of Their Conjecture Generalisations

Based on their empirical observations – which were true for some particular cases, and having validated them empirically for new particular cases – the MPTs were asked to write down their discoveries so far as one or more conjectures (which are considered conjecture generalisations in this report), using complete sentences. All of the MPTs managed to capture the salient aspects in their conjecture as reflected in the following typical responses:

Case: Shannon

Shannon	The discovery is the total sum of the distances from a point inside an equilateral triangle to the sides of a triangle is a constant, irrespective of where the point is in the triangle.

Case: Trevelyan

Trevelyan	For any equilateral triangle, if you take a point inside that triangle then the sum of the distance from the point, say the point is P, from P to all three sides, stays the same irrespective of where that point is located inside the triangle.

9.4.2.3 Findings Based on GSP Context

1. All the MPTs were quite surprised to find that point P, which represented a position of where Sarah could build her house, could be located anywhere inside the triangle to yield a constant result, namely the sum of the distances from the house to all three beaches remains constant.
2. The cognitive conflict they experienced between their initial conjecture and their new observations seemed to have served as a driving force in getting the MPTs to quickly modify their initial non-*GSP* conjecture (which is correct) to capture their new experience, namely from any position of point P within the equilateral triangle, the sum of the distances remains constant.
3. All MPTs made their generalisations on empirical (experimental) grounds only.

9.4.3 Certainty

Although the MPTs were quite surprised that Sarah's house could be built anywhere as a result of experimentation in a *GSP* context, their expressions and use of phrases like 'irrespective of where the point is in the triangle' suggested that in most cases the MPTs were reasonably confident that their conjecture was true in general. Nevertheless, to check their level of certainty, every MPT was requested to indicate their level certainty on the given number line (see Task 1(c)(i) in Annexure X).

The MPTs' responses indicated that four out of eight students were 100% certain (convinced) that their discovered conjecture generalisation was always true, without any desire for further experimentation. Three out of the eight MPTs expressed high levels of conviction (85%, 75% and 70%) and one MPT, who expressed a medium level of conviction (50%), said he/she would move on to expressing a 100% level of certainty in his/her conjecture generalisation level, only after a little further experimentation and probing.

The following response by Shannon is representative of the responses of those four MPTs who were fully convinced of their conjecture generalisation without the need for any further exploration, discussion, or probing.

Case: Shannon

Researcher	You can probably think of times when something that always appeared to be true, turned out to be false some time, right? How certain are you that your conjecture is always true? Record your level of certainty on the number line and explain or justify your choice – from your observation, of course.
Shannon	I think it's a hundred percent.
Researcher	Are you sure?
Shannon	Yes.

Within the group of MPTs who wanted to experiment further, two MPTs, Logan and Victor, just wanted to experiment further with the given equilateral triangle. This entailed dragging the vertex of the given equilateral triangle and/or point P to further different positions within the given equilateral triangle. It seems more supporting empirical examples, with the invariant property being maintained, were necessary to fully convince these two MPTs that their conjecture generalisation was true for equilateral triangles.

For example, the following extract from the task-based interview with Logan represents his set of actions and responses, which moved him from an 85% conviction level to a 100% conviction level:

Case: Logan

Logan	So I must indicate how true I think it is? So I must make a dot where I think it is? I'll say I'm 85% certain.
Researcher	If you suspect your conjecture is not always true, try to supply a counter-example. Do you want to investigate more? Do you want to experiment further?
Logan	I just want to take another point of this ... Okay. We used only point A to change the shape, so I thought I'd try another point to see [Logan dragged point B and increased the size of the equilateral triangle and then dragged point P around the interior of the equilateral triangle].
Researcher	And now?
Logan	I'm 100% convinced.
Researcher	So what is your response to Question 2?
Logan	At this point I agree 100%. I don't have a counter-example.

The other two MPTs, Tony and Alan, did not initially express 100% certainty in their conjecture generalisation, because they were not completely sure as to whether their conjecture generalisation was also true for non-equilateral triangle cases – namely isosceles triangles and scalene triangles. After experimenting within the context of isosceles triangles and/or scalene triangles, both MPTs realised that their conjecture generalisation only held true for equilateral triangles. They consequently expressed a 100% level of certainty in their respective initial posited conjecture generalisations, which were restricted specifically to equilateral triangles. However, one should bear in mind that whether or not the result is true for other types of triangles, it should logically have no effect on their certainty about the truth of the conjecture for equilateral triangles. The conjecture is about equilateral triangles, e.g. "If an equilateral triangle ...", and this says nothing about other triangles and certainty in that proposition ought not to be influenced by whether it is true for other triangles or not. Therefore, it seems more likely that it was not the conjecture about equilateral triangles that they were uncertain about, but about its generalisation to other triangles. Of course, it could be that these two students were not making a distinction between a statement and its converse; and thought the converse also needed to be true, i.e. if the sum of perpendicular distance to sides is constant, then the triangle is equilateral.

The following excerpt from the task-based interview with Tony captures the gist of the MPTs' transition to a 100% level of certainty that their conjecture generalisation is always true for the case of equilateral triangles only.

Case: Tony

Researcher	So, you have an isosceles triangle and now you have the sum of the measurements from point *P.* Drag point *P* and see what happens to the sum.
Tony	It's changing …
Researcher	So, the sum of the distances is changing?
Tony	Yes.
Researcher	So what do you conclude then? You said you wanted to see if the result is also for an isosceles triangle, so what is your conclusion?
Tony	I think this theory that the total sum of the distances – it only applies for equilateral triangles.

Tony's last remark in the above excerpt, "I think this theory that the total sum of the distances – it only applies for equilateral triangles", suggests that he realised his conjecture generalisation did not hold true for isosceles triangles. However, the use of the word, 'think', prompted the researcher to suspect that Tony was not 100% convinced of his assertion. Hence, the researcher asked Tony, "Do you still want to investigate further?"

Tony	Let's try the scalene, but I think it will still do the same thing that was done with the isosceles.

The remainder of the task-based interview pertaining to the scalene triangle proceeded as follows:

Researcher	Do you still want to check?
Tony	Ja.
Researcher	Here is a scalene triangle … So now we have the measurements of the heights and the sum shown. Drag point.
Tony	It actually changes very fast.

This experience convinced Tony that it was necessary for the triangle to be equilateral for the result to hold.

9.4.3.1 Findings Based on Certainty

Four out of eight MPTs were 100% certain about their conjecture generalisation after their initial set of experimental explorations. Two MPTs required further experimentation within the context of equilateral triangles, while two MPTs wanted further experimentation outside the context of equilateral triangles (such as isosceles and scalene triangles) before pronouncing with a 100% certainty level that their conjecture generalisation was true only for equilateral triangles. The latter two students were either looking at a generalisation to all triangles or the converse, as discussed earlier.

9.4.4 Heuristic Counter-Examples

According to A Mathematical Dictionary for Schools (Bolt & Hobbs 2004), a counter-example is a particular case which disproves a conjecture or claim. In other words, a global counter-example is an example that shows that a given statement, conjecture, hypothesis, proposition or rule is false. Indeed, a single counter-example is sufficient to refute a false statement. A heuristic counter-example, on the other hand, in the Lakatosian sense, may just necessitate the reformulation or refinement of the given conjecture (De Villiers 1996, 2004, 2010). Generally, although not always, counter-examples are produced largely by empirical testing, rather than deductive reasoning.

9.4.5 Refinement/Modification of an MPT's Initial Non-*GSP* Conjecture

The first empirical example constructed through dragging point *P* within the interior of the equilateral triangle within *GSP* served as a heuristic counter-example to the MPTs' assumption that the mid-point (centroid or centre) of the equilateral triangle was the only point that produced the minimum distance (as per their initial conjecture that was made in a non-*GSP* context). The further empirical examples that were constructed through the dragging of point *P* around the interior of the equilateral triangle acted not as heuristic counter-examples any longer, but as supporting evidence for the improvement (modification) of their correct initial non-*GSP* conjecture. This was done to encompass any point within the equilateral triangle to produce the minimum distance sum or generate a constant distance sum (i.e. Sarah could build her house anywhere). Actually, the heuristic counter-example instilled a sense of surprise in the MPTs and the further supporting empirical examples forced them to modify (refine) their initial conjecture that Sarah should build her house in the centre. It was therefore generalised to a new conjecture (or improved conjecture), which says that Sarah could build her house anywhere inside the equilateral triangle-shaped island.

9.5 Discussion of Findings

This section discusses the findings related to the research, with the focus on the development of an inductive generalisation for the equilateral triangle problem.

As described in Section 9.4, the equilateral triangle problem was used as the 'vehicle' to answer this core question. Figure 9.5 provides an overview of the path that the MPTs traversed to construct their inductive generalisation for the equilateral triangle problem. This helped their understanding of the dynamism that evolved with the construction of a generalisation for the equilateral triangle.

At the very start of the task-based activity, the MPTs were first given an opportunity in a non-*GSP* context with an expectation that they would spontaneously use their own intuition to locate a point in the equilateral triangle (which was drawn on the hard copy worksheet), where they thought Sarah should build her house – so that the total sum of the distances from the house to all three beaches is a minimum. All eight of the MPTs located a point in the centre (or middle) of the equilateral triangle (see Finding 1 of Section 9.4.1). Indeed, the choice of the centre (commonly known as midpoint or centroid) is certainly one of the correct positions, among many others, that will create the minimum distance.

When the MPTs were asked to explain or justify why they chose the centre, the explanations of three MPTs (Victor, Logan and Renny) suggested they had been thinking that the distances to the sides should be equal to minimise the sum (i.e. they displayed a misconception that the distances have to be equal in order to minimise the sum). Although some of the other five MPTs may have also been intuitively thinking along the same lines, none of them provided a reason to justify their choice. In particular, none of the MPTs offered symmetry as a reason for their initial choice.

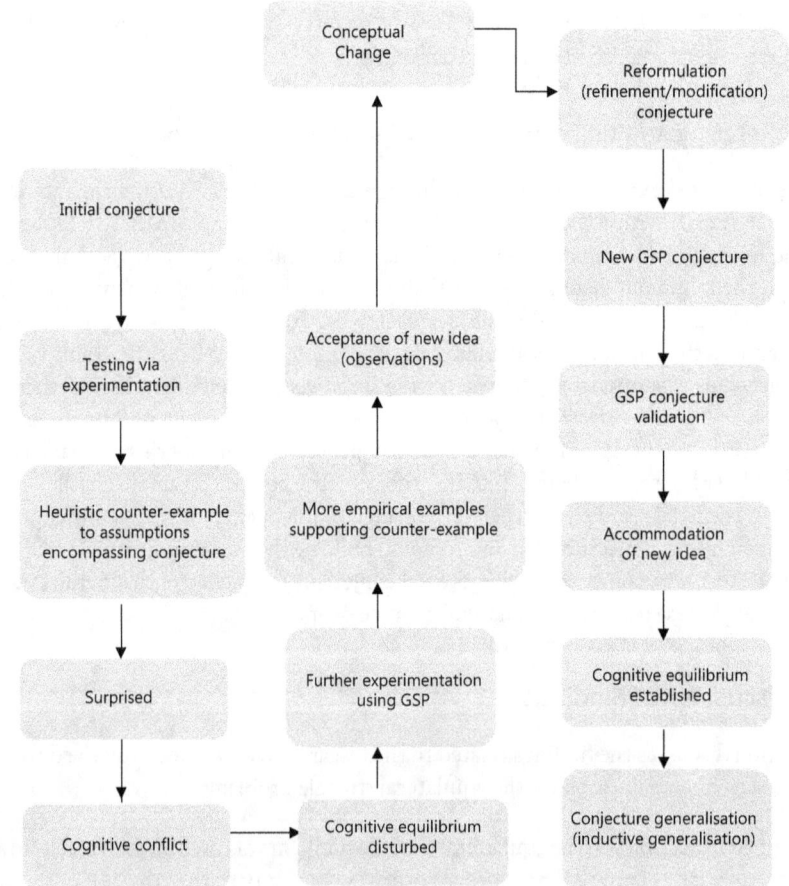

Figure 9.5   A Trajectory of the MPTs' Inductive Generalisation

Consistent with a constructivist perspective of learning, which suggests that learning should occur through the active involvement of learners, the MPTs were provided with an opportunity to explore and experiment with their initial conjecture using *GSP*. In this instance, during their one-to-one task-based interview, each MPT was given a ready-made sketch containing an equilateral triangle with a point P inside the triangle representing a possible position of the house. As per Task 1(b) in Appendix A through dragging point P, the MPTs constructed a visual continuum of cases with each having a different location of point P; and hence observed the invariance of the distance sum, namely the sum of the distances was constant.

As discussed, the first visual example acted as a heuristic counter-example not only to their initial non-*GSP* conjecture but also to the assumption that the centre was the only point creating the minimum distance. Although the further experienced empirical examples supported their acceptance of their heuristic counter-example, this occurred with a degree of surprise to all MPTs and prevailed across the cases as described. This surprise can be attributed to the MPTs seeing that the displayed dynamic empirical examples contradicted an assumption in their initial conjecture, namely that point P should be at the centre.

As per Piaget's equilibration theory (Berger, 2004; Piaget, 1978, 1985), the experienced contradiction seemed to have caused some cognitive conflict within their cognitive structures and therefore disturbed their cognitive equilibrium – i.e. it brought about cognitive disequilibrium, which is commonly known as cognitive conflict. In an attempt to resolve their internal conflict, each MPT abandoned their initial conjecture and through accommodation of the new idea within their cognitive structures, reconstructed a new conjecture that embraced the invariance of the distance sum. In this way, each MPT restored his/her cognitive equilibrium. Thus, within this context, it seems that the heuristic counter-example was the underlying cause of the cognitive conflict. This cognitive conflict forced the MPTs to reject their earlier conjecture and generalise to a new conjecture that says that Sarah could build her house anywhere inside the equilateral triangle-shaped island. The aforementioned MPTs' modification (refinement) of their initial non-*GSP* conjecture in favour of their new conjecture, portrays cognitive conflict as a key driver of conceptual change (see Ausubel 1968; Biemans & Simons 1999; Duit 1999; Di Sessa 2006). Through further experimentation with new particular cases, and seeing that their *GSP* conjecture was still true for such new cases, the MPTs began to see and believe that their *GSP* conjecture was true in general. In particular, the visual empirical examples thus provided the necessary warrants for all eight MPTs to eventually be completely convinced that there were no counter-examples to their conjecture generalisations.

Returning to Research Question 1, the results that accrued from the equilateral problem task demonstrated that the MPTs were able to construct a conjecture generalisation, namely that the sum of the distances from a point inside an equilateral triangle to its sides is constant. This conjecture generalisation was arrived at inductively, not through one single process but rather a set of complementary processes, as represented by the multi-faceted trajectory depicted in Figure 9.5.

9.6 Conclusion

In this qualitative study, which was governed by a constructivist framework, eight MPTs were involved in typical mathematical processes that mathematicians normally traverse in their endeavour to develop an inductive generalisation. This study investigated the active engagement of eight MPTs in the processes associated with the development of an inductive generalisation using a task-based activity worksheet located within a dynamic geometry environment. In doing so, the research attempted to determine and explain how the MPTs developed SMK, PCK and TPACK; that is, inductive generalisation in a dynamic context including *GSP*. In the process, this study explored how the MPTs experienced counter-examples (particularly heuristic counter-examples to assumptions embodying the development of their initial conjectures) from a conceptual change perspective and how they modified their conjecture generalisations as a result of such experiences. To this end, the chapter provided a model for integrating the knowledge mixes as required by the MRTEQ policy.

The analysis of the data was grounded in an analytical-inductive method governed by an interpretive paradigm. The results of this part of the study showed that the MPTs first experienced a heuristic counter-example to the assumptions defining their initial conjectur, which resulted in cognitive conflict. Subsequently, through further experimental exploration and reformulation of their initial conjecture, the MPTs finally re-established their cognitive equilibrium.

The study showed that mathematical teaching and learning is a complex activity and requires various knowledge mixes and skills. The study indicated that advanced mathematical teaching and learning require allowing students to work actively with mathematical objects and when they do so, they are able to question their reasoning and move to more advanced mathematical reasoning. The study also indicated that TPACK is a useful tool to enhance advanced mathematical teaching, learning and thinking. TPACK, which entails the use of technology, was also shown to be helpful in enabling students to work actively with mathematical objects and to achieve more advanced mathematical learning and thinking.

Due to the nature of the chapter, how student teachers use the knowledge gained in this process in the classroom could not be examined. It is, however, anticipated that due to the vast inequalities in classrooms, the application, particularly of TPACK, could prove to be challenging. Further research that probes the processes examined in this chapter in classroom practice is essential for ultimately improving mathematics teaching and learning.

References

Ausubel, D.P. 1968. *Educational psychology: A cognitive view*. New York: Holt, Rinehart & Winston.

Ball, D.L.; Thames, M.H. & Phelps, G. 2008. Content knowledge for teaching: What makes it special? *Journal of Teacher Education*, 59(5): 398-407.

Battista, M.T. & Clements, D.H. 1995. Geometry and proof. *Mathematics Teacher*, 88(1): 48-54.

Berger, K.S. 2004. *The developing person through the lifespan (6th ed.)*. New York: Worth Publishers.

Biemans, H.J.A. & Simons, P.R.J. 1999. Computer-assisted instructional strategies for promoting conceptual change. In: W. Schnotz & M. Carretero (eds). *Advanced learning and instruction series: New perspectives on conceptual change*. New York: Elsevier Science Ltd, 247-262.

Bolt, B. & Hobbs, D. 2004. *A mathematical dictionary for schools*. New York: Cambridge University Press.

Cañadas, M.C. & Castro, E. 2005. A proposal for the categorisation for analysing inductive reasoning. In: M. Bosch (ed.). *Proceedings of Congress of European Research in Mathematics Education (CERME) 4 International Conference*. Spain: Sant Feliu de Guixols, 401-408. Available at: https://ermeweb.free.fr/CERME4.

Cañadas, M.C.; Deulofu, J.; Figuerias, L.; Reid, D. & Yevdokimov, A. 2007. The conjecturing process: Perspectives in theory and implications in practice. *Journal of Teaching and Learning*, 5(1): 55-72.

Carraher, D.W.; Martinez, M.V. & Schliemann, A.D. 2008. Early algebra and mathematical generalization. ZDM *Mathematics Education*, 40: 3-22. https://doi.org/10.1007/s11858-007-0067-7

Carter, P.; Govender, R. & Heany, F. 2007. *Focus on Mathematics Grade 12*. Cape Town: Maskew Miller & Longan.

Concise Oxford dictionary. 1995. (10th ed.). Cape Town: Oxford University Press.

Contreras, J. & Martinez-Cruz, A. 2009. Representing, modeling and solving problems in interactive geometry environments. In: T.V. Craine & R. Rubenstein (eds). *Understanding geometry for a changing world: Seventy-first yearbook*. Reston, VA: NCTM, 233-252.

Creswell, J.W. 2003. *Research design: Qualitative, quantitative, and mixed-methods approaches (2nd ed.)*. Thousand Oaks, CA: Sage Publications.

Denzin, N.K. & Lincoln, Y.S. 2005. Introduction: The discipline and practice of qualitative research. In: N. Denzin & Y.S. Lincoln (eds). *The Sage handbook of qualitative research (3rd ed.)*. Thousand Oaks, CA: Sage Publications, 1-32.

Department of Basic Education (DBE). 2011a. *Curriculum and assessment policy statement for further education and training phase Grades 10-12: Mathematics*. Pretoria: DBE.

Department of Basic Education (DBE). 2011b. *Curriculum and assessment policy statement for senior phase Grades 7-9: Mathematics*. Pretoria: DBE.

Department of Basic Education (DBE). 2011c. *Curriculum and assessment policy statement for intermediate phase Grades 4-6: Mathematics*. Pretoria: DBE.

Department of Basic Education (DBE). 2011d. *Curriculum and assessment policy statement for intermediate phase Grades 1-3: Mathematics*. Pretoria: DBE.

Department of Basic Education and Department of Higher Education and Training (DBE & DHET). 2011. *Integrated strategic planning framework for teacher education and development in South Africa, 2011-2025*. Pretoria: Government Printer.

Department of Education (DoE). 2002a. *National curriculum statement: Overview*. Pretoria: DoE.

Department of Education (DoE). 2002b. *Revised National Curriculum Statement for Grades R-9 (schools): Mathematics*. Pretoria: DoE.

Department of Education (DoE). 2003a. *National Curriculum Statement for Grades 10-12 (schools): Mathematics*. Pretoria: DoE.

Department of Education (DoE). 2003b. *Revised National Curriculum Statement for Grades R-9 (schools): Teacher's guide for the development of learning programmes: Mathematics.* Pretoria: DoE.

Department of Education (DoE). 2003c. *Revised National Curriculum Statement for Grades 10-12 (schools): Teacher's guide for the development of learning programmes: Mathematics.* Pretoria: DoE.

Department of Education and Science and the Welsh Office. 1995. *Mathematics in the national curriculum.* London, United Kingdom: Her Majesty's Stationery Office.

Department of Higher Education and Training (DHET). 2015. National Qualifications Framework Act, 2008 (Act No. 67 of 2008): Revised Policy on the Minimum Requirements for Teacher Education Qualifications. *Government Gazette*, 38487, 19 February. Pretoria: Government Printer.

De Villiers, M. 1992. Inductive and deductive reasoning: Logic and proof. In: M. Moodley, R.A. Njisane & N.C. Presmeg (eds). Mathematics education for in-service and pre-service teachers. Pietermaritzburg: Shuter & Shooter, 45-59.

De Villiers, M. 1996. *Some adventures in Euclidean geometry.* Durban, South Africa: University of Durban-Westville.

De Villiers, M. 1998. An alternative approach to proof in dynamic geometry. In: R. Lehrer & D. Chazan (eds). *Designing learning environments for developing and understanding of geometry and space.* Mahwah, NJ: Lawrence Erlbaum Associates, 369-394.

De Villiers, M. 1999. *Rethinking proof with the Geometer's Sketchpad 3.* Emeryville, CA: Key Curriculum Press.

De Villiers, M. 2003a. *Rethinking proof with Geometer's Sketchpad 4.* Emeryville, CA: Key Curriculum Press.

De Villiers, M. 2003b. *The value of experimentation in mathematics.* Paper presented at the 9th National congress of AMESA, 30 June-4 July 2003. Available at: https://mzone.mweb.co.za/ residents/profmd/homepage.html

De Villiers, M. 2004. The role and function of quasi-empirical methods in mathematics. *Canadian Journal of Science, Mathematics and Technology Education*, 4(3): 397-418. https://doi.org/10.1080/14926150409556621

De Villiers, M. 2007. Some pitfalls of dynamic geometry software. *Teaching and Learning Mathematics*, 4: 46-52.

De Villiers, M. 2010. Experimentation and proof in mathematics. In: G. Hanna, H.N. Janke & H. Pulte (eds). *Explanation and proof in mathematics: Philosophical and educational perspectives.* New York: Springer, 205-221. https://doi.org/10.1007/978-1-4419-0576-5_14

Di Sessa, A.A. 2006. A history of conceptual change research: Threads and fault lines. In: R.K. Sawyer (ed.). *The Cambridge handbook of the learning sciences.* New York: Cambridge University Press, 265-281.

Douek, N. 2009. Approaching proof in school: From guided conjecturing and proving to a story of proof construction. In: V. Durand-Guerrier, S. Soury-Lavergne & F. Arzarello (eds). *Proceedings of Congress of European Research in Mathematics Education (CERME) 6.* 28 January-1 February. Lyon: France, 332-342. Available at: https://ife.ens-lyon.fr/publications/edition-electronique/cerme6/cerme6.pdf

Driscoll, M.P. 2000. *Psychology of learning for instruction.* Massachusetts: Pearson Education.

Driscoll, M.P.; Egan, M.; DiMatteo, R.W. & Nikula, J. 2009. Fostering geometric thinking in the middle grades: Professional development in Grades 5-10. In: T. Craine & R. Rubenstein (eds). *Understanding geometry for a changing world: 71st yearbook*. USA: NCTM, 155-172.

Duit, R. 1999. Conceptual change approaches in science education. In: W. Schnotz, S. Vosniadou & M. Carretero (eds). *New perspectives on conceptual change (Advances in Learning and Instruction Series, 1st ed.)*. New York: Elsevier Science Ltd, 263-282.

Education Development Centre Inc. 2002. *Examples, patterns, and conjectures*. Available at: https://www2.edc.org/makingmath/Handbook/Teacher/Conjectures/Conjectures.pdf

Flick, U. 2007. *Designing qualitative research*. Thousand Oaks, CA: Sage Publications. https://doi.org/10.4135/9781849208826

Giamatti, C. 1995. Conjectures in geometry and the Geometer's Sketchpad. *Mathematics Teacher*, 88(6): 456-458.

Govender, R. 2002. *Student teachers' understanding and development of their ability to evaluate and formulate definitions in a Sketchpad context*. Master's thesis. Durban: University of Durban-Westville.

Govender, R. & De Villiers, M. 2002. Constructive evaluations of definitions in a Sketchpad context. Paper presented at the Association for Mathematics Education of South Africa National conference. Durban: University of Natal, July 2002. Available at: mweb.co.za/residents.profmd/rajen.pdf

Gray, D. 2008. *Using The Geometer's Sketchpad in the math classroom to improve engagement, transform the learning environment and enhance understanding*. Available at: https://discoverarchive.vanderbilt.edu/handle/1803/571.

Hiebert, J.; Morris, A.K. & Glass, B. 2003. Learning to teach: An "experiment" model for teaching and teacher preparation in mathematics. *Journal of Mathematics Teacher Education*, 6(3): 201-222. https://doi.org/10.1023/A:1025162108648

Hitchcock, G. & Hughes, D. 1995. Research and the teacher: *A qualitative introduction to school-based research (2nd ed.)*. London: Routledge.

Hobson, A.J.; Malderez, A.; Tracey, L.; Giannakaki, M.S.; Pell, R.G.; Kerr, K.; Chambers, G.N.; Tomlinson, P.D. & Roper, T. 2006. *Becoming a teacher: Student teachers' experiences of initial teacher training in England*. Research report RR744. United Kingdom: The Department for Education and Skills, University of Nottingham.

Houston, K. 2009. *How to think like a mathematician: A companion to undergraduate mathematics*. Cape Town: Cambridge University Press. https://doi.org/10.1017/CBO9780511808258

Hoyles, C. & Noss, R. 1994. Dynamic geometry environments: What's the point? *Mathematics Teacher*, 87(9): 716-717.

Hummel, K.E. 2000. *Introductory concepts for abstract mathematics*. USA: Chapman & Hall.

Izen, S.P. 1998. Proof in modern geometry. *Mathematics Teacher*, 91(8): 718-721.

Jackie, N. 1991. *The Geometer's Sketchpad learning guide*. Emeryville, CA: Key Curriculum Press.

Jackie, N. 1995. *The Geometer's Sketchpad*. Berkeley, CA: Key Curriculum Press.

James, N. 1992. Investigative approaches to the learning and teaching of mathematics. In: M. Moodley, R.A. Njisane & N.C. Presmeg (eds). *Mathematics education for inservice and pre-services teachers*. Pietermaritzburg: Shuter and Shooter Publishers, 60-67.

Jansen, J. 2013. Personal reflections on policy and school quality in South Africa: When the politics of disgust meets the politics of distrust. In: Y. Sayed, A. Kanjee & M. Nkomo (eds). *The search for quality education in post-apartheid South Africa: Interventions to improve learning and teaching.* Cape Town: HSRC Press, 81-89.

Kilpatrick, J.; Swafford, J. & Findell, B. (eds). 2001. *Adding it up: Helping children learn mathematics.* Washington, D.C.: National Academy Press.

Klymchuk, S. 2008. *Using counter-examples to enhance learners' understanding of undergraduate mathematics.* Available at: https://akoaotearoa.ac.nz/download/ng/file/group-3300/using-counter-examples-to-enhance-learners-understanding-of-undergraduate-mathematics.pdf

Leedy, P. 1993. *Practical research: Planning and design (5th ed.).* USA: Macmillan Publishing Company.

MacBeath, J. 2012. *The future of the teaching profession.* Brussels: Education International Research Institute.

MacLeod, G. & Cebula, K.R. 2009. Experiences of disabled students in initial teacher education. *Cambridge Journal of Education,* 39(4): 457-472. https://doi.org/10.1080/03057640903352465

Mariotti, M.A. 2001. Justifying and proving in the Cabri environment. *International Journal of Computers for Mathematical Learning,* 6(3): 257-281. https://doi.org/10.1023/A:1013357611987

Mariotti, M.A. 2007. Geometrical proof: The mediation of a microworld. In: P. Boero (ed.). *Theorems in schools: From history, epistemology and cognition to classroom practice.* The Netherlands: Sense Publishers, 285-304.

Mason, J. 1999. *Learning and doing mathematics (2nd revised ed.).* York, United Kingdom: QED.

Mason, J.; Burton, L. & Stacey, K. 1982. *Thinking mathematically.* London: Addison-Wesley.

McMillan, J.H. & Schumacher, S. 2010. *Research in education (7th ed.).* New York: Longman.

Mishra, P. & Koehler, M.J. 2006 Technological pedagogical content knowledge: A framework for teacher knowledge. *Teachers College Record,* 108(6): 1017-1054. https://doi.org/10.1111/j.1467-9620.2006.00684.x

Morrow, W. 1989. *Chains of thought: Philosophical essays in South African education.* Johannesburg: Southern Book Publishers.

Mudaly, V. & De Villiers, M. 2002. *Mathematical modeling and proof.* Paper presented at the 10th AMESA congress. University of the North-West, Potchefstroom, 30 June-4 July. Available at: https://mysite.mweb.co.za/residents/profmd/vimmodel.pdf

National Council of Teachers of Mathematics (NCTM). 2000. *Principles and standards for school mathematics.* Reston, VA: NCTM.

Njisane, R.A. 1992. Mathematical thinking. In: M. Moodley, R.A. Njisane & N.C. Presmeg (eds). *Mathematics education for in-service and pre-service teachers.* Pietermaritzburg: Shuter & Shooter, 26-37.

November, I. 2010. The teacher as an agent of transformation. In: L. Conley, J. de Beer, H. Dunbar-Krige, E. du Plessis, S. Gravett, L. Lomofsky, V. Merckel, I. November, R. Osman, N. Petersen, M. Robinson & M. van der Merwe (eds). *Becoming a teacher.* Cape Town: Pearson Education, 183-196.

O'Connell, J. 2013. The education quality improvement partnership programme: A whole-school development framework. In: Y. Sayed, A. Kanjee & M. Nkomo (eds). *The search for quality education in post-apartheid South Africa: Interventions to improve learning and teaching.* Cape Town: HSRC Press, 121-146.

Oxford dictionary. 2004. (2nd ed.). Cape Town: Oxford University Press.

Piaget, J. 1978. *The development of thought: Equilibrium of cognitive structures.* New York: Viking.

Piaget, J. 1985. *The equilibration of cognitive structures: The central problem of intellectual development.* Chicago: University of Chicago Press.

Polya, G. 1954. *Mathematics and plausible reasoning: Induction and analogy in mathematics (vol. 1).* Princeton, NJ: Princeton University Press.

Pólya, G. 1967. *Le Découverte des Mathématiques. [The discovery of mathematics.]* París: DUNOD.

Robinson, M. & Lomofsky, L. 2010. The teacher as educational theorist. In: L. Conley, J. de Beer, H. Dunbar-Krige, E. du Plessis, S. Gravett, L. Lomofsky, V. Merckel, I. November, R. Osman, N. Petersen, M. Robinson & M. van der Merwe (eds). *Becoming a teacher.* Cape Town: Pearson Education, 31-51.

Scher, D. 2002. *Students' conceptions of geometry in a dynamic geometry software environment.* PhD dissertation. New York University, New York.

Schwarz, C. 1993. *Chambers dictionary.* New Delhi: Allied Publishers Ltd.

Schwartz, J.L. & Yerushalmy, M. 1986. *The Geometric Supposer series.* Pleasantville, N.Y.: Sunburst Communications.

Sinclair, M.; De Bruyn, Y.; Hanna, G. & Harrison, P. 2004. Cinderella and the Geometer's Sketchpad. *Canadian Journal of Science, Mathematics and Technology Education,* 4(3): 423-437. https://doi.org/10.1080/14926150409556623

Sowder, L. & Harel, G. 1998. Types of students' justifications. *Mathematics Teacher,* 91(8): 670-675.

Tall, D. 1988. Concept image and concept definition. In: J. de Lange & M. Doorman (eds). *Senior secondary mathematics education.* Utrecht: OW & OC, 37-41.

Taylor, N. 2014. *Initial Teacher Education Research Project: An examination of aspects of initial teacher education curricula at five higher education institutions.* Summary report. Johannesburg: JET Education Services.

Vincent, J.; Chick, H. & McCrea, B. 2005. Argumentation profile charts as tools for analysing student's argumentation. In: H.L. Chick & J.L. Vincent (eds). *Proceedings of the 29th Conference for the Psychology of Mathematics Education (PME) (vol. 4).* Melbourne: PME, 281-288.

Whiteley, W. 2000. *Dynamic geometry programs and the practice of geometry.* Available at: https://www.researchgate.net/publication/237370692_Dynamic_Geometry_Programs_and_the_Practice_of_Geometry

Yerushalmy, M. 1993. Generalization in geometry. In: J.L. Schwartz, M. Yerushalmy & B. Wilson (eds). *The geometric supposer: What is it a case of?* New Jersey: Lawrence Erlbaum Associates Inc, 57-84.

Appendix 1

Session one task-based activity – Equilateral Triangle Problem

Task 1 Shipwreck problem

Sarah, a shipwreck survivor manages to swim to a desert island. As it happens, the island closely approximates the shape of an equilateral triangle. She soon discovers that the surfing is outstanding on all three of the island's coasts and crafts a surfboard from a fallen tree and surfs everyday. Where should Sarah build her house so that the total sum of the distances from the house to all three beaches is a minimum? (She visits them with equal frequency).

Task 1-(a): Locating a point in the triangle not using Sketchpad.

1. Before you proceed further, locate a point in the triangle at the point where you think Sarah should build her house.

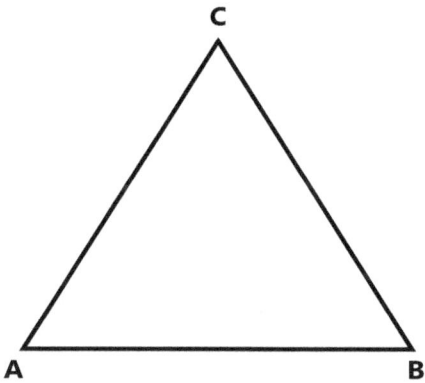

2. Why did you choose that position? Explain or justify your choice.

Task 1-(b): Using *Sketchpad* to develop a conjecture

Open the sketch **Distances.gsp**. Drag point P to experiment with your sketch.

1. Press the button to show the distance sum. Drag point P around the interior of the triangle. What do you notice about the sum of the distances?
2. Drag a vertex of the triangle to change the triangle's size. Again, drag point P around the interior of the triangle. What do you notice?
3. Write your discoveries so far as one or more conjectures. Use complete sentences.

Task 1-(c)   Certainty, counter examples and logical explanations

1. You probably can think of times when something that always appeared to be true turned out to be false sometimes. How certain are you that you conjecture is always true? Record your level of certainty on the number line and explain (or justify) your choice.

```
•————————•————————•————————•————————•
0%         25%        50%        75%       100%
```

2. If you suspect your conjecture is not always true, try to supply a counter-example.

If you are fully convinced of the truth of your conjecture, do you still have a need for an explanation (i.e. do you want know why it is true)?.

Chapter 10

Learning to Teach Language in the Further Education & Training Phase

Hanlie Dippenaar, Azeem Badroodien & Nomakhaya Mashiyi

10.1 Introduction

In contemporary South Africa most learners are taught (and learn) through a second language. This poses brings enormous challenges for them in their everyday schooling lives. A number of studies have shown that, alongside the lack of human and material resources for supporting and implementing initial literacy skills, being taught in a second language has a significant (mostly negative) influence on the overall schooling performances of South African learners (Alidou & Brock-Utne 2006; Smits, Huisman & Kruijff 2008; Pinnock & Vijayakumar 2009). In that respect, language in South Africa has always been deeply implicated in marginalising, alienating and elevating or sidelining different groups of language speakers in different contexts and spaces. This is done to the extent that "those that were most marginalised during apartheid often continue to be those who are most marginalised in the post-apartheid education system" (Heugh 2013:23).

In line with key discussions in this book that concentrate on teacher preparedness, confidence and competence to teach in South African schools, this chapter focuses specifically on current ITE practice concerns that influence the ways in which teachers are prepared to teach language (as a functional tool and as a tool for communication) in South Africa – especially for reading and writing. In doing so, the chapter builds on and explores a number of factors that have been used to explain South Africa's poor literacy outcomes, such as:

- ✓ many teachers and students battle to communicate in the dominant language of instruction;
- ✓ LiEPs are not clearly articulated in CAPS documents;
- ✓ misunderstandings of the early literacy-to-academic literacy continuum within the formal schooling system;
- ✓ challenges tied to the re-introduction of African languages, like isiXhosa at primary school for three years, instead of the recommended eight years; and
- ✓ varied interpretations of "multilingualism" and too much "terminological slippage" (Heugh 2013:23; Taylor 2014).

For this chapter, and pertinently for learners learning in a second language, it is notable that teachers in South Africa are not sufficiently trained in how to teach language, especially reading and writing, in ways that constructively engage with the above factors (Taylor 2014). To explore this, this chapter explores the views and reflections (collected via particular instruments) of a group of student teachers who were enrolled for a one-year PGCE programme (at one university in the Western Cape) on how they were assisted to become language educators in the FET phase.

These insights contribute to key discussions in this book. The discussions include understanding student teacher experiences of ITE programmes as a way of ascertaining teacher preparedness, confidence and competence to teach in South African schools.

This chapter draws on data collected in a larger regional study exploring experiences of Foundation Phase and FET student teachers, and which included responses on FET language teaching. Specifically, it engages with the views and reflections (collected via particular instruments) of a group of student teachers who were enrolled for a one-year PGCE programme at one university in the Western Cape. It also analyses what they stated about being assisted to become language educators in the FET Phase.

The data were collected via two questionnaires and a number of focus group interviews. The first questionnaire investigated the beliefs of student teachers regarding language and teaching language. The second questionnaire sought to ascertain their experience of teaching practice and how this affected their confidence to teach various linguistic skills in their major subject areas (English and some isiXhosa). The subsequent focus groups probed similar themes, with a particular inclination towards giving student teachers the opportunity to develop their initial views about the ITE programme and languages and how the programme prepared them to teach languages in the FET Phase.

In analysing the above three datasets, the chapter first places student teachers' beliefs and practices against the broader landscape of language teaching in South Africa and the pressure associated with developing linguistic (and multiple literacies) competency in the 21st century.

10.2 Teaching Languages Post-Apartheid

10.2.1 Challenges for Teaching

Napier (2011) argues that although a range of language transformation policies are in place in South Africa – with much progress achieved since 1994 – there remain a number of hurdles that obstruct the full implementation of the South African LiEP. These include: (i) the ways in which globalisation discourses privilege English as the language of communication, (ii) the difficulties attached to embedding multilingualism in such a climate, (iii) the many challenges tied to embedding mother-tongue instruction, and (iv) pedagogical or transmission issues within mediums of instruction.

The above contexts and challenges are not helped by language policy practices in South Africa that focus narrowly on language planning, or lean towards what Kubanyiova and Crookes (2016:118) refer to as a "passive-technician view of language teaching". The latter refers to an approach to language teaching that foregrounds or privileges the ways in which teachers select and arrange materials and how they organise the curriculum, motivate students, manage classrooms, liaise with parents and assess students (Kubanyiova & Crookes 2016).

In the later data sections, it is shown how many of the abovementioned approaches to language teaching have tended to predominate in the Western Cape (as opposed to approaches that develop, prepare and skill student teachers with a variety of different proficiencies, techniques and insights).

10.2.2 Dilemmas Tied to Language Policy

Since 1994 (with the promulgation of 11 official languages and the crafting of a multilingual LiEP in 1997) schools and, more recently, universities have wrestled with how to enhance student learning and promote "epistemological access" (Hibbert & Van der Walt 2014). The lack of success of the various approaches adopted thus far highlights key struggles in implementing post-apartheid LiEPs and the continuing inequities that current LiEPs and current conceptions of language seem to mask.

In the above regard, two approaches have primarily been undertaken. In the first instance, many argue for indigenous languages to be treated as fully fledged mediums of instruction based on research that has shown that learners perform better when taught in their home language (Bender, Dutcher, Klaus, Shore & Tesar 2005; Brock-Utne 2007; Prah 2009). This is so, it is argued, because it avoids learners having to decode a language that they do not understand before they have made the necessary connections between spoken and written language (Smits et al. 2008:8). It is often argued that learners are able to at least understand their teachers in a common language at crucial moments in their development. However, despite indigenous languages being recognised as official languages in South Africa, this approach is rarely followed and indigenous languages beyond the Foundation Phase are not used regularly as fully fledged media of instruction.

In the second instance, teachers often adopt multilingualism as a key resource in teaching and learning (Brock-Utne 2007; Prah 2009; Makoe & McKinney 2014; Krog 2017), doing so mainly through code switching. Baker (1993:76) defines code switching as "when an individual more or less deliberately alternates between two or more languages". Teachers use this approach to mediate learning in cases where learners have limited proficiency in the LoLT (Moyo 2000; Setati et al. 2002). In that respect, Garcia and Flores (2012:232) remind us of the following:

> Unless teachers' pedagogies include the language practices of students, and unless all students are taught in ways that support and develop their diverse language practices, there cannot be any meaningful participation in education, and thus in society. Multilingual pedagogies are at the centre of all education that meaningfully includes learners; that is, education that is not simply done to students, but in which students do and participate.

Notably, code switching is practised differently in various teaching contexts. For higher education settings where code switching is often used, Van der Walt (2013, citing Garcia 2009:303) refers to a number of teaching-learning strategies that educators at universities have adopted to attempt to shift language practices so that "full multilingual repertoires can legitimately be used as resources for learning" (Makoe & McKinney 2014). These include: 'responsible code switching' (sometimes referred to as instructional code switching/ code alternation); 'translanguaging' (no functional separation of languages); 'co-languaging' (comparing and contrasting languages); 'preview-view-review', and 'cross-linguistic' work and awareness. From among these, translanguaging practices are viewed as particularly fluid and dynamic since the different languages are not approached as if they require autonomous skills, and "the complex fluid language practices of students" are recognised (Garcia & Flores 2012).

10.2.3   Approaches and Concerns Tied to the Teaching of Language

The fact that the technique of code switching is applied quite differently when student teachers are taught and developed at the university level, as opposed to when teachers use code switching as a pedagogical device at the school level, provides a huge challenge in preparing student teachers to teach language.

At the university level two schemes predominate. The first is where bilingual lecturers use code switching randomly in spontaneous and intuitive ways, in contexts where they presume students are able to understand lecturers equally well in different languages. This approach is not appropriate, however, when students are not bilingual or where the development of a particular academic language is paramount or needs to be prioritised (Van der Walt 2013:143). The second approach is where lecturers utilise code switching in responsible and purposive ways, knowing that students have acquired the adequate academic literacy skills, and thereafter apply code switching in 'deliberate' ways to serve particular *purposes* (Van der Walt 2013:143). In both instances, lecturers utilise code switching as a teaching technique and rarely as a model that student teachers can or should use in their classrooms.

At the school level, the literature reveals that code switching, code mixing, translation, repetition and township lingo are mostly used at the rural and township school level in South Africa – with the main purpose to make the curriculum more accessible to learners whose second (or third) language is English. In urban and desegregated school settings, English as a main language of instruction is hegemonic, with very little value attached to code switching (Chick & McKay 2001).

A number of studies reveal that code switching, when used in township settings, is extensively used in contexts where the teacher and learners share a first language or home language to facilitate learning and make up for learners' lack of English language competence (Adendorff 1993; Adler 1998; Probyn 2001). This is particularly evident in cases where learners share a home language or first language with a teacher, with the first language becoming the *de facto* medium of instruction (Setati & Adler 2000; Setati et al. 2002; Brock-Utne & Holmarsdottir 2003). Ironically, where code switching is used to teach in this way, assessments are often still conducted in English (Mashiyi 2011).

As such, several South African small-scale studies have revealed inconsistencies and contradictions in how multilingualism is conceived, with the quality of teacher training often very poor in preparing teachers to enter schools with adequate linguistic repertoires and skills. These latter two processes are influenced by: issues of human and infrastructural resources in schools; the contexts in which language policies are implemented; perceptions of the power of English and whether it should be used as a medium of instruction; teachers' linguistic insecurities; and often quite low levels of learner proficiency in all languages (Setati 2000; Setati & Adler 2000; Probyn 2001; Setati et al. 2002).

Furthermore, with regard to the language preparation of student teachers for the FET Phase, Nomlomo (2013) reveals through her study of ITE programme-level student teachers' use of isiXhosa home language that language teaching often mainly focuses on the development of oral skills and grammar, with too little attention paid to reading and writing. According to Nomlomo (2013), this adds to or exacerbates the literacy problems and challenges that FET learners face at the school level when taught by such student teachers. Nomlomo (2013) argues that because FET learners in particular are at the tail end of their school education and would need advanced academic literacy skills when entering the tertiary level, all language teachers (including student teachers) should be exposed to pedagogies that adequately prepare learners for the 21st century. For her, teacher training in languages (like isiXhosa) needs to be offered by competent language lecturers who are able to mediate learning effectively, as well as reflect on their own practices.

In the above respect, the variously noted policies, challenges and concerns shape in different ways how student teachers in South Africa are prepared at the ITE level in South Africa, and how they navigate current language policies and their implementation. For the chapter, it is anticipated that the above also influence how student teachers perceive and approach their preparation and development at the FET level (with specialisation in English and isiXhosa) within an ITE programme. The remainder of the chapter engages with three research instruments conducted with student teachers in an ITE programme and trained at the FET level in 2016 and examines and analyses these student teachers' experiences of 'being taught to teach language'.

10.2.4 Teacher Education Policy for the FET Phase

The MRTEQ policy (DHET 2015a:5) determines the design and categorisation of ITE programmes at university level. This policy document articulates the required knowledge and practice standards for professional educators and teachers in the schooling system, at both the BEd degree level and the PGCE level. As NQF level-7 professionally focused qualifications that confer on graduates their beginner teacher status, the function of ITE programmes is to develop a level of teacher professional expertise regarded as crucial to the success of the schooling system.

The underlying purpose of the qualifications is to develop focused knowledge and skills within classroom teachers with "a specific depth and specialisation of subject knowledge" within different specialisations, together with practical skills and workplace experience to enable them to apply their "learning as beginner teachers in schools in varying contexts" (DHET 2015a:26). The MRTEQ policy requires that beginner teachers also attain a level of proficiency in the LoLT that as newly qualified FET teachers they have specialised to teach. This is alongside being fully proficient in the two specialist South African official languages that they attained as part of the qualification (As such, in attempting to guarantee that NQTs in languages are always able to teach in the LoLT, the MRTEQ policy not only seeks to ensure proper certification but also to ensure that teachers have a variety of necessary skills to teach in diverse contexts. Indeed, a closer examination of the Basic Competences of Beginner Teachers (DHET 2015b) reveals a fairly sound attempt to "realise the importance of ITE in playing its proper part in the rescue of schooling from its present predicament" (Taylor 2014).

For this chapter, the student teachers in the ITE programme commented on three instruments related specifically to specialist teaching in English and some isiXhosa for secondary school teaching (FET Phase) – with both language departments at the relevant university having very similar pedagogical and academic aims. The main focus of both academic departments is facilitating critical thinking and analysis around language policies and curricula in the South African context and having students analyse key principles (pertaining to language) inherent in the National Curriculum. They do so by looking closely at theories of teaching and learning, and teaching students how to apply these skills required in their method subjects. Learning how to teach these subject methods as a home language is seemingly part of both components, with the teaching of assessment skills apparently regarded as an important practical dimension within each of the university departmental courses.

In the three instruments, student teachers were asked questions that related specifically to the roles they envisioned for language teachers and whether they thought they were taught enough practical skills to teach language, or whether the focus was more on critical thinking and reflection and how these contribute to the development of learners (as envisaged by Crookes 2013; Hawkins & Norton 2009, in Kubanyiova & Crookes 2016:119).

The following section discusses the kinds of data that were examined for this chapter to gain a sense of what student teachers thought about their preparation. Thereafter follows a report on and analysis of what this may mean for teachers learning to teach language in the FET Phase.

10.3 Methodology

The focus of this chapter draws from data collected by CITE (cf Chapter One) across three universities in the Western Cape (and one in Gauteng) that collects and analyses the perceptions of student teachers regarding their teacher preparation in ITE programmes. For this chapter, the focus is only on what student teachers at one university noted regarding language in the FET Phase. This draws on three sets of data, namely (i) a survey conducted in 2016 with 68 student teachers about their beliefs regarding teaching, (ii) a second survey conducted later in 2016 with 45 participants, which focused mainly on their teaching practice experiences and (iii) a set of focus group interviews that explored how student teachers felt about their experiences across their ITE preparation.

Drawing from the above, instruments focused solely on questionnaire items that related to the teaching of language (in this case English and some isiXhosa) and provided an analysis of a variety of tables that captured the data according to a four-point Likert-scale.

Some important and notable characteristics about the sample used in this chapter include the following:
- ✓ The majority of the student teachers were female and under 30 years of age.
- ✓ The majority of the respondents were coloured and the remainder predominantly African.
- ✓ Just over 50% of the respondents recorded English as their primary home language, about 30% indicated Afrikaans and 16% isiXhosa.
- ✓ Much of the descriptions of the sample on English are based on a global view of English and isiXhosa language student teachers.

Importantly, the data for the surveys were collected from student respondents whose subject specialisation was English or isiXhosa, which are two of the three main languages of learning and instruction in the Western Cape.

In analysing the data in the sections that follow, the data is separated out as per key identified themes. The relevant findings are then interpreted according to the view that teacher education programmes must be able to combine SMK, PCK and knowledge of context (Shulman 1987) in synergistic ways that effectively prepare student teachers at the ITE stage. This approach is applied specifically to the teaching of the English language at the FET level.

10.4 Student Teacher Reflections on Language Teaching Preparation

The chapter explores in three subsections how student teachers responded to the various questionnaires and focus group discussions to questions about (i) their beliefs about language and teaching language when they entered the ITE programme, (ii) their pedagogical preparation and experiences of teaching practice and how this affected their confidence to teach various linguistic skills in their major subject areas (English and some isiXhosa), and (iii) their views of the ITE programme and whether it prepared them to teach languages in the FET Phase. The aim of the subsections is to show what student teachers believe about language teaching and how this may influence their development of the kinds of pedagogical, linguistic and literacy competencies needed for teaching language at the FET level.

10.4.1 Student Teacher Beliefs

Some student teacher beliefs are crucial to their eventual practice and for the development of the kinds of proficiencies they will need to teach. These include: student teacher beliefs about the importance of language and its teaching; the kinds of teaching strategies they think are needed to teach language; and their views of the contribution of language to the development of different elements of teaching.

10.4.1.1 Beliefs About the Role of Language in Teaching and Learning

For example, when asked about the importance of language as a subject, student teachers strongly acknowledged (over 76%) that languages facilitate understanding across the curriculum and that they are important tools for thought and communication. They also acknowledged that they offer important ways for learners to make sense of the worlds they live in and in the shaping of their identities.

However, while 81% of student teachers strongly believed that language plays a key role in assisting learners to listen, speak, read and write, they did not overwhelmingly (or strongly) believe that the subject of language is key to learner development, or (in a later question) that every teacher needs to be a language teacher. Ironically, only 27 of the 58 (46,6%) student teachers strongly believed this to be the case, with five student teachers suggesting that language is not key to learner development. Also, only 28 of the 58 (48,3%) student teachers strongly agreed that language is important for learner identity. This is an important and interesting formulation when combined with the views of the majority of student teachers (77,6%) that parents play a bigger role in teaching language at home.

Notably, these views are often presented somewhat differently for the English language, where student teachers (in later questions) believed that English is extensively used across the South African curriculum and thus imperative for teaching and learning.

Table 10.1   Student Teacher Beliefs about Language as a Subject

Student teacher beliefs	Strongly disagree N (%)	Disagree N (%)	Agree N (%)	Strongly agree N (%)
Language is a tool for thought.	0 (0)	0 (0)	23 (40,4)	34 (59,6)
Language is a tool for communication.	0 (0)	0 (0)	14 (24,1)	44 (75,9)
Language is a shared means to make better sense of the world we live in.	0 (0)	0 (0)	22 (37,9)	36 (62,1)
Language is important for one's identity.	0 (0)	0 (0)	30 (51,7)	28 (48,3)
Language is the most important subject taught at school.	0 (0)	5 (8,6)	26 (44,8)	27 (46,6)
Language assists learners to listen, speak, read and write.	0 (0)	0 (0)	11 (19)	47 (81)
Language facilitates understanding across the curriculum.	0 (0)	0 (0)	14 (24,1)	44 (75,9)

10.4.1.2 Beliefs about the Teaching of Language and its Role in Developing the Skills of Reading, Writing, Speaking and Listening

Also, as opposed to the strong role foreseen (81%) for language in assisting learners to listen, speak, read and write (as noted above), student teachers offered a quite different perspective when prompted on the main role of language teaching (see Table 10.2). Only 44,8% of the student teachers strongly believed that the main goal of teaching languages is to help learners think and reason. Also, only 56,9% strongly believed that there is a close correlation between understanding languages and being able to read and write.

Table 10.2   Student Teacher Beliefs about Teaching Language

Student teacher beliefs	Strongly disagree N (%)	Disagree N (%)	Agree N (%)	Strongly agree N (%)
The goal of teaching language is to help learners think and reason.	1 (1,7)	3 (5,2)	28 (48,3)	26 (44,8)
There is a correlation between reading and writing, and understanding languages.	0 (0)	2 (3,4)	23 (39,7)	33 (56,9)

Learning to Teach Language in the Further Education & Training Phase

Table 10.2   Student Teacher Beliefs about Teaching Language (cont)

Student teacher beliefs	Strongly disagree N (%)	Disagree N (%)	Agree N (%)	Strongly agree N (%)
Teaching literature is about expecting the right answer.	0 (0)	19 (32,8)	36 (62,1)	3 (5,2)
Classroom discussion is useful.	0 (0)	0 (0)	22 (37,9)	36 (62,1)
Language is a tool for thought and communication.	0 (0)	0 (0)	21 (36,8)	36 (63,2)
Prescribed language textbooks are the most important resources a teacher has.	3 (5,2)	29 (50)	24 (41,4)	2 (3,4)
Exposure to many different types of text is useful for learning a language.	0 (0)	0 (0)	21 (36,2)	37 (63,8)
Parents should be involved in teaching languages at home.	0 (0)	0 (0)	13 (22,4)	45 (77,6)

Furthermore, with regard to the teaching of languages (as captured in Table 10.3), over 80% of the student teachers strongly believed it is important to learn to speak and write and being able to comprehend when listening and reading. However, only 58,6% strongly believed that it is important to learn grammatical structures. This has serious implications for how student teachers think about the teaching of language, the abilities and techniques they need to teach it and the ways in which they ought to mainly assist and develop learners. This concern is further reinforced (see Table 10.4) by the student teachers' responses to questions about their ability to teach grammatical structures (tied to learning to write), with only 35,7% very confident in doing so and as many as 19,6% of the respondents revealing little confidence in doing so.

Table 10.3   Beliefs about the Importance of Developing Language Teaching Skills

Student teacher beliefs	Not at all N (%)	Somewhat important N (%)	Important N (%)	Very important N (%)
Learning to speak	0 (0)	1 (1,7)	13 (22,4)	44 (75,9)
Learning to listen with comprehension	0 (0)	0 (0)	8 (14)	49 (86)
Learning grammatical structures	0 (0)	5 (8,6)	19 (32,8)	34 (58,6)
Learning to read with comprehension	0 (0)	0 (0)	6 (10,5)	51 (89,5)
Learning to write	0 (0)	0 (0)	12 (20,7)	46 (79,3)

10.4.2 Student Teacher Confidence in Developing the Four Skills of Language and in Teaching these Skills

As noted above, the student teachers considered learning to read, write, speak and listen as important skills that need to be consciously fashioned within all learners. Yet, their big challenge is that they were not always confident about their ability to develop these, nor did they think the ITE programme has concentrated enough on developing these skills in their individual preparation.

When prompted in this regard in the questionnaires, the student teachers suggested limited confidence in having the necessary skills to teach learners how to read, write, listen or speak languages. As noted in Table 10.3, less than 50% of the student teachers indicated that they were very confident in being able to impart these skills, with between 10-20% of them noting little confidence in doing so. This speaks to both how they felt about their own abilities, as well as their assessment of the extent to which the ITE programme has prepared them for this. Many, in fact, indicated that they would expect to undergo further CPD to address these deficiencies when they become formally employed teachers. Notably, the student teachers seemed to be far more comfortable teaching learners how to read – rather than to write, speak or to listen. This suggests a tendency on their part to rely on generic or generalised skills rather than on actual established or taught pedagogical techniques.

Table 10.4 Student Teacher Confidence in Developing Language Teaching Skills

Confidence to teach	Not at all N (%)	Somewhat confident N (%)	Confident N (%)	Very confident N (%)
Learning to speak	0 (0)	6 (10,7)	30 (53,6)	20 (35,7)
Learning to listen with comprehension	0 (0)	8 (14,5)	23 (41,8)	24 (43,6)
Learning grammatical structures	0 (0)	11 (19,6)	25 (44,6)	20 (35,7)
Learning to read with comprehension	0 (0)	6 (10,7)	22 (39,3)	28 (50)
Learning to write	0 (0)	6 (10,7)	23 (41,1)	27 (48,2)

10.4.2.1 Teaching Strategies and Resources for Teaching English

Allied to the above skills, teachers are thought to need three further skills in teaching language: (i) being able to generate classroom discussion effectively, (ii) being able to provide learners with multiple texts and other resources to help them learn a language, and (iii) working with prescribed textbooks as their main supporting resource.

With regard to the latter, as captured in Table 10.2, more than 50% of the student teachers unexpectedly did not believe that prescribed language textbooks were their most important resource. With that, only 62-64% of them strongly believed in the value of class discussions or that learners need to be provided with multiple and different types of learning texts to learn a language.

The direct implication of the above sets of beliefs is that the student teachers did not seem fully confident in their own skills or abilities to teach learners how to systematically read, write, speak and listen. They were also not very convinced of the value of established resources (like textbooks) normally relied on to convey or support the development of these skills. The magnitude of these different beliefs has immediate implications for how student teachers are prepared for teaching language at the FET level.

10.4.3 Student Teacher Experiences of ITE Programmes and Views about their Development of Key Pedagogical Skills

10.4.3.1 Student Teachers Indicate what they were Taught, and its Value to them

The student teachers were also questioned about their preparation to teach language through the ITE programme – whether through lectures, the development of (and their confidence and willingness to implement) different teaching strategies or their experiences of teaching practice. For this chapter, only questionnaire items relating to language teaching were identified and analysed, with questions mainly exploring the student teachers' views of their preparation for language teaching practice.

Perhaps the more interesting data in Table 10.5 are the lesson strategies that the student teachers indicated were taught (or not taught) to them in ITE classes and their views of these. A large majority of the student teachers, for instance, recorded that whole-class teaching, how to facilitate a class discussion, and using multimodal and visual text were definitely and widely taught. Only 45-55% of them noted that they were taught how to group learners according to their ability, how to group learners according to mixed ability, use of the chalkboard, use of the whiteboard, and use of drama and role play.

Notably, with regard to the former (most taught), only 25,6% of the student teachers found the whole-class strategy very useful, while 43,2% and 52,6% respectively found the use of multimodal and visual text, and facilitating a class discussion, very useful. On the other hand, a significant proportion (close to 30%) also did not always regard the strategies as particularly useful.

Furthermore, with regard to the least-taught strategies, where these were taught, only 18-35% of the student teachers found the strategies very useful and 23-42% did not find the strategies useful.

The above suggest two further issues:
- ✓ Even though much attention was given to the most-taught strategies, many student teachers were not convinced about the usefulness of some of them or the preoccupation of ITE programmes with them.
- ✓ Given the limited attention given to the least-taught strategies, the teaching thereof was also probably not very convincing or useful.

On the other hand, the student teachers indicated that they found the lesson strategies that focused on how to get learners to work individually, to work in pairs, having them work in groups, how to use worksheets, how to use prescribed textbooks and how to use educational technology, more helpful. Here up to 50% of the student teachers found the teaching of these strategies very useful.

Interestingly, while the student teachers indicated that there was not a big focus on the use of the chalkboard (44,4%) or the whiteboard (55,6%), many of them found the teaching thereof fairly useful (76% and 70% respectively).

Worryingly, however, the student teachers did not find the lesson strategies of how to group learners according to their abilities (43%), how to get learners to work individually (26,5%) or how to do drama and role play (35,8%), very helpful. Alternatively, they noted that there was not a big focus on these in the ITE programme. This is notwithstanding the three strategies seemingly having significant roles to play in the effective teaching of language at the FET level.

Table 10.5   Student Teacher Views of Teaching Strategies

Teaching lesson strategies	Yes, it was taught	Not at all	Somewhat useful	Useful	Very useful
Whole-class teaching	77,8%	2,6%	23,1%	48,7%	25,6%
Group learners according to their ability	46,7%	10,7%	32,1%	39,3%	17,9%
Group learners according to mixed ability	57,8%	11,8%	14,7%	44,1%	29,4%
Use of multimodal and visual text	71,1%	5,4%	24,3%	27%	43,2%
Use of drama and role play	51,1%	12,9%	22,9%	32,3%	32,3%
Use of the chalkboard	44,4%	10,3%	13,8%	41,4%	34,5%
Use of the whiteboard	55,6%	12,1%	18,2%	39,4%	30,3%
Have learners work individually	62,2%	2,9%	23,5%	35,3%	38,2%
Have learners work in pairs	66,7%	0%	8,6%	48,6%	42,9%
Have learners work in groups	68,9%	0%	13,9%	36,1%	50%
Use of worksheets	68,9%	5,6%	13,9%	44,4%	36,1%
Use of prescribed textbooks	68,9%	2,7%	16,2%	37,8%	43,2%
Use of educational technology	62,2%	8,8%	11,8%	32,4%	47,1%
Facilitate a class discussion	73,3%	0%	13,2%	34,2%	52,6%

10.4.3.2 Student Teachers' Responses Regarding their Confidence to Implement and Teach Different Strategies

It is assumed that where student teachers are confident about teaching a lesson strategy or skill that they would tend to use it in or during their own teaching. This clearly emerges in the sections below, where the student teachers consistently noted less intent to use lesson strategies at times when they had less confidence in their own abilities to use such strategies (see Table 10.6).

The responses from the student teachers on their confidence and intent to use strategies provide a number of interesting outlooks and also some potential contradictions in the correlation between student teacher confidence and utility.

First, where the student teachers were not adequately exposed to or did not find certain lesson strategies particularly useful (such as grouping learners according to their ability or grouping learners according to mixed ability), only about 11% felt very confident about using the strategies; and between 30-35% of them indicated that they would use the strategies frequently. Lower optimism seems to suggest low intended use among student teachers.

Second, where the student teachers found the teaching of certain strategies in ITE programmes helpful (as with having learners work individually, getting them to work in pairs or having learners work in groups), only between 34-44% of the student teachers felt very confident about using these strategies in class. Also, only about 60% of them noted the likelihood to frequently use the strategies in their practice.

Third, similar to the above, with the use of multimodal and visual texts and facilitating class discussions, the student teachers seemed relatively confident about using certain lesson strategies (between 33-39% very confident), with just over 60% also indicating that they would use these strategies frequently. The same is noted for the use of worksheets, prescribed textbooks, educational technology, chalkboard and whiteboard (33-41% very confident), where 60-70% of the student teachers indicated a particular inclination to frequently utilise these in their teaching. Cautious optimism therefore does not translate into cautious utilisation, with the student teachers generally keen to use the strategies frequently.

Fourth, as with the use of drama and role play in the classroom, when the student teachers indicate less of a passion for a strategy (28,9% very confident), this can often translate into a similarly muted percentage (38,5%) saying that they would use it frequently.

Conversely, as noted in the previous subsection where the student teachers showed a more cautious attitude towards whole-class teaching, even when they indicated they were only quietly confident about practising a lesson strategy (28,2% very confident), many could still be keen to frequently (74,4%) use the strategy. This may probably be linked to anticipated class sizes and school contexts when student teachers start teaching – rather than their standpoints on the value or effectiveness of whole-class teaching.

Overall, the data in Tables 10.6 and 10.7 suggest that confidence to utilise lesson strategies and the likelihood of student teachers practising them in schools are closely tied to both the attention paid to these strategies within ITE programmes and how useful and pertinent student teachers consider the teaching thereof. This suggests that good (better) language teaching in ITE preparation can make a meaningful impact on whether and how student teachers include certain lesson strategies in their practice, as well as on their confidence in doing so. It speaks to the influence that prioritising certain lesson strategies could have on teaching student teachers how to teach language more effectively.

Table 10.6   Student Teacher Confidence to Teach Specific Teaching Strategies

Confidence to use lesson strategies	Not confident	Somewhat confident	Confident	Very confident
Whole-class teaching	0%	20,5%	51,3%	28,2%
Group learners according to their ability	5,4%	35,1%	48,6%	10,8%
Group learners according to mixed ability	2,6%	34,2%	52,6%	10,5%
Use of multimodal and visual text	0%	23,1%	43,6%	33,3%
Use of drama and role play	5,3%	34,2%	31,6%	28,9%
Use of the chalkboard	7,9%	15,8%	42,1%	34,2%
Use of the whiteboard	5,1%	15,4%	38,5%	41%
Have learners work individually	2,6%	10,5%	52,6%	34,2%
Have learners work in pairs	0%	10,3%	53,8%	35,9%
Have learners work in groups	2,6%	7,7%	46,2%	43,6%
Use of worksheets	2,6%	7,7%	56,4%	33,3%
Use of prescribed textbooks	5,1%	12,8%	43,6%	38,5%
Use of educational technology	0%	18,9%	40,5%	40,5%
Facilitate a class discussion	2,6%	10,3%	48,7%	38,5%

Learning to Teach Language in the Further Education & Training Phase

Table 10.7   Student Teachers' Views on whether they will Implement Teaching Strategies

Intent to use lesson strategies	Never	Occasionally	Frequently
Whole-class teaching	0%	25,6%	74,4%
Group learners according to their ability	29,7%	40,5%	29,7%
Group learners according to mixed ability	18,4%	47,4%	34,2%
Use of multimodal and visual text	2,6%	33,3%	64,1%
Use of drama and role play	10,3%	51,3%	38,5%
Use of the chalkboard	2,6%	50%	47,4%
Use of the whiteboard	2,6%	35,9%	61,5%
Have learners work individually	0%	30,8%	69,2%
Have learners work in pairs	0%	41%	59%
Have learners work in groups	2,6%	36,8%	60,5%
Use of worksheets	2,6%	28,9%	68,4%
Use of prescribed textbooks	0%	36,8%	63,2%
Use of educational technology	0%	38,9%	61,1%
Facilitate a class discussion	2,6%	34,2%	63,2%

10.4.3.3   Assessment Preparation as Indicative of Confidence, Ability and Intent

As noted previously, it is widely anticipated that the individual confidence of student teachers to speak, listen, write and read influences their ability to teach these skills and other knowledge areas during language lessons. What they are confident to teach with regard to language teaching shapes what learners are able to access and use in the classroom. A key way of finding out these latter abilities lies in the confidence that the student teachers express about what they are able to teach and how they are able to assess this.

Disconcertingly, most student teachers indicated a confidence level of just 50-60% in having the necessary skills in terms of writing, reading, speaking and listening to share with their learners, with only 46-59% indicating that the ITE programme totally focused on preparing them for this. About 13% of the student teachers claimed that they have not been adequately prepared to teach languages, with the student teachers observing that they were the least prepared in the knowledge of grammar and the teaching thereof. Notably, the student teachers felt best prepared at the FET level to teach literature and poetry, even though they did not seem to have developed the necessary techniques and pedagogical skills to teach these topics appropriately. Indeed, the student teachers often expressed high confidence (between 53-74%) in having been prepared to do certain tasks, yet did not seem to be very confident in having absorbed these abilities.

Table 10.8 Student Teachers' Views on whether they were Taught the Necessary Skills during Language Teaching

Skills developed in student teachers	Not at all	Somewhat	Moderately	Totally
Speaking	0%	10,3%	30,8%	59%
Listening with comprehension	0%	17,9%	25,6%	56,4%
Understanding grammatical structures	0%	10,3%	43,6%	46,2%
Reading with comprehension	0%	15,4%	30,8%	53,8%
Writing	0%	10,3%	30,8%	59%

Table 10.9 Student Teacher Preparedness to Perform certain Tasks

Preparedness to perform certain tasks	Not at all	Somewhat	Moderately	Totally
Ask questions that get learners to reflect about and interpret what they are reading	0%	5,1%	28,2%	66,7%
Get learners interested in reading	0%	7,7%	23,1%	69,2%
Know which learner needs help with reading	0%	10,3%	23,1%	66,7%
Meet the needs of the individual learners in a language class	0%	10,3%	28,2%	61,5%
Get learners to speak in the class	0%	5,3%	21,1%	73,7%
Get learners to feel confident in reading	0%	5,4%	21,6%	73%
Get learners to listen	0%	2,6%	26,3%	71,1%
Get learners to write	0%	13,2%	18,4%	68,4%
Get learners to understand how to put sounds together	0%	15,8%	26,3%	57,9%
Use language to stimulate learners' imaginations	0%	2,6%	31,6%	65,8%
Teach in multilingual classrooms	2,6%	13,2%	31,6%	52,6%

This is also most evident in what the student teachers stated about their ability to assess the various skills and the extent to which the ITE programme prepared them to assess these. When questioned on their ability and knowledge to assess reading, writing, listening and speaking, the majority of the student teachers indicated that they were very confident to do so. Yet, when questioned about the extent to which they could assess individual skills, the student teachers indicated that they were only able to between 36% and 39% state very confidently that they could assess these skills.

Table 10.10 Confidence to Assess the Skills during Language Teaching

Ability to assess skills	Not at all	Somewhat confident	Confident	Very confident
Speaking	0%	15,4%	51,3%	33,3%
Listening with comprehension	0%	23,1%	46,2%	30,8%
Understanding grammatical structures	0%	28,2%	35,9%	35,9%
Reading with comprehension	0%	15,4%	46,2%	38,5%
Writing	0%	17,9%	43,6%	38,5%

This hardly suggests a grasp of the knowledge or ability to assess learners, nor does it point to the skills needed to analyse or interpret the work of different learners. In fact, only 33% of the student teachers noted being able to even interpret the assessments of learners adequately, being able to use peer assessments well or provide decent feedback (as noted in Table 10.11).

Table 10.11 Knowledge and Skills Gained to Assess Language

Knowledge and skills gained	Not at all	To some extent	To a large extent	Completely
I learned to develop assessments (e.g. tests, assignments, etc.).	27,8%	38,9%	16,7%	16,7%
I learned to develop assessment memoranda.	27,8%	38,9%	16,7%	16,7%
I learned to use assessment results for teaching.	27,8%	38,9%	16,7%	16,7%
I learned to report assessment results.	27,8%	27,8%	27,8%	16,7%
I learned to identify learners' strengths and weaknesses.	27,8%	33,3%	33,3%	5,6%
I learned to provide effective feedback during lessons.	27,8%	38,9%	27,8%	5,6%
I learned to ask higher-order thinking questions.	27,8%	33,3%	27,8%	11,1%
I learned to train learners to conduct peer assessment.	27,8%	33,3%	33,3%	5,6%
I learned to train learners to conduct self-assessment.	26,3%	36,8%	21,1%	15,8%

This concern about not having been taught the necessary skills to teach the four main skills in language teaching or being able to assess them, was also apparent in the student teachers' responses to questions about the kinds of CPD they think they would need in formal teaching. More than 40% of them indicated the need for substantial further development across all four skills once having left the ITE programme. In fact, 84,5% of the student teachers felt that they probably learned more about how to do this during teaching practice, where their mentor teachers helped them to substantially understand the language curriculum.

Table 10.12   Envisaged CPD as a Language Teacher

Skill	Not at all	Some development	Substantial development	A lot
Teaching learners to speak	0%	28,2%	46,2%	25,6%
Teaching learners to listen with comprehension	0%	20,5%	41%	38,5%
Teaching grammatical structures	0%	23,7%	44,7%	31,6%
Teaching reading	0%	23,1%	43,6%	33,3%
Teaching writing	0%	25,6%	33,3%	41%

10.5 Student Teacher Preparedness to Teach Language in the FET Phase

Given the beliefs that the student teachers voiced about teaching language and the abilities and skills they highlighted as needed in teaching language, this third subsection discusses elements of the ITE programme and the teaching of language as noted by seven student teachers during focus group interviews. These highlight the contributions of an ITE programme to the preparation of student teachers to teach language in the FET Phase. The aim is to show its influence on how they thought about developing the different pedagogical, linguistic and literacy competencies required for language teaching at the FET level.

Notably, the student teachers all acknowledged that teaching language in South Africa, especially to isiXhosa-speaking learners who wrestle with Afrikaans and English fluency in the classroom, is deeply challenging. For them – while language is critical to the development of each learner – for second-language learners who struggle to read and write, it is even more important for student teachers to be grounded in the foundational dimensions of language and to be made comfortable in working with these skill requirements.

This is an enormously difficult task, as it requires teachers to have a solid grasp of the language that they teach, as well as abilities to weave together a variety of pedagogical practices in ways that suit their specific learners. Cushioned within the debate about the balance of theory and practice within teacher preparation, student teachers are often challenged with which element to privilege in relation to their own development – keeping in mind the different teaching contexts that they will enter.

As such, different student teachers during focus group interviews had differing views about theory and practice in their tertiary education. Some complained about tertiary knowledge being too theoretical, and that there was not enough emphasis on practice and their practicum and how to teach language to school learners. Others felt that having a strong grounding in the conceptual dimensions of language with its corresponding philosophical, social and theoretical parts, as well as its psychology, provides them as teachers with the confidence and the expertise to share the key tenets of language and its value and to build this within learners. Many, however, could not express a clear preference, but noted the following:

- ✓ Where language is mainly taught within a bachelor's degree, there needs to be greater attempts to cover some materials that are included in the CAPS curriculum. This would assist student teachers to have deeper insight into the materials and knowledge when they teach it.
- ✓ Whereas the current PGCE course on language mainly focuses on developing the attitudes, empathy and professionalism of student teachers and providing them with the skills to positively reinforce and motivate learners, there needs to be a bigger focus on how to teach language itself and how to approximate and convey what they were taught in their overall language degree.
- ✓ Where provided with lesson plan templates and other applied instruments during the PGCE course – and given their previous learning at university level – the student teachers felt they needed to be taught how to implement and assess them.

Fundamentally, the student teachers noted that they could not be allowed to draw on learning experiences during their own schooling (where they teach like they were taught), or on how they were taught during their undergraduate degrees in language. The student teachers cautioned that greater emphasis needs to be placed on helping them to convert their university knowledge base into meaningful teaching moments, and to be provided with the appropriate techniques that help them do this. This, many student teachers noted, is not a priority or skill focus within the current PGCE course.

In that regard, the student teachers observed that the teaching practicum (or teaching practice) has a particularly important role to play in the development of PGCE student teachers. Teaching practice is the one element of student teacher preparation where they have the opportunity to take initiative, make their own CK relevant and practical and tease out some of the challenges that they will encounter when they enter schools. Teaching practice also gives them the opportunity to witness first-hand the many difficulties of teaching language within the school context and to think through how they will address issues of (the lack of) textbooks, demotivated or disinterested learners and/or often highly bureaucratic institutional spaces when they get to teach language in schools. Furthermore, teaching practice gives student teachers access to real-life teachers and mentors whose practices could either motivate them (and be copied) or used to critically reflect on what 'not to do'.

In terms of developing the necessary subject knowledge, PCK and social context knowledge needed to effectively teach language in schools. The student teachers also provided a number of insights in the focus groups that usefully highlight key challenges raised in the overall literature on teaching language. These are explored below.

10.5.1 Curriculum and Subject Content Matter

How important is language as a subject to the development of learners in schools? Does it provide key tools for critical thought and introspection and help learners to make sense of the worlds that they live in? Or is language simply a form of communication and a way of accessing other knowledge forms? What are student teachers expected to process during ITE programmes and what is the expected CK base they need to accumulate to teach language at the FET level?

The above are questions that fundamentally shape and inform how student teachers approach the issue of SCK in language teaching. Often, where they believe that language is critical to the overall development of learners and the shaping of their identities, student teachers are more comfortable with broader exposure to a language and its different dimensions; and where student teachers emphasise language as a communicative tool, they seem more keen on the technical aspects of language teaching. For the former, the focus is invariably on how to marry specialist knowledge to school content knowledge and texts being utilised at the school level, as well as how to teach this. In the latter, the focus is normally on the finer and more structured details of teaching and how to organise language teaching in the classroom.

In both instances, however, the student teachers accentuated the need to always develop items like grammatical structure and its unconditional importance both to effectively learning and teaching a language. Experiences of this are more apparent during teaching practice where student teachers are exposed to what might (or might not) work for them in the classroom. A key challenge for language in PGCE courses is that student teachers are often not sufficiently exposed to a particular (CAPS) school curriculum and struggle with how to teach this when they enter schools during teaching practice.

Indeed, the key challenge for ITE programmes is how to best prepare student teachers to approach these kinds of encounters. It requires student teachers to be able to assess particular learner strengths, weaknesses and needs in language – as well as in other subjects – and to teach in ways that get learners to absorb the more detailed aspects of a language. They must then merge this with what they know, are comfortable with and use in their everyday lives. This would be particularly difficult for student teachers who do not see a correlation between learning a language completely and being able to read and write.

10.5.2 Pedagogy and PCK

A key prerequisite in teaching a language is to be able to understand its logics and nuances and to prepare ways of teaching these and sharing key concepts and techniques with learners. Teaching language can be an even more onerous encounter in a situation where many student teachers are themselves not completely comfortable with the language they are teaching and where their learners are predominantly engaging with their subject as a second language.

Previous subsections showed that the student teachers seemed to struggle with the concept of pedagogy and 'how to teach'. The student teachers noted that they were not overly confident in their individual skills to teach language to learners, nor in understanding key aspects of prescribed texts that they were meant to completely rely on in their teaching. They suggested that the ITE programme has not sufficiently prepared them to teach in either area.

The student teachers noted that the ITE programme also did not sufficiently engage with how to teach in situations where English is a second or third language for both student teachers and learners, as well as in contexts where the LoLT is predominantly English. They noted that whereas in such cases multilingualism would be a key resource in teaching and learning, and code switching the preferred linguistic device, this approach did not work well when student teachers did not have a good grasp of the language they were teaching or its particular needs, and where they used code switching merely to make the curriculum more accessible to learners.

As required by the MRTEQ policy (DHET 2015a:26), student teachers need a full repertoire of skills to engage in multilingual teaching, which includes being able to alternate between languages, not privilege one above another and being able to compare the constructs and practices of one language against another. ITE programmes do not generally prepare teachers in this way. In many cases, lecturers use code switching as a technique to convey their teaching in the tertiary environment, but often do not have the necessary expertise to empower student teachers with the required linguistic range and skills to use code switching as a useful pedagogical model in the classroom.

This deficit is even more palpable in relation to the oral skills, grammar, reading and writing abilities that student teachers must master to be able to teach a language (and in a language). Many of the student teachers did not have either the associated CK or detailed pedagogical skills to teach a language, but then invariably noted that they have also not mastered how to specifically teach reading, writing, listening or speaking in the FET Phase.

In that respect, the student teachers reflected that ITE programmes were also quite poor at preparing them to engage with the functional, boring tasks of teaching language. It was poor to the extent that they were not able to do basic things like prepare proper lesson designs and plans at the PGCE level, or mastered how to systematically assess learners in the four key skill areas of language.

10.6 Conclusion

Language is what makes each learner in each school uniquely human and is what 'dresses up' each of their thoughts in ways that give substance to their education and individual development (Heidegger 2000:83). Language is also critical for effective learning, made more special when learners achieve fluency in a language that is not their first language. In that regard, post-apartheid language policies in South Africa have sought since 1994 to enable democratic, efficient and pragmatic language use. It claims to do so in ways that also reconcile inequalities between languages (De Kock 2017) by casting them (policies) within values of respect, diversity and efficiency, as well as promoting multilingualism as a social good and recognising the speaking and practices of historically marginalised languages as legitimate and valid. In doing so, language policies claim to provide opportunities for learners to access education in the language of their choice (DoE 1996). In reality however, the consequences of not interrupting a largely bifurcated education system and an enduring preoccupation with English as a dominant language have meant that the teaching of language has quite different difficulties attached to it in different contexts.

With linguistic inequalities bound up in language in ways that reflect particular forms of race privilege and economic opportunity, the value afforded to particular languages often corresponds closely with the value afforded to the standing or social position of different groups – invariably located in quite different schools (De Kock 2017:2-3). This places significant pressure on language teaching in previously disadvantaged schools.

It also creates particular challenges for university educators, student teachers, teachers in schools, and learners. For example, it requires ITE programmes to critically engage with the symbolic value of the different languages of their student teachers, while equipping them with the linguistic skills that enable them to teach effectively in multiple contexts (De Kock 2017: 2-3). It further requires the focus on English proficiency to be contextualised for all users – with each student teacher being orientated to its contextual history, its underlying and dominant value and its relationship and contribution to the underdevelopment of other local linguistic forms. In so doing, student teachers are then apparently equipped with the critical and transformative attitudes about the status quo of dominant languages (like English) and understand its role as a primary driver of economic success and social mobility (De Kock 2017:2-3).

Indeed – with student teacher practices and their teaching of languages so crucial to educational transformation – school learners cannot take on the kinds of linguistic identities and senses of belonging that will empower them in their everyday lives, unless ITE programmes do not address key responsibilities within their programme delivery. In that respect, preparing future teachers to teach language in the FET Phase needs to be approached as part of a national effort to locate language teaching and multilingualism within the national consciousness. How well teachers teach language will ultimately determine whether learners in schools access and prosper in that language and use this to shape their futures.

This chapter sought to ascertain the beliefs and views of student teachers within an ITE programme regarding their key language challenges; in so doing highlighting some of their experiences and challenges when formulating the required competencies to teach language in the FET Phase (Grades 10 to 12). Their beliefs and views pose a number of important questions for how language courses are currently offered at tertiary institutions.

There is little doubt that there is an urgent need for student teachers to develop the relevant pedagogical techniques and practical skills during their tertiary preparation. However, if this orientation to language teaching is to take hold and be meaningful and effective, a better balance needs to be struck within ITE programmes between how language is approached, conceptualised and taught at the tertiary level; and how student teachers are taught to teach language in schools. It furthermore needs a much deeper conversation between policymakers, university lecturers, subject advisers, teachers and schools on how this can most effectively be achieved.

Reference

Adendorff, R. 1993. Code-switching among Zulu-speaking teachers and their pupils. *Language Education*, 7(3): 141-162. https://doi.org/10.1080/09500789309541356

Adler, J. 1998. Languages of teaching dilemmas: Unlocking the complex multilingual secondary mathematics classroom. *An International Journal of Mathematics Education*, 8(1): 24-33.

Alidou, H. & Brock-Utne, B. 2006. Experience I – Teaching practices – Teaching in a familiar language. In: H. Alidou, A. Boly, B. Brock-Utne, Y.S. Diallo, K. Heugh & H. Wolff (eds). *Optimising learning and education in Africa – the language factor. A stock taking of research on mother-tongue and bilingual education in sub-Saharan Africa*. Paris: ADEA, 85-100.

Baker, C. 1993. *Foundations of bilingual education and bilingualism*. Clevedon: Multilingual Matters.

Bender, P.; Dutcher, N.; Klaus, D.; Shore, J. & Tesar, C. 2005. *In their own language: Education for all*. Washington, D.C.: World Bank.

Brock-Utne, B. 2007. Language of instruction and student performance: New insights from research in Tanzania and South Africa. *International Review of Education*, 53(5): 509-530. https://doi.org/10.1007/s11159-007-9065-9

Brock-Utne, B. & Holmarsdottir, H. 2003. Language policies and practices: Some preliminary results from a research project in Tanzania and South Africa. In: B. Brock-Utne, Z. Desai & M. Qorro (eds). *Language of Instruction in Tanzania and South Africa*. Dar es Salaam: E&D Limited, 80-101.

Chick, K. & McKay, S. 2001. Teaching English in multi-ethnic schools in the Durban area: The promotion of multilingualism or monolingualism? *Southern African Linguistics and Applied Language Studies Journal*, 19(34): 179-196.

Crookes, G. 2009. The practicality and relevance of second language critical pedagogy. *Language Teaching*, 43(3): 333-348. https://doi.org/10.1017/S0261444809990292

Crookes, G. 2013. *Critical ELT in action: Foundations, promises, praxis*. London: Routledge.

De Kock, T. 2017. *Linguistic identity and social cohesion in three Western Cape schools*. Master's thesis. Cape Town: Cape Peninsula University of Technology.

Department of Education (DoE). 1996. Curriculum 2005: *A discussion document*. Pretoria: DoE.

Department of Higher Education and Training (DHET). 2015a. National Qualifications Framework Act, 2008 (Act No. 67 of 2008): Revised Policy on the Minimum Requirements for Teacher Education Qualifications. *Government Gazette*, 38487, 19 February. Pretoria: Government Printer.

Department of Higher Education and Training (DHET). 2015b. Basic competences of beginner teachers. In: Department of Higher Education and Training (DHET). National Qualifications Framework Act (67/2008): *Revised policy on the minimum requirements for teacher education qualifications*. Pretoria: DHET. Appendix C.

Garcia, O. 2009. *Bilingual education in the 21st century: A global perspective*. London: John Wiley & Sons.

Garcia, O. & Flores, N. 2012. Multilingual pedagogies. In: M. Jones, A. Blackledge & A. Creese (eds). *The Routledge handbook of multilingualism*. New York: Routledge, 232-246.

Hawkins, M. & Norton, B. 2009. Critical language teacher education. In: A. Burns & J. Richards (eds). *Cambridge guide to second language teacher education.* Cambridge: Cambridge University Press, 30-39.

Heidegger, M. 2000. Letter on humanism. *Journal of Global Religious Vision,* 1(1): 83-109.

Heugh, K. 2013. Literacy and languages in school education in South Africa. In: V. Reddy, A. Juan & T. Meyiwa (eds). *Towards a 20 year review: Basic and post school education.* Pretoria: HSRC Press, 18-33.

Hibbert, L. & Van der Walt, C. (eds). 2014. *Multilingual universities in South Africa.* Bristol: Multilingual Matters. https://doi.org/10.21832/9781783091669

Krog, A. 2017. *Universities should reflect multilingual South Africa.* Sunday Times, 19 March.

Kubanyiova, M. & Crookes, G. 2016. Re-envisioning the roles, tasks and contributions of language teachers in the multilingual era of language education research and practice. *The Modern Language Journal,* 100(S1): 117-132. https://doi.org/10.1111/modl.12304

Mahofa, E. 2014. *Code-switching in the learning of mathematics word problems in Grade 10.* Master's thesis. Cape Peninsula University of Technology, Cape Town.

Makoe, P. & McKinney, C. 2014. Linguistic ideologies in multilingual South African suburban schools. *Journal of Multilingual and Multicultural Development,* 35(7): 658-673. https://doi.org/10.1080/01434632.2014.908889

Mashiyi, F.N. 2011. *How South African teachers make sense of language-in-education policies.* PhD dissertation. Pretoria: University of Pretoria.

Moyo, T. 2000. Language use in the neighbourhood of Empangeni and Richards Bay. *South African Journal of African Languages,* 20(2): 123-133.

Napier, D.B. 2011. Critical Issues in language and education planning in twenty first century in South Africa. U.S. *China Education Review,* B(1): 58-76.

Nomlomo, V. 2013. Preparing isiXhosa home language teachers for the 21st-century classroom: Student teachers' experiences, challenges and reflections. *South African Linguistics and Applied Language Studies,* 31(2): 207-217. https://doi.org/10.2989/16073614.2013.815887

Pinnock, H. & Vijayakumar, G. 2009. *Language and education: The missing link.* London: Save the Children Alliance.

Prah, K.K. 2009. Mother-tongue education in Africa for emancipation and development: Towards the intellectualization of African languages. In: B. Brock-Utne & I. Skattum (eds). *Languages and education in Africa: A comparative and trans-disciplinary analysis.* Oxford: Oxford Symposium Books, 83-104.

Probyn, M. 2001. Teachers' voices: Teachers' reflections on learning and teaching through the medium of English as an additional language in South Africa. *International Journal of Bilingual Education,* 4(4): 249-266. https://doi.org/10.1080/13670050108667731

Setati, M. 2000. Between languages and discourses: Language practices in primary multilingual classrooms in South Africa. *Educational Studies in Mathematics,* 43(2): 243-259.

Setati, M. & Adler, J. 2000. Between languages in South Africa. *Educational Studies in Mathematics,* 43(1): 243-269. https://doi.org/10.1023/A:1011996002062

Setati, M.; Adler, J.; Reed, Y. & Bapoo, A. 2002. Incomplete journeys: Code-switching and other language practices in mathematics, science and English language classrooms in South Africa. *Language and Education,* 16(2): 128-149. https://doi.org/10.1023/A:1011996002062

Shulman, L. 1987. Knowledge and teaching: Foundations of the new reform. *Harvard Educational Review*, 57(1): 1-22. https://doi.org/10.17763/haer.57.1.j463w79r56455411

Smits, J.; Huisman, J. & Kruijff, K. 2008. *Home language and education in the developing world.* Nijmegen: UNESCO.

Taylor, N. 2014. *Thinking, language and learning in initial teacher education. Paper presented to the Seminar on Academic Depth and Rigour in ITE.* University of the Witwatersrand, 30-31 October. Available at: https://www.jet.org.za/resources/taylor-thinking-language-and-learning-in-ite-for-web.pdf

Van der Walt, C. 2013. *Multilingual higher education: Beyond English orientations – multilingual higher education.* Bristol: Multilingual Matters. https://doi.org/10.21832/9781847699206

Chapter 11

A Prospective 21st Century Post-apartheid Teacher Education Agenda

Yusuf Sayed, Nazir Carrim & Azeem Badroodien

11.1 Introduction

This chapter examines the consistent themes that emerged from the study data on which this book is based. It scrutinises models of ITE for the 21st century and asks what drives them. It also considers policy implications and recommendations that could take ITE programmes and prospective teachers forward into the 21st century. It concludes with a discussion of some of the limitations of the overall study, and areas that may need to be considered for future research in these areas.

The cohort of student teachers that were reached through this study are those who entered ITE programmes in the post-apartheid moment. They are students that may not have necessarily experienced living in apartheid South Africa and as such have had their own schooling and ITE training in post-apartheid South Africa. As students who were born in a new democratic post-apartheid South Africa, these student teachers do not have the history, experience or understanding of how education under apartheid was constructed, or an understanding of how ITE programmes worked and what they covered under apartheid. While they may share similar experiences with students who studied under apartheid, they are a distinct cohort that represents the 'first generation' of post-apartheid teachers. The study on which this book is based was initiated precisely to bring to the fore these experiences as the student cohorts become the new generation of teachers entering schools after more than two decades of democracy; carrying with them into their teaching the hopes and frailties of a society still in transition and scarred by new and old conflicts and tensions. As argued in this book, becoming a teacher in post-apartheid South Africa requires facing the dynamics, forces and developments of the 21st century and the conditions that prospective teachers in the 21st century are likely to face in their school contexts and their teaching practice.

11.2 Emerging Themes

The focus in this book was on two ITE programmes: BEd Foundation Phase and PGCE FET focusing on student teacher learning to teach languages and mathematics. The focus on these two areas is important for two reasons. Firstly, languages and mathematics have been identified as priority areas for education quality in South Africa. Learner performances in both local national tests and international standardised tests in these subjects are poor. Secondly, learner competency in both languages and mathematics are considered crucial skills in order to successfully navigate the 21st century. This point will be discussed later in this chapter in more detail.

The focus on the Foundation and FET phases of schooling aimed to capture what skills NQTs would be equipped with in order to deal with learners who enter and exit the schooling system, given that the Foundation Phase begins with primary schooling and the FET Phase completes the schooling phase in the current structure of the South African education system. As such, this focus has enabled this study to gauge what kind of teaching, and teachers, learners are likely to encounter when they enter and leave schools as they progress through their basic education academic careers.

The first issue emerging from this book is the importance of evaluating student teacher experiences. In a policy climate of derision of ITE programmes and providers and thin research that seeks to evaluate the efficacy of such programmes, this book gives primary credence to the voices of prospective teachers. As the future corps of post-apartheid prospective teachers, their experiences of ITE matter particularly in policy determination and provider practices.

Second, the findings revealed by the data in this study strongly suggest that all the student teachers reached in this study consistently and unambiguously agreed that the ITE programmes were necessary for them to obtain the training and development they needed to become teachers. This was indicated in Chapters 5 and 6 where ITE programmes in the Foundation and FET phases were indicated as being important. The BEd and PGCE programmes were consistently found to be useful and important in developing them as professional teachers and developing their professional knowledge and practice. They were 'happy' to have enrolled in these ITE programmes, even in cases where teaching may not have been their first choice.

Third, contrary to popular perception, the student teachers in this study, as discussed in Chapter 3, were largely motivated by intrinsic reasons to become teachers. The desire to help young children and to give back to the community and society were important drivers in the decision to enrol in ITE programmes, as also indicated in Chapter 4. The sense of idealism – for many, but certainly not for all – suggests that post-apartheid prospective teachers seek to effect positive change in society through their practices as teachers. They seek to better the lives of the young, uplift their communities and bring about social cohesion and unity in society. The extent to which these values and ideals are nurtured in ITE remains an issue.

Fourth, given the varied landscape of how prospective teachers have been educated and socialised, it was expected that the student teachers' beliefs about knowledge and teaching in general would follow this trajectory. The data showed that in the absence of student teachers being challenged about their beliefs regarding teaching and what constitutes professional knowledge, they reverted back to traditional teaching practices – which may or may not be suitable to create a democratic classroom environment. This was shown in Chapters 5, 6 and 7. The study also revealed that not all student teachers felt competent or confident to teach language and mathematics skills to learners, which could impact negatively on teachers' classroom practices and overall learner performance, as indicated in Chapter 6. The dynamic relationship between student teachers' beliefs and their classroom practices complicates the development of ITE programmes as it would be imprudent to think the former does not hugely impact the latter. A distinction is also made between student teachers' general beliefs and student teachers' pedagogical beliefs, which are both context bound. If the aim of ITE programmes is to develop the skills, knowledge and attitudes to be able to teach in the varied educational context of South Africa, individual characteristics and group dynamics (in terms of race, culture, ethnicity and religion) need to be considered in order to suitably realise the aims and objectives of the programme.

Fifth, the ITE curricula of the BEd provided the student teachers with SCK and PCK and equipped them with an understanding of the school curriculum that they were expected to teach. It also assisted them with designing assessment tasks and helped with issues related to classroom management and understanding the various issues that are related to learners' learning. Specifically for SCK, BEd students experienced this as part of the core modules that they had in these programmes. In contrast, the PGCE programmes begin with the assumption that the student teachers already possessed SCK. Yet both groups felt that they had a varying extent of sufficient education content and specialist SCK, which in these cases were in language and mathematics, to teach. The covering of content to be taught in different subject areas is tied to the methodology modules covered in the programmes. However, prospective teachers indicated that they would have liked to have learned more of how to deliver such content. This was evident in the discussion of the data in Chapters 5, 6 and 7. In other words, they would have wanted more PCK and the various teaching rituals that it accompanies in order to successfully teach this learning area. The MRTEQ policy currently emphasises the need for prospective teachers to have sufficient SCK as well as PCK to be effective teachers. What additional PCK would mean for programmes is crucial for this policy directive.

Sixth, for many student teachers, the teaching practice component is considered to be immensely helpful in preparing them to become teachers. As prospective teachers, the practicum affords them the opportunity to practise their learning in the ITE programmes as well as encouraging reflection on their own practices, creating the possibility of student teachers to become reflexive practitioners. Key to the practicum is the support of their school-based mentors and university supervisors. In general, prospective teachers viewed support from mentors in schools to be useful and helpful. Yet they pointed out that mentoring support during the practicum could be strengthened to make it a more valuable and meaningful learning experience for translating theory into practice. Chapters 5 and 6 pointed to these emphases in the teaching practicum and student teachers wanting more exposure to teaching practice.

Seventh, the data revealed that some student teachers experienced their ITE as preparing for a teaching context in which issues of diversity and equity are important. As indicated in Chapters 5 and 6, this is due to the orientation of some of ITE programmes of institutions and in the orientation of some of the prospective teachers. The data revealed a strong commitment among prospective teachers to deal with diversity and inclusive education in their teaching – see for example Chapters 3, 4, 5 and 6. However, they did not all necessarily feel well prepared for this, although their experiences of teaching in diverse schooling contexts during the practicum supported them to some extent, in this respect. However, it would be reasonable to argue that an explicit and strong social justice orientation is not central to ITE programmes, nor is it a core aim in the approaches used by prospective students. Considering the reasons why they decided to become teachers and the beliefs student teachers hold prior to entering the programme, ITE programmes could benefit from paying greater attention to this.

The themes emerging from this book suggest that prospective teachers need further input that cuts across all the sets of knowledge outlined in Chapter 1. In the first knowledge set, prospective teachers need more PCK. In the second knowledge set, prospective teachers need ways of dealing with complexities of their classroom and school contexts. In the third knowledge set, prospective teachers need space and time to enable their teaching to contribute to the aims of social justice.

In relation to the first knowledge set, which refers to specialist and subject specific knowledge, prospective teachers' need for more PCK refers to being given more time to practise their teaching, to be exposed to more of teaching as a discursive practice and to develop skills using ICT in their teaching.

The data also indicated that while prospective teachers had a reasonable sense of SCK and PCK, they did not seem to be getting sufficient exposure to teaching as a discursive practice. In the data this was indicated as something that would reinforce prospective teachers' PCK and would assist in making their lessons more coherent and to make connections better, as shown in Chapter 7. The data also indicated that if this is done, it would also lead to increasing prospective teachers' confidence in their own teaching.

In the second knowledge set, which refers to the space and place where pedagogy is enacted, prospective teachers indicated that they did not always feel equipped to deal with the complexities of their classrooms and school contexts. The first area where the data indicated this need was in the area of multilingualism. This was shown in Chapters 6 and 10. Teachers do not always speak the first language of learners in their classrooms, and because the medium of instruction used is not the learners' first language, this causes complications for prospective teachers to ensure that such learners gain access to the knowledge that is taught.

Prospective teachers also indicated that multilingualism is also about recognising the diversity of the cultures in their classrooms. The BEd and PGCE ITE programmes cover such issues in their programmes, as indicated above. However, the prospective teachers felt that they needed to be better equipped with how to deal with these issues in their teaching.

Multilingualism and recognising cultural diversity are increasing in the 21st century and are linked to what has been described as the "politics of identity" (see Hall et al. 1992, for example). Prospective teachers' need in this regard is thus important to recognise. In Chapter 6 it was indicated that prospective teachers, according to the data, were in agreement with the principles of inclusive education and positively recognising differences as they are covered in the ITE programmes. However, they seemed to need further assistance with strategies they can use in their teaching to deal with these in their classrooms.

Prospective teachers moreover indicated that when they were placed in schools that were either located in low socio-economic areas or where most of their learners came from low socio-economic backgrounds, they found it difficult to deal with such learners' problems – as shown in Chapters 6 and 10. In this regard, if the socio-economic inequalities and backgrounds of learners are not addressed by governments, then the effects of these on teaching and learning are likely to continue.

This leads to the third knowledge set – which refers to aims, purposes and goals of education – where being able to use teaching to contribute to the aims of social justice and social cohesion seemed difficult for the prospective teachers to realise in practice. This commitment to social justice by prospective teachers rubs against the fact that the BEd and PGCE ITE programmes are not aligned to a social justice model of ITE. Furthermore, the CAPS curriculum, as discussed in Chapter 2 and which is supported by the MRTEQ policy, stipulates the content to be covered in each subject area. Its pacing as well as sequencing, complemented by a narrow system of ANAs, do not afford prospective teachers the time and space to develop social cohesion and social justice in their classrooms. As such, it puts in play a culture of performativity (see Ball 2000) in which a social justice and social cohesion approach to pedagogy is reduced.

Globally, as noted in Chapter 2, there is an increasing concern with teachers, teaching and teacher education tied to a new global education agenda which commits all countries to achieving equitable and quality lifelong learning for all by 2030. A core target of the 10 education targets is increasing the supply of qualified teachers by 2020. This focus on teachers predating the SDG agenda is positively making teachers and their work visible but not always in productive ways – as argued below.

This agenda is occurring in a global context marked by a discursive space in which teachers are derided and regarded as the main/part of the problem for poor education quality. Thus, it is argued that declining education quality and poor learning attainment are the result of ineffective teacher governance and accountability systems and measures manifested in teacher absences, for example. The blaming of teachers for poor education quality is also argued to be a result of weaknesses in teacher knowledge about their subjects or how to teach their subjects, evident in teacher performance on standardised tests, for example. Furthermore, it is argued that teachers are poorly motivated in the public sector and that their status as full-time civil servants results in teachers focusing more on their own needs rather than the needs of learners. In such a discursive space, questions are raised about whether ITE has any bearing on what happens in schools and whether providers of ITE programmes are responsive to the needs of schools that employ their prospective teachers.

This discursive space is not only negative. Teachers are also positioned as the solution to the education crisis. Sayed and Ahmed (2015) note how the (then) deputy president of South Africa, Cyril Ramaphosa, argues that teachers needed to be approached as the "solution to the current crisis in education and not the problem", and that South Africa needed teachers that have "the ability and commitment to nurture and develop young people to their full potential" (City Press 2014). Sayed and Ahmed (2015) further note that the paradoxical nature of this discursive space imagines teachers as superheroes who have the agential space and capacity to fulfil a vast and broad range of expectations. It also imagines that they possess knowledge of a broad range of content and how to teach it, including, but not limited to: life skills, citizenship and peace education, moral and ethical education, child protection, human rights and skills for sustainable livelihoods. Teacher agency in this discursive space overestimates what teachers are able to do in challenging contexts, which sets them up to fail, and creates the vicious cycle of a 'teacher blame and teacher possibility', as the deputy president's intervention in South Africa does.

In the context sketched above, a series of education policy reforms concerning the work of teachers has emerged. This consequently bears down on the nature, form and content of ITE programmes. There are several directions which these reforms take in a neo-liberal global order, namely: performativity (Ball 2003), managerialism (Robertson 2012), testing and evaluation of teachers (National Planning Commission 2013), and standardisation and specifications of outcome measures for ITE programmes. These changes are described by Robertson (2012:591) as a set "of neo-liberal projects and flanking mechanisms, including choice, vouchers, charters, devolved governance, global rankings, privatization, public-private partnerships, management-by-audit, and self-management (the list goes on)".

Several features of this neo-liberal global order impact the work of teachers. First, there has been an increasing emphasis in policy on what Ball (2003) terms a "culture of performativity". Ball (2003:216) notes that "performativity is a technology, a culture and a mode of regulation that employs judgements, comparisons and displays as means of incentive, control, attrition and change based on rewards and sanctions (both material and symbolic)". The culture of performativity employs procedures and technologies, to use Ball's (2003) terms, which subject teachers to targets/indicators to be achieved as outcomes of teaching and learning – as in the case of systematic tests and ANAs in South Africa. Performativity also operates on a pedagogy which is where teaching and learning are viewed only in terms of the acquisition of skills and knowledge that are stipulated as priority areas in the areas of mathematics, science, technology and languages. As a result, space and time for social cohesion and social justice to be developed through teaching and learning, are delegitimised and marginalised. It is done to the point where prospective teachers find they do not, in practice, have any time or space to develop social cohesion and social justice through their teaching. The most obvious form of the technology of pedagogic performativity is scripted pedagogy – a policy gaining much favour in the work of international development agencies (Robertson 2012) and manifesting in the work of low-cost private school providers such as *Bridge Academies*.

Secondy managerialism seeks to regulate the work of teachers through two principal mechanisms. The first is the promotion of performance-related pay with teacher contracts being tied to learner performance. It is argued that by doing so, teacher accountability is enhanced and becomes an in-built feature of teacher conditions of their employment. In tying teacher pay to performance, it is implied that there is a direct and linear correlation between how teachers perform and how students learn. The second mechanism is by de-linking entry into teaching from qualification. Various international agencies and groups (cf. Robertson 2012) argue that teacher qualifications have no real impact on how teachers perform. Moreover, some policymakers have embraced approaches that permit teachers with no preparation in pedagogy or child/adolescent development to be classified as "highly qualified", if they pass a test of SMK (usually a licensing exam) (NCATE 2013). While such assertions are debatable (cf. Naylor & Sayed 2014), it is common in policy to remove or reduce entry qualifications for teachers. The most prominent of such schemes are Teach First (UK), Teach America and Teach India; many of which are part of the Teach for All (TFA) Network and which place in public schools unqualified or underqualified teachers. Such schemes tap into newly qualified graduates from any discipline as teachers. McConney et al. (2012) note that TFA teachers stay for short periods in schools. McConney et al. (2012) further note that there are some positive features of this model in terms of, for example, increasing supply. However, teacher unions and professional associations critique this approach given its threat of teaching as a profession and its technicist approach to teaching which undervalues intital teacher preparation.

On the negative side, a high proportion of TFA-prepared teachers leave teaching after two years. It is a design feature of the TFA strategy that its teachers need only make a two-year commitment to teaching in the schools. This revolving-door approach to teacher retention necessarily means both direct and hidden costs to the schools and students of TFA teachers and these costs would seem particularly burdensome for schools in challenging circumstances. In addition to high turnover, many traditional teacher education stakeholders have observed TFA's apparent alignment with the rise of deregulation, choice and marketisation, and key factors in a neo-liberal/neoconservative educational reform agenda.

Similarly, in low-fee private schools, many teachers who are employed are underqualified and unqualified. The employment of such teachers is to break what is considered to be producer capture. Such teachers are argued to be well motivated, if not more so, than qualified teachers. However, the evidence of their impact on learning attainment in such schools is not conclusive and mixed at best (Day et al. 2014).

Managerialism as an approach also reshapes how teacher education is provided; such as the 'apprenticeship' model of teacher preparation and devolution of teacher training to schools as currently being attempted in UK schooling contexts. In this apprenticeship model, prospective teachers are placed with practising teachers as their apprentices and it is assumed that this is all that is needed to be an effective teacher. In this regard, then, how such programmes are designed structurally, are also what should constitute teacher preparation and ITE programmes. In deregulating teacher entry, ideologically a market approach to education is constructed, which implicitly or explicitly erodes the public democratic model of education in general and teacher education in particular.

Thirdly, NCATE (2013) points out that although existing evidence indicates that teacher preparation "does make a difference", some policymakers have recently advocated that a passing score on a test of SMK and a background check are all that are needed to become an effective teacher. In South Africa, the NDP (2013) proposes testing teachers regularly and using such results to determine the registration status of teachers. Thus, teachers who wish to be licensed to teach should at a minimum pass centrally prescribed teacher tests.

Testing of teachers is advocated for and managed by large corporations such as Pearson (2007), which notes that they offer testing services for the 21st century teacher:

> Working closely with educators, Pearson offers dynamic teacher licensing and performance assessment solutions. Our custom teacher licensure testing programmes are 100 percent aligned to state standards. We also provide a wide variety of teacher licensure testing services such as test development, administration, and scoring [...] Our state-of-the-art assessments are a fitting match for the next generation of teachers. The NES® (National Evaluation Series™) is a comprehensive, dynamic testing programme aligned to national subject and pedagogy standards. The edTPA™ assessment process provides a deeper look at performance and includes a review of a teacher candidate's authentic teaching materials.

Teacher testing suffers from the same problems as that of testing learners. It is assumed that there is a direct correlation between how a teacher performs on a test and how they perform in classroom settings and consequently how learners perform. Moreover, it ignores the ways in which the contexts in which teachers teach impact learner performance. Moreover, testing teachers is an unhelpful policy proposition in itself if it is not tied to effective and empowering forms of professional support for teachers. While not advocating abandoning assessment that focuses on what teachers know and how capable they are in their practices, it is important to develop systems, as Darling-Hammond (2012) note, that are clearly tied to a transparent set of teacher standards. These standards are supported by teachers and their professional associations, are sensitive to context and are tied to effective forms of professional support. Only in this way is it possible to develop high-quality, effective, fair and teacher-owned forms of teacher tests.

Finally, linked to the idea of testing teachers, is creating standards and outcome measures for ITE programmes that assess the extent to which prospective teachers are school-ready. These suggested measures are usually accompanied by systems of teacher licensing. Outcome measures for ITE are in the main predicated on national teacher standards and on policy specifications such as the NSE in South Africa. Interest in outcome measures in ITE is often driven by a concern that prospective teachers are not being prepared well to teach and by a concern of declining education quality, as noted above. In this context, there is a great deal of advocacy for more robust and fine-grained measures of ITE outcome measures. The NCTAF (2016:12-13) states that

> [f]inally, to ensure that new teachers are 'profession ready', performance assessments need to be in place as a condition of full licensure. Studies have found that teachers' scores on performance-based assessments are positively associated with their effectiveness when they later become full-time teachers.

The NCTAF (2016:13) further bemoans the fact that in the USA only "12 states have policies in place requiring a state-approved performance assessment as part of programme completion, for state licensure, and/or for teacher preparation programme accreditation/review". While needed, outcome measures in ITE are a form of regulating the professional work of teachers and are symbiotically linked, as noted above, to testing and evaluating regimes. As such, they narrow measures of teacher performance in ITE programmes to an input-output model. Moreover, they run the risk of individualising assessing teacher preparation for practice and consequentially do not take into account what institutions that provide ITE programme do and should do. Unless ITE outcome measures are focused on institutional as well as individual development, accompanied by professional support and build the "professional capital" of prospective teachers (Fullan & Hargreaves 2012; Fullan, Rincón-Gallardo & Hargreaves 2015), they are unlikely to be effective mechanisms of assuring standards as they purport to do. The failure to do so is likely to result in contestations, by providers, professional associations and the prospective teachers themselves, to a narrow ITE outcome measures approach as policy suggests.

Collectively, the measures discussed in this section are marked by a hard-edged economic emphasis on individualism, flexibility, competition and incentives, which are features of a turn to the marketisation of teacher education specifically and education more generally.

This is likely to undermine the basis of learning as a structured social encounter between the teacher and the learner. As such, the neo-liberal emphasis – on performativity, managerialism, deregulation, teacher tests and testing and measurable outcomes – as discussed above, structurally and in the policy contexts, undermine the willingness and need of prospective teachers to develop social cohesion and social justice through their teaching. These measures also do not assist prospective teachers in dealing with the complexities in their classrooms and school contexts in a highly unequal global order.

11.3 Teacher Education Models and Approaches in the Post-apartheid 21st Century

Becoming a teacher in post-apartheid South Africa is also becoming a teacher in the challenging times of the 21st century. This suggests that when viewing ITE programmes that certify prospective teachers, such programmes need to be accompanied by an examination of the extent to which such ITE programmes prepare prospective teachers for dealing with the challenges of being a teacher in the 21st century in a post-apartheid South Africa. To address such issues, one needs to look at the type(s) of model(s) of ITE that would most suit the demands of the 21st century – which this section now turns its attention to.

There are multiple and competing models of ITE, as alluded to in Chapter 1. Models of ITE capture what prospective teachers are exposed to and shape what they do as teachers in diverse classroom contexts. One such model is that of Whitcomb (2010), who indicates that at the end of the 20th century four dominant approaches to teacher education prevailed, which were taken forward into the 21st century. For Whitcomb (2010:598), these four conceptions of teacher education are:

1. social justice;
2. teaching for understanding;
3. contemplative; and
4. clinician-professional.

The *social justice* conception of teacher education is one which "begins with the idea that the central purpose of education is to redress the social, economic, and political inequities" (Whitcomb 2010:598). In this approach, not only is the teacher aware of such inequities but raises their learners' consciousness about such inequities. This approach also highlights the importance of changing such unequal social orders, and both the teacher and the learners in their classes are viewed as activists who are committed to social justice and change.

In the teaching for understanding approach to teacher education, the central focus is on the teaching of academic content. In this approach, the teacher facilitates their learners' understanding of and engagement with the disciplinary content in their subjects. Rather than merely imparting or transmitting such content to their learners, teachers in the teaching-for-understanding approach attempt to "structure engaging problems or essential questions that guide learners to construct understanding of disciplinary concepts rather than receive finished knowledge" (Whitcomb 2010:600). It is in this approach that Shulman's

(1986) theories of SCK and PCK gain their importance. How best to get learners to engage with problems and issues, and how best to make knowledge and concepts accessible to learners, are issues that relate to PCK and Shulman's work in this regard and have been significant in developing this teaching-for-understanding approach to teacher education.

The contemplative approach to teacher education is one that is based on the idea of "cultivating self-knowledge, developing an emotional and compassionate presence, and tapping into one's sense of vocation or mission" (Whitcomb 2010:601). The contemplative approach is also "personalistic". Whitcomb (2010) notes, that the contemplative approach to teacher education, has not been dominant within the mainstream of teacher education.

The clinician-professional approach to teacher education is one that draws on views of medical education. It claims to be scientific and utilises "behavioural, cognitive and sociocultural orientations in psychology" and has informed "process-product research", which has focused on "teachers' observed behaviours" and "tested students using standardised tests to measure student performance" (Whitcomb 2010:602).

One way of engaging with the four models and approaches above is to consider three interrelated questions. First, what reform imperatives and discourses drive teacher education and the different models and approaches? The second is to use Cochran-Smith's (2001) words: What are the 'warrants' made for one or more of the models above? The third question is: What constitutes a quality teacher and quality teaching?

Turning to the first question, the reform imperatives that drive models which focus on content and practice tend to construct teacher education as deficient in training or learning (Cochran-Smith 2004). In this scenario, teacher education is perceived as failing to provide prospective teachers with sufficient content and pedagogical knowledge, as well as failing to provide sufficient training and practice for the classroom. As concerns mount over learner performance, the perception of failure to provide knowledge and skills intensifies. Thus, the black box of what happens inside ITE programmes becomes a matter of concern and attention among policymakers and administrators.

In societies in or emerging from conflict, reform imperatives to promote national unity and reconciliation drive ITE models that focus on social justice. In this scenario, teacher education is regarded as deficient in supporting prospective teachers with the skill, knowledge and disposition to ensure national unity and promote reconciliation and tolerance. Cast in this way, teacher education programmes are called upon to equip prospective teachers with the necessary tools to overcome violence and conflict in and through education. Teacher education policy is thus orientated to a focus on social justice. However, this is often dealt with at the individual, and not systemic, level.

In teacher education reform discourses, the state tends to construct teacher education as a 'policy problem' in which policymakers seek to find feasible solutions to factors which it can control; such as what is taught in ITE programmes and how, and who is recruited into teacher education (Cochran-Smith 2004). As a 'policy problem', the state offers neutral solutions to the problems such as enhancing CK, increasing the practice component of ITE programmes and infusing social justice concerns into such programmes. Thus, teacher education policy focuses on a narrow agenda that emphasises the acquisition of CK and PCK, albeit expanded to include social justice concerns. Collectively, the policy prescriptions tightly specify what providers should do and how, leading arguably to the regulation or perhaps overregulation of ITE programmes. However, all solutions to the 'policy problem' of ITE are ideological in nature. In tightly regulating the nature and content of ITE programmes, the state not only disempowers providers. It also narrows the agential space of prospective teachers, making it difficult to realise a reflective and contemplative model of teacher education that Whitcomb (2010) and others note as lacking. The agential space of prospective teachers is, in this sense, crucial to embedding the idea of teaching as a profession and the teacher as a committed, socially aware, democratic and responsive professional. To regulate/overregulate is to, in the South African context, reduce the act of teaching to a technical activity devoid of the values that drive the activity of teaching.

Turning to the second question, Cochran-Smith and Fries (2001) identify three interrelated warrants for discourses of teacher education reform. The first is the evidentiary warrant, which they note as the justifications and evidence used for policy recommendations. The second is the accountability warrant, which they identify as holding teachers to account through measures such as outcomes and results, being that of the learners or themselves (Cochran-Smith & Fries 2001). The final warrant is the political warrant, in which policy prescriptions and options are justified on the basis of a wider societal and citizen benefit (Cochran-Smith & Fries 2001). Across all these warrants they note that diametrically opposed policy solutions can be offered (Cochran-Smith & Fries 2001). For example, tightly specifying what is taught and how, or providing space for providers to choose what to teach and how, can be justified on the basis of evidence and/or on the basis of accountability and/or the basis of the public benefit. As such, the models and approaches to teacher education discussed above can be justified on one or more or all of these warrants. This suggests that what model or approach to teacher education is 'ideal', is an intensely political issue and shaped by political, social and economic concerns.

Turning to the third question, models of teacher education imply conceptions of what the teacher ought to be or do, what is viewed as the quality of teachers and what would be viewed as quality teaching. There are various and varying ways in which teachers, the quality of teachers and the quality of teaching have been conceptualised across the years in different contexts and from different perspectives. For this study, however, the question has been more of how post-apartheid prospective teachers experience these, rather than what has been used to understand these notions in other views or perspectives. The focus of this study is on the experiences of what constitutes the teacher, the quality of teachers and the quality of teaching that have emerged from the data.

Darling-Hammond (2012) distinguishes between the quality of teachers and quality of teaching in the following way, and these help in clarifying the ways in which prospective teachers in this study have experienced these. For Darling-Hammond (2012:2), teacher quality refers to "the bundle of personal traits, skills, and understandings that an individual brings to teaching, including dispositions to behave in particular ways". These also include

> strong content knowledge related to what is to be taught, knowledge of how to teach others in that area, as well as skill in implementing productive instructional and assessment practices, understanding learners and their development, including how to support learners with learning difficulties and those who are not proficient in the language of instruction, general ability to organise ideas and to observe and think diagnostically, and an adaptive expertise to make judgements of what is likely to work in a given context in response to students' needs (Darling-Hammond 2012:2-3).

Teaching quality, however, refers to "strong instruction that enables a wide range of students to learn. Such instruction meets the demands of disciplines, the goals of instruction, and the needs of students in a particular context" (Darling-Hammond 2012:3). For Darling-Hammond (2012), however, these contexts are more about the 'curriculum and assessment systems'. They do not include the socio-economic, cultural or political contexts in which teachers are expected to teach or the backgrounds from which learners come.

Some of the complexities surrounding quality teaching and teaching quality and their implications for ITE include recognising teaching as a 'complex interpretative social and cultural practice'.

For Cochran-Smith et al. (2012), these complex practices include: classroom relations, classroom management and classroom environments; content and curriculum; pedagogy and practice; student learning, opportunities and responsibilities; professionalism; emotional identities; school context and mission; resilience; hard work; and management of the curriculum. This suggests that ITE and the preparation of prospective teachers are more than just being about ensuring learner achievement levels. Improving learner achievement levels go beyond the pedagogy and SCK of teachers and these have an effect on learners' achievement levels. In this regard, then, ensuring quality teaching and teacher quality and improving learner achievement levels, are far more complex issues and need to be treated as issues that are influenced by various factors and which operates on several levels.

The prospective teachers in this study indicated that teacher quality was more than just having SCK and PCK. Chapters 4, 5 and 6 emphasised this too. Teaching quality, the data suggested, is far more than recognising the curriculum and assessment demands, as Darling-Hammond (2012) suggests. It also significantly includes dealing with factors external to formal curriculum and recognising not only the learning difficulties that learners may face, but also the contexts – socio-economic, political and cultural – that schools are located in and from which learners come.

In the context of the discussion above, which model of teacher education is appropriate, as articulated by Whitcomb (2010), is not merely a technical question. It is an intensely political question and reflects diverse and contested normative understandings of what is desirable and valued. The evidence in this book, which reflects elements of each model, can only be understood in the context of changing education and teacher education policy priorities. The fluctuations in ITE programmes in South Africa and learners' experiences thereof, as this book reports, can be explained by the shifting teacher education reform discourses.

Whitcomb (2010:603) notes that "most teacher education programmes reflect a blending of such conceptual approaches". However, it is also the case that some models and approaches are more dominant. In the South African case, as alluded to above, the training/content and the clinician/practices models are more dominant and are driven by a discourse of teacher education reform which sees existing programmes as deficient and lacking. This blaming of ITE for the failing of education is part of a wider discourse that blames teachers while also seeing them as saviours. As ITE moves into the post-apartheid 21st century in South Africa, it is increasingly becoming clearer that using only one approach to ITE is insufficient. A 'blending' of approaches is more likely and more appropriate, but anchored within a democratic, social justice and public-good understanding of teacher education. The ITE models for the 21st century would be amiss if they only promoted one approach at the expense of others. Prospective teachers, as the data indicated, benefit from each of the approaches; see for example Chapters 5 to 10. Prospective teachers need to know how to ensure that their learners gain CK; how to measure their learners' learning; how to make their classrooms more inclusive, democratic and anti-discriminatory; and how to be self-reflexive so that they can develop and improve their own practices.

11.4 Moving Forward with Policy, Practice and Research

We end this book by considering how models of teacher education and reform discourses speak to what ITE provisions are needed in relation to systemic interventions at various levels of educational systems. We also consider the kinds of policy provisions that need to be put in place to realise the aims of equipping prospective teachers and educational systems to effectively deal with the challenges of being a teacher working towards providing access to equitable and quality education for all in the 21st century. The following section discusses such policy and research implications and recommendations that can be made in the light of the discussions in this book and the data upon which they are based.

11.4.1 A Democratic Public-Good Approach

Approaches and models of ITE programmes and teacher education in general are inherently matters of values and politics. They cut to the heart of what are considered to be desirable values of an education system, what are considered to be an ideal quality teacher and quality teaching, what values and dispositions should be promoted and developed in prospective teachers in ITE programmes, who is recruited to become a prospective teacher and how NQTs are deployed and managed. Policy determinations about such issues must foreground – as the South African Constitution and National Education Policy Act do – the values of equity and redress, which seek to develop a democratic and public-good approach to teacher education. Being anchored in such an approach allows policymakers, providers and prospective teachers to judge the efficacy of ITE programmes in relation to the extent to which they promote a democratic and public-good vision of professional practice, as noted in Chapter 1.

11.4.2 A Joined up and Comprehensive Teacher Education Policy Approach

Developing high-quality ITE programmes requires a joined and comprehensive teacher education policy framework which places equitable and quality student learning at the core of professional practice. In such a teacher policy framework attention is paid to all aspects of teachers' work, beginning with recruitment, to deployment and governance. ITE programmes as such are integrally linked to a teacher education policy framework that ensures that the best teachers are recruited and deployed to schools where they are needed. Such a framework, as Chapter 1 indicated, requires actions and interventions at all levels. Reforming ITE programmes, as suggested below, cannot be disconnected from wider reforms. Only in this way can problems such as out-of-field placement for new graduates be overcome.

11.4.3 High-Quality ITE Programmes

At the core of a comprehensive teacher education policy framework are high-quality ITE programmes which foreground the three knowledge sets that this book outlined. Prospective teachers entering schools in the post-apartheid 21st century need to be competent in their SMK and how to teach it, have deep and insightful understanding of the context of their learners and the society they are part of and be confident in and committed to social justice. All these sets of knowledge, as this book suggests, should be treated as integrated. In this the fragmentation of ITE programmes as a series of discrete and disconnected modules may be overcome.

At the heart of high-quality ITE programmes is the teaching practicum, which provides meaningful opportunities to practise and put theory into practice. For this to occur requires ITE providers developing strong and durable partnerships with schools and school staff committed to making teaching practice a meaningful and valuable learning opportunity. In this respect, a national framework in South Africa that is provincially adapted and clarifies university and school partnership responsibilities to maximise learning opportunities that the practicum offers for prospective teachers, is required. To this end, there is a need for ITE providers in different provinces to coordinate and collectively manage the teaching practicum component of the programme.

High-quality ITE programmes are only possible if there is a democratic and social justice vision of professional practice that sees teachers as both competent 'technicians' as well as professionally capable activists. Both national and state providers should thus ensure that programmes are structured in such a way as to give material effect to this vision.

11.4.4 Strong and Capable ITE Providers

High-quality ITE programmes are not possible without strong and capable providers. This implies that the best should be recruited as teacher educators, who are secure in their knowledge and who are competent and capable teachers. ITE programmes, as straddling the theory/practice divide, require academics whose teaching is based on research about professional practice and vice versa.

Strong ITE programmes are managed by visionary and dedicated leaders who share and consensually develop a democratic vision of teacher education. Deans of Faculties of Education in South Africa should thus be leading processes of transforming programmes in ways that produce capable, competent and confident graduates with the three knowledge sets discussed above.

The role of the state in this context should be to support and nurture capable ITE providers, aligned to a coherent and comprehensive teacher education policy framework. Such a framework should be adequately resourced and consensually developed, buttressed by a concrete and feasible implementation strategy.

Ongoing and continuous teacher professional development targeted at different stages of a teacher's career is also important. High-quality ITE programmes are necessary but not sufficient conditions for effective and quality teaching. Ongoing professional development opportunities for learning should also be made available to all teachers – including new ITE graduates.

The research reported in this book is part of a larger research project which notes that NQTs are often the awkward relative of the teacher education system. Not only is there a lack of a comprehensive and effective induction system in South Africa, there are few targeted professional development opportunities for NQTs. An important starting point would be to create a formal and structured induction system for NQTs and they need to be given the time and space to capitalise on professional development opportunities that support them to develop and refine their teaching skills. This could take multiple forms, including working with more experienced teachers and with peers, as well as attending workshops.

Teacher professional development is an ongoing process of inquiry and learning. To this end, national and provincial governments in South Africa and schools need to create the space and time for teachers to continue to learn professionally. Ongoing professional development works best when it is resourced and when it is provided when needed. This requires a demand-driven rather than a supplier-based model of CPD that puts teachers in charge of their own development – in context and on site.

11.4.5 Credible Prospective Teacher Evaluation Systems in ITE

Assessing teacher performance to teach as an outcome of ITE programmes is an important priority to raise the quality of teaching and learning. To this end, it is necessary to develop common and agreed-upon methods of assessing prospective teachers' readiness to teach.

To begin with, it is necessary to develop in South Africa transparent and teacher-owned teacher standards that connect what happens in the classroom and in the university to student learning. However, as noted above, these standards should not be expansive in nature, recognise context as shaping practice and avoid causally determinist associations between teaching and student learning.

Teacher standards should be aligned to clear and transparent ITE outcome measures as argued above. Robust outcome measures in ITE are characterised by meaningful assessments that assess: (i) prospective teachers' knowledge of their subject and how to teach it, (ii) prospective teachers' knowledge of context and (iii) prospective teachers' knowledge of social justice, which collectively assesses prospective teachers' readiness to practice. The forms of assessments that measure such outcomes should be authentic and aligned to practice.

11.4.6 Developing the Knowledge Base

In the South African context, there is a dearth of systematically collected data about ITE programmes, particularly in relation to student teacher experiences. This is a gap that this study seeks to fill and which future research can complement.

Building on the idea of the three knowledge sets developed in Chapter 1, three areas/assemblages of important research warrant further work in ITE – recognising that teacher preparation research is a "historically situated social practice" (Cochran-Smith & Villegas 2015b:8).

The first research assemblage calls research attention to how, in what ways and to what extent ITE programmes support prospective teachers in acquiring CK, PKC and general pedagogical skills. Such research focuses on what skills and knowledge prospective teachers should acquire as a result of their training. It also considers how national and global policy impacts the acquisition of such knowledge.

The second assemblage encompasses research that covers how context and the macro policy environment impact what ITE providers and programmes can achieve. Such research would cover: new entry routes into teaching; the regulation of ITE providers and programmes; how ITE programmes engage with and prepare prospective teachers for teaching in diverse school contexts; and testing and evaluation of teachers and prospective teachers' performance.

The third research assemblage may align with what Cochran-Smith and Villegas (2015b) might refer to as research on diversity, inclusion and equity. In the context of this book, this research assemblage would encompass research on how and in what ways teacher education policy and ITE programmes hinder or support prospective teachers' acquisition of skills and dispositions for social justice. It calls particular attention to how ITE programmes prepare prospective teachers for democracy and for the values of equity and redress in the South African context.

Across all three assemblages, there are several crucial cross-cutting areas of research. These include the role of teacher educators, the role and place of the teaching practicum in supporting prospective teachers and how ITE programmes prepare prospective teachers for a changing 21st century.

In the South African context, developing the knowledge base for and about ITE is particularly important, given the dearth of large-scale and systematically collected research. Moreover, the absence of longitudinal research about ITE needs addressing. Only by addressing the gaps noted above can the field of teacher education become an important national and institutional research priority.

This chapter draws this book to a close by highlighting the diverse ways in which prospective teachers are prepared to teach, outlining the contexts which impact their future work and ending with suggestions for the future. However, none of these suggestions outlined above in themselves will result in a high-quality teacher education system unless they are implemented collectively and as part of wider reforms in education systems at large. Reforms of education systems should in turn be tied to national transformation agendas that seek to reinvigorate and defend education as a public good tied to the rights of all citizens in a democratic society. In this way, it is possible to reinvigorate and recover a transformative teacher education agenda, which lays the basis for a more egalitarian society.

References

Ball, S.J. 2000. Performativities and fabrications in the education economy: Towards the performative society. *Australian Educational Researcher*, 27(2): 1-23. https://doi.org/10.1007/BF03219719

Ball, S.J. 2003. The teacher's soul and the terrors of performativity. *Journal of Education Policy*, 18(2): 215-228. https://doi.org/10.1080/0268093022000043065

Bourgonje, P. & Tromp, R. 2011. *Quality educators: An international study of teacher competencies and standards*. Brussels: Education International & Oxfam Novib.

Carrim, N. & Taruvinga, M. 2015. Using ICTs (educationally) for development in an African context: Possibilities and limitations. *Perspectives in Education*, 33(1): 100-116.

Castells, M. 2001. The new global economy. In: J. Muller, N. Cloete & S. Badat (eds). *Challenges of globalisation: South African debates with Manuel Castells*. Cape Town: Maskew Miller Longman, 2-22.

City Press. 2014. *Teachers are the solution, not the problem*. Interview with Cyril Ramaphosa. Available at: https://www.news24.com/Archives/City-Press/Teachers-are-the-solution-not-the-problem-Cyril-Ramaphosa-20150429

Cochran-Smith, M. 2001. The outcomes question in teacher education. *Teaching and Teacher Education*, 17(5): 527-546. https://doi.org/10.1016/S0742-051X(01)00012-9

Cochran-Smith, M. 2004. *Walking the road: Race, diversity, and social justice in teacher education*. New York: Teachers College Press.

Cochran-Smith, M. & Fries, M.K. 2001. Sticks, stones, and ideology: The discourse of reform in teacher education. *Educational Researcher*, 30(8): 3-15. https://doi.org/10.3102/0013189X030008003

Cochran-Smith, M.; McQuillan, P.; Mitchell, K.; Gahlsdorf-Terrell, D.; Barnatt, J.; D'Souza, L.; Jong, C.; Shakman, K.; Lam, K. & Gleeson, A. 2012. A longitudinal study of teaching practice and early career decisions: A cautionary tale. *American Educational Research Journal*, 49(5): 844-880. https://doi.org/10.3102/0002831211431006

Cochran-Smith, M. & Villegas, A.M. 2015a. Studying teacher preparation: The questions that drive research. European *Educational Research Journal*, 14(5): 379-394. https://doi.org/10.1177/1474904115590211

Cochran-Smith, M. & Villegas, A.M. 2015b. Framing teacher preparation research: An overview of the field, part 1. *Journal of Teacher Education*, 66(1): 7-20. https://doi.org/10.1177/0022487114549072

Darling-Hammond, L. 2012. *Creating a comprehensive system for evaluating and supporting effective teaching*. California: Stanford Centre for Opportunity Policy in Education.

Day, A.L.; McLoughlin, C.; Aslam, M.; Engel, J.; Wales, J.; Rawal, S.; Batley, R.; Kingdon, G.; Nicolai, S. & Rose, P. 2014. *The role and impact of private schools in developing countries: A rigorous review of the evidence.* Final report. London: Department for International Development (DFID).

Department of Basic Education (DBE). 2012a. *Action plan 2014: Towards the realisation of schooling 2025.* Pretoria: DBE.

Department of Basic Education (DBE). 2012b. *Annual National Assessment: A guideline for the interpretation and use of ANA results.* Pretoria: DBE.

Department of Basic Education (DBE). 2015. *Minimum requirements for teacher education qualifications policy.* Pretoria: DBE.

Department of Education (DoE). 2008. Foundation for learning campaign. *Government Gazette*, 30880(306), 14 March. Pretoria: Government Printer, 3-23.

Fullan, M. & Hargreaves, A. 2012. Reviving teaching with 'professional capital'. *Education Week*, 31(33): 30-36.

Fullan, M.; Rincón-Gallardo, S. & Hargreaves, A. 2015. Professional capital as accountability. *Education Policy Analysis Archives [Archivos Analíticos de Políticas Educativas]*, 23(15): 153-163. https://doi.org/10.14507/epaa.v23.1998

Hall, S. 1992. The question of cultural identity. In: S. Hall, D. Held & T. McGrew (eds). *Modernity and its futures.* London: Polity Press, 274-316.

Hall, S.; Held, D. & McGrew, T. (eds). 1992. *Modernity and its futures.* London: Polity Press.

Hargreaves, A. & Fullan, M. 2012. *Professional capital: Transforming teaching in every school.* New York: Teachers College Press.

Loughran, J. & Hamilton, M.L (eds). 2016. *International handbook of teacher education (vol. 1).* Singapore: Springer. https://doi.org/10.1007/978-981-10-0369-1

Mansfield, C.F.; Beltman, S.; Price, A. & McConney, A. 2012. Don't sweat the small stuff: Understanding teacher resilience at the chalkface. *Teaching and Teacher Education*, 28(3): 357-367. https://doi.org/10.1016/j.tate.2011.11.001

McConney, A.; Price, A. & Woods-McConney, A. 2012. *Fast-Track teacher education: A review of the research literature on Teach for all Schemes.* Perth: Murdoch University, Centre for Learning, Change and Development.

National Commission on Teaching & America's Future (NCTAF). 2016. *What matters now: A new compact for teaching and learning.* Arlington: NCTAF. Available at: https://nctaf.org/wp-content/uploads/2016/08/NCTAF_What-Matters-Now_A-Call-to-Action.pdf

National Council for the Accreditation of Teacher Education (NCATE). 2013. *What makes an effective teacher?* USA: NCATE.

National Planning Commission (NPC). 2013. *National development plan vision 2030: Our future – make it work.* Available at: https://nationalplanningcommission.wordpress.com/the-national-developme nt-plan/

Naylor, R. & Sayed, Y. 2014. *Teacher quality: Evidence review.* Canberra: Office of Development Effectiveness.

Pearson.com. 2007. *Assessment: Ensuring teacher quality*. Available at: https://www.pearson assessments.com/teacherlicensure.html

Republic of South Africa (RSA). 1996a. National Education Policy Act, no. 27 of 1996. Pretoria: Government Printer.

Republic of South Africa (RSA). 1996b. South African Constitution, act no. 108 of 1996. Pretoria: Government Printer.

Robertson, S. 2012. Placing teachers in global governance agendas. *Comparative Education Review*, 56(4): 584-607. https://doi.org/10.1086/667414

Sayed, Y. & Ahmed, R. 2015. Education quality, and teaching and learning in the post-2015 education agenda. *International Journal of Educational Development (IJED)*, 40: 330-338. https://doi.org/10.1016/j.ijedudev.2014.11.005

Shulman, L. 1986. Those who understand: Knowledge growth in teaching. *Educational Researcher*, 15(2): 4-14. https://doi.org/10.3102/0013189X015002004

Shulman, L. 1987. Knowledge and teaching: Foundations of the new reform. *Harvard Educational Review*, 57(1): 1-22. https://doi.org/10.17763/haer.57.1.j463w79r56455411

Whitcomb, J.A. 2010. Conceptions of teacher education. In: P. Peterson, E. Baker & B. McGraw (eds). *International encyclopaedia of education (3rd ed.)*. Philadelphia: Elsevier Science and Technology Books, 598-603. https://doi.org/10.1016/B978-0-08-044894-7.00665-5

Appendix 2

Mapping Education Policies Relating to Teachers and Teacher Education in South Africa

Policy	Year	Link
Reconstruction and Development Programme	1995	https://www.sahistory.org.za/sites/default/files/the_reconstruction_and_development_programm_1994.pdf
South African Qualifications Authority Act	1995	https://www.saqa.org.za/show.php?id=5469
White Paper 1: Education and Training	1995	https://www.thedti.gov.za/sme_development/docs/White_paper.pdf
South African Constitution	1996	https://www.justice.gov.za/legislation/constitution/SAConstitution-web-eng.pdf
White Paper 2: Organisation, Governance and Funding of Schools	1996	https://www.education.gov.za/Portals/0/Documents/Legislation/White/paper/white/paper/.pdf
South African Schools Act	1996	https://www.gov.za/sites/www.gov.za/files/Act84of1996.pdf
National Education Policy Act	1996	https://www.gov.za/sites/www.gov.za/files/Act27of1996.pdf
Green Paper on the Transformation of Higher Education	1996	https://www.gov.za/sites/www.gov.za/files/Green/Paper/on/Higher/Education/Transformation_0.pdf
Higher Education Qualification's Framework (HEQF)	1997	www.dhet.gov.za/Policy/and/Development/Support/The/High/Education/Qualifications/Framework/(HEQF).pdf
Higher Education Act	1997	https://www.ul.ac.za/research/application/downloads/Policy/and/Procedures/for/the/Measurement/of/Research/Outputs/for/Public/Higher/Education/Institutions.pdf
Education Laws Amendment Act	1997	https://saflii.org/za/legis/num_act/elaa1997235.pdf
White Paper 3: Programme for the Transformation on Higher Education	1997	https://www.che.ac.za/media_and_publications/legislation/education-white-paper-3-programme-transformation-higher-education
Curriculum 2005 (C2005) (OBE)	1997	https://www.education.gov.za/
Employment of Educators Act	1998	https://saflii.org/za/legis/num_act/eoea1998265.pdf
Development Appraisal System (DAS)	1998	www.education.gov.za/FLinkClick.aspx

Policy	Year	Link
National Student Financial Aid Scheme Act	1999	https://www.dhet.gov.za/Legal/and/Legislative/Services/National/Student/Financial/Aid/Scheme/Act20No.//of201999/(GG2)Amended.pdf
South African Council for Educators Act	2000	https://www.acts.co.za/south-african-council-for-educators-act-2000/index.html
Norms and Standards for (Teacher) Education	2000	www.gov.za/documents/national-education-policy-act-norms-and-standards-educators
White Paper 5 on Early Childhood Education	2001	www.gov.za/documents/education-white-paper-5-early-childhood-education
White Paper 6: Special Needs Education	2001	www.gov.za/documents/special-needs-education-education-white-paper-6
Education Laws Amendment Bill	2001	www.dhet.gov.za/LegislationActs/Education/Laws/Amendment/Act/No.24/of/2005.pdf
Whole School Evaluation (WSE)	2001	https://www.education.gov.za
Performance Management and Development System (PMDS)	2002	https://www.dpsa.gov.za/dpsa2g/documents/sms/pmds_ch_4.pdf
Systemic Evaluation Framework (SEF)	2002	www.saide.org.za/
Revised National Curriculum Statement (RNCS)	2002	https://wcedonline.westerncape.gov.za/ncs/rncs.html
Integrated Quality Management System (IQMS)	2003	www.dhet.gov.zaIntegrated/Quality/Management/System
Education Laws Amendment Act	2005	saflii.org/za/legis/num_act
NCS	2005	https://www.westerncape.gov.za/information-about-revised-national-curriculum-state
Ministerial Committee on Teacher Education	2005	https://www.education.gov.za/Portals/0/Documents/Reports/Ministerial/Committee/on/Teacher/Education.pdf
Education Laws Amendment Act	2007	https://saflii.org/za/legis/num_act/elaa2007235/
National Policy Framework for Teacher Education	2007	https://www.che.ac.za/media_and_publications/frameworks-criteria/national-policy-framework-teacher-education
National Qualifications Framework Act	2008	https://www.saqa.org.za/docs/legislation/2010/act67.pdf
National Strategy on Screening, Identification, Assessment, and Support (SIAS)	2008	www.ibe.unesco.org/curricula/southafrica/sa_ie_str_2008_eng.pdf
Curriculum Assessment Policy Statement (CAPS)	2011	https://www.education.gov.za/Curriculum/CurriculumAssessmentPolicyStatements(CAPS)
Minimum Requirement for Teacher Education Qualification (MRTEQ)	2011	www.gov.za/files/34467_gon583.pdf

Appendix 2

Policy	Year	Link
Integrated strategic planning framework for Teacher Education and Development in SA (ISPFTED)	2011	www.dhet.gov.za/Teacher/Education/Technical/Report/Intergrated/Strategic/Planning/Framework/for/Teacher/Education/and/Development
National Development Plan (NDP)	2012	www.nationalplanningcommission.org.za/Documents/devplan_ch12_0.pdf
Higher Education Qualification's Sub-framework (HEQSF)	2013	www.che.ac.za/announcements/revised-heqsf-was-gazetted-2nd-august-2013
Minimum Requirement for Teacher Education Qualification (MRTEQ)	2015	www.dhet.gov.za/Teacher/Education/National/Qualifications/Framework/Act67_2008/Revised/Policy/for/Teacher/Education/Quilifications.pdf

Appendix 3

Overview of Research Questionnaires

Below is a summary of the questionnaires (and the number of respondents for each) administered to the exit-level students completing their initial teacher education (ITE) programme. There were two cohorts. One cohort of student teachers was completing a Bachelor of Education (BEd) specialising in the Foundation Phase and the second cohort was completing a Postgraduate Certificate in Education (PGCE) specialising in the Further Education and Training (FET) phase. Three questionnaires were administered to the BEd student teachers and two questionnaires were administered to the PGCE student teachers.

The Number of Respondents per Questionnaire is Listed Below:

Questionnaire	Questionnaire focus	Cohort	No. of respondents
Questionnaire 1	Motivation for becoming a teacher and beliefs about teaching	BEd	259
Questionnaire 2	Experiences related to the academic programme	BEd	223
Questionnaire 3	Teaching practice and confidence to teach in the Foundation Phase	BEd	243
Questionnaire 1	Motivation for becoming a teacher and beliefs about teaching	PGCE	66
Questionnaire 2	Teaching practice and confidence to teach	PGCE	45

The Tables below provide a brief summary of each questionnaire used.

BEd Foundation Phase

BEd: Foundation Phase Instruments	
Questionnaire 1:	Motivation for becoming a teacher and beliefs about teaching
Synopsis	This questionnaire examined student teachers' motivations for becoming a teacher and their beliefs about teaching. The questionnaire also placed specific emphasis on the beliefs of teaching language and mathematics.
Section 1	Background information: this section asked student teachers descriptors about their background; including age, race, gender, home language, ITE programme, funding, etc. Respondents were given a selection of closed-ended options to choose from.
Section 2	Reasons for studying to become a teacher: this section asked student teachers to rate in order of importance the reasons why they chose to become teachers. Participants responded by selecting one option from a four-point Likert-scale that ranged from low importance to high importance.

Section 3	My beliefs about teaching: this section asked student teachers to best describe their beliefs about teachers and teaching. Respondents could select their answers from a four-point Likert-scale that ranged from 'Strongly disagree' to 'Strongly agree'.
Section 4	Beliefs about language and teaching language(s) in the Foundation Phase: this section asked student teachers about their beliefs regarding language teaching, views on teaching language(s), the importance of various language-related skills development, their competence to develop language skills and their confidence in developing learners' language skills. Participants were given the option to select their responses from a four-point Likert-scale. The scale for each item differed between 'Strongly disagree', 'Strongly agree', 'Not at all' and 'Very competent'.
Section 5	Beliefs about mathematics and teaching mathematics in the Foundation Phase: this section asked student teachers about their beliefs regarding the subject of mathematics, beliefs regarding the goal of teaching mathematics, views on teaching mathematics, the importance of developing Foundation Phase learners' mathematical knowledge, their competence in developing mathematical skills in learners and their confidence in developing mathematics skills in Foundation Phase learners. Participants were given the option to select their responses from a four-point Likert-scale. The scale for each item differed between 'Strongly disagree', 'Strongly agree', 'Not at all' and 'Very competent'.
Section 6	My career plan: this section asked student teachers about their professional development as they complete the final leg of their ITE programme. The respondents were asked about their expectations of what they would learn in their final year of their ITE programme and what their concerns were about teacher education in 2016.
Section 7	Invitation to participate in the research: this section asked respondents if they would like to participate in further research such as interviews and focus groups. Respondents who responded positively had to provide their details.

BEd Foundation Phase

BEd: Foundation Phase Instruments	
Questionnaire 2:	Experiences related to the academic programme
Synopsis	This questionnaire asked student teachers to respond to prompts relating to items taught to them in the academic programme, about language and teaching language and about mathematics and teaching mathematics.
Section 1	Background information: this section asked student teachers descriptors about their background – including age, race, gender, home language, ITE programme, funding, etc. Respondents were given a selection of closed-ended options to choose from.
Section 2	The Foundation Phase programme: this section asked student teachers whether they had covered certain aspects relating to teaching in their academic programme. Respondents could answer 'Yes' or 'No' regarding covering a certain aspect and also rate the usefulness of an item. This scale ranged from 'Not at all' to 'Very Useful'. This section also asked respondents about teaching strategies employed by their trainers, about the usefulness of these strategies, the kinds of assessment tools used in the programme, the number of hours spent on academic work and how they felt about the programme in general. This section made use of both closed-ended and open-ended questions.

Appendix 3

Section 3	Learning about language and teaching language in the Foundation Phase: this section asked student teachers about language-related items taught to them in the programme. It also investigated the kinds of language-related teaching strategies they had been taught to prepare them for teaching in the classroom. Respondents could answer either 'Yes' or 'No' and also rate the level to which these aspects had been addressed on a scale that ranged from 'Not at all' to 'Totally'. The latter part of this section contained two open-ended question asking respondents to list the most valuable thing they have been taught relating to teaching learners to read and listen.
Section 4	Learning about mathematics and teaching mathematics in the Foundation Phase: this section asked student teachers about mathematics-related items taught to them in the programme. It asked them to what extent certain mathematical concepts had been taught to them that they would need to teach learners. It asked them about how to assess learners' mathematical skills and if they required any additional assistance to teacher learners mathematics. This section asked respondents about which lesson strategies related to teaching mathematics were taught to them and also how useful these lesson strategies were. Respondents could respond with 'Yes' or 'No' and rate the level of usefulness from 'Not at all' to 'Very Useful'. The latter part of this section asked student teachers to list one of the most valuable things they had learned relating to teaching mathematics.
Section 5	Invitation to participate in the research: this section asked respondents if they would like to participate in further research such as interviews and focus groups. Respondents who responded positively had to provide their details.

BEd Foundation Phase

BEd: Foundation Phase Instruments	
Questionnaire 3:	Teaching practice and confidence to teach in the Foundation Phase
Synopsis	This questionnaire asked student teachers about their views on teaching practice, their confidence to enter the teaching profession and about their career plans. It also asked about what they learned about teaching language and mathematics whilst in teaching practice and their final views on the academic programme.
Section 1	Background information: this section asked student teachers descriptors about their background; including age, race, gender, home language, ITE programme, funding, etc. Respondents were given a selection of closed-ended options to choose from.
Section 2	My experience of teaching practice in the Foundation Phase: this section asked respondents to list the school(s) at which they completed their teaching practice, how their ITE programme prepared them to teach during this time, what they had learned in their teaching practice, the teaching activities they participated in, about their relationship with learners and mentor teachings and about their support system that assisted them to develop their professional knowledge. Scales in this section focused on usefulness, whether items were learned or not and the extent to which the respondent developed.
Section 3	Teaching languages in the Foundation Phase: this section asked student teachers about their confidence to teach language(s), the skills they acquired to assess language(s), the level of confidence relating to developing learners' language skills, what kind of development they would like to receive to improve their language teaching skills and how they felt they were best and least prepared for teaching language(s). Scales in this section ranged from 'Not Confident' to 'Very Confident', 'Not at all' to 'Completely', and 'Never' to 'Occasionally'.

Section 4	Teaching mathematics in the Foundation Phase: this section asked students about their confidence to teach various mathematical items. It also asked them about the teaching strategies employed in their teaching of mathematics, their knowledge gained in assessing mathematics, their level of confidence to teach mathematical concepts to learners, the kinds of professional development they would like to have to improve their teaching skills, and what aspects of mathematics they were best and least prepared to teach. Scales in this section ranged from 'Not Confident' to 'Very Confident', 'Not at all' to 'Completely', and 'Never' to 'Occasionally'.
Section 5	Experience of the academic programme: this section asked student teachers about their experience of the whole academic programme. It asked them to rate themselves against the MRTEQ policy and about the institutional environment. The scales in this section ranged from 'Strongly Disagree' to 'Strongly Agree' and 'Not at all' to 'Not Applicable'.
Section 6	Next year: this section asked student teachers if they intended to teach after graduation and if they had already applied for teaching positions in schools.
Section 7	Invitation to participate in the research: this section asked respondents if they would like to participate in further research such as interviews and focus groups. Respondents who responded positively had to provide their details.

PGCE FET Phase

PGCE: FET	
Questionnaire 1:	Motivation for becoming and teacher and beliefs about teaching
Synopsis	This questionnaire examined student teachers' motivations for becoming a teacher and their beliefs about teaching. The questionnaire also placed specific emphasis on the beliefs of teaching language and mathematics.
Section 1	Background information: this section asked student teachers descriptors about their background; including age, race, gender, home language, funding sources, subjects completed in Grade 12 and details of their undergraduate degree. Respondents were given a selection of closed-ended options to choose from.
Section 2	Reasons for studying to become a teacher: this section asked student teachers to rate in order of importance the reasons why they chose to become teachers. Participants responded by selecting one option from a four-point Likert-scale that ranged from low importance to high importance.
Section 3	My beliefs about teaching: this section asked student teachers to best describe their beliefs about teachers and teaching. Respondents could select their answers from a four-point Likert-scale that ranged from Strongly disagree to Strongly agree.
Section 4	Beliefs about language(s) and language(s) teaching in FET: this section asked student teachers about their beliefs about language as a subject and teaching language, the importance of developing language skills and confidence to develop language skills in learners. Scales in this section ranged from 'Strongly Disagree' to 'Strongly Agree', 'Not at all' to 'Very Important', and 'Not at all' to 'Very Confident'.

Appendix 3

Section 5	Beliefs about mathematics and teaching mathematics in FET: this section asked student teachers about their beliefs about mathematics as a subject and about teaching mathematics, about their views on the goals of teaching mathematics, the importance of developing learners' mathematical knowledge and about their confidence to develop learners' mathematical knowledge. Scales in this section ranged from 'Strongly Disagree' to 'Strongly Agree', 'Not at all' to 'Very Important', and 'Not at all' to 'Very Confident'.
Section 6	My career plan: this section asked student teachers what they expected to learn in the programme, what their concerns were relating to teacher education and where they planned to teach after graduation. Most of the items in this section were open-ended.
Section 7	General experience: this section asked student teachers to list any experience about their programme that they thought might be useful for the study. This was an open-ended question.
End of questionnaire	Invitation to participate in the research: this section asked respondents if they would like to participate in further research such as interviews and focus groups. Respondents who responded positively had to provide their details.

PGCE FET Phase

PGCE	
Questionnaire 2:	Teaching practice and confidence to teach
Synopsis	This questionnaire asked student teachers about their views on teaching practice, their confidence to enter the teaching profession, and about their career plans. It also asked about what they learned about teaching language and mathematics whilst in teaching practice and their final views on the academic programme.
Section 1	Background information: this section asked student teachers descriptors about their background; including age, race, gender, home language, funding sources, subjects completed in Grade 12 and details of their undergraduate degree. Respondents were given a selection of closed-ended options to choose from.
Section 2	My experience of the academic programme: this section asked about items and concepts covered in the programme, about strategies used by trainers in the programmes, about the usefulness of these strategies, the kinds of assessment tools they were exposed to and the usefulness thereof. It also asked about time spent on academic work, their learning experiences in the programme, the institutional environment and how they would describe their programme in general. The scales in this section included 'Yes' and 'No', 'Not at all' and 'Very Useful', 'Strongly disagree' to 'Strongly Agree', and 'Not at all' and 'Not applicable'.
Section 3	My experience of teaching practice in the PGCE: this section asked respondents to list the school(s) at which they completed their teaching practice, how their ITE programme prepared them to teach during this time, what they had learned in their teaching practice, the teaching activities they participated in, about their relationship with learners and mentor teachings and about their support system that assisted them to develop their professional knowledge. Scales in this section focused on usefulness, whether items were learned or not and the extent to which the respondent developed.

Section 4	Teaching language in the FET phase: this section asked respondents about skills they were taught to teach language, about their confidence to teach various linguistic items, their teaching habits in relation to teaching language, their level of preparedness to teach languages, their skills gained in teaching languages, their confidence to assess language skills, the kind of professional development they would like to receive in relation to teaching language and the area they felt best and least prepared to teach. Scales in this section included 'Yes' and 'No', 'Not at all' to 'Not covered yet', 'Not confident' to 'Very Confident', 'Never' to 'Frequently', and 'Not at all' to 'Totally'.
Section 5	Teaching mathematics in the FET Phase: this section asked respondents about skills they were taught to teach mathematics, about their confidence to teach various mathematical items, their teaching habits in relation to teaching mathematics, their level of preparedness to teach mathematics, their skills gained in teaching mathematics, their confidence to assess mathematical skills, the kind of professional development they would like to receive in relation to teaching mathematics and the area they felt best and least prepared to teach. Scales in this section included 'Yes' and 'No', 'Not at all' to 'Not covered yet', 'Not confident' to 'Very Confident', 'Never' to 'Frequently', and 'Not at all' to 'Totally'.
Section 6	Next year: this section asked respondents about whether they will teach after they graduate and if they had already applied for teaching posts.
Section 7	Invitation to participate in the research: this section asked respondents if they would like to participate in further research such as interviews and focus groups. Respondents who responded positively had to provide their details.

www.ingramcontent.com/pod-product-compliance
Lightning Source LLC
Chambersburg PA
CBHW080407230426
43662CB00016B/2343